THE
WORKS
OF
CHARLES SUMNER.

Veniet fortasse aliud tempus, dignius nostro, quo, debellatis odiis, veritas triumphabit. Hoc mecum opta, lector, et vale.

LEIBNITZ.

VOL. II.

BOSTON:
LEE AND SHEPARD.
1875.

University Press: Welch, Bigelow, & Co.,
Cambridge.

CONTENTS OF VOLUME II.

FAME AND GLORY.

An Oration before the Literary Societies of Amherst College at their Anniversary, August 11, 1847.

But if there be in Glory aught of good,
It may by means far different be attained,
Without ambition, war, or violence, —
By deeds of peace, by wisdom eminent,
By patience, temperance.
Milton, *Paradise Regained.*

Da veniam scriptis, quorum non gloria nobis
Causa, sed utilitas officiumque fuit.
OVID, *Epist. ex Ponto*, III. ix., 55, 56.

Singulari in eo negotio usus opera Flacci Pomponii, consularis viri, nati ad omnia quæ recte facienda sunt, simplicique virtute, merentis semper quam captantis gloriam. — VELLEIUS PATERCULUS, *Hist.*, Lib. II. Cap. 129.

Non privatim solum, sed publice *furimus.* Homicidia compescimus, et singulas cædes; quid bella, et occisarum gentium *gloriosum scelus?* — SENECA, *Epist.* XCV. § 30.

Tanto major famæ sitis est quam
Virtutis! Quis enim virtutem amplectitur ipsam,
Præmia si tollas?
JUVENAL, *Sat.* X. 140–142.

Wealth and children are the ornament of this present life; but good works, which are permanent, are better, in the sight of thy Lord, with respect to the reward, and better with respect to hope. — *Koran*, tr. Sale, Ch. 18.

For ages mingled with his parent dust,
Fame still records Nushirovan the Just.
From the PERSIAN, by Sir William Jones: *Life*, p. 98.

Then Peredur returned to his mother and her company, and he said to her, "Mother, those were not angels, but honorable knights." Then his mother swooned away. — *The Mabinogion*, tr. Lady Charlotte Guest, Vol. I. p 300.

One day he met a poor woman weeping bitterly; and when he inquired the cause, she told him that her only brother, her sole stay and support in the world, had been carried into captivity by the Moors. Dominick could not ransom her brother; he had given away all his money, and even sold his books, to relieve the poor; but he offered all he could, — he offered up himself to be exchanged as a slave in place of her brother. The woman, astonished at such a proposal, fell upon her knees before him. She refused his offer, but she spread the fame of the young priest far and wide. — JAMESON, *Legends of the Monastic Orders: St. Dominick.*

Lord! what honor falls to a knight that he kills many men! The hangman killeth more with a better title. It were better to be butchers of beasts than butchers of our brethren, for this were more unnatural. — WYCLIFFE, *Of the Seven Deadly Sins.*

Gueres ou peu il s'est aydé des gens d'espée en ses ambassades, si-non que de ses gens de plume, ayant opinion que l'espée ne sceut tant bien entendre ses affaires, ny les conduire et démesler, comme la plume. — BRANTÔME, *Vies des Hommes Illustres et Grands Capitaines François*, Discours XLV.

He lives in fame that died in virtue's cause.
SHAKESPEARE, *Titus Andronicus*, Act I. Sc. 2.

Honors thrive,
When rather from our acts we them derive
Than our foregoers.
All's Well that Ends Well, Act II. Sc. 3.

The purest treasure mortal times afford
Is spotless reputation: that away,
Men are but gilded loam or painted clay.
Richard II., Act I. Sc. 1.

'T is death to me to be at enmity:
I hate it, and desire all good men's love.
Richard III., Act II. Sc. 1.

Never any state
Could rise or stand without this thirst of glory,
Of noble works, as well the mould as story.
For else what governor would spend his days
In envious travel for the public good?
Who would in books search after dead men's ways?
F. GREVILLE, LORD BROOKE, *Fame and Honor*.

Boccaline has this passage of soldiers. They came to Apollo to have their profession made the eighth liberal science, which he granted. As soon as it was noised up and down, it came to the butchers, and they desired their profession might be made the ninth. "For," say they, "the soldiers have this honor for the killing of men: now we kill as well as they; but we kill beasts for the preserving of men, and why should not we have honor likewise done to us?" Apollo could not answer their reasons, so he reversed his sentence, and made the soldier's trade a mystery, as the butcher's is. — SELDEN, *Table Talk: War*.

The soldiers say they fight for honor, when the truth is they have their honor in their pocket. — *Ibid.*

Certainly, as some men have sinned in the principles of Humanity, and must answer for not being men, so others offend, if they be not more. . . . . For great constitutions, and such as are constellated unto knowledge, do nothing, till they outdo all; they come short of themselves, if they go not beyond others. . . . . A man should be something that all men are not, and individual in somewhat beside his proper name.
SIR THOMAS BROWNE, *Vulgar Errors: Of Credulity and Supinity*.

Fame, if not double-faced, is double-mouthed,
And with contrary blast proclaims most deeds;
On both his wings, one black, the other white,
Bears greatest names in his wild aëry flight.
MILTON, *Samson Agonistes*, 971-974.

The extremes of glory and of shame,
Like East and West, become the same;
No Indian prince has to his palace
More followers than a thief to the gallows.
BUTLER, *Hudibras*, Part II. Canto I. 271-274.

Who fears not to do ill, yet fears the name,
And free from Conscience, is a slave to Fame.
DENHAM, *Cooper's Hill*, 129, 130.

The secret pleasure of a generous act
Is the great mind's great bribe.
DRYDEN, *Don Sebastian*, Act V. Sc. 1.

On pend un pauvre malheureux pour avoir volé une pistole sur le grand chemin, dans son besoin extrême; et on traite de héros un homme qui fait la conquête, c'est-à-dire qui subjugue injustement les pays d'un état voisin. . . . . Prendre un champ à un particulier est un grand péché; prendre un grand pays à une nation est *une action innocente et glorieuse.* — FÉNELON, *Examen de Conscience sur les Devoirs de la Royauté*, Direction XXV.

Content thyself to be obscurely good;
When vice prevails, and impious men bear sway,
The post of honor is a private station.
ADDISON, *Cato*, Act IV. Sc. 4.

Nor Fame I slight, nor for her favors call;
She comes unlooked for, if she comes at all.
POPE, *Temple of Fame*, 513, 514.

To glory some advance a lying claim,
Thieves of renown and pilferers of fame.
YOUNG, *Sat.* III. 87, 88.

Ah! who can tell how hard it is to climb
The steep where Fame's proud temple shines afar?
BEATTIE, *Minstrel*, I. 1.

I would wish for immortality on earth for no other reason than for the power of relieving the distressed. — MARIA THERESA: Coxe's *History of the House of Austria*, Vol. II. Ch. 44.

Adieu, mon cher et illustre maître; nous avons fait un beau rêve, mais il a été trop court. Je vais me remettre à la géométrie et à la philosophie. Il est bien froid de ne plus travailler que pour la gloriole, quand on s'est flatté pendant quelque temps de travailler pour le bien public. — CONDORCET, *à Voltaire*, 1776: *Œuvres*, Tom. I. p. 115.

Un temps peut arriver, où les princes, lassés de l'ambition qui les agite, et de ce retour habituel des mêmes inquiétudes et des mêmes projets, tourneront davantage leurs regards vers les grandes idées d'Humanité; et si les hommes du temps présent ne doivent pas être spectateurs de ces heureuses révolutions, il leur est permis du moins de s'unir par leurs vœux à la perfection des vertus sociales, et aux progrès de la bienfaisance publique. — NECKER, *De l'Administration des Finances de la France*, Part. I. Ch. 13.

Les nations ne doivent porter que le deuil de leurs bienfaiteurs. Les représentans des nations ne doivent recommander à leur hommage que les héros de l'humanité. — MIRABEAU, *Éloge Funèbre de Franklin.*

I have had occasion to know many thousand persons in the course of my travels on this subject [of the Slave-Trade], and I can truly say that the part which these took on this great question was always a true criterion of their moral character. — CLARKSON, *History of the Abolition of the African Slave-Trade*, Vol. II. p. 460.

Not thus the schoolmaster in his peaceful vocation. . . . . His is a progress not to be compared with anything like a march; but it leads to a far more brilliant triumph, and to laurels more imperishable than the destroyer of his species, the scourge of the world, ever won. Such men — men deserving the glorious title of Teachers of Mankind — I have found laboring conscientiously, though perhaps obscurely, in their blessed vocation. . . . . Their calling is high and holy; their fame is the property of nations; their renown will fill the earth in after ages, in proportion as it sounds not far off in their own times. — LORD BROUGHAM, *Speech at Liverpool, July* 20, 1835.

Lieutenant-Colonel Wheeler, in his despatch (Camp Cudjah, August 24, 1840) to Captain Douglas, describing the storming of an Affghanistan fort, says: "I directed Lieutenant Paterson to concentrate as heavy a volley as he could close to the gate: this had the desired effect, shook the gate, and enabled the Grenadiers of the Forty-Eighth, under that officer, to force it, and carry the fort *in beautiful style, bayoneting all within it!*" — HAYDON, *Lectures on Painting and Design*, Vol. II. p. 262.

ORATION.

THE literary festival which we are assembled to commemorate is called Commencement. To an interesting portion of my hearers it is the commencement of a new life. The ingenuous student, having completed his term of years — a classical Olympiad — amidst the restraints of the academy, in the daily pursuits of the lecture-room, observant of forms, obsequious to the college curfew, at length renounces these restraints, heeds no longer the summoning bell, throws off the youthful gown, and now, under the auspices of Alma Mater, assumes the robe of manhood. At such a change, the mind and heart open to impressions which may send an influence through remaining life. A seasonable word to-day may, peradventure, like the acorn dropped into propitious soil, shoot upward its invigorating growth, till its stately trunk, its multitudinous branches, and sheltering foliage become an ornament and protection of unspeakable beauty.

Feeling more than I can express the responsibility of the position in which I am now placed by your partial kindness, I trust that what I shall say may be not unworthy of careful meditation, and that it may ripen in this generous soil with no unwelcome growth. I address the literary societies of Amherst College, and my subject will naturally bear some relation to the occasion and to the assembly. But though addressing literary societies, I feel that I should inadequately perform my duty at this time, if I spoke on any topic of mere literature, without moralizing the theme; nor could I satisfy myself, — I think I should not satisfy you, — if I strove to excite merely a love of knowledge, of study, of books, or even of those classics which, like the ancient Roman roads, the Appian and Flaminian Ways, once trod by returning proconsuls and tributary kings, still continue the thoroughfares of nations. These things I may well leave to the lessons of your able instructors and to the influences of this place; nor, indeed, can I expect to touch upon any topic which, under the mingled teachings of the pulpit and the chair, has not been already impressed upon your minds with more force than I can command. Still, I may not vainly indulge the hope, by singling one special theme, to present it with distinctness and unity, so that it will be connected hereafter, in some humble measure, with the grave and the pleasant memories of this occasion.

To you now standing on the threshold of life, anxious for its honors, — more anxious, I hope, for its duties, — nothing can be more important or interesting than the inquiry, what should be your aims, and what your motives of conduct. The youthful bosom throbbing with historic examples is stirred by the praises lavished upon those who have gone before, and pants for fresh fields. The laurels of Miltiades would not suffer Themistocles to sleep. Perhaps a kindred sleeplessness consumes the early thoughts of our day, and, in those visions which it is said young men shall see, Fame and Glory too often absorb the sight. Turning the attention in this direction, we may, perhaps, ascertain the true nature of these potent attractions, and to what extent they can be justly regarded.

My subject is FAME AND GLORY. As I undertake this discussion, I feel that I enter upon a theme which has become a commonplace of declamation, while it has filled the aspirations of many of the noblest natures that have lived. The great Roman orator, whose essay *De Gloria*, surviving the wreck of antiquity, was lost in the darkness of the Middle Ages, cannot claim exclusive possession of the topic he had fondly made his own; nor is there enough in the chapter *De Cupiditate Gloriæ*, by the Roman historiographer,[1] to supersede inquiry, especially in a Christian age, when a speaker may hope to combine lights and illustrations which had not dawned upon the Heathen.

Three questions present themselves: *First*, What, in the more popular acceptation, are Fame and Glory? *Secondly*, To what extent, if any, are they proper motives of conduct or objects of regard? and, *Thirdly*, What are True Fame and Glory, and who are the men most worthy of honor? Already, in stating these questions, scenes and characters memorable in history rise before us, while from a distance we discern the dazzling heights of human ambition.

I.

WHAT, in the more popular acceptation, are Fame and Glory? In considering this question we must look beyond the verses of poets, the eulogies of orators, and

[1] Valerius Maximus, Lib. VIII. c. 14.

the discordant voices whether of history or philosophy. We must endeavor to observe these nimble-footed phantoms from a nearer point of view, to follow their movements, to note their principle of life, and to direct upon them the light of truth. Thus we may hope to arrive at a clear perception of their character, and perhaps do something by which to disenchant their pernicious power and break their unhappy sorcery.

Fame was portrayed by the poets of antiquity as a monster, with innumerable eyes to see, innumerable ears to hear, and innumerable tongues to declare what she had seen and heard: —

> "Monstrum horrendum, ingens, cui quot sunt corpore plumæ,
> Tot vigiles oculi subter (mirabile dictu),
> Tot linguæ, totidem ora sonant, tot subrigit aures." [1]

In this character her office was different from that commonly attached to Glory. She was the grand author and circulator of reports, news, tidings, good or bad, true or false. Glory seems to have escaped the unpleasing personification of her sister, Fame. These two names were often used in the same sense; but the former more exclusively designated that splendor of renown which was so great an object of heathen ambition. For the present purpose they may be regarded as synonymous, denoting, with different degrees of force, the reputation awarded on earth for human conduct.

Glory, in common acceptance, is a form or expression of public opinion. It is the judgment uttered by fellow-mortals upon our lives or acts. It is the product of their voices. It is the echo of their characters and minds. Its value and significance are, therefore, measured by the weight justly attached to this opinion. If

[1] Æneid, IV. 181-183.

those from whom it proceeds are enlightened, benevolent, and just, it may be the mark of honor. If, on the other hand, they are ignorant, heartless, or unjust, it must be an uncertain index, varying always in accordance with the elevation, mediocrity, or degradation of the intellectual and moral nature.

This explanation enables us to appreciate different foundations of Fame. In early and barbarous periods homage is rendered exclusively to achievements of physical strength, chiefly in slaying wild beasts or human beings termed "enemies." The feats of Hercules, filling the fable and mythology of early Greece, were triumphs of brute force. Conqueror of the Nemean lion and the many-headed hydra, strangler of the giant Antæus, illustrious scavenger of the Augean stables, grand abater of contemporary nuisances, he was hailed as hero and commemorated as god. At a later time honor was still continued to mere muscular strength of arm. The most polite and eminent chief at the siege of Troy is distinguished by Homer for the ease with which he hurled a stone such as could not be lifted even by two strong men of his day: —

> "A ponderous stone bold Hector heaved to throw,
> Pointed above, and rough and gross below;
> Not two strong men the enormous weight could raise,
> Such men as live in these degenerate days;
> Yet this, as easy as a swain could bear
> The snowy fleece, he tossed and shook in air."[1]

This was Glory in an age which had not learned to regard the moral and intellectual nature, or that which distinguishes man from the beast, as the only source of conduct worthy of just renown.

As we enter the polished periods of antiquity, ambi-

[1] Iliad, tr. Pope, XII. 537-542.

tion gleams in new forms, while we still discern the barbarism that slowly yields to advancing light. The Olympic games echoed to the Isthmian in shouts of praise. All Greece joined in competition for prizes awarded to successful charioteers and athletes; and victory was hailed as a great Glory. Poets did not disdain to sing these achievements; and the odes of Pindar — the Theban eagle, whose pride of place is still undisturbed in the Grecian firmament — are squandered in commemoration of these petty or vulgar contests. In Sparta honor was the monopoly of the soldier returning with his shield, or on it. The arts of peace yielded servile precedence to the toils of war, in which were absorbed life and education. Athens, instinct with the martial spirit, did not fail to cherish the owl with the spear that belonged to her patron goddess; poetry, eloquence, philosophy, history, art, held divided empire with arms; so that this city is wreathed with a Glory other and higher than that of Sparta. And yet this brilliant renown, admired through a long succession of ages, must fade and grow dull by the side of triumphs grander and holier than any achieved by force or intellect alone.

Rome slowly learned to recognize labors not employed in war. In her stately and imperatorial tongue, *virtue*, that word of highest import, was too often restricted to martial courage. Her much-prized crowns of honor were all awarded to the successful soldier. The title to a triumph, that highest object of ambition, was determined by the number of enemies destroyed, and at least five thousand must have been slain in battle without any considerable detriment to the Roman power. Her most illustrious characters cherished this barbarous spirit. Cato the Censor, that model Roman, hearing that the Athenian ambassadors had captivated the youth of Rome by the charms of philosophy, abruptly dismissed them, and, with the spirit of a Mohawk Indian, declared his reprehension of such corrupting influence on a people whose only profession was war. Even Cicero, in his work of beautiful, but checkered morals, where heathenism blends with truth almost Christian, commends to youth the Glory of war, while he congratulates his son Marcus on the great praise he had obtained from Pompey and the whole army, " by riding, hurling the javelin, and enduring every kind of military labor."[1]

The Roman, taught the Glory of war, was also told, as a last resort, to balk the evils of the world by taking his own life, — falling on his sword, like Brutus, or opening his veins, like Seneca. Suicide was honorable, glorious. A grave historian has recorded the melancholy end of Cato at Utica, whose philosophical suicide is so familiar to English readers from Addison's tragedy: first, the calm perusal of Plato's Dialogue on the Immortality of the Soul; then the plunging of the dagger into his body; the alarm of friends; the timely presence of aid, by which the wound was closed; and when the determined patriot was again left alone, a further ferocious persistence in his purpose till life was extinct: yet this recital is crowned by the annunciation, that Cato, " even by his death, gained great Glory."[2]

Other stages show other elements of renown. The Huns bestowed Glory upon the successful robber; the Scandinavians, upon the triumphant pirate; while in

[1] De Officiis, Lib. II. c. 13.
[2] Dion Cassius, Lib. XLIII. c. 11.

Wales petty larceny and grossness of conduct were the foundations of Fame. In the Welsh tale of "The Mabinogion," where are stories of King Arthur, so famous in song and legend, Peredur, whose dead father had owned "the earldom of the North," is sent by his mother to visit where lived "the best and the boldest and the most bountiful of men." As the son is about to leave, the mother instructs him how to secure an honorable name. "Now hear," says the ambitious mother to her child. "If by chance thou comest by a church, there chant thy paternoster. When thou seest victuals and drink to satisfy thy appetite, help thyself thereto. If thou shouldest hear a cry of distress, go and know the cause, but in particular if it is the voice of a female. Should any precious jewel attract thy eyes, take it; and bestow on others also. *Thus shalt thou acquire Fame.*"[1] The processes of Fame thus rudely displayed were refined by chivalry; but the vivid page of Froissart shows, that, while courtesy became a fresh and grateful element, petty personal encounters with spear and sword were the honorable feats by which applause was won and a name extended after death. And we learn from old Michael Drayton, the poet who has pictured the Battle of Agincourt, something of the inhuman renown there obtained: —

> "Who would have Fame full dearly here it bought,
> For it was sold by measure and by weight;
> And at one rate the price still certain stood, —
> *An ounce of honor cost a pound of blood.*"[2]

From the early literature of Spain, where Chivalry

[1] Southey, Chronicles of the Cid, Note 53. — In the translation by Lady Charlotte Guest this passage is somewhat mitigated. The Mabinogion, Vol. I. p. 300.

[2] Battle of Agincourt, st. 287.

found a favorite haunt, it appears that brutality, assassination, and murder were glorious, while adventure in robbery and promptitude in vengeance were favorite acts of heroism. "The Life of the Valiant Cespedes," a Spanish knight of renown, by Lope de Vega, reveals exploits which were little better than performances of a brawny porter and a bully. Passions of a rude nature were gratified at will. Sanguinary revenge and inhuman harshness were his honorable pursuits. A furious blow of his clenched fist, in the very palace of the Emperor at Augsburg, knocked out the teeth of a heretic, — an achievement hailed with honor and congratulation by the Duke of Alva, and by his master, Charles the Fifth. Thus did a Spanish gentleman acquire Fame in the sixteenth century ![1]

Such, in other places and times, have been objects of praise. Such is the Glory achieved. Men have extolled what, according to their knowledge or ignorance, they could best appreciate. Nor does this rule fail in our day. The ends of pursuit vary in different parts of the globe and among different persons; and Fame is still awarded to conduct which reason condemns as barbarous. The North American savage commemorates the chief who hangs at the door of his wigwam a heavy string of scalps, the spoils of war. The New-Zealander honors the champion who slays and then eats his enemy. The cannibal of the Feejee Islands, only recently explored by an expedition from our shores, is praised for his adroitness in lying, — for the dozen men he has killed with his own hand, — for triumphant capture, in battle, of a piece of tapa-cloth attached to a staff, not unlike one of our flags; and when dead, his

[1] Sismondi's Literature of the South of Europe, Vol. IV. pp. 8 – 16.

club is placed in his hand, and extended across the breast, to indicate in the next world that the deceased was a chief and a warrior.[1] This is barbarous Glory! But among nations professing Christianity, in our day, there is a powerful public opinion exulting in conduct from which we turn with disgust, as we discern it among the savages of our forest, or the cannibals of the Pacific. The triumphs of animal strength and of brutal violence are hailed as famous. With perverse insensibility to the relative value of human acts, the chances and incidents of war are exalted above the pursuits of peace. Victors from fields moistened with a brother's blood are greeted with grateful salutations, justly due to those only who have triumphantly fulfilled the grand commandments on which hang all the law and the prophets.

Such is controlling public opinion in our age and country. A people that regards success rather than those objects for which alone success is worthy of desire, — that has not yet discerned the beauty of humble and disinterested labor in the great causes by which mankind is advanced, — that has not yet admired the golden link of harmony by which all efforts of usefulness are bound together, — that has not yet recognized the peculiar Christian sentiment of Human Brotherhood, without difference of country, color, or race, — that does not feel, in the concerns of state, as of private life, the enkindling supremacy of those principles of Justice and Benevolence which send their heavenly radiance into the home of poverty, the darkness of ignorance, and the solitude of the prison, which exhibit the degradation

[1] Narrative of the United States Exploring Expedition, Vol. III. pp. 76, 80 98.

of the slave and the wickedness of war, while they exalt scholarship, invigorate eloquence, extend science and all human knowledge, — such a people, not unnaturally, applauds conduct less in harmony with truth, virtue, goodness, than with its own imperfect spirit. And this is what is called Reputation, Fame, Glory, — fickle as a breeze, unsubstantial as a shadow. Well does the master poet of Italy say, —

> "Nought is this mundane Glory but a breath
> Of wind, that comes now this way and now that,
> And changes name because it changes side."[1]

II.

In determining that Glory is but a form or expression of public opinion, valuable only according to those from whom it proceeds, the way is prepared for the second question, — To what extent, if any, is it a proper motive of conduct or object of regard?

If we were ready to follow implicitly those simple precepts of Christianity which ordain exalted duties as the rule of life, this inquiry might be answered shortly. It is well to pursue it in other aspects.

Glory occupied the philosophers of antiquity, who disputed much on its value. Chrysippus and Diogenes held it in unbounded contempt, declaring that it was not worth extending a finger for.[2] Epicurus, under the natural guidance of principles enjoining repose and indifference to public affairs, inculcated a similar contempt. His views were expressed sententiously in the precept of his school, *Conceal thy life;* and he did not hesitate to warn against regulating conduct by the opinion of oth-

[1] Dante, Divina Commedia: *Purgatorio*, Canto XI. 100-102.
[2] Cicero, De Finibus, Lib. III. c. 17.

ers or the reputation of the world. Montaigne has pleasantly remarked, that even this philosopher, when death was at hand, relaxed from the insensibility he had enjoined, — dwelling upon the memory of his teachings, and by his will ordering his heirs to provide, in every recurring January, a festival to honor the day of his birth.[1]

On the other hand, Carneades maintained that Glory is to be sought for its own sake, — an opinion which has not failed to find much sympathy and many followers.[2] Aristotle regarded it as the greatest and most invaluable of external goods, and warned against two extremes, both, in his opinion, equally vicious, — excess in seeking and in avoiding.[3] But it is to the Roman orator that we are to look for the most vivid defence of this, the master passion of his youth, manhood, and age.

The influence exerted by Cicero over the opinions of mankind renders this feature of his character important. Of a less solid understanding than Demosthenes and Aristotle, — the former of whom, in his most masterly oration, vindicated for himself a crown, the badge of Glory, while the latter, as we have already seen, was not insensible to its attractions, — he is more conspicuous than either for the earnestness and constancy with which he displays its influence, the frankness with which he recognizes it as a supreme motive and reward, and the seductive eloquence with which he commends it as an object of vehement and perpetual ambition. On his return from those studies in Athens by which his

[1] Essays, Book II. ch. 16: *Of Glory*. The will is preserved in the Life of Epicurus by Diogenes Laertius, Lib. X. c. 10. See also Cicero, De Finibus, Lib. II. c. 30, 31.

[2] Cicero, De Finibus, Lib. III. c. 17.

[3] Ethics, Lib. II. c. 7; Lib. IV. c. 3, 4.

skill as an orator was so much enhanced, he consulted the Oracle at Delphi, not to learn how best his great powers and accomplishments might be devoted to the good of mankind, but by what means he might soonest arrive at the height of Glory. The answer of the Oracle, though imperfect and heathen, was in a higher mood than the inquiry. It was, "By making his own genius, and not the opinion of others, the guide of life." Arrived in Rome, he was fired by the fame of Hortensius at the bar, and commenced his forensic career in emulous rivalry of that illustrious lawyer. In all the manifold labors of subsequent life, as orator, statesman, general, rhetorician, poet, historian, critic, and philosopher, the aspiration for renown was the *Labarum* by which he was guided and inspired. It was to him the cloud by day and the pillar of fire by night.

In Cicero this sentiment was ennobled, so far as possible with a desire so selfish, by the eminent standard which he established for the Glory so much coveted. In one of his orations he characterizes it as "the illustrious and extended Fame of many and great deserts, either towards friends, or towards country, or towards the whole race of men." [1] And again, in the calmness of those philosophical speculations by which his name is exalted, not less than by the eloquence which crushed Catiline, won the clemency of Cæsar, and blasted the character of Antony, he declares that "Glory is the united praise of the good, the incorrupt voice of the true judges of eminent virtue, responding to virtue as an echo, and, being for the most part an attendant on good deeds, ought not to be disdained by good men." [2] This is the picture of True Glory; nor were there any occa-

1 Pro Marcello, 8.

2 Tusc. Quæst., Lib. III. c. 2.

sion of criticism, if he had striven to do the good works to which Fame responds as an echo, without regard to his own advancement.

However elevated his conception of Glory, he sought it for its own sake. He wooed it with the ardor of a lover, and embraced it as the bride of his bosom. In that unsurpassed effort for his early teacher, the poet Archias, where the union of literary and professional studies is vindicated with a beauty equal to the cause, he makes public profession of his constant desire for Fame. In quoting his words on that occasion, I present a vindication of this sentiment which has exerted immeasurable influence over the educated world, and is, beyond question, the most eloquent and engaging that ever fell from mortal lips. "Nor is this," says he, "to be dissembled which cannot be concealed, but it is to be openly avowed: we are all influenced by the love of praise, and the best are chiefly moved by Glory. The philosophers themselves inscribe their names even in those little books which they write on contempt of Glory; in the very productions in which they express disdain of Praise and Fame they wish to gain Praise and Fame for themselves. . . . . And now, O judges, I will declare myself to you, and confess to you my love of Glory, too strong, perhaps, but nevertheless honorable. . . . . For virtue desires no other reward of its toils and dangers than Praise and Glory: this being withdrawn, what is there in our poor brief career of life that can induce us to undertake such great labors? Surely, if the soul did not look forward to posterity, if all its thoughts were confined within the bounds by which the span of life is circumscribed, it would neither waste its strength in labors so arduous, nor vex itself with so many cares and watchings, nor would it fight so often for life itself. But now there is in every good man a certain virtue, stirring the soul night and day with the incentive of Glory, and admonishing us that the remembrance of our name must not be suffered to pass away with our life, but should be made to endure through all futurity."[1] This certainly is frank. And in another oration Cicero sharply declares that no man exerts himself with praise and virtue in the perils of the republic who is not moved thereto by the hope of Glory and a regard to posterity.[2]

Thus distinctly recognizing human applause as an all-sufficient motive of conduct, and professing his own dependence upon it, we cannot be surprised at his sedulous efforts to fortify his Fame, nor even at the iterations of self-praise with which his productions abound. In that interesting collection of letters, so much of which is happily spared to us, disclosing the aims and aspirations of his life, there is melancholy evidence of the pernicious sway of this passion, even in his noble bosom. With an immodest freedom, which he vindicates to himself by the remarkable expression, that *an epistle does not blush,* he invites his friend Lucceius to undertake the history of that portion of his life rendered memorable by the overthrow of the Catilinarian conspiracy, his exile, and return to his country; and, not content with dwelling on the variety and startling nature of the incidents, with the scope they would naturally afford to the accomplished historian, whose Glory, he subtly suggests, may in this way be connected forever with his own, as is that of Apelles with the Glory of Alexander, he proceeds so far as to press his

[1] Pro Archia, 11.

[2] Pro C. Rabirio, 10.

friend, if he does not think the facts worth the pains of adorning, yet to allow so much to friendship, to affection, and to that favor which he had so persuasively condemned in his prefaces, as not to confine himself scrupulously to the strict laws of history or the requirements of truth.[1] Thus, in the madness of his passion for Glory, would he suborn that sacred verity which is higher than friendship, affection, or any earthly favor!

A character like Cicero, compact of so many virtues, resplendent with a genius so lofty, standing on one of the most commanding pinnacles of classical antiquity, still admired by the wide world, hardly less than by the living multitudes that once chafed about the rostrum like a raging sea and were stilled by the music of his voice, — such a character cannot fail to exert a too magical charm over the young, especially where its lessons harmonize with the weakness rather than with the sternness of our nature, — with the instinctive promptings of selfishness, rather than with that disinterestedness which places duty, without hope of reward, without fear or favor, above all human consideration. It is most true that he has kindled in many bosoms something of his own inextinguishable ardors; and the American youth — child of a continent beyond the Atlantis of his imagination, and lifted by institutions he had never seen, even in his vision of a Republic — feels a glow of selfish ambition, as, in tasks of the school, he daily cons the writings of this great master.

1 Epistolæ ad Diversos, Lib. V. 12. — The letter to Lucceius seems to have been a favorite, as it is a most remarkable, production of its author. Writing to Atticus, he says, "*Valde bella est*," and seeks to interest him in the same behalf. (Ad Atticum, Lib. IV. 6.) Pliny, who looked to the pen of Tacitus for Fame, but in a higher spirit than Cicero, expressly declares that he does not desire him to give the least offence to truth. "Quanquam non exigo ut excedas actæ rei modum. Nam nec historia debet egredi veritatem, et honeste factis veritas sufficit." — Plin. Epistolæ, Lib. VII. 33.

His influence is easily discerned in the sentiments of those whose scholarly nurture has brought them within the fascination of his genius. I refer, by way of example, to Sir William Jones, a character of much purity, and of constant sympathy with freedom and humanity, not less than with various labors of learning and literature. In one of his early letters he said that he wished "absolutely to make Cicero his model";[1] while in another he shows himself a true disciple, by loyalty to the same motive of conduct which animated the Roman. "Do not imagine," says Jones, "that I despise the usual enjoyments of youth. No one can take more delight in singing and dancing than I do, nor in the moderate use of wine, nor in the exquisite beauty of the ladies, of whom London affords an enchanting variety; *but I prefer Glory, my supreme delight, to all other gratifications, and I will pursue it through fire and water, by day and by night.*"[2] Here is frankness kindred to that of his Roman exemplar.

It will be proper to pause, in this review of opinion, and endeavor, by careful analysis, to comprehend the just office of this sentiment, which is elevated to be the guide of conduct and aim of life.

Unquestionably, as we are constituted, Glory does exert an imperious control. Its influence is widely and variously felt, though seeming to diminish with advancing years, with the growth of the moral and intellectual nature, with the development of the Christian character, and in proportion as the great realities of existence here and hereafter engross the soul. The child is sensitive to it in earliest dalliance on a parent's

1 Letter to H. A. Schultens, October, 1774: Life, by Lord Teignmouth, p. 126.

2 Letter to C. Reviczki, March, 1771: Ibid., p. 96.

knee. Here is an element of that unamiable selfishness which pervades his crude nature, rendering him jealous and envious of caress and praise bestowed upon another. His little bosom palpitates with unrestrained ardors, which in children of a larger growth animate conquerors, and those whom the world calls "great." As he mingles with playmates, the same passion enters into his sports, and attends the exercises of the school. He is covetous of evanescent applause among his peers. He struggles for this fragile Glory, — a bubble blown by the breath of boys.

In maturer years a similar solicitude continues, modified by period and circumstance. The youth putting away childish things rarely forgets the sentiment of emulation; while not insensible to the desire of *excellence,* he is animated by the desire of *excelling.* I do not mention this for any austere criticism, but as a psychological fact. And when preparation gives place to action, then this same sentiment, which absorbed the child and animated the youth, reappears in the confirmed ambition of manhood. Now, under loftier name, and with mien of majesty, it beckons to competition with the masters of human thought and conduct, filling his bosom with a pleasing frenzy. He is aroused by

> "the spur that the clear spirit doth raise
> (*That last infirmity of noble mind*)
> To scorn delights and live laborious days."[1]

He burns to impress his name upon the age, and to challenge the gratitude of posterity. For this he enters the lists with voice, pen, or, it may be, the sword. Like Themistocles, he is sleepless from the laurels of those who have gone before; like Alexander, he

[1] Milton, Lycidas, 70-72.

sighs for some new world to conquer; like Cæsar, he pours fruitless tears, because, at the age of the dying Alexander, he has done nothing memorable; like Cicero, he dwells upon the applause of men, and draws from it fresh inspiration to labor; and even if he writes against Glory, it is, according to Pascal, for the Glory of writing well. This is the *Love of Glory*, a sentiment which lurks in every stage and sphere of life, — with the young, the middle-aged, and the old, — with the lowly, the moderate, and the great, — under as many *aliases* as a culprit, — but, in all its different forms and guises, having one simple animating essence, the passion for the approbation of our fellow-men.[1] By a touch of exquisite nature, Dante reveals the suffering spirits, in the penal gloom and terror of another world, clothed in the weakness of mortal passion, and, unconscious of the true glories of Paradise, still tormented by the desire to be spoken of on earth.[2] And Pascal echoes Dante, when, with that point which is so much his own, he says that "we lose life itself with joy, provided men speak of the loss."[3]

This desire lies deep in the human heart. It is a sentiment implanted at birth. It is kindred to other sentiments and appetites, whose office is to provide for our protection. It is like the love of wealth or the love of power, desires which all feel in a certain degree to be

1 "Nulla est ergo tanta humilitas, quæ dulcedine gloriæ non tangatur." — Val. Max., Lib. VIII. c. 14, § 5.

2 "Però se campi d 'esti luoghi bui,
E torni a riveder le belle stelle,
Quando ti gioverà dicere: I' fui,
Fa che di noi alla gente favelle."
Inferno, Canto XVI. 82-85.

3 Pensées, Part. I. Art. V. sec. 2: *Vanité de l'Homme.*

part of their being. Recognizing it, then, as an endowment from the hand of God, we may hesitate to condemn its influence at all times and under all circumstances. Implanted for some good, it is our duty to comprehend its true function. This is not difficult.

The Love of Glory, then, is a motive of human conduct. But the same Heavenly Father who endowed us with the love of approbation has placed in us other sentiments of a higher order, more kindred to his own divine nature. These are Justice and Benevolence, both of which, however imperfectly developed or ill directed, are elements of every human soul. The desire of Justice, filling us with the love of Duty, is the sentiment which fits us to receive and comprehend the sublime injunction of doing unto others as we would have them do unto us. In the predominance of this sentiment, enlightened by intelligence, injustice becomes impossible. The desire of Benevolence goes further. It leads all who are under its influence to those acts of kindness, disinterestedness, humanity, love to neighbor, which constitute the crown of the Christian character. Such sentiments are celestial, godlike, in their office.

In determining proper motives of conduct, it is easy to perceive that the higher are more commendable than the lower, and that even an act of Justice and Benevolence loses something of its charm when known to be inspired by the selfish desire of human applause. It was the gay poet of antiquity who said that concealed virtue differed little from sepulchred sluggishness:—

> "Paulum sepultæ distat inertiæ
> Celata virtus."[1]

But this is a heathen sentiment, alien to reason and to

[1] Hor., Carm. IV. ix. 29, 30.

truth. It is hoped that men will be honest, but from a higher motive than because honesty is the best policy. It is hoped that they will be humane, but for nobler cause than the Fame of humanity.

The love of approbation may properly animate the young, whose minds have not yet ascended to the appreciation of that virtue which is its own exceeding great reward.[1] It may justly strengthen those of maturer age who are not moved by the simple appeals of duty, unless the smiles of mankind attend them. It were churlish not to offer homage to those acts by which happiness is promoted, even though inspired by a sentiment of personal ambition, or by considerations of policy. But such motives must always detract from the perfect beauty even of good works. The Man of Ross, who was said to

> "Do good by stealth, and blush to find it Fame,"

was a character of real life, and the example of his virtue may still be prized, like the diamond, for its surpassing rarity. It cannot be disguised, however, that much is gained where the desire of praise acts in conjunction with the higher sentiments. If ambition be our lure, it will be well for mankind, if it unite with Justice and Benevolence.

It may be demanded if we should be indifferent to the approbation of men. Certainly not. It is a proper source of gratification, and is one of the just rewards on earth. It may be enjoyed when virtuously won, though it were better, if not proposed as the object of desire. The great English magistrate, Lord Mansfield, while confessing a wish for popularity, added, in words which

1 "Virtutum omnium pretium in ipsis est. Non enim exercentur ad præmium ; recte facti fecisse merces est." — Seneca, Epist. LXXXI. 17.

cannot be too often quoted, "But it is that popularity which follows, not that which is run after; it is that popularity which, sooner or later, never fails to do justice to the pursuit of noble ends by noble means."[1] And the historian of the Decline and Fall of the Roman Empire, who was no stranger to the Love of Glory, has given expression to the satisfaction which he derived from the approbation of those whose opinions were valuable. "If I listened to the music of praise," says Gibbon, in his Autobiography, "I was more seriously satisfied with the approbation of my judges. The candor of Dr. Robertson embraced his disciple. A letter from Mr. Hume overpaid the labor of ten years."[2] It would be difficult to declare the self-gratulation of the successful author in language more sententious or expressive.

While recognizing praise as an incidental reward, though not a commendable motive, we cannot disregard the evil which ensues when the desire for it predominates over the character, and fills the soul, as is too often the case, with a blind emulation chiefly solicitous for personal success. The world, which should be a happy scene of constant exertion and harmonious coöperation, becomes a field of rivalry, competition, and hostile struggle. It is true that God has not given to all the same excellences of mind and heart; but he naturally requires more of the strong than of the many less blessed. The little we can do will not be cast vainly into his treasury; nor need the weak and humble be filled with any idle emulation of others. Let each act earnestly, according to the measure of his powers, — rejoicing al-

[1] Rex *v.* Wilkes, 4 Burrow's Reports, 2562.
[2] Memoirs: Miscellaneous Works, p. 94.

ways in the prosperity of his neighbor; and though we may seem to accomplish little, yet we shall do much, if we be true to the convictions of the soul, and give the example of unselfish devotion to duty. This of itself is success; and this is within the ambition of all. Life is no Ulyssean bow, to be bent only by a single strong arm. There is none so weak as not to use it.

In the growth of the individual the intellect advances before the moral powers; for it is necessary to know what is right before we can practise it; and this same order of progress is observed in the Human Family. Moral excellence is the bright, consummate flower of all progress. It is often the peculiar product of age. And it is then, among other triumphs of virtue, that Duty assumes her commanding place, while personal ambition is abased. Burke, in that marvellous passage of elegiac beauty where he mourns his only son, says, "Indeed, my Lord, I greatly deceive myself, if, in this hard season, I would give a peck of refuse wheat for all that is called Fame and Honor in the world."[1] And Channing, with a sentiment most unlike the ancient Roman orator, declares that he sees "nothing worth living for but the divine virtue which endures and surrenders all things for truth, duty, and mankind."[2]

Such an insensibility to worldly objects, and such an elevation of spirit, may not be expected at once from all men, — certainly not without something of the trials of Burke or the soul of Channing. But it is within the power of all to strive after that virtue which it may be difficult to reach; and just in proportion as duty becomes the guide and aim of life shall we learn to close

[1] Letter to a Noble Lord: Works, Vol. VII. p. 417.

[2] Letter to James G. Birney: Works, Vol. II. p. 175

the soul against the allurements of praise and the asperities of censure, while we find satisfactions and compensations such as man cannot give or take away. The world, with ignorant or intolerant judgment, may condemn; the countenance of companion may be averted; the heart of friend may grow cold; but the consciousness of duty done will be sweeter than the applause of the world, than the countenance of companion, or the heart of friend.

III.

From this survey of Glory, according to common acceptance, and of its influence as a motive of conduct, I advance to the third and concluding head, — What are True Fame and Glory, and who are the men most worthy of honor? The answer is already implied, if not expressed, in much of the discussion through which we have passed; but it may not be without advantage to dwell upon it more at length.

From the vicious and barbarous elements entering into past conceptions of Glory, it is evident that there must be a surer and higher standard. A degraded public opinion naturally fails to appreciate excellence not in harmony with its own prejudices, while it lavishes regard upon conduct we would gladly forget. Genius, too, in all ages, (such is the melancholy story of Humanity,) has stooped to be sycophant, apologist, or friend of characters never to be mentioned without disgust. Historian, poet, and philosopher, false to every sacred office, have pandered to the praise of those who should have been gibbeted to the condemnation of mankind. Lucan, the youthful poet of Freedom, offers in his "Pharsalia" the incense of adulation to the monster Nero; Quintilian, the instructor, pauses in his grave "Institutes of Oratory" to speak of the tyrant Domitian as *most holy;* Paterculus, the historian, extols Tiberius and Sejanus; Seneca, the philosopher, condescends, in his treatise on Consolation, to flatter the imbecile Claudius; while, not to multiply instances in modern times, Corneille, the grandest poet of France, prefaced one of his tragedies with a tribute to the crafty tyrant Mazarin; and our own English Dryden lent his glowing verse to welcome and commemorate a heartless, unprincipled monarch and a servile court.

Others, while refraining from eulogy, unconsciously surrender to sentiments and influences, the *public opinion,* of the age in which they live, — investing barbarous characters and scenes, the struggles of selfishness and ambition, and even the movements of conquering robbers, with colors too apt to fascinate or mislead. Not content with that candor which should guide our judgment alike of the living and the dead, they yield sympathy even to injustice and wrong, when commended by genius or elevated by success, and especially if coupled with the egotism of a vicious patriotism. Not feeling practically the vital truth of Human Brotherhood, and the correlative duties it involves, they are insensible to the true character and the shame of transactions by which it is degraded or assailed, and in their estimate depart from that standard of Absolute Right which must be the only measure of true and permanent Fame.

Whatever may be temporary applause, or the expression of public opinion, it may be asserted without fear of contradiction, *that no true and permanent Fame can be founded except in labors which promote the happiness of mankind.* If these are by Christian means, with disinterested motives, and with the single view of doing good, they become that rare and precious virtue whose fit image is the spotless lily of the field, brighter than Solomon in all his Glory. Earth has nothing of such surpassing loveliness. Heaven may claim the lustre as its own. Such labors are the natural fruit of obedience to the great commandments. Reason, too, in harmony with these laws, shows that the true dignity of Humanity is in the moral and intellectual nature, and that the labors of Justice and Benevolence, directed by intelligence and abasing that part which is in common with beasts, are the highest forms of human conduct.

In determining the praise of actions, four elements may be regarded: *first,* the difficulties overcome; *secondly,* the means employed; *thirdly,* the motives; and, *fourthly,* the extent of good accomplished. If the difficulties are petty, or the means employed low, vulgar, barbarous, there can be little worthy of highest regard, although the motives are pure and the results beneficent. If the motives are selfish, if a desire of power or wealth or Fame intrude into the actions, they lose that other title to regard springing from beauty and elevation of purpose, even if the conduct be mistaken or weak, and the results pernicious. Horne Tooke claimed for himself no mean epitaph, when he asked for himself after death the praise of good intentions. Still further,—if little or no good arises, and the actions fail to be ennobled by high and generous motives, while the means employed are barbarous and unchristian, and the difficulties overcome are trivial, then surely there is little occasion for applause, although worldly success or the bloody eagle of victorious battle attend them.

Here we encounter the question, What measure of praise shall be accorded to war, or to the profession of arms? Thus far, great generals and conquerors have attracted the largest share of admiration. They swell the page of history. For them is inspiring music, the minute-gun, the flag at half-mast, the trophy, the monument. Fame is a plant whose most luxuriant shoots have grown on fields of blood. Are these vigorous and perennial, or are they destined to perish and fall to earth beneath the rays of the still ascending sun?

There are not a few who will join with Milton in his admirable judgment of martial renown: —

> "They err who count it glorious to subdue
> By conquest far and wide, to overrun
> Large countries, and in field great battles win,
> Great cities by assault. What do these worthies
> But rob and spoil, burn, slaughter, and enslave
> Peaceable nations, neighboring or remote,
> Made captive, yet deserving freedom more
> Than those, their conquerors, who leave behind
> Nothing but ruin, wheresoe'er they rove,
> And all the flourishing works of peace destroy?" [1]

This interesting testimony finds echo in another of England's remarkable characters, Edmund Waller, — himself poet, orator, statesman, man of the world, — who has left on record his judgment of True Glory, in a valedictory poem, written at the age of eighty, when the passions of this world no longer obscured the clear perception of duty. At an earlier period of life he had sung of war. Mark the change in this swan-like note, which might disenchant even the eloquence of Cicero, covetous of Fame: —

[1] Paradise Regained, Book III. 71-80.

"Earth praises conquerors for shedding blood;
Heaven, those that love their foes and do 'em good.
It is terrestrial honor to be crowned
For strewing men, like rushes, on the ground:
True Glory 't is to rise above them all,
Without the advantage taken by their fall.
He that in fight diminishes mankind
Does no addition to his stature find;
But he that does a noble nature show,
Obliging others, still does higher grow:
For virtue practised such an habit gives
That among men he like an angel lives;
Humbly he doth, and without envy, dwell,
Loved and admired by those he does excel.
. . . .
Wrestling with Death, these lines I did indite;
No other theme could give my soul delight.
O that my youth had thus employed my pen,
Or that I now could write as well as then!" [1]

Well does the poet give the palm to moral excellence! But it is from the lips of a successful soldier, cradled in war, the very pink of warlike heroism, that we are taught to appreciate the Fame of literature, which, though less elevated than that from disinterested beneficence, is truer and more permanent than any bloody Glory. I allude to Wolfe, conqueror of Quebec, who has attracted a larger share of romantic interest than any other of the gallant generals in English history. We behold him, yet young in years, at the head of an adventurous expedition, destined to prostrate the French empire in Canada, — guiding and encouraging the firmness of his troops in unaccustomed difficulties, — awakening their personal attachment by his kindly suavity, and their ardor by his own example, — climbing the precipitous steeps which conduct to the heights of the strongest fortress on the American continent, — there, under its walls, joining in deadly conflict, — wounded,

[1] Of the Fear of God, Canto 2.

— stretched upon the field, — faint from loss of blood, — with sight already dimmed, — his life ebbing rapidly, — cheered at last by the sudden cry, that the enemy is fleeing in all directions, — and then his dying breath mingling with the shouts of victory. An eminent artist has portrayed this scene of death in a much admired picture. History and Poetry have dwelt upon it with peculiar fondness. Such is the Glory of arms! Happily there is preserved to us a tradition of this day which affords the gleam of a truer Glory. As the commander, in his boat, floated down the current of the St. Lawrence, under cover of night, in the enforced silence of a military expedition, to effect a landing at an opportune promontory, he was heard repeating to himself, in subdued voice, that poem of exquisite charm, — then only recently given to mankind, now familiar as a household word wherever the mother tongue of Gray is spoken, — the "Elegy in a Country Churchyard." Strange and unaccustomed prelude to the discord of battle! As the ambitious warrior finished the recitation, he said to his companions, in low, but earnest tone, that he "would rather be the author of that poem than take Quebec."[1] He was right. The Glory of that victory is already dying out, like a candle in the socket. The True Glory of the poem still shines with star-bright, immortal beauty.

Passing from these testimonies, I would observe for a moment the nature of Military Glory. Its most conspicuous element is courage, placed by ancient philosophers among the four cardinal virtues: Aristotle seems to advance it foremost. But plainly, of itself, it is neither virtue nor vice. It is a quality in man possessed in common with a large number of animals. It

[1] Grahame, History of the United States, Vol. IV. pp. 51, 52.

becomes virtue, when exercised in obedience to the higher sentiments, with Justice and Benevolence as its objects. It is of humbler character, if these objects are promoted by Force, or by *the beast in man.* It is unquestionably vice, when, divorced from Justice and Benevolence, it lends itself to the passion for wealth, power, or Glory.

It is easy to determine that courage, though of the lion or tiger, when employed in an unrighteous cause, cannot be the foundation of true and permanent Fame. Mardonius and his Persian hosts in Greece, Cæsar and his Roman legions in Britain, Cortés and his conquering companions in Mexico, Pizarro and his band of robbers in Peru, the Scandinavian Vikings in their adventurous expeditions of piracy, are all condemned without hesitation. Nor can applause attend hireling Swiss, or Italian chieftains of the Middle Ages, or bought Hessians of the British armies, who sold their spears and bayonets to the highest bidder. And it is difficult to see how those, in our own day, following *the trade of arms,* careless of the cause in which it is employed, can hope for better sympathy. An early English poet, of mingled gayety and truth, Sir John Suckling, himself a professor of war, makes the soldier confess the recklessness of his life: —

"I am a man of war and might,
And know thus much, that I can fight,
Whether I am i' th' wrong or right,
Devoutly."[1]

In such a spirit no True Glory can be achieved. And is not this plainly the spirit of the soldier, regarded as a "machine" only, and acting in unquestioning obedience to orders? No command of Government, or any human

[1] A Soldier: Works, Vol. I. p. 82.

power, can sanctify wrong; nor can rules of military subordination, or prejudices of an unchristian patriotism, dignify conduct in violation of heaven-born sentiments. The inspiring inscription at Thermopylæ said, "O stranger, tell the Lacedæmonians that we lie here *in obedience to their commands*";[1] but the three hundred Lacedæmonians who there laid down their lives were stemming, in those narrow straits, the mighty tide of Xerxes, as it rolled in upon Greece.

To all defenders of freedom or country the heart goes forth with cordial, spontaneous sympathy. May God defend the right! Their cause, whether in victory or defeat, is invested with the interest which from the time of Abel has attached to all who suffer from the violence of a brother-man. But their unhappy strife belongs to the DISHONORABLE BARBARISM of the age, — like the cannibalism of an earlier period, or the slavery of our own day.

Not questioning the right of self-defence, or undertaking to consider the sanctions of the *Institution* of War as an established Arbiter of Justice between nations, or its necessity in our age, all may join in regarding it as an *unchristian institution*, and a *melancholy necessity*, offensive in the sight of God, and hostile to the best interests of men. A field of battle is a scene of execution *according to the laws of war*, — without trial or judgment, but with a thousand Jack Ketches in the odious work.[2] And yet the acts of hardihood and skill here displayed are entitled "brilliant"; the move-

1 Simonides, apud Herod. Hist., Lib. VIII. c. 229.

2 A brilliant writer, who never fails to exalt war, recognizes the parallel between the soldier and the executioner; but he finds the soldier so noble as to ennoble even the work of the executioner, when called to perform it. — Joseph de Maistre, Les Soirées de Saint-Pétersbourg, Tom. II. pp. 4 – 13.

ments of the executioners in gay apparel are praised as "brilliant"; the destruction of life is "brilliant"; the results of the *auto da fé* are "brilliant"; the day of this mournful tragedy is enrolled as "brilliant"; and Christians are summoned to commemorate with *honor* a scene which should rather pass from the recollection of men.

The example even of martial Rome may here teach us one great lesson. Recognizing the fellowship of a common country, conflicts between citizens were condemned as *fratricidal*. *Civil* war was branded as *guilt* and *crime*. The array of opposing forces, drawn from the bosom of the same community, knit together by the same political ties, was pronounced *impious*, even where they appeared under such cherished names as Pompey and Cæsar: —

"*Impia* concurrunt Pompeii et Cæsaris arma."[1]

As the natural consequence, victories in these fraternal feuds were held to be not only unworthy of praise, but never to be mentioned without blame. Even if countenanced by *justice* or dire *necessity*, they were none the less mournful. *No success over brethren of the same country could be the foundation of honor.* And so firmly was this principle embodied in the very customs and institutions of Rome, that no *thanksgiving* or religious ceremony was allowed by the Senate in commemoration of such success; nor was the *triumph* permitted to the conquering chief whose hands were red with the blood of fellow-citizens. Cæsar forbore even to send a herald of his unhappy victories, and looked upon them with *shame*.[2]

1 Lucan, Pharsalia, Lib. VII. 196.

2 See Illustrations at the end of this Oration.

As we recognize the commanding truth, that God "hath made of one blood all nations of men," and that all his children are brethren, the distinctions of country disappear, ALL WAR BECOMES FRATRICIDAL, and victory is achieved only by shedding a brother's blood. The soul shrinks from contemplation of the scene, and, while refusing to judge the act, confesses its unaffected sadness.

"The pomp is darkened, and the day o'ercast."

It was natural that ancient Heathen, strangers to the sentiment of Human Brotherhood, should limit their regard to the narrow circle of country, — as if there were magical lines within which strife and bloodshed are shame and crime, while beyond this pale they are great Glory. Preparing for battle, the Spartans sacrificed to the Muses, anxious for the countenance of these divinities, to the end that their deeds might be fitly described, and deeming it a heavenly favor that witnesses should behold them. Not so the Christian. He would rather pray that the recording angel would blot with tears all recollection of the fraternal strife in which he was sorrowfully engaged.

This conclusion, however repugnant to the *sentiment* of Heathenism or the *practice* of Christian nations, stands on the Brotherhood of Man. Because this truth is imperfectly recognized, the Heathen distinction between *civil* war and *foreign* war is yet maintained. To the Christian, every fellow-man, whether remote or near, whether of our own country or of another, is "neighbor" and "brother"; nor can any battle, whether between villages or towns or states or countries, be deemed other than *shame*, — like the civil wars of Rome, which the poet aptly said could bear no *triumphs*: —

"Bella geri placuit *nullos habitura triumphos.*"[1]

The same mortification and regret with which we regard the hateful contest between brothers of one household, kinsmen of one ancestry, citizens of one country, must attend every scene of strife; for are we not *all*, in a just and Christian sense, brethren of one household, kinsmen of one ancestry, citizens of one country,—the world? The inference is irresistible, that no success in arms against fellow-men, no triumph over brothers, flesh of our flesh and bone of our bone, no destruction of the life which God has given to his children, no assault upon his sacred image in the upright form and countenance of man, no effusion of human blood, *under whatever apology of necessity vindicated*, can be the foundation of Christian Fame.

Adverse to the prejudices of mankind as such conclusion may be, it must find sympathy in the refined soul and the inner heart of man, while it is in harmony with those utterances, in all ages, testifying to the virtue whose true parent is Peace. The loving admiration, so spontaneously offered to the Christian graces which adorned the Scipios, hesitates at those scenes of blood which gave to them the unwelcome eminence of "the two thunderbolts of war." The homage freely accorded to forbearance, generosity, or forgiveness, when seen in the spectral glare of battle, is a tacit rebuke to the hostile passions whose triumphant rage constitutes the Glory of arms. The wail of widows and orphans, and the sorrows of innumerable mourners refusing to be comforted, often check the gratulations of success. Stern warriors, too, in the paroxysm of victory, by unwilling tears vindicate humanity and condemn their

[1] Lucan, Pharsalia, Lib. I. 12.

own triumphs. More than one, in the dread extremities of life, has looked back with regret upon his career of battle, or perhaps, like Luxembourg of France, confessed that he would rather remember a cup of cold water given to a fellow-creature in poverty and distress than all his victories, with their blood, desolation, and death. Thus speaks the heart of man. No true Fame can flow from the fountain of tears.

The achievements of war and the characters of conquerors have been exposed by satire, under whose sharp touch we see their unsubstantial renown.

> "Heroes are much the same, the point 's agreed,
> From Macedonia's madman to the Swede."

Nobody has done this more plainly than Rabelais, who, in an age when Peace was only a distant vision, gave expression to those sentiments, often vague and undefined, which have their origin in the depths of the human soul. In the Life of Pantagruel, that strange satire, compounded of indecency, humor, effrontery, and learning, one of the characters, after being very merry in hell, talking familiarly with Lucifer, and penetrating to the Elysian Fields, recognizes some of the world's great men, but changed after a very extraordinary manner. Alexander the Great is mending and patching old breeches and stockings, and thus obtains a very poor living. Achilles is a maker of hay-bundles; Hannibal, a kettle-maker, and seller of egg-shells. All the knights of the Round Table are poor day-laborers, employed to row over the rivers Cocytus, Phlegethon, Styx, Acheron, and Lethe, when, according to Rabelais. "my lords the devils have a mind to recreate themselves upon the water, as on like occasion one hires the boatmen at Lyons, the gondoliers of Venice, or oars of London, — but with this difference, that these poor knights have for their fare only a bob or flirt on the nose, and in the evening a morsel of coarse, mouldy bread."[1] Such is the wretched contrast between the judgment of earth and that other judgment, which cannot be arrested when earth has passed away.

Whatever the voice of poets, moralists, satirists, and even of soldiers, it is certain that the Glory of arms still exercises no mean influence over the human mind. The "red planet Mars" is still in the ascendant. The Art of War, which a French divine has happily termed "the baleful art of teaching men to exterminate one another,"[2] is yet held, even among Christians, an honorable pursuit; and the animal courage which it stimulates and develops is prized as transcendent virtue. It will be for another age and a higher civilization to appreciate the more exalted character of Beneficence as an Art, — the art of extending happiness and all good influences, by word or deed, to the largest number of mankind, — while, in blessed contrast with the misery, degradation, and wickedness of war, shines resplendent the True Grandeur of Peace. All then will be willing to join with the early poet in saying, —

> "Though louder Fame attend the martial rage,
> 'T is greater Glory to reform the age."[3]

Then shall the soul thrill with a nobler heroism than that of battle, while peaceful Industry, with untold multitudes of cheerful and beneficent laborers, takes the

1 Pantagruel, Book II. ch. 30.

2 "L'art militaire, c'est à dire, l'art funeste d'apprendre aux hommes à s'exterminer les uns les autres." — Massillon, Oraison Funèbre de Louis le Grand.

3 Waller, Of Queen Catharine, on New Year's Day, 1683.

place of War and its works, — while Literature, full of comfort and sympathy for the heart of man, rejoices in happiest empire, — while Science, with extensive sceptre, advances the bounds of knowledge and power, adding unimaginable strength to the hands of men, opening immeasurable resources in the earth, and revealing new secrets and harmonies in the skies, — while Art, elevated and refined, lavishes fresh images of beauty and grace, — while Charity, in streams of milk and honey, diffuses itself through all the habitations of the world.

Does any one ask for signs of this coming era? The increasing knowledge and beneficence of our own day, the broad-spread sympathy with human suffering, the widening thoughts of men, the longings of the heart for a higher condition on earth, the unfulfilled promises of Christian Progress, are the auspicious auguries of this Happy Future. Not to the Great Navigator alone, but to all now toiling for the new and glorious future, may be addressed the inspiring verses of the German poet: —

> " Steer, bold mariner, on! albeit witlings deride thee,
> And the steersman drop idly his hand at the helm;
> Ever, ever to westward! there must the coast be discovered,
> If it but lie distinct, luminous lie in thy mind.
> Trust to the God that leads thee, and follow the sea that is silent;
> Did it not yet exist, now would it rise from the flood.
> Nature with Genius stands united in league everlasting;
> What is promised by one surely the other performs." [1]

As early voyagers over untried realms of waste, we have already observed the signs of land. The green twig and fresh red berry have floated by our bark; the odors of the shore fan our faces; nay, we descry the

[1] Schiller, Columbus.

distant gleam of light, and hear from the more earnest watchers, as Columbus heard, after midnight, from the mast-head of the Pinta, the joyful cry of *Land! Land!* and, lo! a New World breaks upon our morning gaze.

A new order of heroes and of great men will then be recognized, while the history of the Past will be reviewed, to re-judge the Fame awarded or withheld. There are many, having high place in the world's praise, from whom a righteous Future will avert the countenance, so that they will know at last the neglect which has thus far been the lot of better men; but there are others, little regarded during life, sleeping in humble or unknown earth, who shall become the favorites of True Glory. At Athens there was an altar dedicated to the Unknown God. The time is at hand, when the company of good men whose lives are without record or monument will find at length an altar of praise.

Then will be cherished, not those who, from accident of birth, or by selfish struggle, have succeeded in winning the attention of mankind, — not those who have commanded armies in barbarous war, — not those who have exercised power or swayed empire, — not those who have made the world tributary to their luxury and wealth, — not those who have cultivated knowledge, regardless of their fellow-men. Not present Fame, nor war, nor power, nor wealth, nor knowledge, alone, can secure an entrance to this true and noble Valhalla. Here will be gathered those only who have toiled, each in his vocation, for the welfare of the race. Mankind will remember those only who have remembered mankind. Here, with the apostles, the prophets, and the martyrs, shall be joined the glorious company of the world's benefactors, — the goodly fellowship of truth and duty, — the noble army of statesmen, orators, poets, preachers, scholars, men in all walks of life, who have striven for the happiness of others. If the soldier finds a place in this sacred temple, it will be not *because*, but *notwithstanding*, he was a soldier.

"*God alone is great!*" Such was the admired and triumphant exclamation with which Massillon opened his funeral discourse on the deceased monarch of France, called in his own age Louis *the Great*. It is in the attributes of God that we find the elements of true greatness. Man is great by the godlike qualities of Justice, Benevolence, Knowledge, and Power. And as Justice and Benevolence are higher than Knowledge and Power, so are the just and benevolent higher than those who are intelligent and powerful only. Should all these qualities auspiciously concur in one person on earth, then might we look to behold a mortal, supremely endowed, reflecting the image of his Maker. But even Knowledge and Power, without those higher attributes, cannot constitute true greatness. It is by his Goodness that God is most truly known; so also is the Great Man. When Moses said unto the Lord, "Show me thy Glory," the Lord answered, "I will make all my Goodness pass before thee."[1]

It will be easy to distinguish between those merely memorable in the world's annals and those truly great. Reviewing the historic names to which flattery or a false appreciation of character has awarded this title,

[1] Exodus, xxxiii. 18, 19. — It was a saying of Heathen Antiquity, that to help a mortal was to be a God to a mortal, and this is the way to everlasting Glory: "Deus est mortali juvare mortalem, et hæc ad æternam Gloriam via." — Plin., Nat. Hist., II. 7.

we find its painful inaptitude. Alexander, drunk with victory and with wine, whose remains, after early death at the age of thirty-two, were borne through conquered Asia on a funeral car glittering with massive gold and wonderful in magnificence, was not truly great. Cæsar, ravager of distant lands, and trampler upon the liberties of his own country, with an unsurpassed combination of intelligence and power, was not truly great. Louis the Fourteenth of France, magnificent spendthrift monarch, prodigal of treasure and of blood, always panting for renown, was not truly great. Peter of Russia, organizer of material prosperity in his vast empire, murderer of his own son, despotic, inexorable, unnatural, savage, was not truly great. Frederic of Prussia, heartless and consummate general, skilled in the barbarous art of war, who played the game of robbery with human lives for dice, was not truly great. There is little of true grandeur in any such career. None of the Beatitudes showered upon them a blessed influence. They were not poor in spirit, or meek, or merciful, or pure in heart. They were not peacemakers. They did not hunger and thirst after Justice. They did not suffer persecution for Justice's sake.

It is men like these, that the good Abbé St. Pierre, in works deserving well of mankind, has termed *Illustrious,* in contradistinction to *Great.* Their influence was extensive, their power mighty, their names famous; but they were barbarous, selfish, and inhuman in aim, with little of love to God and less to man.

There is another and a higher company that thought little of praise or power, whose lives shine before men with those good works which glorify their authors. There is Milton, poor and blind, but " bating not a jot of heart or hope," — in an age of ignorance the friend of education, in an age of servility and vice the pure and uncontaminated friend of freedom, tuning his harp to those magnificent melodies which angels might stoop to hear, and confessing his supreme duties to Humanity in words of simplicity and power. "I am long since persuaded," was his declaration, "that, to say or do aught worth memory and imitation, no purpose or respect should sooner move us than simply the love of God and of mankind."[1] There is Vincent de Paul, of France, once a captive in Algiers. Obtaining freedom by happy escape, this fugitive slave devoted himself with divine success to works of Christian benevolence, — the establishment of hospitals, visiting those in prison, the spread of amity and peace. Unknown, he repairs to the galleys at Marseilles, and, touched by the story of a poor convict, takes the heavy chains upon himself, that this fellow-man may leave to visit his wife and children; and then, moved by the sorrows of France bleeding with war, hurries to her powerful minister, the Cardinal Richelieu, and on his knees entreats, — "Give us peace! have pity upon us! give peace to France!"[2] There is Howard, the benefactor of those on whom the world has placed its brand, — whose charity, like that of the Frenchman, inspired by the single desire of doing good, illumined the gloom of the dungeon as with angelic presence. "A person of more ability," he says, in sweet simplicity, "with my knowledge of facts, would have written better; but the object of my ambition was not the Fame of an author. *Hearing the cry of the miserable, I devoted my time to their relief.*"[3] And, lastly, there

1 Of Education: Prose Works, Vol. I. p. 273.
2 Biographie Universelle: Art. *Vincent de Paul.*
3 Howard's State of the Prisons, p. 469.

is Clarkson, who, while yet a pupil of the University, commenced those life-long labors against slavery and the slave-trade which embalm his memory. Writing an essay on the subject as a college exercise, his soul warmed with the task, and, at a period when even the horrors of "the middle passage" did not excite condemnation, he entered the lists, the stripling champion of the Right. He has left a record of the moment when this supreme duty flashed upon him. He was horseback, on his way from Cambridge to London. "Coming in sight of Wade's Mill, in Hertfordshire," he says, "I sat down disconsolate on the turf by the roadside, and held my horse. Here a thought came into my mind, that, if the contents of the Essay were true, *it was time some person should see these calamities to their end*."[1] Pure and noble impulse to a beautiful career!

Such are exemplars of True Glory. Without rank, office, or the sword, they accomplished immortal good. While on earth, they labored for their fellow-men; and now, sleeping in death, by example and works they continue the same sacred office. To all, in every sphere or condition, they teach the universal lesson of magnanimous duty. From the heights of their virtue, they call upon us to cast out the lust of power, of office, of wealth, of praise, of a fleeting popular favor, which "a breath can make, as a breath has made," — to subdue the constant, ever-present suggestions of self, in disregard of neighbors, near or remote, whose welfare should never be forgotten, — to check the madness of party, which so often, for the sake of success, renounces

1 Clarkson's History of the Abolition of the African Slave-Trade, Vol. I. p. 171.

the very objects of success, — and, finally, to introduce into our lives those sentiments of *Conscience* and *Charity* which animated them to such labors. Nor should these be holiday virtues, marshalled on great occasions only. They must become part of us, and of our existence, — present on every occasion, small or great, — in those daily amenities which add so much to the charm of life, as also in those grander duties which require an ennobling self-sacrifice. The former are as flowers, whose odor is pleasant, though fleeting; the latter are like the costly spikenard poured from the box of alabaster upon the head of the Lord.

To the supremacy of these principles let us all consecrate our best purposes and strength. So doing, we must reverse the very poles of worship in the past. Thus far men have bowed down before stocks, stones, insects, crocodiles, golden calves, — graven images, of ivory, ebony, or marble, often of cunning workmanship, wrought with Phidian skill, but all *false gods*. Their worship in the future must be the true God, our Father, as he is in heaven, and in the *beneficent* labors of his children on earth. Then farewell to the Siren song of a worldly ambition! Farewell to the vain desire of mere literary success or oratorical display! Farewell to the distempered longing for office! Farewell to the dismal, blood-red phantom of martial renown! Fame and Glory may continue, as in times past, the reflection of public opinion, — but of an opinion sure and steadfast, without change or fickleness, illumined by those two eternal suns of Christian truth, love to God and love to man.

All things will bear witness to the change, while the busy forms of wrong and outrage disappear like evil spirits at the dawn. Then shall the happiness of the poor and lowly have uncounted friends. The cause of those in prison shall find fresh voices, the education of the ignorant kindly supporters, the majesty of Peace other vindicators, the sufferings of the slave new and gushing floods of sympathy. Then, at last, shall the Brotherhood of Man stand confessed, filling the souls of all with more generous life, prompting to deeds of beneficence, conquering the Heathen prejudices of country, color, and race, guiding the judgment of the historian, animating the verse of the poet and the eloquence of the orator, ennobling human thought and conduct, and inspiring those good works by which alone we attain the summits of True Glory. Good Works! Such even now is the Heavenly Ladder on which angels are ascending and descending, while weary Humanity, on pillows of stone, slumbers heavily at its feet.

ILLUSTRATIONS REFERRED TO ON PAGE 38.

Civil War a Crime. — The terms describing civil war, employed by Roman writers, implicate *both sides* in its guilt and dishonor. Such phrases as the following occur in the "Pharsalia" of Lucan: "*civile nefas*" (Lib. IV. 172); "*civilis Erinnys*" (IV. 187); "*crimen civile*" (VII. 398). Eutropius says: "Hinc jam *bellum civile* successit, *exsecrandum et lacrimabile.*" (Brev. Hist. Rom., Lib. VI. c. 19.) Of the war between Sulla and Marius Florus says: "Hoc deerat unum populi Romani malis, jam ut ipse intra se *parricidale bellum* domi stringeret, et in urbe media ac foro, quasi harena, cives cum civibus suis gladiatorio more concurrerent. Æquiore animo utcumque ferrem, si plebeii duces, aut si nobiles, mali saltem, ducatum *sceleri* præbuissent; cum vero, *pro facinus!* qui viri! qui imperatores! decora et ornamenta sæculi sui, Marius et Sulla, *pessimo facinori* suam etiam dignitatem præbuerunt." (Epit. Rerum Rom., Lib. III. c. 21.) The condemnation of the historian is aroused, not because of the wickedness of a contest among fellow-*men*, but among fellow-*citizens*, and because illustrious personages joined in it. But he is impartial in condemning *both sides*. Marius and Sulla alike are treated as criminals. The same judgment seems to be expressed with regard to Cæsar and Pompey. "*Cæsaris furor atque Pompeii* urbem, Italiam, gentes, nationes, totum denique qua patebat imperium, quodam quasi diluvio et inflammatione corripuit; adeo ut non recte tantum *civile* dicatur, ac ne sociale quidem, sed nec externum, sed potius commune quoddam ex omnibus, et plus quam bellum." (Ibid., Lib. IV. c. 2.) His description of what was called the Social War contains a principle which must condemn equally all strife among cognate nations or states: "Sociale bellum vocetur licet, ut extenuemus invidiam; si verum tamen volumus, illud civile bellum fuit. Quippe cum populus Romanus Etruscos, Latinos, Sabinosque miscuerit, et unum ex omnibus sanguinem ducat, corpus fecit ex membris, et ex omnibus unus est. *Nec minore flagitio socii intra Italiam, quam intra urbem cives rebellabant.*" (Ibid., Lib. III. c. 18.)

No triumph, thanksgiving, or holiday for a conqueror in Civil War. — Valerius Maximus, in his chapter on *Triumphs*, shows how the victories of civil war were regarded in Rome. "Although," he says, "any one should perform illustrious and highly useful acts to the Republic in civil war, he was not on this account hailed as Imperator; nor were any *thanksgivings* decreed; nor did he enjoy a *triumph* or *ovation:* because, *howsoever necessary these victories might be, they were always regarded as mournful,* inasmuch as they were obtained, not by *foreign*, but by *domestic* blood. Therefore Nasica and Opimius *sorrowfully* slew, the one the faction of Tiberius Gracchus, and the other that of Caius Gracchus. Quintus Catulus, after overthrowing his colleague, Marcus Lepidus, with all his seditious forces, returned to the city, *showing only a moderated joy.* Even Caius Antonius, the conqueror of Catiline, made his soldiers wipe their swords before taking them back to the camp. Lucius Cinna and Caius Marius, after eagerly draining the blood of citizens, *did not proceed immediately to the temples and altars of the gods.* So, too, Lucius Sulla, who waged many civil wars, and whose successes were most cruel and insolent, at his triumph, on the establishment of his power, carried in his procession the representations of many Greek and Asiatic cities, *but of no town occupied by Roman citizens.* It were grievous and wearisome to dwell longer on the wounds of the Republic. *The Senate never gave the laurel to any one, nor did any one ever desire that it should be given to himself, while a part of the state was in tears.*" These last words deserve to be repeated in the original text: "Lauream nec Senatus cuiquam dedit, nec quisquam sibi dari desideravit, civitatis parte lacrimante." (Valerius Maximus, Lib. II. c. 8, § 7.) Florus, at the close of his chapter on the War with Sertorius, says, that the victorious leaders wished this to be regarded as a *foreign* rather than a *civil* war, *in order that they might triumph:* "Victores duces *externum* id magis quam *civile* bellum videri voluerunt, *ut triumpharent.*" (Epit. Rerum Rom., Lib. III. c. 22.) Cæsar did not triumph over Pompey, although at a later day he shocked his fellow-citizens by a triumph over the sons of that leader. "*All the world,*" says Plutarch, in his Life of Cæsar, "*condemned his triumphing in the calamities of his country, and rejoicing in things which nothing could excuse, either before the gods or men, but extreme necessity.* And it was the more obvious to condemn it, because, before this, he had never sent any messenger or letter to acquaint the public with any victory he had gained in the civil wars, *but was rather ashamed of such advantages.*" (Lives, tr. Langhorne, Vol. IV. p. 387.)

A similar judgment of contests and battles *between citizens* appears in other writers. Appian, speaking of Caius Gracchus, says, that "all averted their countenances from him, as *a man polluted with the blood of a citizen.*" (De Bellis Civilibus, Lib. I. c. 25.) The same author, in describing the triumphs of Cæsar on his return from Africa, says, that "he took care that there should be no triumphal inscription of his victories over Romans, his fellow-citizens, *as both unbecoming himself, and shameful and of evil omen to the Roman people.*" (Ibid., Lib. II. c. 101.) We may follow this sentiment in the History of Dion Cassius. After describing the victory over Catiline, he says, "The victors themselves greatly bewailed the loss to the Commonwealth of such and so many men, citizens and allies, *although justly slain.*" (Hist. Rom., Lib.

XXXVII. c. 40.) Thus the *justice* of the war did not make it a source of glory. Dion says, that Pompey, after his success over Cæsar at Dyrrachium, "did not speak of it boastfully, *nor did he wreathe his fasces with laurel, feeling a repugnance to doing anything of this sort on account of a victory over citizens.*" (Ibid., Lib. XLI. c. 52.) The manner in which he refers to Cæsar's conduct, also, after the battle of Pharsalia, is in harmony with that of the other classical writers. "Cæsar," he says, "sent no announcement of it to the people, *being unwilling to appear to rejoice publicly over such a victory;* wherefore he did not celebrate any triumph on account of it." (Ibid., Lib. XLII. c. 18.) But he pursued a different course with regard to his victory over the *foreigner* Pharnaces, which he announced in that famous epigrammatic epistle, "*Veni, vidi, vici.*" Dion says, "Cæsar was prouder of this than of any other of his victories, although it was not very splendid." (Ibid., Lib. XLII. c. 48.) The same historian alludes to his triumph over the sons of Pompey, "having conquered no *foreign enemy*, but destroyed so large a number of *citizens.*" (Ibid., Lib. XLIII. c. 42.) Crowns and public thanksgivings were decreed to Octavius Cæsar, after his victories over Antony; "but," says Dion, "they did not expressly name Antony, and the other Romans conquered with him, either at first or then, *as though it were right to celebrate festivities over them.*" (Ibid., Lib. LI. c. 19.)

"The Tatler," in considering the Roman triumph, notices that "it was not allowed in a civil war, lest one part should be in tears, while the other was making acclamations." (No. LXIII.) And Hudibras, in a most suggestive passage, uses language applicable to all civil war: —

> "What towns, what garrisons, might you
> With hazard of this blood subdue,
> Which now ye 're bent to throw away
> *In vain untriumphable fray!*"
>
> Part I. Canto II. 499 - 502.

International War criminal, and as little worthy of honor as Civil War. — Erasmus dealt a blow at the distinction, still preserved among Christians, between *civil* war and *foreign* war. "*Plato civile bellum esse putat, quod Græci gerunt adversus Græcos. At Christianus Christiano propius junctus est quam civis civi, quam frater fratri.*" (Erasmi Epist., Lib. XXII. Ep. 16.) The same idea is found in the Byzantine Gregoras: "Indecorum esse Christianis tanta cum acerbitate inter se armis certare, cum rationes sint conveniendi ad pacem et communes vires in impios vertendi." (Gregoras, Lib. X., De Alexandro Bulgaro, quoted by Grotius, De Jure Belli ac Pacis, Lib. II. cap. 23, § 8, No. 3, note.) Even here it is rather the Brotherhood of Christians than the Brotherhood of Man that is recognized. Assuming the latter, international war becomes criminal, and as little worthy of honor as civil war. It is a war among brothers.

Who can think of that contest between the two brothers Eteocles and Polynices without abhorrence? Who would think of awarding glory to Abel, if, in self-defence, he had succeeded in slaying his hostile brother, Cain? There is a play of Beaumont and Fletcher where two brothers are represented as drawing swords upon each other. When finally separated, they are addressed in words applicable to the contests of nations: —

> "Clashing of swords
> So near my house! Brother opposed to brother!
> . . . . Hold! hold!
> Charles! Eustace!
> . . . . . . But these unnatural jars,
> Arising between brothers, *should you prosper,*
> *Would shame your victory*"
>
> *The Elder Brother*, Act V. Sc. 1.

The unreasonableness of any True Glory in such a contest is felt by all at the present day, though there have been monsters or barbarians who *gloried* even in a kinsman's blood. Massinger, in his play of "The Unnatural Combat," has portrayed such a character. A father and son fight with each other. The father is victorious. His exultation in the death of his son is not unlike that which often attends the victories of Christian nations: —

> "Were a new life hid in each mangled limb,
> I would search and find it; and howe'er to some
> I may seem cruel thus to tyrannize
> Upon this senseless flesh, I *glory* in it,
> . . . . . . my falling *glories*
> Being made up again, and cemented
> With a son's blood."
>
> *The Unnatural Combat,* Act II. Sc. 1.

The father, whose hands are wet with a son's blood, is thus addressed: —

> "The conqueror that survives
> *Must reap the harvest of his bloody labor.*
> *Sound all loud instruments of joy and triumph.*"
>
> *Ibid.*

The soul revolts from such a triumph; but how does this differ from the triumphs of war? The enlightened morality of our age will yet confess that it is equally wrong to commemorate by thanksgiving or holiday any bloody success, even in a *just* contest, over our *brother man.*

NECESSITY OF POLITICAL ACTION AGAINST THE SLAVE POWER AND THE EXTENSION OF SLAVERY.

SPEECH IN THE WHIG STATE CONVENTION OF MASSACHUSETTS, AT SPRINGFIELD, SEPTEMBER 29, 1847.

MR. SUMNER persevered in opposition to the Mexican War, as unjust in character, and waged for the sake of Slavery. At a Whig meeting in Boston, assembled in Washingtonian Hall, September 15, for the choice of delegates to the Annual State Convention, he introduced the following Resolutions.

"*Resolved*, That a war of aggression, conquest, and robbery is a national crime of unquestionable atrocity, which good citizens should strive by unceasing exertion to prevent and arrest.

"*Resolved*, That such a war becomes doubly hateful, when the lust of conquest is inflamed and stimulated by the passion to extend Slavery and to strengthen the Slave Power.

"*Resolved*, That the present war with Mexico is unconstitutional in origin, unjust in character, and detestable in object, and that a regard for the Constitution, which is outraged, for the Union, which is endangered, for the lives of innocent men vainly sacrificed, for the principles of justice wantonly violated, and for the true honor of the country tarnished, should animate us to oppose with uncompromising earnestness the further waste of national treasure for purposes of aggression, and to call for the withdrawal of our troops within the acknowledged limits of the United States.

"*Resolved*, That we are unchangeably opposed to the annexation of any territory to this Union, either directly by conquest, or indirectly as payment for expenses of the war; but if additional territory be forced upon us, or be acquired by purchase, or in any other way, then we will demand that there shall be neither slavery nor involuntary servitude therein, otherwise than for the punishment of crime."

Mr. Sumner, Hon. C. F. Adams, and J. S. Eldridge, Esq., spoke in favor of the Resolutions; Hon. James T. Austin and William Hayden, Esq., against them. They were finally laid on the table. The Whigs of Boston would not commit themselves to these principles. Mr. Sumner's name was placed at the head of the large delegation appointed by the meeting.

The Convention assembled at Springfield, September 29, 1847, and organized with the following officers: Hon. George Ashmun, of Springfield, President; John C. Gray, of Boston, Thomas Emerson, of South Reading, James H. Duncan, of Haverhill, J. T. Buckingham, of Cambridge, Samuel Wood, of Grafton, James White, of Northfield, Theodore Hinsdale, of Litchfield, William Porter, of Lee, Truman Clark, of Walpole, John A. Shaw, of Bridgewater, and Samuel Osborn, of Edgartown, Vice-Presidents; John P. Putnam, of Boston, Linus B. Comins, of Roxbury, Charles R. Train, of Framingham, and S. H. Davis, of Westfield, Secretaries.

Mr. Webster was present, and addressed the Convention, mainly on the Mexican War. Among the Resolutions adopted by the Convention was one recommending him as a candidate for President of the United States. While the Resolutions were pending, the following was moved as an amendment by Hon. John G. Palfrey.

"*Resolved*, That the Whigs of Massachusetts will support no men for the offices of President and Vice-President but such as are known by their acts or declared opinions to be opposed to the extension of Slavery."

This Resolution was the result of a conference among the more earnest Anti-Slavery members, with whom Mr. Sumner acted, in the hope of making opposition to the extension of Slavery a political test at the next Presidential election. It was sustained in speeches by Mr. Palfrey, Hon. C. F. Adams, Mr. Sumner, Hon. William Dwight, and Hon. Charles Allen, and was opposed by Hon. Robert C. Winthrop and Hon. John C. Gray. On the question being taken, the Resolution was declared lost.

Mr. Sumner spoke as follows.

MR. PRESIDENT, — It is late, and I am sorry to trespass on unwilling attention. The importance of the cause is my apology. The question is, How shall we express our opposition to the extension of Slavery? Here it is satisfactory to know that there can be no embarrassment from constitutional scruples. It is not proposed to interfere with Slavery in any constitutional stronghold, or to touch any so-called compromise of the Constitution. Adopting the principle, so often declared by our Southern friends, that Slavery is a local institution, drawing its vitality from the municipal laws of the States in which it exists, we solemnly assert that the power of the Nation, of Congress, of the North as well as the South, shall not be employed for its extension, and that this curse shall not be planted in any territory hereafter acquired.

Is it not strange, Mr. President, that we, in this nineteenth century of the Christian era, in a country whose heroic charter declares that "all men are created equal," under a Constitution one of whose express objects is to "secure the blessings of liberty," — is it not passing strange that we should be occupied now in considering how best to prevent the opening of new markets for human flesh? Slavery, already expelled from distant despotic states, seeks shelter here by the altars of Freedom. Alone in the company of nations our country assumes the championship of this hateful institution. Far away in the East, at "the gateways of the day," by the sacred waters of the Ganges, in effeminate India, Slavery is condemned; in Constantinople, queenly seat of the most powerful Mahometan empire, where barbarism still mingles with civilization, the Ottoman Sultan brands it with the stigma of disapprobation; the Barbary States of Africa are changed to Abolitionists; from the untutored ruler of Morocco comes the declaration of his desire, stamped in the formal terms of a treaty, that the very name of Slavery may perish from the minds of men; and only recently from the Bey of Tunis has proceeded that noble act by which, "for the glory of God, and to distinguish man from the brute creation," — I quote his own words, — he decreed its total abolition throughout his dominions. Let

Christian America be taught by these despised Mahometans. God forbid that our Republic — "heir of all the ages, in the foremost files of time" — should adopt anew the barbarism and cruelty they have renounced or condemned!

The early conduct of our fathers, at the formation of the Constitution, should be our guide now. On the original suggestion of Jefferson, subsequently sustained and modified by others, a clause was introduced into the fundamental law of the Northwest Territory by which Slavery has been forever excluded from that extensive region. This act of wisdom and justice is a source of prosperity and pride to the millions living beneath its influence. And shall we be less true to Freedom than the authors of that instrument? Their spirits encourage us in devotion to this cause. With promptings from their example may properly mingle the testimony given by that evangelist of Liberty, Lafayette, who, though born on a foreign soil, is already, by earnest labors, by blood shed in our cause, by the friendship of Washington, by the gratitude of every American heart, enrolled among our patriots and fathers. His opinions of Slavery are now newly revealed to the world. From the pen of the philanthropist Clarkson we learn that his amiable nature was specially aroused even at its mention. "He was a real gentleman," says Clarkson, "and of soft and gentle manners. I have seen him put out of temper, but never at any time except when Slavery was the subject." The thought of it in the land he had helped to redeem troubled him so that he exclaimed to Clarkson: "*I would never have drawn my sword in the cause of America, if I could have conceived that thereby I was founding a land of Slavery.*" Shall we, whom his sword helped to free, now found a new land of Slavery?

A proposal is made that the Missouri Compromise shall be applied to any territory acquired from Mexico, — in other words, that all south of the parallel of 36° 30′ shall be devoted to Slavery. Are you aware, Sir, that this line, so unhappily notorious in our history, is almost precisely the parallel of Algiers, once the chief seat of White Slavery? It is the proper parallel to mark a boundary so disgraceful. Let it be called the Algerine line. At the present time there can be no compromises. Compromise with Slavery is treason to Freedom and to Humanity. It is treason to the Constitution also. With every new extension of Slavery, fresh strength is imparted to that political influence, monstrous offspring of Slavery, known as the Slave Power. This influence, beyond any other under our government, has deranged our institutions. To it the greater evils which have afflicted the country, the different perils to the Constitution, may all be traced. The Missouri Compromise, the annexation of Texas, the war with Mexico, are only specimens of trouble from the Slave Power. It is an ancient fable that the eruptions of Etna were produced by the restless movements of the giant Enceladus imprisoned beneath.[1] As the giant turned on his side, or stretched his limbs, or struggled, the conscious mountain belched forth flames, red-hot cinders, and fiery lava, carrying destruction and dismay to those who dwelt upon its fertile slopes. The Slave Power is the Imprisoned Giant of our Constitution. It is there confined

1 "Et fessum quoties mutat latus, intremere omnem
Murmure Trinacriam, et cœlum subtexere fumo."
Æneid, III. 581, 582.

and bound. But its constant and strenuous struggles have caused, and ever will cause, eruptions of evil, in comparison with which flames, red-hot cinders, and fiery lava are trivial and transitory. The face of Nature may be blasted, the land may be struck with sterility, villages may be swept by floods of flame, and whole families entombed alive in its burning sepulchre; but all these evils are small, compared with the deep, abiding, unutterable curse from an act of national wrong.

Let us, then, pledge ourselves, in solemn form, by united exertion, to restrain this destructive influence, at least within its original constitutional bounds. Let us at all hazards prevent the extension of Slavery and the increase of the Slave Power. Our opposition must keep right on, and not look back: —

> "Like to the Pontic sea,
> Whose icy current and compulsive course
> Ne'er feels retiring ebb, but keeps due on
> To the Propontic and the Hellespont."

In this contest, we may borrow from the ancient Greek, who, when his hands were cut off, fought with his stumps, and even with his teeth. We may borrow from our party in its defence of the Tariff. We may borrow from the slaveholders themselves, who are united and uncompromising in their unholy cause. Let us struggle for Freedom as they struggle for Slavery. Let us rally under our white pavilion, with its trophies of Justice, Freedom, and Humanity, as enthusiastically as they troop together beneath their black flag pictured over with whips, chains, and manacles.

This brings me directly to the point, How shall we make our opposition felt? How shall it become vital and palpable? On the present occasion we can only declare our course. But this should be in language sternly expressive of our *determination.* It will not be enough merely to put forth *opinions* in well-couched phrase, and add yet other resolutions to the hollow words which have passed into the limbo of things lost on earth. We must give to our opinions that edge and force which they can have only from the declared determination to abide by them at all times. We must carry them to the ballot-box, and bring our candidates to their standard. The recent constitution of Louisiana, to discourage duelling, disqualifies all engaged in a duel from holding any civil office. The Whigs of Massachusetts, so far as in them lies, must pronounce a similar sentence of disqualification upon all not known to be against the extension of Slavery.

It is distinctly proclaimed by the Slave Power, that no person can receive its support who is known to be against the extension of Slavery. The issue here offered we must join. This is due to our character for sincerity. It will show that we are in earnest, and, so doing, we help to check that tyrannical spirit which has thus far intimidated the politicians — I will not say the people — of the Free States. To those now too ready for the part of Grand Compromiser, on a question which admits of no compromise, it will be a warning that they can expect no support for high office from us. Our motto must be, "Principles, and those *only* who will maintain them."

I urge this course, at the present moment, from deep conviction of its importance. And be assured, Sir, whatever the final determination of this Convention, there are many here to-day who will never yield support to any candidate, for Presidency or Vice-Presidency, who is not known to be against the extension of Slavery, even though he have freshly received the sacramental unction of a "regular nomination." We cannot say, with detestable morality, "Our party, *right or wrong.*" The time has gone by when gentlemen can expect to introduce among us the discipline of the camp. Loyalty to principle is higher than loyalty to party. The first is a heavenly sentiment, from God: the other is a device of this world. Far above any flickering light or battle-lantern of party is the everlasting sun of Truth, in whose beams are the duties of men.

THE LATE HENRY WHEATON.

ARTICLE IN THE BOSTON DAILY ADVERTISER, MARCH 16, 1848.

THE death of a person like Mr. Wheaton naturally arrests attention, — even at this period of funereal gloom, when the Angel of Death has overshadowed the whole country with his wings. He was long and widely known in official relations, devoted for many years to the service of his country, studious always of literature and jurisprudence, illustrious as a diplomatist and expounder of the Law of Nations, — with a private character so pure as to make us forget, in its contemplation, the public virtues by which his life was elevated.

He died after a brief illness, accompanied by a disease of the brain, on Saturday evening, March 11, 1848, at Dorchester. On that day the remains of John Quincy Adams, who, as President of the United States, first advanced Mr. Wheaton to a diplomatic place in the service of his country, — after a long procession, through mourning towns and cities, from the Capitol, which had been the scene of his triumphant death, — were brought to their final resting-place in the adjoining town of Quincy. The faithful friend and servant thus early followed his venerable chief to the fellowship of another world.

The principal circumstances in Mr. Wheaton's life may be briefly told. He was born at Providence, on the

27th of November, 1785, and was a graduate of Brown University, in 1802. After admission to the bar, he visited Europe, particularly the Continent, where his mind thus early became imbued with those tastes which occupied so much of his later years. Some time after his return, finding little inducement to continue the practice of the law in Providence, he removed to New York. This was in 1812. Here he became the editor of an important journal, "The National Advocate," — a paper afterwards merged in "The Courier and Inquirer." His experience in this character closed May 15, 1815. As a journalist, he is reputed to have been uniformly discreet, decorous, and able, at a time when the fearful trials of war, in which the country was engaged, added to the responsibilities of his position.

His labors as editor did not estrange him from the law. About this period he became for a short time one of the justices of the Marine Court, a tribunal now shorn of its early dignity. In 1815 he appeared as author of a treatise on jurisprudence. This was a "Digest of the Law of Maritime Captures and Prizes." In the judicial inquiries incident to the administration of the Laws of War — still maintained by the Christian world — such a treatise was naturally of much practical utility. It may also claim the palm of being among the earliest juridical productions of our country. Nor, indeed, has it been without the disinterested praise of foreign nations. Mr. Reddie, of Edinburgh, in his recent work on Maritime International Law, says, "Although it cannot be strictly called a valuable accession to the legal literature of *Britain*, it gives us much pleasure to record our opinion, that, in point of learning and methodical arrangement, it is very superior to any treatise on this department of the law which had previously appeared in the English language."[1] No American contribution to jurisprudence so early as 1815 has received such marked commendation abroad. Kent and Story had not then produced those works which have secured to them their present freehold of European fame.

In 1816 he became Reporter to the Supreme Court of the United States, which office he held till 1827. His Reports are in twelve volumes, and embody what may be called the *golden judgments* of our National Judicature, from the lips of Marshall, Livingston, Washington, Thompson, and Story.

Mr. Wheaton's time was not absorbed by these official duties. He entered much into the practice of his profession. His name appears as counsel in important causes at Washington. He was editor of divers English law books, republished in this country, with valuable notes. On several literary occasions he pronounced discourses of signal merit. One of these, in 1820, before the Historical Society of New York, touches upon his favorite theme, with which his name is now so firmly connected, the Law of Nations; another, in 1824, at the opening of the New York Athenæum, takes a rapid survey of American literature. In 1826 he published his Life of that great lawyer, William Pinkney. It is also understood that during all this period he was a frequent contributor to the "North American Review."

Nor did these accumulated labors, literary and juridical, keep him from other services. He was a member of the Legislature of New York, and in 1821 held a seat in the Convention which remodelled the Consti-

[1] Maritime International Law, Vol. II. p. 298.

tution of that State. In 1825 he was placed on the commission for revising the statutes of New York. This was the first effort of any State professing the Common Law to reduce its disconnected and diffusive legislation to the unity of a code. Thus is his name associated with one of the most important landmarks in American law.

All these duties and callings he relinquished in the summer of 1827, when he entered upon the diplomatic service, which opened before him a new career of usefulness. It was then that he became Chargé d'Affaires at Copenhagen, where he continued till 1835, when he was transferred by President Jackson to Berlin, as Minister Resident. In 1837 he was raised by President Van Buren to the rank of Envoy Extraordinary and Minister Plenipotentiary at the same court. On July 22, 1846, he had his audience of farewell from the King of Prussia, being recalled by President Polk. This long term of service was passed abroad with the intermission of a brief period in 1834, when he revisited his country on leave of absence.

During this protracted career in foreign countries, charged with responsible negotiations, he was not lost in the toils of office, or in the allurements of court life. He was always a student. At Copenhagen he prepared his "History of the Northmen, or Danes and Normans, from the Earliest Times to the Conquest of England by William of Normandy." This was published in 1831, both in England and in America. In 1844 it was much enlarged, and translated into French. At the time of his death he was occupied in preparing another edition. In 1838 he contributed to the Edinburgh Cabinet Library a portion of the volumes entitled "Scandinavia."

By these works he earned an honorable place among our historical writers. His History of the Northmen preceded, in time, the productions of Bancroft and Prescott, which have since achieved so much renown.

From literature he passed again to jurisprudence, where he has won his surest triumphs. His "Elements of International Law" appeared in London and the United States in 1836, and again in 1846, much enlarged. This was followed by a "History of the Law of Nations in Europe and America, from the Earliest Times to the Treaty of Washington," which first appeared in French, at Leipsic, in 1841, under the title of *Histoire des Progrès du Droit des Gens en Europe depuis la Paix de Westphalie jusqu'au Congrès de Vienne, avec un Précis Historique du Droit des Gens Européen avant la Paix de Westphalie.* This was originally written for a prize offered by the French Institute. The question proposed was, *Quels sont les progrès qu'a fait le droit des gens en Europe depuis la Paix de Westphalie?* It was bold and honorable in Mr. Wheaton to venture in a foreign tongue the discussion of so great a subject. The Greek of Cicero excited the admiration of the rhetoricians at Rhodes and Athens, and the French of Gibbon was in harmony with his own swelling English style; but Mr. Wheaton, whether in French or English, is commended by matter rather than manner. On this account he was at disadvantage before the polished French tribunal. His effort received what was called *mention honorable;* but the prize was awarded to a young Frenchman, whose production has never seen the light. An impartial public opinion has awarded our countryman another prize more than academic. The same work in English, much enlarged, is now an authority.

Besides these classical treatises, Mr. Wheaton published an able and thorough Inquiry into the Validity of the Right of Visitation and Search, particularly as recently claimed by Great Britain. Here he upheld the views of the American government. The acknowledged weight of his opinion in the science of law gave to his conclusions commanding influence.

On his recent return to this country, he was welcomed with many manifestations of regard, both public and private. Wherever he appeared, he was a favored guest. At the last Commencement of Brown University, he delivered the Address before the Phi Beta Kappa Society. His subject was Germany. The various departments of thought and conduct, which have been successfully occupied by the "many-sided" mind of that country, were sketched with singular ability. His voice was feeble, and, as he spoke, large numbers of the audience drew near the pulpit, filling the adjacent aisles, and standing in respectful attention, that they might follow his learned discourse.

Such were the important and diversified labors of his valuable life. Without any adventitious aids of fortune, or special favor, he achieved eminent place in the civilized world. By virtue of his office he lived as an equal among nobles and princes, while his rare endowments opened to him at will the fraternities of learning and science. And yet his qualities were not those of the courtier. Nor did any heaven-descended eloquence lend fire to his conversation or style. Both were simple, grave, reserved, like his manners, attractive rather from clearness and matter than from brilliancy or point.

His career abroad as Diplomatist was one of the

longest in our history, — longer even than that of John Quincy Adams. It was not his fortune to affix his name to any treaty, like that of 1783, which acknowledged our Independence, or that of Ghent in 1814, which restored peace to England and the United States. But his extended term of service was filled by a succession of wise and faithful labors, which rendered incalculable good to his own country, while they impressed his character upon the public mind of Europe. His negotiation with Denmark was important. More important still was his careful management of our national interests in connection with the German Zollverein. Besides these conspicuous acts, with which all are familiar, there is his long and constant correspondence with the Department of State at Washington, which is known to comparatively few, although of exceeding merit.

It was his habit, contrary to the usage of many American ministers, by regular authentic communications, to keep the Government at home informed with regard to the position of foreign nations, as observed by him. All the matters which prominently occupied the Continental nations during his residence abroad, particularly those two disputes known as the Belgian question and the Egyptian question, which seemed for a while to fill the firmament of Europe with "portents dire," were discussed in these despatches with instructive fulness. These may be found in the archives of his legation, and in the Department of State at Washington, "enrolled in the Capitol," where they will be studied by the future historian.

His familiarity with the Law of Nations, from his position as a diplomatist, was enhanced by mature and thorough study. For this he was prepared by training at the bar, the influence of which may be discerned in some of his writings. He was master alike of its learning and its dialectics. It happened in Berlin that he was called to defend the rights of ambassadors against an injurious usage established or recognized by the Prussian government. All who have read his paper on this occasion will attest the force and sharpness of his unanswered argument. Strange that this task should have devolved upon an American minister! Strange that the privileges of ambassadors should have found their defender in a Cis-Atlantic citizen! His defence excited the attention of the diplomatic body in Europe. Copies were transmitted to the different courts, where, as I have understood, it was discussed, and generally, if not universally, sanctioned.

Justly eminent as a practical diplomatist, his works derived new value from the position of their author, while even his official rank was aided by his works. His was a solitary example in our age, perhaps the only instance since Grotius, of an eminent minister who was also an expounder of the Law of Nations. His works, therefore, are received with peculiar respect. Already they have become *authorities*. Such they are regarded by the two British writers who have since appeared in this field, Mr. Manning and Mr. Reddie. The former, in his excellent Commentaries, refers to Mr. Wheaton's work on the Elements of International Law as "certainly the best elementary book on the topic that exists";[1] while Mr. Reddie announces that "this work, although not by a British author, was certainly, at the date of its publication, the most able and scientific

[1] Commentaries on the Law of Nations, Preface, p. v.

treatise on International Law which had appeared in the English language."[1] It is admitted that the method is superior to that of Martens, Chitty, Schmalz, or Klüber.

It cannot be disguised that his two works in this department are remarkable for careful statement and arrangement, rather than for that elegance, or glow, or freedom of discussion, by which the reader is carried captive. His Elements afford the best view yet presented of the Law of Nations, as practically illustrated in the adjudged cases of England and the United States, and in recent diplomacy. But we miss in them the fulness and variety of illustration which characterize some of the earlier writers, and especially that genial sentiment which interests us so constantly in Vattel. The History, which first appeared in French, is not less important than the Elements. Here the field is more clearly his own. This work supplies a place never before filled in the literature of the English language, if in that of any language. To all students of jurisprudence, nay, more, to all students of history, who ascend above wars and battles to the principles which are at once parent and offspring of events, this account of the Progress of the Law of Nations is an important guide.

Had Mr. Wheaton's life been longer spared, he would have found it his province, in the discharge of his recently assumed office as Lecturer on the Civil [Roman] and International Law at Harvard University, to survey again the same wide field. What further harvests he might then have gathered it is impossible now to estimate. He never entered upon these labors. The reaper was removed before he began to use the sickle.

[1] Maritime International Law, Vol. II. p. 441.

Such was his life, — passed not without well-deserved honor at home and abroad. In those two great departments of labor, History and the Law of Nations, he is among our American pioneers. Through him the literature and jurisprudence of our country have been commended in foreign lands: —

"Fluminaque in fontes cursu reditura supino."[1]

Others may have done better in the high art of History; but no American historian has, like him, achieved European eminence as a writer on the Law of Nations; nor has any other American writer on the last great theme been recognized abroad as historian. He was a member of the French Institute; and I cannot forget, that, at the time of his admission, the question, so honorable to his double fame, was entertained by the late Baron Degérando, the jurist and philanthropist, whether he should be received into the section of History or of Jurisprudence. He was finally attached to the latter. Prescott and Bancroft belong to the former.

It is as an expounder of Public International Law that his name will be most widely cherished. In the progress of Christian civilization, many of the rules now sustained by learned subtilty or unquestioning submission, shaping the public concerns of nations, will pass away. The Institution of War, with its complex code, now sanctioned and legalized by nations, as a proper mode of adjusting their disputes, will yield to some less questionable arbitrament. But a profound interest must always attach to the writings of those great masters who have labored to explain, to advance, and to refine that system, which, though incomplete, has helped to keep the great Christian Commonwealth in the bonds

[1] Ovid, Epist. ex Ponto, Lib. IV. Ep. v. 43.

of Peace. Among these Mr. Wheaton's place is conspicuous. His name is already inscribed on the same tablet with those of Grotius, Pufendorf, and Vattel.

It were wrong to close this imperfect tribute without a renewed testimony to the purity of his life. From youth to age his career was marked by integrity, temperance, frugality, modesty, industry. His quiet, unostentatious manners were fit companions of his virtues. His countenance, which is admirably preserved in the portrait by Healy, had the expression of thoughtfulness and repose. Nor station nor fame made him proud. He stood with serene simplicity in the presence of kings. In the social circle, when he spoke, all drew near to listen,—sure that what he said would be wise, tolerant, and kind.

UNION AMONG MEN OF ALL PARTIES AGAINST THE SLAVE POWER AND THE EXTENSION OF SLAVERY.

SPEECH BEFORE A MASS CONVENTION AT WORCESTER, JUNE 28, 1848.

THE effort to establish a political test in the Whig party in opposition to the extension of Slavery failed; but the Antislavery sentiment was constantly active. Those who coöperated in the movement were denounced as disturbers, and finally obtained an epithet, applied often in sarcasm, which may be considered their highest praise. They were called *Conscience* Whigs, in contradistinction to *Cotton* Whigs. The contest was continued in the newspapers, and also in the Legislature of Massachusetts. The course of the two great political parties compelled a final break.

General Cass, who had abandoned the Wilmot Proviso, which he once maintained, was nominated by the Democrats as their candidate for the Presidency. General Taylor, who was a considerable slaveholder, was nominated by the Whigs, without any platform. It seemed impossible for persons earnest against Slavery to sustain either. Already, in New York, a considerable portion of the Democratic party, known as "Barnburners," had refused to support General Cass, and nominated Martin Van Buren, adopting at the same time resolutions asserting the power of Congress to prohibit Slavery in the Territories, and calling for the exercise of this power.

At the nomination of General Taylor, Hon. Charles Allen and Hon. Henry Wilson, of Massachusetts, delegates to the National Convention, both refused to support the candidate. This was the signal for movement. A call was issued for a convention to found a new party. It was signed by Mr. Sumner and those with whom he was in the habit of acting. This was the beginning of the separate Free-Soil organization in Massachusetts, which afterwards grew into the Republican party. The call, which was extensively signed, concluded by inviting "fellow-citizens throughout the Commonwealth, who are opposed to the nomination of Cass and Taylor, to meet in convention at Worcester, on Wednesday, the 28th day of June current, to take such steps as the occasion shall demand in support of the PRINCIPLES to which they are pledged, and to coöperate with the other Free States in a convention for this purpose." It will be observed that the people were summoned to support *principles*, and also to coöperate with the Free States generally in this behalf. The response was prompt and enthusiastic. As many as five thousand persons appeared at Worcester, quickened by hostility to Slavery. The City Hall was not large enough, and the excited multitude adjourned to the Common, where they were called to order by Alexander DeWitt, of Oxford. Samuel F. Lyman, of Northampton, was chosen Chairman *pro tem.*, and W. S. Robinson, of Lowell, Secretary *pro tem.* A committee, of which Hon. E. L. Keyes, of Dedham, was chairman, reported the following list of officers: Hon. Samuel Hoar, of Concord, President; David Heard, of Wayland, Alanson Hamilton, of North Brookfield, Joseph L. Richardson, of Medway, Dr. S. G. Howe, of Boston, John Wells, of Chicopee, Joseph Stevens, of Warwick, and R. P. Waters, of Salem, Vice-Presidents; William S. Robinson, of Lowell, William A. Wallace, of Worcester, Allen Shepard, of Ashland, William A. Arnold, of Northampton, Secretaries. On motion of Hon. S. C. Phillips, of Salem, a committee was appointed to draft an address and resolutions, consisting of Mr. Phillips, Erastus Hopkins, of Northampton. D. W. Alvord, of Greenfield, M. M. Fisher, of Medway, A. C. Spooner, of Boston, A. Bangs, of Springfield, and E. Rockwood Hoar, of Concord.

The Convention was first addressed by Samuel Hoar, on taking the chair, — then by Charles Allen, Henry Wilson, Abraham Payne, of Rhode Island, Charles Hart, of Rhode Island, J. C. Woodman, of Maine, Amasa Walker, Lott Poole, Joshua Leavitt, Lewis D. Campbell, of Ohio, Joshua R. Giddings, of Ohio, J. C. Lovejoy, Charles Francis Adams, Charles Sumner, Edward L. Keyes, and E. Rockwood Hoar. The speeches were earnest and determined, and they were received in a corresponding spirit. No great movement ever showed at the beginning more character and power. It began true and strong.

All the speakers united in renouncing old party ties. None did this better than C. F. Adams, who concluded his remarks by saying: "Forgetting the things that are behind, I propose that we press forward to the high calling of our new occupation; and, fellow-citizens, whatever may be the fate of you or me, all I can now add is to repeat the words of one with whom I take pride in remembering that I have been connected: 'Sink or swim, live or die, survive or perish,' to go with the liberties of my country is my fixed determination." To these words Mr. Sumner alluded at the beginning of his speech.

MR. PRESIDENT AND FELLOW-CITIZENS: —

AT the close of a day crowded with exciting interest and full of best auguries, I feel that I can add little to what you have already heard. What can I say that shall enforce the great cause so successfully commended by my friend from Ohio [Mr. GIDDINGS], and, lastly, by my friend [Mr. ADAMS] who has just spoken, with the voice of the American Revolution on his lips? One thing, at least, I can do: I can join them in renunciation of party relations, so plainly inconsistent with the support of Freedom. They have been Whigs; and I, too, have been a Whig, though "not an ultra Whig." I was a Whig because I thought this party represented the moral sentiments of the country, — that it was the party of Humanity. It has ceased to sustain this character. It represents no longer the moral sentiments of the country. It is not the party of Humanity. A party which renounces its sentiments must expect to be renounced. In the coming contest I wish it understood that I belong to the party of Freedom, — to that party which plants itself on the Declaration of Independence and the Constitution of the United States.

The transactions in which we are now engaged recall an incident of French history. It was late in the night, at Versailles, that a courtier of Louis the Sixteenth, penetrating the bed-chamber of his master, and arousing him from slumber, communicated the intelligence, big with destiny, that the people of Paris, smarting under wrong and falsehood, had risen in their might, and, after a severe conflict with hireling troops, destroyed the Bastile. The unhappy monarch, turning upon his couch, said,

"It is an *insurrection.*" "No, Sire," answered the honest courtier, "it is a *revolution.*" And such is our movement to-day. It is a REVOLUTION, — not beginning with the destruction of a Bastile, but destined to end only with the overthrow of a tyranny differing little in hardship and audacity from that which sustained the Bastile of France, — I mean the Slave Power of our country. Do not start at this similitude. I intend no unkindness to slaveholders, many of whom are doubtless humane and honest. Such also was Louis the Sixteenth; and yet he sustained the Bastile, with the untold horrors of its dungeons, where human beings were thrust into companionship with toads and rats.

By the Slave Power I understand that combination of persons, or, perhaps, of politicians, whose animating principle is the perpetuation and extension of Slavery, with the advancement of Slaveholders. That such a combination exists is apparent from our history. It shows itself in the mildest, and perhaps the least offensive form, in the undue proportion of offices held by Slaveholders under the National Constitution. It is still worse apparent in a succession of acts by which the National Government has been prostituted to Slavery. Mindful of the Missouri Compromise, with its sanction of Slavery, — mindful of the annexation of Texas, with its fraud and iniquity, — mindful also of the war against Mexico, in itself a great crime, where wives and sisters have been compelled to mourn sons, husbands, and brothers untimely slain, — as these things, dark, dismal, atrocious, rise before us, may we not brand their unquestionable source as a tyranny hateful as that which sustained the Bastile? The Slave Power is the criminal.

This combination is unknown to the Constitution; nay, it exists in defiance of that instrument, and of the recorded opinions uttered constantly by its founders. The Constitution was the crowning labor of the men who gave us the Declaration of Independence. It was established to perpetuate, in organic law, those rights which the Declaration had promulgated, and which the sword of Washington had secured. "We hold these truths to be self-evident: that all men are created equal; that they are endowed by their Creator with certain unalienable rights; that *among these are life, liberty, and the pursuit of happiness.*" Such are the emphatic words which our country took upon its lips, as it first claimed its place among the nations of the earth. These were its baptismal vows. And the preamble of the Constitution renews them, when it declares its objects, among other things, to "establish justice, promote the general welfare, and *secure the blessings of liberty* to ourselves and our posterity." Mark: not to establish *injustice*, not to promote the welfare of a class, or of a few slaveholders, but the *general* welfare; not to foster the curse of slavery, but to secure the blessings of *liberty*. And the declared opinions of the fathers were all in harmony with these two charters. "I can only say," said Washington, "that there is not a man living who wishes more sincerely than I do to see a plan adopted for the abolition of slavery; but there is only one proper and effectual mode by which it can be accomplished, and that is by legislative authority; and this, as far as my suffrage will go, shall never be wanting." [1] Patrick Henry, while confessing

[1] Letter to Robert Morris, April 12, 1786: Writings of Washington, ed. Sparks, Vol. IX. p. 159.

that he was the master of slaves, said: "I will not, I cannot justify it. However culpable my conduct, I will so far pay my devoir to Virtue as to own the excellence and rectitude of her precepts, and lament my want of conformity to them. I believe a time will come, when an opportunity will be offered to abolish this lamentable evil."[1] And Franklin, as President of the earliest Abolition Society of the country, signed a petition to the first Congress, in which he declared himself "bound to use all justifiable endeavors to loosen the bands of slavery, and promote a general enjoyment of the blessings of freedom."[2] Thus the soldier, the orator, and the philosopher of the Revolution, all unite in homage to Freedom. Washington, wise in council and in battle, Patrick Henry, with tongue of flame, Franklin, with heaven-descended sagacity and humanity, all bear testimony to the times in which they lived, and the institutions they helped to establish.

It is plain that our Constitution was formed by lovers of Human Freedom, — that it was animated by their divine spirit, — that Slavery was regarded by them with aversion, so that, if covertly alluded to, it was not named in the instrument, — and that they all looked forward to an early day when this evil and shame would be obliterated from the land. Surely, then, it is right to say that the combination which seeks to perpetuate and extend Slavery is unknown to the Constitution, — that it exists in defiance of that instrument, and also of the recorded opinions uttered constantly by its founders.

Time would fail me to dwell on the perpetual influ-

1 Letter to Robert Pleasants, January 18, 1779: Goodloe's Southern Platform, p. 79.

2 Annals of Congress, 1st Cong. 2d Sess., 1198.

ence, growing with time, which the Slave Power has exerted from the foundation of the government. In the earlier periods of our history it was moderate and reserved. The spirit of the founders still prevailed. But with the advance of years, and as these early champions passed from the scene, it became more audacious, aggressive, and tyrannical, till at last it obtained the control of the government, and caused it to be administered, not in the spirit of Freedom, but in the spirit of Slavery. Yes! the government of the United States is now (let it be said with shame), not, as at the beginning, a government merely permitting, while it regretted Slavery, but a government openly favoring and vindicating it, visiting also with its displeasure all who oppose it.

During late years the Slave Power has introduced a new test for office, which would have excluded Washington, Jefferson, and Franklin. It applies an arrogant and unrelenting ostracism to all who express themselves against Slavery. And now, in the madness of tyranny, it proposes to extend this curse over new soil not yet darkened by its presence. It seeks to make the flag of our country the carrier of Slavery into distant lands, — to scale the mountain fastnesses of Oregon, and descend with its prey upon the shores of the Pacific, — to cross the Rio Grande, and there, in broad territories, recently wrested from Mexico by robber hands, to plant a shameful institution which that republic has expressly abolished.

In the prosecution of its purposes, the Slave Power has obtained the control of both the great political parties. Their recent nominations were made to serve its interests, to secure its supremacy, and especially to promote the extension of Slavery. Whigs and Democrats, — I use the old names still, — professing to represent conflicting sentiments, concur in being representatives of the Slave Power. General Cass, after openly registering his adhesion to it, was recognized as the candidate of the Democrats. General Taylor, who owns slaves on a large scale, though observing a studious silence on Slavery, as on all other things, is not only a representative of the Slave Power, but an important constituent part of the Power itself.

I will not dwell upon the manner in which General Taylor was forced upon the late Whig party. This has been amply done by others. But you will pardon me, if I allude to the aid his nomination derived from a quarter of the country where it should have encountered inexorable opposition, — I refer to New England, and especially to Massachusetts. I speak only what is now too notorious, when I say that it was the secret influence which went forth from among ourselves that contributed powerfully to this consummation. Yes! it was brought about by an unhallowed union — conspiracy let it be called — between two remote sections: between the politicians of the Southwest and the politicians of the Northeast, — between the cotton-planters and flesh-mongers of Louisiana and Mississippi and the cotton-spinners and traffickers of New England, — between the lords of the lash and the lords of the loom.

And now the question occurs, What is the true line of duty with regard to these two candidates? Mr. Van Buren — and I honor him for his trumpet call to the North — sounded the true note, when he said he could not vote for either. Though nominated by opposite parties, they represent substantially the same interest. The election of either would be a triumph of the Slave

Power, entailing upon the country the sin of extending Slavery. How, then, shall they be encountered? To my mind the way is plain. The lovers of Freedom, from both parties, and irrespective of all party associations, must unite, and by a new combination, congenial to the Constitution, oppose both candidates. This will be the FREEDOM POWER, whose single object will be to resist the SLAVE POWER. We will put them face to face, and let them grapple. Who can doubt the result?

I hear the old political saw, that "we must take the least of two evils." My friend from Ohio [Mr. GIDDINGS] has already riddled this excuse, so that I might well leave it untouched; but I cannot forbear a brief observation. It is admitted, then, that Cass and Taylor both are *evils*. For myself, if two evils are presented to me, I will take neither. There are occasions of political difference, I admit, when it may become expedient to vote for a candidate who does not completely represent our sentiments. There are matters legitimately within the range of expediency and compromise. The Tariff and the Currency are of this character. If a candidate differs from me on these more or less, I may yet vote for him. But the question before the country is of another character. This will not admit of compromise. It is not within the domain of expediency. *To be wrong on this is to be wholly wrong.* It is not merely expedient for us to defend Freedom, when assailed, but our duty so to do, unreservedly, and careless of consequences. Who in this assembly would help to fasten a fetter upon Oregon or Mexico? Who that would not oppose every effort to do this thing? Nobody. Who is there, then, that can vote for either Taylor or Cass?

But it is said that we shall throw away our votes, and that our opposition will fail. Fail, Sir! No honest, earnest effort in a good cause can fail. It may not be crowned with the applause of men; it may not seem to touch the goal of immediate worldly success, which is the end and aim of so much in life. But it is not lost. It helps to strengthen the weak with new virtue, — to arm the irresolute with proper energy, — to animate all with devotion to duty, which in the end conquers all. Fail! Did the martyrs fail, when with precious blood they sowed the seed of the Church? Did the discomfited champions of Freedom fail, who have left those names in history that can never die? Did the three hundred Spartans fail, when, in the narrow pass, they did not fear to brave the innumerable Persian hosts, whose very arrows darkened the sun? Overborne by numbers, crushed to earth, they left an example greater far than any victory. And this is the least we can do. Our example will be the main-spring of triumph hereafter. It will not be the first time in history that the hosts of Slavery have outnumbered the champions of Freedom. But where is it written that Slavery finally prevailed?

Assurances here to-day show that we need not postpone success. It seems already at hand. The heart of Ohio beats responsive to the heart of Massachusetts, and all the Free States are animated with the vigorous breath of Freedom. Let us not waste time in vain speculations between two candidates. Both are bad. Both represent a principle we cannot sanction.

Whatever may be said to the contrary by politicians, Freedom is the only question now before the American people. The Bank is not alone an "obsolete idea."

All the ideas put forward in the controversies of party are now practically obsolete. Peace has come to remove the question of the Mexican War. We are no longer obliged to consider if an unnecessary and unconstitutional war shall be maintained by supplies. There is no question with regard to the Sub-Treasury. This is now firmly established. Then comes the cause of Internal Improvements. This is not unimportant, but happily it is removed from the domain of party. The Chicago Convention for the express consideration of this subject was composed of various political opinions, and I understand that its recommendations are now sustained by opposite parties.

Of the past issues, that of the Tariff excites the most interest. This, it will be remembered, did not find a place in the early history of the country. Only in recent times has it occupied the attention of politicians, and been the occasion of vehement popular appeals. Regret is often expressed that it is the subject of party strife. It will be in the recollection of most persons that Mr. Webster made a vigorous effort to remove it from the list of party questions. What he was unable to do directly has been accomplished indirectly by the Mexican War. The debt of millions now entailed upon the country renders it necessary to impose a tariff which will satisfy the demands of all. Of course the debt must be paid; nor should we lose time in paying it, nor postpone it to the next generation. The people are not ready to meet it by direct taxation,—though, for one, I should be well pleased to see such a corrective applied to war. It can be paid only through the agency of a tariff, which, for this purpose, if for no other, must be supported by all parties. The Tariff, then, like the others, is no longer a political issue. If not obsolete, it is at least in abeyance.

These questions being out of the way, what remains for those who, in casting their votes, regard *principles* rather than *men?* It is clear that the only question of present practical interest arises from the usurpations of the Slave Power and the efforts to extend Slavery. This is the vital question at this time. It is *the question of questions.* It was lately said in the Convention of the New York Democracy at Utica (and I am glad to quote that most respectable body of men), that the movement in which we are now engaged is the most important since the American Revolution. Something more may be said. *It is a continuance of the American Revolution.* It is an effort to carry into effect the principles of the Declaration of Independence, and to revive in the administration of our government the spirit of Washington, Franklin, and Jefferson, — to bring back the Constitution to the principles and practice of its early founders, — to the end that it shall promote Freedom, and not Slavery, and shall be administered in harmony with the spirit of Freedom, and not with the spirit of Slavery.

In the last will and testament of Washington are emphatic words, which may be adopted as the motto for the present contest. After providing for the emancipation of his slaves, to take place on the death of his wife, he says, "And I do hereby expressly forbid the sale or transportation out of the said Commonwealth of any slave I may die possessed of, *under any pretence whatsoever.*"[1] So, at least, should the people of the United States expressly forbid the sale or transportation of any

[1] Writings of Washington, ed. Sparks, Vol. I. p 570.

slave beyond their ancient borders, under any pretence whatsoever.

Returning to our forefathers for their principles, let us borrow also something of their courage and union. Let us summon to our sides the majestic forms of those civil heroes whose firmness in council was equalled only by the firmness of Washington in war. Let us again awake to the eloquence of the elder Adams, animating his associates in Congress to independence; let us listen anew to the sententious wisdom of Franklin; let us be enkindled, as were the men of other days, by the fervid devotion to Freedom which flamed from the heart of Jefferson.

Instructed even by our enemies, let us be taught by the Slave Power itself. The few slaveholders are always united. Hence their strength. Like sticks in a fagot, they cannot be broken. Thus far the friends of Freedom have been divided. *Union*, then, must be our watchword, — union among men of all parties. By such union we consolidate an opposition which must prevail.

Let me call upon you, then, men of all parties, Whigs and Democrats, or howsoever named, to come forward and join in a common cause. Let us all leave the old organizations, and come together. In the crisis before us, it becomes us to forget past differences, and those names which have been the signal of strife. Only remembering our duties, when the fire-bell rings at midnight, we ask not if it be Whigs or Democrats who join us to extinguish the flames; nor do we make any such inquiry in selecting our leader then. To the strongest arm and the most generous soul we defer at once. To him we commit the direction of the engine. His hand grasps the pipe to pour the water upon the raging conflagration. So must we do now. Our leader must be the man who is the ablest and surest representative of the principles to which we are pledged.

Let Massachusetts, nurse of the men and principles that made our earliest revolution, vow herself anew to her early faith. Let her once more elevate the torch which she first held aloft, or, if need be, pluck fresh coals from the living altars of France, proclaiming, "Liberty, Equality, Fraternity," — Liberty to the captive, Equality between master and slave, Fraternity with all men, — the whole comprehended in that sublime revelation of Christianity, the Brotherhood of Man.

In the contemplation of these great interests, the intrigues of party, the machinations of politicians, the combinations of office-seekers, all seem to pass from sight. Politics and morals, no longer divorced from each other, become one and inseparable in the holy wedlock of Christian sentiment. Such a union elevates politics, while it gives a new sphere to morals. Political discussions have a grandeur which they never before assumed. Released from topics which concern only the selfish squabble for gain, and are often independent of morals, they come home to the heart and conscience. A novel force passes into the contests of party, breathing into them the breath of a new life, — of Hope, Progress, Justice, Humanity.

From this demonstration to-day, and the acclaim wafted to us from the Free States, it is easy to see that the great cause of Liberty, to which we now dedicate ourselves, will sweep the heart-strings of the people. It will smite all the chords with a might to draw forth emotions such as no political struggle ever awakened before. It will move the young, the middle-aged, and the old. It will find a voice in the social circle, and mingle with the flame of the domestic hearth. It will touch the souls of mothers, wives, sisters, and daughters, until the sympathies of all swell in one irresistible chorus of indignation against the deep damnation of lending new sanction to the enslavement of our brother man.

Come forward, then, men of all parties! let us range together. Come forth, all who thus far have kept aloof from parties! here is occasion for action. Men of Peace, come forth! All who in any way feel the wrong of Slavery, take your stand! Join us, lovers of Truth, of Justice, of Humanity! And let me call especially upon the young. You are the natural guardians of Freedom. In your firm resolves and generous souls she will find her surest protection. The young man who is not willing to serve in her cause, to suffer, if need be, in her behalf, gives little promise of those qualities which secure an honorable age.

THE LAW OF HUMAN PROGRESS.

AN ORATION BEFORE THE PHI BETA KAPPA SOCIETY OF UNION COLLEGE, SCHENECTADY, JULY 25, 1848.

Secta fuit servare modum, finemque tenere,
Naturamque sequi, patriæque impendere vitam,
Nec sibi, sed toti genitum se credere mundo.
LUCAN, *Pharsalia*, Lib. II. 381-383.

Plus les lumières se répandent, plus les écarts de la moyenne vont en diminuant; plus, par conséquent, nous tendons à nous rapprocher de ce qui est beau et de ce qui est bien. La perfectibilité de l'espèce humaine résulte comme une conséquence nécessaire de toutes nos recherches.— QUETELET, *Sur l'Homme*, Tom. II. p. 326.

But at my back I always hear
Time's wingèd chariot hurrying near:
And yonder all before us lie
Deserts of vast eternity.

MARVELL, *To his Coy Mistress.*

ORATION.

FROM opposite parts of the country, from various schools of sentiment, we have come together, at this happy anniversary, to interchange salutations, to mingle in friendly communion, and to catch such words of cheer as the occasion shall convey. Here are the young, with freshest laurel of Alma Mater, with joy brightening and hope elevating the countenance, still unconscious of the toils which enter into the duties of the world. Here are they, too, of middle life, on whose weary foreheads the sun now pours his meridian ray, resting for a moment in these pleasant retreats to renew their strength. Here, also, are the fathers, crowned with length of days, and rich with ripened wisdom, withdrawn from active struggle, and dwelling much in meditation upon the Past. The Future, the Present, and the Past, all find their representatives in our Fraternity.

I speak of *our* Fraternity; for, though a stranger among you, yet, as a member of this society in a sister University, and as a student of letters in moments snatched from other pursuits, I may claim kindred here. Let me speak, then, as to my own brethren. Invited by your partial kindness, it is my privilege to unfold some subject, which, while claiming your attention during this brief hour, may not improperly mingle with the memories of this anniversary. I would, if I could, utter truth which, while approved by the old, should sink deep into the souls of the young, filling them with strength for all good works. Mindful, then, of the occasion, deeply conscious of its requirements, solicitous of the harmony which becomes our literary festivals, I cannot banish from my thoughts a topic which is intimately connected with the movements of the present age, — nay, which explains and controls these movements, whether in the march of science, the triumphs of charity, the wide-spread convulsions of Europe, or the generous uprising of our own country in behalf of Freedom.

Wherever we turn is Progress, — in science, in literature, in knowledge of the earth, in knowledge of the skies, in intercourse among men, in the spread of liberty, in works of beneficence, in the recognition of Human Brotherhood. Thrones, where Authority seemed to sit secure, with the sanction of centuries, are shaken, and new-made constitutions come to restrain the aberrations of unlimited power. Men everywhere, breaking away from the Past, are pressing on to the things that are before.

Recall for one moment what has taken place during a brief span of time, hardly exceeding a year. I do not dwell on that mighty revolution in France, with whose throes the earth still shakes, and whose issues are yet unrevealed; I do not pause to contemplate the character of that Pontifical Reformer who has done so much to breathe into Europe the breath of a new life; I can only point to Sicily and Naples, rising against a besotted tyranny, — to Venice and Lombardy, claiming long-lost rights, — to all Italy, filled with the thought of Unity, —

to Hungary, flaming with republican fires,—to Austria, roused at last against a patriarchal despotism,—to Prussia, taking her place among constitutional states,—to Germany, in its many principalities, throbbing with the strong pulse of Freedom. These things are present to your minds.

Other events, of a different character, are not less signs of the age. Discovery has achieved one of its most brilliant, as also one of its most benign results. The genius of Leverrier, traversing the spaces of the heavens, has disclosed a new planet. By the application of ether, the dreaded pain of the surgical knife, and even the pangs of Nature, are soothed or removed, while Death is disarmed of something of its terrors.

These latter times have witnessed two spectacles of another nature and less regarded, which are of singular significance,—harbingers, I would call them, of those glad days of promise which we almost seem to touch. I would not exaggerate, and yet I must speak of them as they impress my own mind. To me they are of a higher order than any discovery in science, or any success in the acquisition of knowledge, or any political prosperity, inasmuch as they are the tokens of that moral elevation, and of that Human Brotherhood, without distinction of condition, nation, or race, which it is the supreme office of all science, all knowledge, and all politics to serve. I refer to the sailing of the Jamestown from Boston with succor to the starving poor of Ireland, and to the meeting of the Penitentiary Congress at Frankfort. All confess the beauty of that act, where prophecy seems fulfilled, by which a Ship of War was consecrated to a purpose of charity. Hardly less beautiful is the contemplation of that assembly at Frankfort (perhaps it is new to some whom I have the honor of addressing), where were delegates from most of the Christian nations,—from military France, Holland, Belgium, Switzerland, the States of Germany, England, Spain, Italy, Denmark, Poland, distant Russia, and frozen Norway,— convened for no purpose of war or diplomacy,— not to agitate selfish coalitions, not to adjust or disturb the seeming balance of Europe, not to exalt or abase the vaulting ambition of potentate or state, but calmly and in fraternal council to consider what could be done for those who are in prison, to hear the recital of efforts in their behalf among all the nations, and to encourage each other in this work. Such a Congress forms a truer epoch of Christian Progress — does it not? — than the Congress of Vienna, with the bespangled presence of great autocrats distributing the spoils of war, as the sailing of the Jamestown is a higher Christian triumph than any mere victory of blood.

Profoundly penetrated by these things, you will confess the Progress of Man. The earnest soul, enlightened by history, strengthened by philosophy, nursed to childish slumber by the simple prayer, "Thy kingdom come, thy will be done on earth as it is in heaven," confident in the final, though slow, fulfilment of the daily fulfilling promises of the Future, looks forward to the continuance of this Progress during unknown and infinite ages, as a *law* of our being.

It is of this that I shall speak to-day. My subject is THE LAW OF HUMAN PROGRESS. In selecting this theme, I would not minister to the pride or gratulation of the Present, nor would I furnish motives for indifference or repose. Rather would I teach how small is the

Present and all it contains, compared with the Future, and how duties increase with the grandeur upon which we enter, while we derive new encouragement from knowledge of the law which is our support and guide.

The subject is vast as it is interesting and important. It might well occupy a volume, rather than a brief discourse. In unfolding it, I shall speak *first* of the history of this law, as seen in its origin, gradual development, and recognition, — and *next* of its character, conditions, and limitations, with the duties it enjoins and the encouragements it affords.

I.

AND, first, of its history. The recognition of this law has been reserved for comparatively recent times. Like other general laws governing the courses of Nature, it was unknown to Antiquity. The ignorance and prejudice which then prevailed with regard to the earth, the heavenly bodies, and their relations to the universe, found fit companionship with the wild speculations concerning the Human Family. The ignorant live only in the Present, whether of time or place. What they see and observe bounds their knowledge. Thus to the early Greek the heavens were upborne by the mountains, and the sun traversed daily in fiery chariot from east to west. So things seemed to him. But the true Destiny of the Human Family was as little comprehended.

Man, in his origin and history, was surrounded with fable; nor was there any correct idea of the principles determining the succession of events. Revolutions of states were referred sometimes to chance, sometimes to certain innate elements of decay. Plutarch did not hesitate to ascribe the triumphs of Rome, not to the operation of immutable law, but to the fortune of the Republic. And Polybius, whom Gibbon extols for wisdom and philosophical spirit, said that Carthage, being so much older than Rome, felt her decay so much the sooner; and the survivor, he announced, carried in her bosom the seeds of mortality. The image of youth, manhood, and age was applied to nations. Like mortals on earth, they were supposed to have a period of life, and a length of thread spun by the Fates, strong at first, but thinner and weaker with advancing time, till at last it was cut, and another nation, with newly twisted thread, commenced its career.

In likening the life of a nation to the life of an individual man, there was error, commended by seeming truth, not yet entirely banished. It prevails still with many, who have not received the Law of Human Progress, teaching that all revolutions and changes are but links in the chain of development, or, it may be, turns in the grand *spiral*, by which the unknown infinite Future is connected with the Past. Nations have decayed, but never with the imbecility of age.

The ancients saw that there were changes, but did not detect the principles governing them, while a favorite fable and popular superstition conspired to turn attention back upon the Past, rather than forward to the Future. In the dawn of Greece, Hesiod, standing near the Father of Poetry, sang the descending mutations through which Mankind had seemed to travel. First came the Golden Age, so he fabled, when men lived secure and happy in pleasant association, without discord, without care, without toil, without weariness, while good of all kinds abounded, like the plentiful fruits which the earth spontaneously supplied. This was followed by the Silver Age, with a race inferior in form and disposition. Next was the Brazen Age, still descending in the scale, when men became vehement and robust, strong in body and stern in soul, building brazen houses, wielding brazen weapons, prompt to war, but not yet entirely wicked. Last, and unhappily his own, according to the poet, was the Iron Age, when straightway all evil raged forth; neither by day nor yet by night did men rest from labor and sorrow; discord took the place of concord; the pious, the just, and the good were without favor; the man of force and the evil-doer were cherished; modesty and justice yielded to insolence and wrong. War now prevailed, and men lived in wretchedness.[1]

Such, according to the Greek poet, was the succession of changes through which mankind had passed. This fable found a response. It was repeated by philosophy and history. Plato adorned and illustrated it. Strabo and Diodorus imparted to it their grave sanction. It was carried to Rome, with the other spoils of Greece. It was reproduced by Ovid, in flowing verses that have become a commonplace of literature. It was recognized by the tender muse of Virgil, the sportive fancy of Horace, and the stern genius of Juvenal. Songs and fables have ever exerted a powerful control over human opinion; nor is it possible to estimate the influence of this story in shaping unconsciously the thoughts of mankind. It is easy to understand that the youth of Antiquity, — let me say, too, the youth of later ages, — nay, of our own day, in our own schools and colleges, — nurtured by this literature, should learn to neglect the Future, and rather regard the Past. The words of

[1] Hesiod, Opera et Dies, 109 - 201.

Horace have afforded a polished expression to this prejudice of education: —

> "Damnosa quid non imminuit dies?
> Ætas parentum, pejor avis, tulit
> Nos nequiores, mox daturos
> Progeniem vitiosiorem." 1

Barren as is classical literature in any just recognition of the continuity of events, any true appreciation of the movement of history, or any well-defined confidence in the Future, it were wrong to say that it never found a voice which seemed, in harmony with the Prophets and the Evangelists, to proclaim the advent of a better age. Virgil, in his Eclogue to Pollio, — the exact meaning of which is still a riddle, — breaks forth in words of vague aspiration, which have been sometimes supposed to herald the coming of the Saviour. The blessings of Peace are here foreshadowed, while the Golden Age seems to be not only behind, but also before. Thus, notwithstanding the prejudice of superstition and the constraint of ignorance, has the human heart, in longings for a better condition on earth, gone forward as the pioneer of Humanity.

To the superstition of Heathenism succeeded that of the Christian Church. The popular doctrine of an immediate millennium, inculcated by a succession of early fathers, took the place of ancient fable; and a Golden Age was placed in advance to animate the hope and perseverance of the faithful. It was believed that the anxieties and strifes filling the lives of men were all to be lost in a blissful Sabbath of a thousand years, when Christ with the triumphant band of saints would return to reign upon earth until the last and general

1 Hor., Carm. III. vi. 45 – 48.

resurrection. Vain and irrational as was the early form of this anticipation, it was not without advantage. It filled the souls of all who received it with aspirations for the Future, while it rudely prefigured that promised period — then, alas! how distant! — when the whole world will glow in the illumination of Christian truth. Among the means by which the Law of Human Progress has found acceptance, it is only just to mention this prophetic vision of the ancient Church.

All the legitimate influences of Christianity were in the same direction. Christianity is the religion of Progress. Here is a distinctive feature, which we vainly seek in any Heathen faith professed upon earth. Confucius, in his sublime morals, taught us not to do unto others what we would have them not do unto us; but the Chinese philosopher did not declare the ultimate triumph of this law. It was reserved for the Sermon on the Mount to reveal the vital truth, that all the highest commands of religion and duty, drawing in their train celestial peace, and marking the final goal of all Progress among men, shall one day be obeyed. "For verily I say unto you," says the Saviour, "till heaven and earth pass, *one jot or one tittle shall in no wise pass from the Law, till all be fulfilled.*"

There is nothing of good so vast or beautiful, nothing so distant or seemingly inaccessible, as to fall beyond the reach of these promises. Though imperfectly understood, or recognized, in the night of ignorance and prejudice, they were heralds of the dawn. In the advance of Modern Europe, they led the way, whispering, *Onward forever!* Long before Philosophy deduced the Law of Human Progress from the history of man, the Gospel silently planted it in the human heart. There it rested, influencing powerfully, though gently, the march of events.

Slowly did it pass from the formularies of devotion into the convictions of reason and the treasury of science. Strange blindness! They, who, repeating the Lord's Prayer, daily called for *the coming of his kingdom on earth*, who professed implicit faith in the final fulfilment of the Law, still continued in Heathen ignorance of the significance and spirit of the Prayer they daily uttered and of the Law they daily recognized. They did not perceive that the kingdom of the Lord was to come, and the Law to be fulfilled by a continuity of daily labor. As modern civilization gradually unfolded itself amidst the multiplying generations of men, they witnessed the successive manifestations of power,— but perceived no Law. They looked upon the imposing procession of events, but did not discern the rule which guided the mighty series. Ascending from triumph to triumph, they saw dominion extended by the discoveries of intrepid navigators,— saw learning strengthened by the studies of accomplished scholars, — saw universities opening their portals to ingenuous youth in all corners of the land, from Aberdeen and Copenhagen to Toledo and Ferrara,— saw Art put forth new graces in the painting of Raffaelle, new grandeur in the painting, the sculpture, and the architecture of Michel Angelo,— caught the strains of poets, no longer cramped by ancient idioms, but flowing sweetly in the language learned at a mother's knee,— received the manifold revelations of science in geometry, mathematics, astronomy,— beheld the barbarism of the barbarous Art of War changed and refined, though barbarous still, by the invention of gunpowder,— witnessed knowledge of all kinds springing to unwonted power through the marvellous agency of the printing-press, — admired the character of *the Good Man of Peace*, as described in that work of unexampled circulation, translated into all modern languages, the "Imitation of Christ," by Thomas à Kempis, — listened to the apostolic preaching of Wyckliffe in England, Huss in Bohemia, Savonarola in Florence, Luther at Worms; and yet all these things, the harmonious expression of *progressive* energies belonging to Man, token of an untiring advance, earnest of a mightier Future, seemed to teach no certain lesson.

The key to this advance had not been found. It was not seen that the constant desire for improvement implanted in man, with the constant effort consequent thereon in a life susceptible of indefinite Progress, caused, naturally, under the laws of a beneficent God, an indefinite advance, — that the evil passions of individuals, or of masses, while retarding, could not permanently restrain this divine impulse, — and that each generation, by irresistible necessity, added to the accumulations of the Past, and in this way prepared a higher Future. To all ignorant of this tendency, history, instead of a connected chain, with cause and effect in natural order, is nothing but a disconnected, irregular series of incidents, like separate and confused circles having no common bond. It is a dark chaos, embroiled by "chance, high arbitress," or swayed by some accidental man, fortunate in position or power. Even Macchiavelli, the consummate historian and politician of his age, — Bodin, the able speculator upon Government, — Bossuet, the eloquent teacher of religion and history, — Grotius, the illustrious founder of the Laws of Nations, — whose large intelligence should have grasped the true philosophy of events, — all failed to recognize in them any prevailing law or governing principle.

It was reserved for a professor at Naples, Giambattista Vico, in the early part of the last century, to review the history of the Past, analyze its movements, and finally disclose the existence of a primitive rule or law by which these movements were effected. His work, entitled "The Principles of a New Science concerning the Common Nature of Nations,"[1] first published in 1725, constitutes an epoch in historical studies. Recent Italian admirers vindicate for its author a place among great discoverers, by the side of Descartes, Galileo, Bacon, and Newton.[2] Without undertaking to question, or to adopt, this lofty homage to a name little known, it will not be doubted, that, as author of an elaborate work devoted expressly to the philosophy of history, at a period when history was supposed to be without philosophy, he deserves honorable mention.

Vico taught regard not merely for the individual and the nation, but the race, and showed, that, whatever the fortunes of individuals, Humanity advances, — that no blind or capricious chance controls the course of human affairs, but that whatever is done proceeds directly, under God, from the forces and faculties of men, and thus can have no true cause except in the nature of things, — excluding, of course, the idea of chance. He recognized three principles at the foundation of civilization: first, the existence of Divine Providence; secondly, the necessity of moderating the passions; and, thirdly, the

1 Principj di una Scienza nuova d' intorno alla comune Natura delle Nazioni. The fourth book is entitled *Del corso che fanno le nazioni;* the fifth book, *Del ricorso delle cose humane nel risurgere che fanno le nazioni.*

2 Cataldo Jannelli, Cenni sulla Natura et Necessità della Scienza delle Cose et delle Storie Umane. Cap. 3, sec. 6.

immortality of the soul: three primal truths, answering to three historical facts of universal acceptance, — religion, marriage, and sepulture. Three stages marked the history of mankind: first, the divine, or theocratic; next, the heroic; and, lastly, the human. These appeared in Antiquity, and were reproduced, as he fancied, in modern times. Ingenuity and novelty are stamped upon this exposition, which is elevated by the exclusion of chance and the recognition of God.

While recognizing Humanity as governed by law, and with a common dependence, the Neapolitan professor failed to perceive that this same law and this common dependence promise to conduct it through unknown and infinite stages. Believing monarchy a perfect government, he did not see beyond the time of kings. Like others before him, and even in our own day, he was perplexed by the treacherous image of youth, manhood, and age, which he applied to nations, as to the individual man. No discovery is complete, and that of Vico, while most ingenious and fruitful, failed to grasp the whole law of the Future.

Meanwhile a gigantic genius in Germany, — whose vision, no less comprehensive than penetrating, embraced the whole circumference of knowledge and reached into the undiscovered Future, to whom the complexities of mathematics, the subtilties of philology, the mazes of philosophy, the courses of history, the rules of jurisprudence, and the heights of theology were all equally familiar, — Leibnitz, that more than imperial conqueror in the realms of universal knowledge, — the greatest, perhaps, of Human Intelligences, — enunciated the Law of Progress in all the sciences and all the concerns of life. The Present, born of the Past, he said, is pregnant with the Future. It is by a sure series that we advance, using and enjoying all our gifts for health of body and improvement of mind. Everything, from the simplest substance up to man, progresses towards God, the Infinite Being, Source of all other beings; and in bold words, which may require explanation, he says, "Man seems able to arrive at perfection": *Videtur homo ad perfectionem venire posse.*[1]

Leibnitz saw the Law of Progress by intuition, and became its herald. But there is no reason to believe that he appreciated its transcendent importance as a rule of conduct, and submitted his great powers to its influence. He saw more than Vico, but he did not discern the practical guide he had discovered. And yet, recognizing this law, the gates of the Future were open to him, and he saw Man in distant perspective, arrived at heights of happiness which he cannot now conceive. The vision of Universal Peace was to him no longer a vision, but the practical idea of humane statesmen, while he bent his incomparable genius to the discovery of a new agent of intercourse among men, — the aspiration of other philosophers since his day, — a Universal Language, where the confusion of tongues will be forgotten, and the union of hearts be consummated in the union of speech.

Close upon Leibnitz came Lessing, whose genius, less universal, but more exquisite, made him the regenerator of German literature. His soul was touched by sympathy for all mankind, and he saw its sure advance. Almost by his side was Herder, gifted among a gifted

[1] Leibnitz. Opera Omnia (ed. Dutens), Tom. VI. p. 309: *Leibnitiana*, Art. LXXIV. — "Ut semper *certa serie progredi* valeamus." Opera Philosophica, p. 85, Art. XI., *De Scientia Universali.* — See also *Théodicée*, § 341.

people, who in his "Philosophy of History" portrays Humanity in its incessant progress from small beginnings of ignorance and barbarism, when wrong and war and slavery prevail, to the recognition of reason and justice as the rule of life. "There is nothing enthusiastical," he says in that work, which is a classic of German prose, "in the hope, that, wherever men dwell, at some future period will dwell men rational, just, and happy,— happy, not through the means of their own reason alone, but of the common reason of their whole fraternal race."[1] In these last words the Law of Progress is announced, with all its promises.

In France we trace this law through a succession of master minds,—first of whom in time, as in authority, is Descartes, the chief of French philosophy. His life was crowded with triumphs of intellect, and after death his spirit seemed for a time to rule all departments of study. Like the universal soul of the Stoics, it was everywhere. Though not formally enunciating the Law of Progress, his "Discourse on Method," first published in 1637, acknowledged its influence in natural science. "The experience which I have in physics," he says, "teaches me that it is possible to arrive at a knowledge of many things which will be very useful to life, and that we may yet discover methods by which man, comprehending the force and the action of fire, water, air, stars, skies, and all the other bodies which environ us, as distinctly as we comprehend the different trades of our artisans, shall be able to employ them in the same fashion for all the uses to which they are appropriate, and thus shall render himself master and possessor of Na-

[1] Philosophie der Geschichte der Menschheit, tr. Churchill, Book XV. ch. 5, § 12.

ture." In these new triumphs of knowledge, he says, "men may learn to enjoy the fruits of the earth without trouble; their health will be preserved, and they will be able to exempt themselves from an infinitude of ills, as well of body as of mind, and even, perhaps, from the weakness of old age." As I repeat these words, uttered long before the steam-engine, the railroad, the electric telegraph, and the use of ether, I seem to hear a prophecy, the prophecy of Science, which each day helps to fulfil. "Without intending any slight," he continues, "I am sure that even those engaged in these matters will confess that all that they know is almost nothing in comparison with what remains to be known."[1] There is grandeur in the assurance with which the great philosopher announces the Future.

From Descartes I come to Pascal, never to be mentioned without a tribute to the early genius which, though removed from life at the age of thirty-nine, left an ineffaceable trace upon the religion, science, and literature of his time. The Law of Progress received from him its earliest and most distinct statement as a rule of philosophy applicable to all the sciences depending upon experience and reason. This is to be found in that posthumous work of eloquent piety and sentiment, *Les Pensées*, first published by his companions of Port Royal, in 1669, some time after his death; and it is not a little curious, as an illustration of the prejudices this truth has encountered, that the chapter where it is set forth, entitled *Of Authority in Matters of Philosophy*, was in this early edition suppressed. Not until the next century was the testimony of Pascal disclosed to the world. "By a special prerogative of the human

[1] Descartes, Discours de la Méthode, Part. 6: Œuvres, Tom. I. pp. 192, 193.

race," says he, "not only each man advances day by day in the sciences, but all men together make continual progress therein, as the universe grows old; because the same thing happens in the succession of men which takes place in the different ages of an individual. So that the whole succession of men in the course of so many ages may be regarded as *one man who lives always and who learns continually.* From this we see with what injustice we respect Antiquity in its philosophers; for, since old age is the period most distant from infancy, who does not see that the old age of this *universal man* must not be sought in the times nearest his birth, but in those which are the most remote? They whom we call the Ancients were indeed new in all things, and properly formed the infancy of mankind; and since to their knowledge we have joined the experience of the ages which have followed, it is in ourselves that is to be found that Antiquity which we revere in the others."[1] We cannot admire too much this splendid inspiration, where the expression is in harmony with the thought. When it was said that mankind may be regarded "as one man who lives always and who learns continually," there was indeed a new discovery, as great as if a new continent or a new planet had been disclosed.

The age enlightened by the genius of Pascal was ready to discuss the question then at hand, on the comparative merits of Ancients and Moderns, involving an inquiry into the principles of Progress, particularly in art and literature. The close of the seventeenth century witnessed this memorable debate, which extended

[1] Pascal, Pensées, Part. I. Art. 1, *De l'Autorité en Matière de Philosophie*: Œuvres (ed. Bossut, 1779), Tom. II.

from France to England. French critics, under the lead of Boileau, espoused the cause of the Ancients. Against them was Charles Perrault, conspicuous at the time among academicians, and still remembered as author of those Fairy Tales, including "Cinderella" and "Blue-beard," which have given him a fame not inferior to that of his brother, Claude Perrault, with whom he is sometimes confounded, to whom France is indebted for that perpetual triumph in architecture, the unsurpassed front of the Louvre. In an elaborate work, published in 1688 – 92, entitled "Parallel between the Ancients and Moderns in regard to the Arts and Sciences,"[1] where the debate is in the form of dialogue, he vindicates the Moderns in comparison with the Ancients, and insists, that, notwithstanding the perfection at which the latter arrived, the Moderns have an advantage from prolonged experience and its necessary accumulations. Like Pascal, whose remarkable words were still unpublished, he, too, sees the life of Humanity *as the life of an individual man eternal*, and, though recognizing epochs of retrogression in history, asserts the continuous progress of the race, not only in the sciences, but also in morals and the arts, not forgetting the art of the kitchen.

This sentiment found similar utterance in a lively contemporary, Fontenelle, an honored academician, whose life extended to a length of days unequalled in the history of literature, having accomplished one hundred years, after devoting that century of existence to the exclusive pursuit of letters. "A good mind cultivated," says this exceptional veteran, "is, so to

1 Parallèle des Anciens et des Modernes, en ce qui regarde les Arts et les Sciences.

speak, composed of all the minds of the preceding ages: it is but one and the same mind that has been cultivated during all this period. So that this man, who has lived from the beginning of the world to the present time, has had his infancy, when he was occupied only with the more pressing wants of life, — his youth, when he has succeeded pretty well in matters of imagination, such as poesy and eloquence, and when he has even begun to reason, but with less solidity than fire. He has now reached the age of manhood, when he reasons with more force and more intelligence than ever; but he would be yet further advanced, if the passion for war had not for a long time possessed him, and given him a contempt for the sciences, to which he has at last returned. . . . . *This man will have no old age;* he will be ever equally capable of the things to which his youth was fitted, and ever more and more so of those which belong to the age of manhood: that is to say, — to quit the allegory, — men will never degenerate, but the sound views of the entire succession of good minds will always be added to one another."[1] — Titian, like Fontenelle, was remarkable for unusual length of days; but the consummate artist, among his immortal pictures, has left hardly one more worthy of immortality than this brilliant statement, where the discovery of Pascal is affirmed and presented with singular clearness and precision.

Thus, in France, was the Law of Progress confessed in the sciences by Descartes and Pascal, — in literature, in arts, and even in morals, by Perrault and Fontenelle. This was before the expiration of the seventeenth cen-

[1] Fontenelle, Digression sur les Anciens et les Modernes: Œuvres, Tom. II. p. 249.

tury. It remained that it should be announced, not only as a special law applicable to certain departments, but as a general Law of Humanity, universal in application, guiding men in all their labors, and erecting before them a goal of aspiration and of certain triumph. This was done by another, who was not philosopher only, nor statesman only, nor philanthropist only, but in whom this triumvirate of characters blended with rare success, — Turgot, the well-loved minister of Louis the Sixteenth. It was said of him by Voltaire, that "he was born wise and just"; and this tribute has especial point, when it is considered that his acceptance of this law was first announced in an essay[1] written in 1750, at the age of twenty-three, while he was yet at the Sorbonne. Let it be mentioned in his praise, that, as he grew in years, in power, and in fame, he did not depart from the happy intuitions of early life, or forget the visions which, as a young man, he had seen. Perceiving clearly the advance already made, he drew from it the assurance of yet further advance. In reason, knowledge, and virtue he did not hesitate to place his own age before preceding ages. "The corrupt of to-day," he was accustomed to say, "would have been Capuchins a hundred years ago." He declared the capacity for indefinite improvement a distinctive quality of the human race, belonging to the race in general, and to each individual in particular. He did not doubt that the progress of the physical sciences, of education, of method in the sciences, or the discovery of new methods, would enlarge the powers of man, rendering him capable of preserving a larger number of ideas in

[1] Sur les Progrès successifs de l'Esprit Humain: Œuvres (ed. Daire), Tom. II. pp. 597 - 611.

the memory, and of multiplying their relations. Nor did he doubt that the moral sense was equally capable of improvement, — that man would become constantly better in proportion as he was enlightened, — that the advance of society would necessarily keep pace with the advance of morals, — that politics, founded, like other sciences, upon observation and reason, would advance also, — that all useful truths must be finally known and adopted, while ancient errors are by degrees annihilated, or give place to new truths, — and that this Progress, increasing always from age to age, has no term, or none at least which can be assigned in the present state of human intelligence.

The early testimony of Turgot was repeated at a later day in his precious fragment on Universal History, which, when compared with the Introductory Discourse of Bossuet on the same theme, shows how superior in the philosophy of history was the layman to the bishop. All ages, says Turgot, are enchained by a succession of causes and effects uniting the present with what has preceded, and all accumulated knowledge is a common treasure, transmitted from generation to generation, as an inheritance, augmented by the discoveries of each age. In this spirit he inaugurates Universal History, giving to it a just elevation, as the exhibition of Human Progress in all its epochs, with all its hindrances, and crowned by all its triumphs.[1]

Such testimony, commended by the earnestness of conviction, was not without influence on the great movement which culminated in the earlier revolution of

[1] Plan de Deux Discours sur l'Histoire Universelle: Œuvres, Tom. II pp. 626 - 667.

France, or rather it was part of that movement. It found welcome in many bosoms, and helped stir the vast mass. Among those especially penetrated by it was the friend and biographer of Turgot, who was not behind his master in this loyalty: I refer to Condorcet. This unfortunate nobleman, conspicuous for learning and genius, particularly in mathematics, and for honest devotion to the principles of the Revolution, when at last proscribed, and compelled to flee for life, — pursued by the very dogs he had helped to arouse, but was impotent to restrain, — sought shelter with a friend, where, in concealment, he passed the last eight months before his mournful death. His first thought was, to send forth a vindication of himself, addressed to his fellow-citizens; but soon renouncing this design, he devoted what remained to him of life — during that most hateful passage of human history, the Reign of Terror — to the preparation of a work in which he brought his various powers to the development of the Law of Human Progress. It is entitled "Sketch of an Historical Table of the Progress of the Human Mind,"[1] and reviews human society in its different stages, unfolding the order of its changes and the influences transmitted from age to age, pointing out the different steps in the march towards truth and happiness. From observation of man as he has been, and as he is to-day, the author passes naturally to those new triumphs which are his certain destiny, so long as he continues to possess the faculties with which he is endowed, and to be governed by the same universal laws.

Thus wrote Condorcet, while the hand of Death yet waited. He died; but the return to reason in France

[1] Esquisse d'un Tableau Historique des Progrès de l'Esprit Humain.

was signalized by unaccustomed homage to the victim. The Committee of Public Instruction reported, that the sketch was "a classical work offered to republican schools by an unfortunate philosopher, that everywhere in it the improvement of society was recognized as the object most deserving the activity of the human intelligence, and that pupils studying here the history of the sciences and the arts would learn to cherish liberty and to detest and vanquish all tyrannies"; and thereupon the National Convention ordered three thousand copies to be distributed at the expense of the nation.[1] And here properly closes this branch of our subject.

The high lineage and authority of this law I have traced, not by the enthusiasts of Humanity, not by Fénelon or Saint-Pierre, not by Diderot or Rousseau, but by a succession of masters who are our acknowledged guides in science, philosophy, and history. In Italy the torch was held aloft by Vico; in Germany, by Leibnitz, Lessing, and Herder; in France it passed through the hands of Descartes, Pascal, Perrault, Fontenelle, Turgot, and Condorcet: —

"Et quasi cursores, vitaï lampada tradunt,"[2]

till at last, at the close of the eighteenth century, its flame was seen from afar. To England we seem little indebted; and yet, when I think of Lord Bacon, I am disposed to say that we are much indebted. This law inspired his great work on the "Advancement of Learning," and is expressed in its very title. It entered into his aspiration to deliver man from present weakness by

1 Rapport fait à la Convention Nationale, au Nom du Comité d'Instruction Publique, etc.: Œuvres de Condorcet (ed. O'Connor et Arago, Paris, 1847 - 49), Tom. VI. pp. 3 - 5.

2 Lucretius, De Rerum Natura, Lib. II. 78.

extending his power over Nature. It is foreshadowed in his great declaration, antedating Pascal, that Antiquity was the youth of the world, — "*Antiquitas sæculi, juventus mundi.*" [1] For a time Bacon had no successors in England. At a later day this law was cordially embraced by Dr. Price,[2] the friend and correspondent of Turgot. Dr. Johnson, who surely did not accept it, shows an unconscious sympathy with it, when he says of life in pastoral countries, that it "knows nothing of progression or advancement." [3] Unhappy people, thus without visible Future on earth!

To the eighteenth century belongs the honor — signal honor I venture to call it — of first distinctly acknowledging and enunciating that Law of Human Progress, which, though preached in Judea eighteen hundred years ago, failed to be received by men, — nay, still fails to be received by men. Writers in our own age, of much ability and unexampled hardihood, while adopting this fundamental law, proceed to arraign existing institutions of society. My present purpose does not require me to consider these, whether for censure or praise, — abounding as they do in evil, abounding as they do in good. It is my single aim to trace the gradual development and final establishment of that great law which teaches that "there is a good time coming," — a Future even on earth, to arouse the hopes, the aspirations, and the energies of Man.

1 De Augmentis Scientiarum, Lib. I.: Works, Vol. IV. p. 34.

2 There is a sermon by Dr Price, published in 1787, on *The Evidence of a Future Period of Improvement in the State of Mankind.*

3 Journey to the Hebrides: Works (Oxford, 1825), Vol. IX. p. 98.

II.

THE way is now prepared to consider the character, conditions, and limitations of this law, the duties it enjoins, and the encouragements it affords.

Let me state the law as I understand it. Man, as an individual, is capable of indefinite improvement. Societies and nations, which are but aggregations of men, and, finally, the Human Family, or collective Humanity, are capable of indefinite improvement. And this is the destiny of man, of societies, of nations, and of the Human Family.

Restricting the proposition to the capacity for indefinite improvement, I believe I commend it to the candor and intelligence of all who have meditated upon this subject. And this brings me to the remarkable words of Leibnitz. He boldly says, as we have already seen, that man seems able to arrive at perfection. Turgot and Condorcet also speak of his "perfectibility," — a term adopted by recent French writers. If by this is meant simply that man is capable of indefinite improvement, then it will not be questioned. But whatever the heights of virtue and intelligence to which he may attain in future ages, who can doubt that to his grander vision new summits will ever present themselves, provoking him to still grander aspirations? God only is perfect. Knowledge and goodness, his attributes, are infinite; nor can man hope, in any lapse of time, to comprehend this immensity. In the infinitude of the universe, he will seem, like Newton, with all his acquisitions, only to have gathered a few pebbles by the seaside. In a similar strain Leibnitz elsewhere says that the place which God assigns to man in space and time necessarily limits the perfections he is able to acquire. As in Geometry the asymptote constantly approaches its curve, so that the distance between them is constantly diminishing, and yet, though prolonged indefinitely, they never meet, so, according to him, are infinite souls the asymptotes of God.

There are revolutions in history seeming on a superficial view inconsistent with this law. From early childhood attention is directed to Greece and Rome; and we are sometimes taught that these two powers reached heights which subsequent nations cannot hope to equal, much less surpass. I would not disparage the triumphs of the ancient mind. The eloquence, the poetry, the philosophy, the art, of Athens still survive, and bear no mean sway upon earth. Rome, too, yet lives in her jurisprudence, which, next after Christianity, has exerted a paramount influence over the laws of modern communities.

But exalted as these productions may be, it is impossible not to perceive that something of their present importance is derived from the early period when they appeared, something from the unquestioning and high-flown admiration of them transmitted through successive generations until it became a habit, and something also from the disposition, still prevalent, to elevate Antiquity at the expense of subsequent ages. Without undertaking to decide if the genius of Antiquity, as displayed by individuals, can justly claim supremacy, it would be easy to show that the ancient plane of civilization never reached our common level. The people were ignorant, vicious, and poor, or degraded to abject slavery, — itself the sum of all injustice and all vice. Even the most illustrious characters, whose names still shine from that distant night, were little more than splendid barbarians. Architecture, sculpture, painting, and vases of exquisite perfection attest an appreciation of beauty in form; but our masters in these things were strangers to the useful arts, as to the comforts and virtues of home. Abounding in what to us are luxuries, they had not what to us are necessaries.

Without knowledge there can be no sure Progress. Vice and barbarism are the inseparable companions of ignorance. Nor is it too much to say, that, except in rare instances, the highest virtue is attained only through intelligence. This is natural; for to do right, we must first understand what is right. But the people of Greece and Rome, even in the brilliant days of Pericles and Augustus, could not arrive at this knowledge. The sublime teachings of Plato and Socrates — calculated in many respects to promote the best interests of the race — were limited in influence to a small company of listeners, or to the few who could obtain a copy of the costly manuscripts in which they were preserved. Thus the knowledge and virtue acquired by individuals were not diffused in their own age or secured to posterity.

Now, at last, through an agency all unknown to Antiquity, knowledge of every kind has become general and permanent. It can no longer be confined to a select circle. It cannot be crushed by tyranny, or lost by neglect. It is immortal as the soul from which it proceeds. This alone renders all relapse into barbarism impossible, while it affords an unquestionable distinction between ancient and modern times. The Press, watchful with more than the hundred eyes of Argus, strong with more than the hundred arms of Briareus, not only guards all the conquests of civilization, but leads the way to future triumphs. Through its untiring energies, the meditation of the closet, or the utterance of the human voice, which else would die away within the precincts of a narrow room, is prolonged to the most distant nations and times, with winged words circling the globe. We admire the genius of Demosthenes, Sophocles, Plato, and Phidias; but the printing-press is a higher gift to man than the eloquence, the drama, the philosophy, and the art of Greece.

There is yet another country which presents a problem for the student of Progress. In vivid phrase Sir James Mackintosh pictures the "ancient and *immovable* civilization of China."[1] But in these words he spoke rather from impressions than from actual knowledge. By the side of the impulsive movement of modern Europe, the people of this ancient empire may appear stationary; but it can hardly be doubted that they have advanced, though according to a scale unlike our own. It is difficult to assign satisfactory reasons for the seeming inertness of their national life. Perhaps I shall not err, if I refer it to peculiar constitutional characteristics, — to inherent difficulties of their language as an instrument of knowledge, — to national vanity on an exaggerated scale, making them look down upon others, — to an insulation excluding all others, — and also to the habit of unhesitating deference to Antiquity, and of "backward-looking thoughts," cultivated by the Chinese from the distant days of Confucius. They do not know the Law of Human Progress.

1 Discourse on the Study of the Law of Nature and Nations, p. 34.

In receiving this law, two conditions of Humanity are recognized: first, its unity or solidarity; and, secondly, its indefinite duration upon earth. And now of these in their order.

1. It is true, doubtless, that there are various races of men; but there is but one great Human Family, in which Caucasian, Ethiopian, Chinese, and Indian are all brothers, children of *one* Father, and heirs to *one* happiness. Though variously endowed, they are all tending in the same direction; nor can the light obtained by one be withheld from any. The ether discovery in Boston will soothe pain hereafter in Africa and in Asia, in Abyssinia and in China. So are we all knit together, that words of wisdom and truth, which first sway the hearts of the American people, may help to elevate benighted tribes of the most distant regions. The vexed question of modern science, whether these races proceeded originally from one stock, does not interfere with the sublime revelation of Christianity, the Brotherhood of Man. In the light of science and of religion, Humanity is an organism, complex, but still one, — throbbing with one life, animated by one soul, every part sympathizing with every other part, and the whole advancing in one indefinite career of Progress.

2. And what is the measure of this career? It is common to speak of the long life already passed by man on earth; but how brief and trivial is this, compared with the countless ages before him! According to received chronology, six thousand years have not yet elapsed since his creation. But the science of Geology, that unimpeached interpreter of the Past, now demonstrates (and here the geology of New York furnishes im-

portant evidence), that, anterior to the commencement of human history, this globe had endured for ages upon ages, baffling human calculation and imagination. Without losing ourselves in the stupendous speculations with regard to different geological epochs, before the earth assumed its present figure, and when it was occupied only by races of animals now extinct, it may not be without interest to glance at the age of the epoch in which we live. This, happily, we are able to do.

From the flow of rivers we have a gigantic measure of geological time. It is supposed that the Falls of Niagara were once at Queenstown, and that they have gradually worn their way back in the living rock, for a distance of seven miles, to the place where they now pour their thunders. An ingenious English geologist, a high authority in his science, Sir Charles Lyell, assuming that this retreat might have been at the rate of one foot a year, shows that the cataract must have poured over that rock for a period of at least 36,960 years. And the same authority teaches us that the alluvion at the mouth of the Mississippi, the delta formed by the deposits of that mighty river (here let it be remarked that alluvions and sand-banks are the most recent geological formations on the surface of the earth, being nearest to our own age), could not have been accumulated within a shorter period than 100,500 years.[1] Even this term, so vast to our small imagination, is only one of a series composing the present epoch; and the epoch itself is but a unit in a still grander series. These measurements, adopted

[1] Lyell's Principles of Geology (7th ed.), Vol I. p. 216. Lyell's Travels in North America, Ch. 2 Horner's Anniversary Address, for 1847, before the London Geological Society, pp. 23 – 27. D'Archiac, Histoire des Progrès de la Géologie, Tom. I. p. 358.

in this branch of knowledge, can be little more than vague approximations; but they teach, from the lips of Science, as perhaps nothing else can, the infinite ages through which this globe has already travelled, and the infinite ages which seem to be its future destiny.

Thus we stand now between two infinities, — the infinity of the Past, and the infinity of the Future; and the infinity of the Future is equal to the infinity of the Past. In comparison with these untold spaces before and after, what, indeed, are the six thousand years of human history? In the contemplation of Man, what littleness! what grandeur! how diminutive in the creation! how brief his recorded history! and yet how vast in hopes! how majestic and transcendent in the Future!

If there be any analogy between his life on earth and that of the frailest plant or shell-fish, as now seen in the light of science, he must still be in his earliest and most helpless infancy. In vain speak of Antiquity in his history; for all his present records are as a day, an hour, a moment, in the unimaginable immensity of duration which seems to await the globe and its inhabitants. In the sight of our distant descendants, successive eras of the brief span which we call History will melt into one; and as to present vision stars far asunder seem near together, so Nimrod and Sesostris, Alexander and Cæsar, Tamerlane and Napoleon, will seem to be contemporaries. Nor is it any exaggeration to suppose that in the unborn ages, illumined by a truth now, alas! too dimly perceived, the class of warriors and conquerors, of which these are signal types, will become extinct, — like the gigantic land reptiles and monster crocodileans belonging to a departed period of zoölogical history.

Admitting the Unity of Mankind, and an Indefinite Future on earth, it becomes easy to anticipate triumphs which else were impossible. Few will question that Man, as an individual, is capable of indefinite improvement, so long as he lives. This capacity is inborn. None so poor as not to possess it. Even the idiot, so abject in condition, is found at last to be within the sphere of education. Circumstances alone are required to call this capacity into action; and in proportion as knowledge, virtue, and religion prevail in a community will that sacred atmosphere be diffused under whose genial influence the most forlorn may grow into forms of unimagined strength and beauty. This capacity for indefinite improvement, which belongs to the individual, must belong also to society; for society does not die, and through the improvement of its individuals has the assurance of its own advance. It is immortal on earth, and will gather constantly new and richer fruits from the teeming generations, as they stretch through unknown time. To Chinese vision the period of the present may seem barren, but it is sure to yield its contribution to the indefinite accumulations which are the token of an indefinite Progress.

Tables speak sometimes as words cannot. From statistics of life, as recorded by Science, we learn the capacity for progress in the Human Family; the testimony is authentic, as it is interesting. A little more than two centuries have passed since Descartes predicted that improvement in human health which these figures exhibit. Could this seer of Science revisit the scene of his comprehensive labors and divine aspirations, he might well be astonished to learn how, in the lapse of so short a period in the life of Humanity, his glowing anticipations have been fulfilled. From the following tables[1] we learn that even the conqueror Death has been slowly driven back, and his inevitable triumph postponed.

Table showing the Diminution of Mortality in different Countries.

Deaths in	England,	in 1690, 1 in 33,	in 1848, 1 in 47.
"	France,	in 1776, 1 in 25½,	in 1848, 1 in 42.
"	Germany,	in 1788, 1 in 32,	in 1848, 1 in 40.
"	Sweden,	in 1760, 1 in 34,	in 1848, 1 in 41.
"	Roman States,	in 1767, 1 in 21½,	in 1829, 1 in 28.

Diminution of Mortality in Cities.

Deaths in	London,	in 1690, 1 in 24,	in 1844, 1 in 44.
"	Paris,	in 1650, 1 in 25,	in 1829, 1 in 32.
"	Berlin,	in 1755, 1 in 28,	in 1827, 1 in 34.
"	Vienna,	in 1750, 1 in 20,	in 1829, 1 in 25.
"	Rome,	in 1770, 1 in 21,	in 1828, 1 in 31.
"	Geneva,	in 1560, 1 in 18,	in 1821, 1 in 40.

Glancing at the cradle of nations and races risen to grandeur, and observing the wretchedness by which they were originally surrounded, we learn that no lot is removed from the influence of this law. The Feejee Islander, the Bushman, the Hottentot, the Congo negro, is not too low for its care. No term of imagined "finality" can arrest it. The polished Briton, whose civilization we now admire, traces his long-descended lineage from one of those painted barbarians whose degradation still lives in the pages of Julius Cæsar. Slowly, and by

[1] Supplied to me by the late Professor H. D. Rogers, from the notes of his Lectures.

degrees, he has reached the height where he now stands; but this is no "finality." The improvement of the Past is the earnest of yet further improvement in the long ages of the Future. And who can doubt, that, in the lapse of time, as the Christian Law is gradually fulfilled, the elevation of the Briton will be shared by all his fellow-men?

The tokens of improvement may appear at a special period, in a limited circle only, among the people, favored of God, enjoying peculiar benefits of commerce and Christianity; but the happy influence cannot be narrowed to any time, place, or people. Every victory over evil redounds to the benefit of all. Every discovery, every humane thought, every truth, when declared, is a conquest of which the whole Human Family are partakers, extending by so much their dominion, while it lessens by so much the sphere of future struggle and trial. Thus, while Nature is always the same, the power of Man is ever increasing. Each day gives him some new advantage. The mountains have not diminished in size; but Man has overcome the barriers they interpose. The winds and waves are not less capricious now than when they first beat upon the ancient Silurian rocks; but the steamboat,

> "Against the wind, against the tide,
> Now steadies on with upright keel."

The distance between two points on the surface of the globe is the same to-day as when the continents were upheaved from their ocean-bed; but the art of man triumphs over such separation, and distant people commune together. Much remains to be done; but the Creator did not speak in vain, when he blessed his earliest children, and bade them "multiply, and replenish the earth, and *subdue it.*"

There will be triumphs nobler than any over inanimate Nature. Man himself will be subdued, — subdued to abhorrence of vice, injustice, violence, — subdued to the sweet charities of life, — subdued to all the requirements of duty, — subdued, according to the Law of Human Progress, to the recognition of that Gospel Law of Human Brotherhood, by the side of which the first is only as the scaffolding upon the sacred temple. To labor for this end was man sent forth into the world, — not in the listlessness of idle perfections, but endowed with infinite capacities, inspired by infinite desires, and commanded to strive perpetually after excellence, amidst the encouragements of hope, the promises of final success, and the inexpressible delights from its pursuit. Thus does the Law of Human Progress

> "assert eternal Providence,
> And justify the ways of God to men,"

by showing Evil no longer a gloomy mystery, binding the world in everlasting thrall, but an accident, under benign Power destined to be surely subdued, as the Human Family press on to the promised goal of happiness.

While recognizing Humanity as progressive, it is important to consider a condition or limitation which may justly temper the ardors of the reformer. Nothing is accomplished except by time and exertion. Nature abhors violence and suddenness. Nature does everything slowly and by degrees. It takes time for the seed to grow into "the bright consummate flower." It is many years before the slender shoot grows into the tree. It is slowly that we pass from infancy and imbecility to manhood and strength. Arrived at this stage, we are still subject to the same condition of Nature. A new temperature or a sudden stroke of light may shock us. Our frames are not made for extremes; so that death may come, according to the poet's conceit, "in aromatic pain."

Gradual change is a necessary condition of the Law of Progress. It is only, according to the poetical phrase of Tacitus, *per intervalla ac spiramenta temporum,* "by intervals and breathings of time," that we can hope to make a sure advance. Men grow and are trained in knowledge and virtue; but they cannot be compelled into this path. This consideration teaches candor and charity towards all who do not yet see the truth as we do. It admonishes us also, while keeping the eye steadfast on the good we seek, to moderate our expectations, and be content when the day of triumph is postponed, for it cannot be always.

This essential condition of the Law of Progress serves to reconcile movement with stability, and to preserve order even in change; as in Nature all projectile forces are checked and regulated by the law of inertia, and the centrifugal motion of the planets is restrained by the attraction of gravitation. In this principle of moderation, honestly pursued, from proper motives, and promising the "well-ripened fruits of wise delay," we find a just Conservatism, which, though not always satisfying our judgment, can never fail to secure our respect.

But there is another Conservatism, — and its treatment belongs to this occasion, — of a different character, which performs no good office, and cannot secure respect.

Child of indifference, of ignorance, of prejudice, of selfishness, it seeks to maintain things precisely as they are, deprecates every change, and, disregarding the *transitory* condition of all that is human, blindly prays for the *perpetuity* of existing institutions. Such an influence is productive of disorder rather than order, and is destructive rather than justly conservative. Contrary to the Law of Progress, it plants itself upon ancient ways, and vainly exalts all that was done by our ancestors, as beyond addition and above amendment. It is well illustrated in the early verses, —

> "Some ther be that do defye
> All that is newe, and ever do crye,
> The old is better, awaye with the newe,
> Because it is false and the old is true";

and again, in the conversation between two eminent English ecclesiastics. "Brother of Winchester," said Cranmer to Lord Chancellor Gardyner, "you like not anything new, unless you be yourself the author thereof." "Your Grace wrongeth me," replied the inveterate Conservative. "I have never been author yet of any one new thing; for which I thank my God."[1] Such a Conservatism is the bigotry of science, of literature, of jurisprudence, of religion, of politics. An example will exhibit its character.

When Sir Samuel Romilly proposed to abolish the punishment of death for stealing a pocket-handkerchief, the Commons of England consulted certain officials of the law, who assured the House that such an innovation would endanger the whole criminal law of the realm. And when afterwards this illustrious reformer and model lawyer (for, of all men in the his-

[1] Campbell's Lives of the Lord Chancellors, Vol. II. ch. 40, p. 51.

tory of the English law, Romilly is most truly the model lawyer) proposed to abolish the obscene punishment for high treason, requiring the offender to be drawn and quartered, and his bowels to be thrown into his face, while his body yet palpitates with life, the Attorney-General of the day, in opposing this humane amendment, asked, "Are the safeguards, the ancient landmarks, the bulwarks of the Constitution, to be thus hastily removed?" Which gave occasion for the appropriate exclamation in reply, "What! to throw the bowels of an offender into his face, one of the safeguards of the British Constitution! I ought to confess that until this night I was wholly ignorant of this bulwark!"[1] An irrational enormity, with a fit parallel only in our own country, where Slavery is called a "divine institution," and important to the stability of our Constitution!

"*Esto perpetua!*" was the dying conservative ejaculation of Paul Sarpi, the Venetian friar, over the constitution of his atrocious republic; and this same phrase is invoked by Sir William Blackstone for the British Constitution, enfolding so many inequalities and so many abuses. It were well — and here all must agree — to exclaim of Truth, of Justice, of Peace, of Freedom, *May it be perpetual!* But is it not irrational to make this claim for any institutions of human device, and therefore finite? How can they provide for the Infinite Future? The Finite cannot measure the Infinite. Nothing from Man's hands — nor laws, nor constitutions — can be perpetual. It is God alone who builds for eternity. His laws are everlasting.

Out of this pernicious prejudice have proceeded that

[1] Essays of Basil Montagu, p. 69.

persecution and neglect which are the too frequent lot of the world's pioneers. Among the ancient Greeks, the wisdom which first assigned the natural cause of thunder and storm was condemned by conservative savages as impiety to the gods. In the eighth century, an ignorant conservative Pope persecuted a priest who declared that the world was round. At a later day, to the everlasting scandal of mankind, the book of Copernicus, unfolding the true system of the universe, was branded by a conservative Papal bull as heretical and false, and Galileo, after announcing the annual and diurnal motions of the earth, was sentenced to the dungeons of the conservative Inquisition. This was in Italy; but in England — and here we come nearer home — Harvey was accustomed to say, that, after the publication of his book on the circulation of the blood, — one of the epochs of modern discovery, — "he fell mightily in his practice, and it was believed by the vulgar that he was crack-brained, and all the physicians were against his opinion." [1] According to him, nobody older than forty, at the time of his discovery, received it as true. The age of forty was the dividing line of life, — a Mason and Dixon's line, — determining the capacity to receive that discovery. This little story may admonish all who have passed that conservative line to be careful how they are inhospitable to any new truth.

This same undue tenacity to existing things and repugnance to what is new threw impediments in the way of successive improvements by which travel and intercourse among men are promoted. Surely stage-coaches, when first introduced into England, must have been wel-

[1] Aubrey's Letters and Lives, Vol. II. p. 383.

come, though novel, as contributing to the comfort of men. But this was not the case universally. An early writer calls for their suppression, breaking forth against them in this wise. "These coaches," he says, "are one of the greatest mischiefs that hath happened of late years to the kingdom, — mischievous to the public, destructive to trade, and prejudicial to lands. First, by destroying the breed of good horses, the strength of the nation, and making men careless of attaining to good horsemanship, a thing so useful and commendable in a gentleman: for, hereby they become weary and listless, when they ride a few miles, and unwilling to get on horseback, not able to endure frost, snow, or rain, or to lodge in the fields; and what reason, save only their using themselves so tenderly, and their riding in these stage-coaches, can be given for this their inability? Secondly, by hindering the breed of watermen, who are the nursery for seamen, and they the bulwark of the kingdom: for, if these coaches were down, watermen, as formerly, would have work, and be encouraged to take apprentices, whereby their number would every year greatly increase. Thirdly, by lessening of his Majesty's revenues: for now four or five travel in a coach together, without any servants, and it is they that occasion the consumption of beer and ale on the roads; and all inn-keepers do declare that they sell not half the drink nor pay the king half the excise they did before these coaches set up."[1] Such was the conservative bill of indictment against stage-coaches. The history of canals, of steamboats, and, lastly, of railways, shows similar prejudices. Even Mr. Jefferson (and I cannot mention him as an immoderate conservative),

[1] The Grand Concern of England, 1673: Harleian Miscellany, Vol. VIII. pp. 539, 540.

when told that the State of New York had explored the route of a canal from the Hudson to Lake Erie, and found it practicable, — that same canal which now, like a thread of silver, winds its way through your imperial State, — replied, that "it was a very fine project, and might be executed a century hence." This is only a little better than the observation of the Greenwich pensioners, who, on first seeing the steamboat upon the waters of the Thames, as they looked out from their palatial home, said, "We do not like the steamboat, it is so contrary to Nature." In our own country, Fitch brought forward the idea of a steamboat amidst ill-disguised sneers; and at a later day, Fulton, while building his first experiment at New York, was viewed with indifference or contempt, as a visionary; and when, at last, he accomplished the long distance to Albany, distrust of the Future still prevailed, and it was doubted if the voyage could be accomplished again, or, if successful again, it was still doubted if the invention could be of permanent value. Thus did this evil spirit perplex noble aims! And in England, as late as 1825, railways were pronounced "altogether delusions and impositions," and the conservative "Quarterly Review," alluding to the opinion of certain engineers that the railway engine could go eighteen or twenty miles an hour, says: "These gross exaggerations may delude for a time, but must end in the mortification of those concerned. . . . . We should as soon expect the people of Woolwich to suffer themselves to be fired off upon one of Congreve's ricochet rockets, as trust themselves to the mercy of such a machine, going at such a rate."[1]

[1] Quarterly Review, Vol. XXXI. pp. 361, 362. Illustrations of this spirit might be indefinitely extended. One, made familiar to the world by Mac-

It is related that the Arve, a river of Switzerland, swollen by floods, sometimes drives the waters of the Rhone back into the Lake of Geneva; and the force is sometimes so great as to make the mill-wheels revolve in a contrary direction. There are too many in the world who by their efforts would cause the stream to flow back upon the fountain, and even make the mill-wheels revolve in a contrary direction.

Unhappily, this same bigotry, — conservatism, if you will, — which has blindly opposed improvement in physical comforts, sets its face more passionately still against those movements whose direct object is the elevation of the race. In all times and places it has persecuted the prophets and stoned the gifted messengers of truth. Of its professors Milton pictures the boldest type in Satan, who, knowing well the sins and offences of mortals, would keep them ever in their present condition, holding them fast in degradation, binding them in perpetual slavery, nor indulging in any aspiration, except of long dominion over a captive race, whose sorrows and hopes cannot touch his impenetrable soul. From a sketch by another hand we learn something of his activity. With honest plainness,

aulay's History, since this Address was delivered, has too much point to be omitted. As late as the close of the reign of Charles the Second, the streets of London, with a population of half a million, were not lighted at night, and, as a natural consequence, became the frequent scene of assassination and outrage, perpetrated under the shelter of darkness. At last, in 1685, it was proposed to place a light, on moonless nights, before every tenth door. This projected improvement was enthusiastically applauded and furiously attacked. "The cause of darkness," says Macaulay, "was not left undefended. There were fools in that age who opposed the introduction of what was called the new light, as strenuously as fools in our age have opposed the introduction of vaccination and railroads, as strenuously as the fools of an age anterior to the dawn of history doubtless opposed the introduction of the plough and of alphabetical writing." — *History of England*, Vol. I. ch. 3.

characteristic of himself and his age, the early English prelate, Latimer, says, in one of his sermons, "The Devil is the most diligentest bishop and preacher in all England."[1] It may be said with equal truth, — and none can question it, — that he is the busiest and most offensive Conservative.

Time forbids my dwelling longer on the ample illustrations of this influence: nor need I. One world-renowned example shall suffice. The early efforts in England for the overthrow of the slave-trade were encountered by an enmity black as the bad passions of the crime itself. In Liverpool the excited slave-traders threatened to throw Clarkson into the dock. But gradually the heart of the nation was touched, until at last the people of England demanded the abolition of this Heaven-defying traffic.

Thus ever has Truth moved on, — though opposed and reviled, still mighty and triumphant. Rejected by the rich and powerful, by the favorites of fortune and of place, she finds shelter with those who often have no shelter for themselves. It is such as these that most freely welcome moral truth, with its new commandments. Not the dwellers in the glare of the world, but the humble and lowly, most clearly perceive this truth, — as watchers placed in the depths of a well observe the stars which are obscured to those who live in the effulgence of noon. Free from egotism and prejudice, whether of self-interest or of class, without cares and temptations, whether of wealth or power, dwelling in the mediocrity or obscurity of common life, they discern the new signal, and surrender unreservedly to its guidance. The Saviour knew this. He did not call upon

[1] Of the Plough: Sermons, Vol. I. p. 65.

Priest or Levite or Pharisee to follow him, but upon the humble fishermen by the Sea of Galilee.

Let us, then, be of good cheer. From the great Law of Progress we derive at once our duties and our encouragements. Humanity has ever advanced, urged by instincts and necessities implanted by God, — thwarted sometimes by obstacles, causing it for a time, a moment only in the immensity of ages, to deviate from its true line, or seem to retreat, but still ever onward. At last we know the law of this movement; we fasten our eyes upon that star, unobserved in the earlier ages, which lights the way to the Future, opening into vistas of infinite variety and extension. Amidst the disappointments which attend individual exertions, amidst the universal agitations which now surround us, let us recognize this law, let us follow this star, confident that whatever is just, whatever is humane, whatever is good, whatever is true, according to an immutable ordinance of Providence, in the sure light of the Future, must prevail. With this faith, we place our hands, as those of little children, in the great hand of God. He will guide and sustain us — through pains and perils it may be — in the path of Progress.

In such a faith there are motives to beneficent activity which will endure to the last syllable of life. Let the young embrace this law; it shall be to them an ever-living spring. Let the old cherish this law; it shall be to them a staff for support. It will give to all, young and old, a new appreciation of their existence, a new sentiment of their force, a new revelation of their destiny. It will be as another covenant, witnessed by the bow in the heavens, not only that no honest, earnest effort for the welfare of man can be in vain, but that it shall send a quickening influence through uncounted ages, and contribute to the coming of that Future of Intelligence, Freedom, Peace we would now secure for ourselves, but cannot. Though not ourselves partakers of these brighter days, ours may be the pleasure at least of foreseeing them, of enjoying them in happy vision, or the satisfaction, sweeter still, of hastening by some moments the too distant epoch.

A life filled with this thought will have comforts and consolations else unknown. In the flush of youthful ambition, or in the self-confidence of success, we may be indifferent to the calls of Humanity; but history, reason, and religion all speak in vain, if any selfish works, not helping the Progress of Man, although favored by worldly smile, can secure that happiness and content so much coveted as the crown of life. Look at the last days of Talleyrand, and learn the wretchedness of an old age enlightened by no memory of generous toil, by no cheerful hope for our fellow-men. When the weakness of years rendered him no longer able to grasp power or hold the threads of intrigue, he surrendered himself to discouragement and despair. By the light of a lamp trimmed in solitude he traced these lines, the most melancholy ever written by an old man,—think of them, politician!—"Eighty-three years of life are now passed! filled with what anxieties! what agitations! what enmities! what troublous complexities! *And all this with no other result than a great weariness, physical and moral, and a profound sentiment of discouragement with regard to the Future and of disgust for the Past.*"[1] Poor old man! Poor indeed! In loneliness, in failing age, with death

[1] Louis Blanc, Histoire de Dix Ans, Tom. V. ch. 10.

waiting at his palace-gate, what to him were the pomps he had enjoyed? what were titles? what were offices? what the lavish wealth in which he lived? More precious far at that moment the consolation that he had labored for his fellow-men, and the joyous confidence that all his cares had helped the Progress of his race!

Be it, then, our duty and our encouragement to live and to labor, ever mindful of the Future. But let us not forget the Past. All ages have lived and labored for us. From one has come art; from another jurisprudence; from another the compass; from another the printing-press; from all have descended priceless lessons of truth and virtue. The most distant are not without a present influence on our daily lives. The mighty stream of Progress, though fed by many tributary waters and hidden springs, derives something of its force from the earlier currents which leap and sparkle in distant mountain recesses, over precipices, among rapids, and beneath the shade of the primeval forest.

Nor should we be too impatient to witness the fulfilment of our aspirations. The daily increasing rapidity of discovery and improvement, and the daily multiplying efforts of beneficence, outstripping the imaginations of the most sanguine, furnish assurance that the advance of man will be with a constantly accelerating speed. The extending intercourse among the nations of the earth, and all the children of the Human Family, gives new promise of the complete diffusion of Truth, penetrating the most distant places, chasing away the darkness of night, and exposing the hideous forms of Slavery. War, and Wrong, which must be hated in proportion as they are seen. And yet, while confident of the Future, and surrounded by heralds of certain triumph, it becomes us to moderate our anticipations, nor imitate those children of the Crusades, who, in their long journey from Western Europe,

> "to seek
> In Golgotha him dead who lives in Heaven,"

hailed each city and castle which they approached as the Jerusalem that was to be the end of their wanderings. Though the goal is distant, and ever advancing, the march is none the less certain. As well attempt to make the sun stand still in his course, or restrain the sweet influences of the Pleiades, as arrest the incessant, irresistible movement which is the appointed destiny of man.

Cultivate, then, a just moderation. Learn to reconcile order with change, stability with progress. This is a wise conservatism; this is a wise reform. Rightly understanding these terms, who would not be a conservative, who would not be a reformer? — a conservative of all that is good, a reformer of all that is evil, — a conservative of knowledge, a reformer of ignorance, — a conservative of truths and principles whose seat is the bosom of God, a reformer of laws and institutions which are but the wicked or imperfect work of man, — a conservative of that divine order which is found only in movement, a reformer of those earthly wrongs and abuses which spring from a violation of the great Law of Human Progress? Blending these two in one, may we not seek to be, at the same time, *Reforming Conservatives and Conservative Reformers?*

And, finally, let a confidence in the Progress of our race be, under God, a constant faith. Let the sentiment of loyalty, earth-born, which once lavished itself on King or Emperor, give place to that other sentiment, heaven-born, of devotion to Humanity. Let loyalty to one man be exchanged for Love to Man. And be it our privilege to extend these sacred influences throughout the land. So may we open to our country new fields of peaceful victory, which shall not want the sympathies and gratulations of the good citizen or the praises of the just historian.

Go forth, then, my country, "conquering and to conquer!" — not by brutal violence, not by force of arms, not, oh! not on dishonest fields of blood, — but in the majesty of Peace, Justice, Freedom, by the irresistible might of Christian Institutions!

THE PARTY OF FREEDOM.

SPEECH ON TAKING THE CHAIR AS PRESIDING OFFICER OF A PUBLIC MEETING TO RATIFY THE NOMINATIONS OF THE BUFFALO CONVENTION, AT FANEUIL HALL, AUGUST 22, 1848.

A CONVENTION of the Free States was held at Buffalo, August 9, 1848, where Martin Van Buren was nominated as President of the United States, and Charles Francis Adams as Vice-President. Resolutions, known as the Buffalo Platform, were adopted, declaring opposition to Slavery wherever we are responsible for it. Among those who took part in the Convention were S. P. Chase, of Ohio, and Preston King, of New York. The proceedings were marked by great unanimity and enthusiasm.

A mass meeting was held at Faneuil Hall on the evening of August 22, 1848, to receive the report of the delegates at Buffalo. The meeting was organized by the choice of the following officers: — Charles Sumner, President; — Dr. John Ware, Franklin Haven, Levi Boles, William Washburn, S. D. Bates, Sumner Crosby, Benjamin Rogers, Henry Lee, Jr., Joseph Willard, Samuel Neal, Dr. Walter Channing, Allen C. Spooner, William B. Spooner, Rev. J. W. Olmstead, Dr. S. G. Howe, Lemuel Capen, Simeon Palmer, Dr. H. I. Bowditch, S. P. Adams, Thomas Bulfinch, Charles G. Davis, Bradford Sumner, David H. Williams, and James M. Whiton, Boston; John C. Dodge, Cambridge; Samuel S. Curtis, Samuel Downer, Jr., William Richardson, Dorchester; William S. Damrell, John Shorey, Dedham; William C. Brown, Chelsea; T. P. Chandler, Brookline; Charles Shute, Hingham; F. A. Kingsbury, Weymouth; Theodore Otis, Charles Ellis, George W. Bond, Elijah Lewis, Roxbury; John B. Alley, Lynn; Thomas S. Harlow, Medford; Charles Foster, Somerville; William H. Keith, Jas. G. Fuller, Charlestown; George Newcomb, Quincy; Vice-Presidents; — Marcus Morton, Jr., John S. Eldridge, Charles W. Slack, David Thaxter, Francis Standish, J. Otis Williams, Dr. W. J. Whitney, Charles A. Phelps, Boston; Charles Ingersoll, Cambridge; Secretaries.

This catalogue may have an interest for persons curious to know who at that time enlisted in the movement.

On taking the chair, Mr. Sumner made the speech below, and then introduced Richard H. Dana, Jr., Esq., of Boston, a delegate to the Buffalo Convention, who reported what had been done there. He was followed by John A. Andrew, Esq., who moved a series of resolutions affirming the principles declared at Buffalo and ratifying the nominations. The reading of these was continually interrupted by applause. Mr. Sumner then introduced David Dudley Field, Esq., of New York, who insisted at length upon the prohibition of slavery in the Territories. Then came Rev. Joshua Leavitt, representing the Liberty Party, now dissolved in the Free-Soil Party. The meeting was singularly auspicious.

FELLOW-CITIZENS, FRIENDS OF FREEDOM: —

GRATEFUL for this cordial welcome, I must consider it offered, not to myself, but to the cause, whose humble representative I am. It is the cause, the good old cause of Freedom, so familiar to early echoes of this hall, which justly awakens your regards, irrespective of men. We are nothing; the cause is everything.

And why, in this nineteenth century, are we assembled here in Faneuil Hall, to vow ourselves to Freedom? Because Freedom is now in danger. The principles of our fathers, of Washington, Franklin, and Jefferson, nay, the self-evident truths of the Declaration of Independence, are assailed. Our Constitution, which was the work of Freedom-loving men, which was watched by Freedom's champions, which, like the Ark of the Covenant, was upborne by the early patriarchs of our Israel, is now prostituted to the uses of Slavery. A body of men, whose principle of union was unknown to the authors of the Constitution, have seized the government, and caused it to be administered, not in the spirit of Freedom, but in the spirit of Slavery. This combination is known as the Slave Power.

The usurpation has obtained sway in both the great

political factions. I say *factions;* for what are factions, but combinations whose sole cement is selfish desire for place and power, in disregard of principles? Whatever may be said of individuals belonging to these opposing combinations, it would be difficult to say whether Whigs or Democrats, in their recent conduct as national parties, had most succumbed to this malign influence. The late Conventions held at Baltimore and Philadelphia were controlled by it. At Baltimore the delegation of the most important State in the Union, known to be in favor of the Wilmot Proviso, was refused admission to the Convention. At Philadelphia the Wilmot Proviso itself was stifled, amidst cries of "Kick it out!" General Cass was nominated at Baltimore, pledged against its whole principle. At Philadelphia, General Taylor, without any pledge on this all-important question, was forced upon the Convention by the Slave Power; nor were principles of any kind declared by this body of professing Whigs. These two candidates, apparently representing opposite parties, both concur in being representatives of Slavery. They are but leaders of the two contending factions into which the Slave Power is divided. And this was fully proved by the action of the Conventions at Baltimore and Philadelphia.

In marked contrast was the recent Convention at Buffalo, where were represented the good men of all the parties, — Whigs, Democrats, and Liberty men, — forgetting alike all former differences, and uniting in common opposition to the Slave Power. There, by their delegates, was the formidable and unsubdued Democracy of New York; there also was the devoted, inflexible Liberty party of the country; there, too, were the true-hearted Whigs and Democrats of all the Free

States, who in this great cause of Freedom are, among the faithless, faithful found; there likewise were welcome delegates from the Slave States, from Maryland and Virginia, anxious to join in this new and holy alliance. In uncounted multitude, mighty in numbers, mightier still in the harmony and unity of their proceedings, this Convention consummated the object for which it was called. It has presented to the country a platform of principles, and *candidates who are the exponents of these principles.* The representatives of the parties there assembled, Whigs, Democrats, and Liberty men, all united. In the strength and completeness of this union I am reminded of the Mississippi, Father of Rivers, where the commingling waters of the Missouri and Ohio are lost in a broad, united, irresistible current, descending in one channel to the sea.

The principles which caused this union are already widely received, and will be proclaimed by this vast assembly. Look at them. They are frankly and explicitly expressed. They were solemnly and deliberately considered by a large committee, and enthusiastically adopted in the Convention. They propose not only to guard the Territories against Slavery, but to relieve the National Government from all responsibility therefor everywhere within the sphere of its constitutional powers. On the subject of Slavery they adopt substantially the prayer of Franklin, who by formal petition called upon the first Congress under the Constitution to "step to the very verge of the power vested in them *for discouraging* every species of traffic in the persons of our fellow-men."[1] They propose to bring back the government to the truths of the Declaration of Indepen-

[1] Annals of Congress, 1st Cong. 2d Sess., 1198.

dence and to the principles of the fathers, so that it shall be administered no longer in the spirit of Slavery, but in the spirit of Freedom.

Other important subjects received attention: cheap postage for the people; retrenchment of the national patronage; the abolition of unnecessary offices; the election of civil officers by the people in all practicable cases; improvement of rivers and harbors; free grant to actual settlers of the public lands; and, lastly, payment of the national debt by means of a tariff. But these matters are all treated as subordinate to the primal principle of opposition to Slavery and the Slave Power. No longer will banks and tariffs occupy the foremost place, and, sounding always with the chink of dollars and cents, give their tone to the policy of the country. Henceforward PROTECTION TO MAN will be the true AMERICAN SYSTEM.

The candidates selected as exponents of these principles have claims upon your support, in forgetfulness of all former differences of opinion. They were brought forward, not because of *the Past*, but *the Present*; I may add, they were sustained by many persons in the Convention *notwithstanding* the Past: Martin Van Buren, the New York Democrat, and Charles Francis Adams, the Massachusetts Whig. But these designations can no longer denote different principles. Those to whom they are applied, whether Democrat or Whig, concur in making opposition to Slavery and the Slave Power the paramount principle of political action. The designations may now be interchanged: Mr. Adams may be hailed as a New York Democrat, and Mr. Van Buren as a Massachusetts Whig.

Many here, once connected with the Whig party, like

myself, have voted on former occasions against Mr. Van Buren, and regard some portions of his career with anything but satisfaction. Mr. Adams is a younger man; but there are some, doubtless, once connected with the Democratic party, who have voted against him. These differences, and the prejudices they have engendered, are all forgotten, absorbed, and lost in entire sympathy with their present position. Time changes, and we change with it. He has lived to little purpose, whose mind and character continue, through the lapse of years, untouched by these mutations. It is not for the Van Buren of 1838 that we are to vote, but for the Van Buren of *to-day*, — the veteran statesman, sagacious, determined, experienced, who, at an age when most men are rejoicing to put off their armor, girds himself anew, and enters the lists as champion of Freedom. Putting trust in the sincerity and earnestness of his devotion to the cause, and in his ability to maintain it, I call upon you, as you love Freedom, and value the fair fame of your country, now dishonored, to render him your earnest and enthusiastic support.

Of Mr. Adams I need say nothing in this place, where his honorable and efficient public service and his private life are so familiar. Standing, as I now do, beneath the images of his father and grandfather, it will be sufficient, if I say that he is heir not only to their name, but to the virtues, the abilities, and the indomitable spirit that rendered that name so illustrious.

Such are our principles, and such our candidates. We present them fearlessly. Upon the people depends whether their certain triumph shall be immediate or postponed: for triumph they must. The old and ill-compacted party organizations are broken, and from their ruins is now formed a new party, *The Party of Freedom*. There were good men who longed for this, and died without the sight. John Quincy Adams longed for it. William Ellery Channing longed for it. Their spirits hover over us, and urge us to persevere. Let us be true to the moral grandeur of our cause. Have faith in Truth, and in God, who giveth the victory.

Fellow-citizens, seeing the spirit which animates your faces, I am tempted to exclaim, that the work is already done to-night, — that the victory is achieved. But I would not lull you to the repose which springs from too great confidence. Rather would I arouse you to renewed and incessant exertion. A great cause is staked upon your constancy: for, except you, where among us would Freedom find defenders?

The sentiment of opposition to the Slave Power, to the extension of Slavery, and to its longer continuance, wherever under the Constitution the National Government is responsible for it, though recognized by individuals, and adopted by a small and faithful party, is now for the first time the leading principle of a broad, resolute, and national organization. It is, indeed, as Mr. Webster lately said, no new idea; it is old as the Declaration of Independence. But it is an idea now for the first time proclaimed by a great political party: for, if the old parties had been true to it, there would have been no occasion for our organization. It is said, our idea is sectional. How is this? Because the slaveholders live at the South? As well might we say that the tariff is sectional, because the manufacturers live at the North.

It is said that we have but one idea. This I deny. But admitting that it is so, are we not, with our one idea, better than a party with no ideas at all? And what is our one idea? It is the idea which combined our fathers on the heights of Bunker Hill, — which carried Washington through a seven years' war, — which inspired Lafayette, — which with coals of fire touched the lips of Adams, Otis, and Patrick Henry. Ours is an idea at least noble and elevating; it is an idea which draws in its train virtue, goodness, and all the charities of life, all that makes earth a home of improvement and happiness.

> "Her track, where'er the goddess roves,
> Glory pursue, and generous Shame,
> The unconquerable Mind, and Freedom's holy flame."

We found now a new party. Its corner-stone is Freedom. Its broad, all-sustaining arches are Truth, Justice, and Humanity. Like the ancient Roman Capitol, at once Temple and Citadel, it shall be the fit shrine for the genius of American institutions.

PARTIES, AND IMPORTANCE OF A FREE-SOIL ORGANIZATION.

LETTER ADDRESSED TO A COMMITTEE OF THE FREE-SOIL PARTY IN BOSTON, OCTOBER 26, 1848.

IN the political campaign which followed the nominations at Buffalo Mr. Sumner took an active part, addressing large audiences at all the principal places in Massachusetts, beginning at Plymouth. On these occasions he discussed at length the failure of the two old parties, and the political character of their candidates, especially in contrast with those of the Free-Soil party, vindicating the necessity of political action against the Slave Power and the extension of Slavery. Contemporary newspapers show the impression produced, and, in the absence of any authentic report, are quoted here. Of his address at Springfield one of his hearers says in a newspaper: —

"It was a speech which, for beauty, eloquence, and convincing argument, I never heard equalled. With the utmost candor, with a power of argument not to be answered, with an array of facts which cannot be met, he examined the position occupied by Cass and Taylor. Refraining from all abuse, on the contrary dealing out praise where praise is due, he yet showed most conclusively that on the great question, the only question of importance now in issue, neither of these candidades could be trusted. He then spoke in a most beautiful manner of our candidate, Martin Van Buren, and his position. Extenuating nothing in his former action or opinion, he spoke of him *as he now is*, the true exponent of the glorious principles of the Buffalo Platform, which he called the Second Declaration of Independence. Mr. Sumner spoke for three hours, and to the close the hall was crowded. The bitterest opponents speak in the highest terms of the speech and the meeting."

Another hearer at Amherst, writing in another newspaper, is equally enthusiastic.

"For three hours the multitude was swayed to and fro by his resistless eloquence. No description can do justice to the address. Its framework was logic and high moral principle, ornamented with refined and classical allusions and glowing images. Through the whole he was interrupted by long and hearty cheers. Toward the close he expressed a fear that he was detaining his audience too long (the clock was then striking midnight) but he was answered by cries from all parts of the house, 'Oh, no! go on! go on! talk all night!' "

This introduction may explain what ensued. Mr. Sumner was nominated for Congress, and, under the circumstances, did not feel authorized to decline. Earnestly urging others to active support of the cause, he could not refuse the post assigned to himself. His letter accepting the nomination, after giving reasons for the step, proceeds to consider at some length the philosophy of parties and the necessity for the new organization in which he was enlisted. The nomination was communicated to him in a letter, which is given below, with his answer. The result will appear in the sequel.

" Boston, October 23, 1848.

"Charles Sumner, Esq.

"Dear Sir,—At a meeting of the Ward, County, and District Convention of the Free-Soil Party of Suffolk, held on Thursday last, it being proposed to go into a nomination of candidate for Representative to Congress, and nominations being called for, your name, and yours only, was placed upon the list.

"A member of the Convention, who represented himself as authorized by you for that purpose, urged, in the strongest terms, your disinclination to be a candidate, growing out of an early formed and long cherished resolution never to hold any political office; but, notwithstanding all that could be urged, the Convention nominated you, by acclamation, the Free-Soil candidate for Congress from District Number One, and appointed us a committee to inform you of the fact.

"It seems to us, as it did to the Convention, that a political crisis has come which calls upon every man to forego his personal wishes, without regard to resolutions formed under circumstances totally different; and considering the extreme importance of a permanent Free-Soil organization, firm, enthusiastic, and united, we trust we shall have the great pleasure of conveying to the Convention your acceptance of their nomination.

"S. G. Howe,
"Otis Turner,
"Matthew Bolles,
"Charles A. Phelps,
"Richard Hildreth."

BOSTON, October 26, 1848.

GENTLEMEN,—I have received your communication of October 23d, informing me that I have been nominated by the Ward, County, and District Convention of the Free-Soil Party of Suffolk as their candidate for Congress, and requesting my acceptance of that nomination.

You state, that a member of the Convention, who represented himself as authorized by me for that purpose, urged in the strongest terms my disinclination to be a candidate, growing out of an early formed and long cherished resolution never to hold political office; but notwithstanding all that could be urged, I was nominated by acclamation.

The member of the Convention who spoke for me, at my special request, did not go beyond the truth. I have never held political office of any kind, nor have I ever been a candidate for any such office. It has been my desire and determination to labor in such fields of usefulness as are open to every private citizen, without the honor, emolument, or constraint of office. I would show by example (might I so aspire!) that something may be done for the welfare of our race, without the support of public station or the accident of popular favor. In this course I hoped to persevere.

I was aware of the readiness with which the world attributes to candidates motives inconsistent with singleness and uprightness; I knew the viperous malignity of a party press, ready to shoot its venom upon those who oppose its course; for a succession of years I saw friends, of whose purity I was assured, a prey to the vampire ferocity of political partisans. Observing these things, I found in them fresh reason for my original determination to keep aloof from office, and from being a candidate for office.

The active part which I have taken in our recent movement, resulting in the formation of a separate organization, has exposed me to something of that animosity usually reserved for candidates. Desirous to avoid any position suggesting desire for office, I have felt an additional motive for adherence to my original purpose. I wished to occupy such a place in our contest, as, while it left me free to labor, should put me above suspicion.

You now bid me renounce the cherished idea of my life, early formed, and strengthened by daily experience, especially by circumstances at the present moment. In support of this request, you suggest that a political crisis has come which calls upon every man to forego his personal wishes.

Upon serious deliberation, anxious to perform my duty, I feel myself unable to resist this appeal. In my view a crisis has arrived which requires the best efforts of every citizen; nor should he hesitate with regard to his peculiar post. Happy to serve in the cause, he should shrink from no labor and no exposure. When the fire-bell rings at midnight, when the ship which bears us drives furious upon a lee shore, there is no time to select the manner in which we will work. Not without dereliction of duty can we be indifferent to the call then addressed to us, nor can we fail to assume the responsibility or service, unwelcome though it be, which is cast upon us.

This is the case now. The principles of Washington, Jefferson, and Franklin, the security of our Constitution, the true fame of our country, the interests of labor, the cause of Freedom, Humanity, Right, Morals, Religion, God, all these are now at stake. Holier cause has never appeared in history. To it I offer not vows only, but my best efforts, wherever they can be effectual.

Accepting, as I now do, the nomination as Free-Soil candidate for Congress from our District, I might properly close this communication; but a topic in the letter with which you have honored me leads me further. While urging my consent, you allege "the extreme importance of a permanent Free-Soil organization, firm, enthusiastic, and united." Even at the hazard of wearying your attention, I would give you my own views.

I agree with the Convention in the importance of the new organization; nor do I think there are many candid persons, recognizing morals as the soul of all true politics, who will hesitate in this conclusion.

The evils of party organization have often been deprecated. Some there are, who, in visions of possible good, think these evils may be entirely removed. They suppose that men may be left to vote, as they act in other concerns, without the constraint of those giant combinations by whose struggle the whole land is uptorn. Some go so far as to oppose all associated action, as interfering with proper freedom and individuality of conduct. On the other hand, there are many who regard the phalanx and antagonism of party as a necessary agency in the administration of free governments. It is supposed that there must be two sides, whose constant watchfulness will prevent abuse and misrule. This idea was pointedly expressed by an eminent British statesman, when he gave as a toast, "A strong Administration and a strong Opposition."

Without yielding to any of these extreme views with regard to the mischiefs or the benefits of party, all should agree that the only true and legitimate object of such an association is to uphold, advance, and develop certain principles, regarded by the members of the party as important to the well-being of the state. So far forth as the members honestly concur in these principles they may properly unite in action. But when they cease to join in their support, or when new principles are called into activity, then the common bond is dissolved, and a new association must be formed.

This law, which is recognized by all intelligent minds, was developed by Mr. Webster at Faneuil Hall in 1825. "*New parties*," he said, "may arise, growing out of new events or new questions; but as to those old parties which have sprung from controversies now no longer pending, or from feelings which time and other causes have now changed or greatly allayed, I do not believe that they can long remain. Efforts, indeed, made to that end, with zeal and perseverance, may delay their extinction, but, I think, cannot prevent it. There is nothing to keep alive these distinctions in the interests and objects which now engage society. New questions and new objects arise, having no connection with the subjects of past controversies, and present interest overcomes or absorbs the recollection of former controversies. All that are united on these existing questions and present interests are not likely to weaken their efforts to promote them by angry reflections on past differences. If there were nothing in *things* to divide about, I think the people not likely to maintain systematic controversies about *men*. They have no interest in so doing. Associations formed to support *principles* may be called *parties;* but if they have no bond of union but adherence to particular *men,* they become *factions.*"[1]

In obedience to this law, political parties in France and England, the only countries besides our own where experience is of service to us on this occasion, have undergone mutations with time. From the reign of Charles the Tenth to the Republic of February, the former country witnessed a succession of parties, representing the different principles struggling for mastery. It was rare that there were two parties only. In England the lines were more distinctly drawn, and the early division into two great parties was more strictly maintained. But here also it is found impossible to stand always upon the ancient ways. Much of the old distinction between Whig and Tory has already become traditional; the members of these two great antagonist combinations have recently united in measures demanded by the law of Human Progress. The monopoly of the Corn Laws, first assailed by Radicals, and then condemned by aristocratic Whigs, was finally overthrown by the leader of the Tories, who marshalled in this cause various forces never before associated.

In our own country parties have undergone changes. It would be difficult to find in the modern Democratic party, rejecting the Wilmot Proviso, that early party which recognized as its chief Jefferson, the original author of the Proviso. It would be equally difficult to find in the modern Whig party, which ignobly trampled upon the Wilmot Proviso, that other early party which aided in the election of Washington, the emancipator of his slaves, and the advocate of Emancipation.

[1] Speeches and Forensic Arguments, p. 98.

The party lately known as Whig is recent in origin. It cannot plead prescription in its favor. Twenty years have not yet elapsed since its birth. It is still in its minority, without any promise that it can reach the *age of freedom*.

From this survey we are admonished not to hesitate in support of the new organization, from any vain idea of necessary permanence in the two old parties. Encouragement also may be drawn from the insufficiency of these parties as representatives of existing public sentiment.

It is a humiliating reflection, forced upon us by the history of parties, that the professions of principle are often a mere cover to selfish efforts for place and power. Politics become a game, and principles are the counters which are used. The apparent contests of principle are made subservient to the contests of interest, and the latter is pursued to the neglect of the former. As this subservience becomes manifest, and as it clearly appears that fidelity to principle is merged in selfish ambition, surrendering all things to the pursuit of barren "availability," party loses title to the countenance of honest men. It is a faction, a cabal. It is an engine of mere political brokerage, by which preferment is procured. If I used a stronger word, I should only borrow the language of the great poet patriot, in describing his own Italy, defiled by noxious factions, whose prostitution of sacred principles filled the whole land with noisome odor.

Without undertaking to apply this language in all its force to either of the parties convened at Baltimore or Philadelphia, it will be sufficient to say that they do not now embody, if they ever did, those principles which are accepted by large numbers of good men as vital and paramount. The question, then, arises, Shall these principles continue without any national organ? Shall they find no voice? Shall they be stifled? Clearly not.

Such precisely is our condition. The important sentiment of hostility to the Slave Power, to the extension of Slavery, and to its longer continuance under the Constitution wherever the National Government is responsible for it, though recognized by individuals, and by a small, but respectable, political organization, was never till now put forth as the paramount principle of a large and national party. It is true, indeed, that here is no new idea. It is as old as the Revolution, — as old as Washington, Jefferson, and Franklin; but it is an idea neglected by both the great parties which have recently swayed the country. Were it recognized by either, there would be no occasion for the new party whose existence has so auspiciously begun.

No person is so hardy as to assert that the present Democratic party embodies this idea. But there are partisans, who, in disregard of well-known facts, claim it as the property of the late Whig party, even in its present metamorphosis into the Taylor faction. It is sometimes proclaimed as their "thunder." How is this?

It is well known that the Whigs of Massachusetts, in local conventions, and also in formal legislative proceedings, have avowed hostility to the Slave Power, to the extension of Slavery, and to its longer continuance under the Constitution, wherever the National Government is responsible for it; but the *National* Whig party, or what Mr. Webster has called "the *united* Whig party of the United States," has never recognized any such principles. Search its history, and you will find that it has been false to them.

As a party, it has never sustained any measure for the abolition of Slavery in the District of Columbia. On the contrary, it has discountenanced all proceedings in this direction. General Harrison, the only President it has succeeded in electing, covertly took ground against it in his Inaugural Message, and Mr. Clay, the acknowledged representative of the party, expressed himself to the same effect, with a warmth which better became a better cause. Nor did either of these Whig statesmen admit, what Mr. Van Buren more than once distinctly declared, that Congress possessed the constitutional power to abolish Slavery in the District. That part of our principles, then, which touches this topic, has formed no portion of the *National* Whig doctrines.

The claim to proprietorship in the principle of opposition to the extension of Slavery is equally vain. Florida and Arkansas have both been admitted as States with slaveholding Constitutions, and the *National* Whig party made no opposition.

The annexation of Texas, when first presented, was opposed by many Whigs of the Slave States, *but on grounds irrespective of Slavery.* It was finally consummated through the agency of John Tyler, President by the act of the Whig party, and of John C. Calhoun, Secretary of State by the unanimous vote of the *Whig* and Democratic members of the Senate, *through joint resolutions, moved in the House by Mr. Milton Brown, a Slaveholding Whig from Tennessee, and in the Senate by Mr. Foster, a Slaveholding Whig from the same State.* Thus even against the annexation of Texas the

Whig party did not present a constant and uniform front.

The question of the extension of Slavery was distinctly presented, on the application of Texas for admission into our Union, with a Constitution which not only established Slavery, but took from the Legislature all power to abolish it. The spirit of New England was aroused. Remonstrances went up to Congress on the single ground of opposition to the extension of Slavery. John Quincy Adams undertook to present them. But, notwithstanding his earnest efforts, the measure was hurried through the House by the vote of every slaveholder present, Whig and Democrat. It went to the Senate, where it was ushered under the sanction in part of Mr. Berrien, a slaveholding Whig from Georgia, and finally triumphed in that body, notwithstanding the opposition of Mr. Webster, by the vote of every slaveholder present, Whig and Democrat. Let it be mentioned to their credit, that Mr. Thomas Clayton, of the Senate, and Mr. John W. Houston, of the House, from Delaware, and Mr. John G. Chapman, of the House, from Maryland, united with the friends of Freedom; but I understand that they are not slaveholders. The associations of the day on which this deed was done added to its character as a mockery of Human Rights. It was on the 22d of December, 1845, the anniversary of the landing at Plymouth Rock.

At a later day this great question again entered Congress, overshadowing all others. In 1846, Mr. Wilmot, a Democrat, of Pennsylvania, in order to secure the Territories for Freedom, moved his Proviso, borrowed from the Ordinance of 1787. The motion was sustained by Northern Whigs, but opposed by slaveholders *without distinction of party.* Exertions were made to rally the Free States on this ground; but the *National* Whig party, anxious to avoid the issue, strove, through the agency of Mr. Berrien and Mr. Webster, to substitute the question of *No more Territory,*—thus avoiding the issue upon the paramount principle, now vaunted as theirs, of opposition to the extension of Slavery.

At the Whig Convention in Philadelphia two different efforts were made to obtain the recognition of this principle; but it was laid upon the table, or stifled amidst unseemly noises and cries of "Kick it out!"

This same Convention nominated for the Presidency General Taylor, who is justly supposed, by his position, to be against the Wilmot Proviso, and who has been advocated recently by Mr. Berrien, a leading slaveholding Whig, remarkable for hostility to the Proviso, on the ground, thus candidly expressed, that "the Southern man who is farthest from us is nearer to us than any Northern man can be,—that General Taylor is identified with us in feeling and interest, was born and educated in a slave-holding State, is himself a slaveholder,—that his slave property constitutes the means of support to himself and family,—*that he cannot desert us,* without sacrificing his interest, his principles, the habits and feelings of his life,—and that with him, therefore, our institutions are safe." In sustaining such a candidate, while professing to be a Free-Soil party, the Whigs imitate those barbarians who elevate in their temple a Pagan idol, while professing to serve, in Gospel light, the only true God.

There are leading supporters of General Taylor, not slaveholders, but acknowledged Whigs, who frankly disclaim the Wilmot Proviso. Mr. Clayton, of Delaware, is reported as declaring to the Senate, July 5, 1848, — "No man has a right to say that the Wilmot Proviso is a Whig principle, or that its opposite is a Whig principle. We repudiate the question altogether, as a political question. Neither the one side nor the other of the question forms any part of our platform." And my friend Mr. Choate, the accomplished orator, is reported as saying, in one of his recent speeches: "On all the great questions of the day BUT JUST SLAVERY, we mean to remain the same party of Whigs, one and indivisible, from Maine to Louisiana; upon this question alone *we always differ from the Whigs of the South*, and on that one we propose simply to vote them down."

I conclude, then, that the principle of opposition to the extension of Slavery, like that of opposition to its longer continuance under the Constitution, wherever the National Government is responsible for it, is not recognized by the national political combination which supports General Taylor. None will say that this combination will oppose the Slave Power, of which their candidate is a component part.

It is to uphold and advance these principles, thus neglected by others, that we have come together, leaving the parties to which we have been respectively attached. Now, in the course of human events, it has become our duty to dissolve the political bands which have hitherto bound us to the old organizations, and to assume a separate existence. Our Declaration of Independence was put forth at Buffalo. Let us, in the spirit of the fathers, pledge ourselves to sustain it with lives, fortunes, and sacred honor. Our cause is holier than theirs, inasmuch as it is nobler to struggle for the freedom of others than for our own. Full of reverence for the fathers, I here repeat what in this contest cannot be too often declared. The love of Right, which is the animating principle of our movement, is higher than the love of Freedom. But both Right and Freedom inspire our cause.

Taking our place as a new party, we fulfil the desires of many good men, living and dead, who have longed to see the thraldom of the old organizations broken. Such was the earnest hope of John Quincy Adams, expressed more than once. "God grant that it may come!" was his devout wish.

Another person, not a politician, whose opinions exercise a wide influence over the present generation, the late William Ellery Channing, has left on record a similar aspiration. In a letter dated January 11, 1840, recently published in his biography, he says: "The Whig interest seems to be too strong to be put down at once. This party has the wealth, and in so rich a State [Massachusetts] has great advantages for perpetuating its power. No party, however, which thinks only of securing wealth can last long. There must be some higher principle."[1] And in another letter, dated March 1, 1842, the same patriot and philanthropist says: "The political state of the country is exceedingly perplexed. *The Whig party has little unity, and is threatened with dissolution. . . . . Would the Democrats break up too, and could we start afresh, the Government would probably be less of an evil than it is.*"[2]

Another eminent person, honored wherever the pulpit and philosophy of our country are known, Rev. Francis Wayland, of the Baptist denomination, has recently put forth sentiments in a similar strain. "But," says he,

[1] Memoir, Vol. III. p. 262. [2] Ibid., p. 263.

"it may be said that a course of conduct like this would destroy all political organizations, and render nugatory the designations in which we have for so very long prided ourselves. If this be all the mischief that is done, the Republic, I think, may very patiently endure it. . . . . If a disciple of Christ has learned to value his political party more highly than he does truth and justice and mercy, it is surely time that his connection with it were broken off. Let him learn to surrender party for moral principle. . . . . *Let all good men do this, and they will form a party by themselves, a party acting in the fear of God, and sustained by the arm of Omnipotence.* . . . .

"Let virtuous men, then, unite on the ground of *universal moral principle*, and the tyranny of party will be crushed. Were the virtuous men of this country to carry their moral sentiments into practice, and act alone rather than participate in the doing of wrong, all parties would, from necessity, submit to their authority, and the acts of the nation would become a true exponent of the moral character of our people."[1]

I would add, that I am glad to adduce this high testimony from the pulpit. The Gospel is never more truly or sublimely preached than when the politician is told that he, too, is bound by its laws, and communities, whether villages, towns, states, or nations, are summoned, like individuals, to obey its sacred behests.

In such a spirit our organization has been established. It is sometimes said, that it does not recognize certain measures of public policy, deemed by certain persons of special importance. If this be so, it does what is better, and what other organizations fail to do: it acknowledges those high principles which, like the

[1] The Duty of Obedience to the Civil Magistrate, pp. 38–40.

great central light, vivify all, and without which all is dark and sterile.

Surely the people will not be diverted from these truths by holding up the Sub-Treasury and the Tariff. The American people are intelligent and humane; they are not bulls, to be turned aside by shaking in their eyes a bit of red cloth, or whales, to be stopped by a tub. In listening to the recent pertinacious and exclusive advocacy which these questions have received, in disregard of Freedom, I am reminded of the scene, so vividly portrayed by Mr. Wirt, where the humor and eloquence of Patrick Henry exhibited an effort of selfishness in the midst of the Revolution. The American army was in great distress, exposed almost naked to the rigor of a winter sky, and marking the frozen ground over which it marched with the blood of unshod feet. "Where was the man," said Patrick Henry, "who would not have thrown open his fields, his barns, his cellars, the doors of his house, the portals of his breast, to receive the meanest soldier in that little band of famished patriots? Where is the man? There he stands; but whether the heart of an American beats in his bosom you are to judge." It was to John Hook that he pointed, who had brought a vexatious suit for two steers taken for the use of the troops. "What notes of discord do I hear?" said the orator. "They are the notes of John Hook, hoarsely bawling through the American camp, *Beef! Beef! Beef!*"[1]

As a separate party, following the example of other parties, and recognizing the necessity of such a course, we nominate candidates for the Presidency, Vice-Presidency, and for all State offices. We cannot support

[1] Wirt's Life and Character of Patrick Henry, pp. 373, 374.

Taylor or Cass, nor can we support the supporters of Taylor or Cass. We cannot sustain men who contribute votes to place the power and patronage of the highest offices in hands which may exercise them against Freedom. I know there are some who will do this, wishing well to Freedom; but her friends should be of sterner stuff. Nor is it easy to put confidence in the moral firmness of men who, while this great cause is pending, can sustain any party or individual not unequivocally pledged to its support.

From this statement you will perceive, Gentlemen, that I am convinced, with you, of "the extreme importance of a permanent Free-Soil organization, firm, enthusiastic, and united." In this conviction I find an additional motive, now that this organization is commencing its most difficult struggle, to accept the nomination which you have tendered. Let us labor together. Confident in the justice of our cause, we will dedicate to it our best powers, careless of opposing factions or the misrepresentations of a mendacious press, — sustaining it with enthusiasm, and yet with candor, with firmness, and yet with moderation. The great law of Human Progress, the all-prevailing might of truth and of God, are on our side.

I have the honor to be, Gentlemen,
Your faithful friend and servant,
CHARLES SUMNER.

S. G. HOWE, OTIS TURNER, MATTHEW BOLLES, CHARLES A. PHELPS, RICHARD HILDRETH, Esquires.

APPEAL FOR THE FREE-SOIL PARTY.

ADDRESS OF THE STATE COMMITTEE TO THE PEOPLE OF MASSACHUSETTS, NOVEMBER 9, 1848.

THE Presidential election took place on Tuesday, November 7, 1848. It was soon apparent that General Taylor was chosen President. The large vote of the Free-Soil Party of Massachusetts gave encouragement for the future. The election of State officers, including Governor and Lieutenant-Governor, and also Members of Congress, was to take place a week after. Mr. Sumner, who had become Chairman of the Free-Soil State Committee, at once prepared an Address to the people of the Commonwealth, rallying them to the polls, which was adopted by the State Committee.

TO THE PEOPLE OF MASSACHUSETTS.

THE FREE-SOIL STATE COMMITTEE offer their congratulations to the people of Massachusetts on the result of the recent election in our Commonwealth.

Nearly FORTY THOUSAND Freemen have, by their votes, borne testimony against the two old political organizations, and for the new party of FREEDOM. They have branded *Taylorism* and *Cassism* as unworthy of support. In doing this they have encountered prejudices and difficulties of a peculiar kind, in addition to the constant, indefatigable, and well-sustained exertions of both the old organizations.

Whatever may be the result in other parts of the country, Massachusetts, by a majority of votes, has rejected both Taylor and Cass.[1] She has declared her want of confidence in their principles, and her unwillingness to recognize either as the representative and impersonation of American institutions.

Still further, she has declared, by the vote of nearly FORTY THOUSAND Freemen, that Slavery shall not be extended, — that Slavery shall not be allowed to continue under the National Government, wherever that Government is responsible for it, — and that the Slave Power shall no longer control the policy of our country.

To support these paramount principles, without equivocation or compromise, at all times and in every way, she has now given her first earnest and determined pledge. Freemen of Massachusetts! it remains with you to redeem this pledge by further exertions.

An election of State officers and of Members of Congress will take place on Monday, November 13th. The principles which we have upheld in the Presidential election, as paramount to all others, let us continue to uphold and advance through the new organization now happily established. Following the example of the other parties, and recognizing the necessity of such a course, we can sustain those only who sustain this organization. We are a separate party, and, as such, have separate candidates.

Remember, then, to vote for no man who is not willing to unite with us in declaring opposition to Slavery and the Slave Power to be above all other questions, and who cannot be relied upon to sustain those men only who join in this alliance of principle.

Vote for STEPHEN C. PHILLIPS, of Salem, our candi-

[1] The votes, as officially determined, stood: For Taylor, 61,072; Cass, 35,284; Van Buren, 38,133.

date for Governor, and for JOHN MILLS, of Springfield, our candidate for Lieutenant-Governor, — men familiar with all the concerns of the Commonwealth, of well-tried prudence, of best capacity, and of inflexible devotion to FREEDOM.

Vote, also, for the Congressional Candidates nominated by the Free-Soil District Conventions.

Vote, likewise, for the Senatorial Candidates nominated by the Free-Soil County Conventions.

And, in your respective towns, vote for such Representatives only as may be relied upon to sustain, in the Legislature of the Commonwealth, the principles which we have at heart, and the new organization dedicated to their support. The final success of our candidates for Governor and Lieutenant-Governor may depend upon the firmness of these men.

Freemen of Massachusetts! Three months only have elapsed to-day since the Convention at Buffalo. In this brief period we have taken our place as one of the great parties of the country. With one bound we have leaped to our present position. In Massachusetts we are not the *third party*. Let our efforts in the next election show us to be FIRST.

First in principles we already are, — *first* in devotion to those truths which give dignity and security to our common country: let us be FIRST also in numbers and power.

Stand firm, Freemen of Massachusetts! Your fidelity now will be the cement of our new organization, and a token of that mutual confidence which shall assure speedy success. Ours is the cause of truth, of morals, of religion, of God. Let us be united in its support! "A stout heart, a clear conscience, and never despair." These were the last words addressed in writing by JOHN QUINCY ADAMS to a person deeply interested in our movement. Let us each consider them addressed directly to himself.

CHARLES SUMNER, *Chairman.*

JOSHUA LEAVITT,
JOHN A. ANDREW,
MARCUS MORTON, Jr.,
EDWARD L. KEYES,
DANIEL W. ALVORD,
ANSON BURLINGAME,
SIDNEY HOMER,
JAMES M. WHITON,
JOHN B. ALLEY,
BENJAMIN F. NEWHALL,
JOSIAH G. ABBOTT,
SHUBAEL P. ADAMS,
JOHN G. WHITTIER,
E. ROCKWOOD HOAR,
JOHN A. SHAW,
GEORGE MINOT,
ALEXANDER DEWITT,
AMASA WALKER,
CHARLES WHITE,
ALLEN BANGS,
WM. H. STODDARD,
H. G. NEWCOMB,
LYMAN C. THAYER,
CALVIN MARTIN,
GEORGE W. STERLING,
WILLIAM JACKSON,
WILLIAM J. REYNOLDS,
SAMUEL DOWNER, Jr.,
CALEB SWAN,
ANDREW L. RUSSELL,
LEWIS LAPHAM,
JOHN A. KASSON,
EDWARD W. GARDNER.

BOSTON, November 9, 1848.

A LAST RALLY FOR FREEDOM.

Letter to the Chairman of the Free-Soil Meeting at Faneuil Hall, November 9, 1848.

Besides speaking at all the principal centres in the State, Mr. Sumner made what was called a "campaign speech" at Faneuil Hall on the evening of October 31st, occupying the whole evening. John A. Andrew, Esq., was in the chair. Of this meeting, and of Mr. Sumner's speech, the *Boston Republican* used strong language. "Mr. Sumner's reception was most gratifying. The cheering was long continued and unanimous, and burst forth at intervals during the speech, which was of surpassing ability and eloquence. During the peroration the audience attained the highest pitch of enthusiasm; deafening and tumultuous shouts resounded, cheer upon cheer, until it seemed as if they would never stop."

Though this speech was never reported, Mr. Sumner was not inclined to speak again in Faneuil Hall before the election, when he found himself advertised for another meeting on the evening of November 9th. The notice was in these words, which were duly capitalized: "Rally to Faneuil Hall! Adams and Sumner, Richard H. Dana, Jr.! Once more to the rescue!" Mr. Adams and Mr. Dana spoke, but Mr. Sumner appeared by letter.

In the absence of the last, Mr. Adams alluded to him as a candidate in language which belongs to this record.

"And what shall I say of Charles Sumner? (Cheers.) From a feeling of delicacy he is not here to-night, and it gives me an opportunity to say that which I should not say to his face. Charles Sumner is a man of large heart, — not of that class of politicians who calculate availability, and the numbers of the opposition, but a man who takes an enlarged view of a noble system of action, and places his shoulder to the wheel to move it forward. He is now doing more to impress on the country a new and powerful moral sentiment in connection with the movement than any man or any ten men in the country. If Boston is what Boston was, she would be doing herself honor and the country benefit by electing him."

The letter of Mr. Sumner, when read to the audience, was received with applause.

BOSTON, November 9, 1848.

MY DEAR SIR, — It was without my knowledge — doubtless through some misapprehension of the Committee — that my name was announced among those to speak in Faneuil Hall to-night.

As a candidate, I feel disposed during the present week to follow what I believe has been the usage in our District, and to avoid meeting my fellow-citizens in public assemblies. I am happy that there are others whose eloquent voices will rally them in the good cause.

Here in Massachusetts our new party, while yet in its cradle, shows a giant's strength. Its enemies look on with amazement, while its friends rejoice. Let us continue to do as we have already done.

True to the principles which have led her by a majority of her votes to reject both Taylor and Cass, Massachusetts cannot uphold their supporters. Her opposition to the old and vicious organizations can be made effectual only by opposing all who sustained these obnoxious candidates. Nor can any candid person object to this course. We are a separate party, and as such have separate candidates. A member of the Taylor faction might complain as well of the Cass party as of the Free-Soil party, for not sustaining his candidate.

Our party is composed of persons from all the other parties, — drawn together by no consideration of mere expediency or personal advantage, but united by a common bond of principle to promote that great cause of Freedom with whose triumph is indissolubly connected the highest welfare of our country. Such a cause is worthy of all our energies. It appeals to good men in the name of virtue and religion. It appeals to the young by the best instincts of their nature. It appeals to those who call themselves Whigs by all the professions of their party here in times past. It appeals to those who call themselves Democrats by all those principles which give life, dignity, and truth to the Democratic character.

With such a cause, at the present moment, we cannot hesitate. In the words of Patrick Henry, which, on the eve of our earlier Revolution, sent a thrill through the Continent, "we must fight, I repeat it, Sir, we must fight," — not with fire and sword, not with weapons of flesh, but with earnest words, with devout aspirations, with sincere and determined souls. Thus shall we conquer that opposing power, which, through the agency of both the old political parties, now seeks to trample down the rising struggle for Freedom.

Faithfully yours,

CHARLES SUMNER.

To the Chairman of the Free-Soil Meeting, Faneuil Hall.

The nomination of Mr. Sumner to Congress in Boston was like a forlorn hope. The vote stood 7,726 for Mr. Winthrop, 1,460 for Mr. Hallett, and 2,336 for Mr. Sumner. At the Presidential election, the week before, the vote was 8,427 for General Taylor, 2,997 for General Cass, and 1,909 for Mr. Van Buren.

WAR SYSTEM OF THE COMMONWEALTH OF NATIONS.

ADDRESS BEFORE THE AMERICAN PEACE SOCIETY, AT ITS ANNIVERSARY MEETING IN THE PARK STREET CHURCH, BOSTON, MAY 28, 1849.

That it may please Thee to give to all nations unity, peace, and concord. — THE LITANY.

What angel shall descend to reconcile
The Christian states, and end their guilty toil ?
WALLER.

Quæ harmonia a musicis dicitur in cantu, ea est in civitate concordia. — CICERO, *De Republica*, Lib. II. Cap. 42.

Una dies Fabios ad bellum miserat omnes,
Ad bellum missos perdidit una dies.
OVID, *Fasti*, Lib. II. 235, 236.

Cum hac persuasione vivendum est: Non sum uni angulo natus; patria mea totus hic mundus est. — SENECA, *Epistola* XXVIII.

Illi enim exorsi sunt non ab observandis telis aut armis aut tubis; id enim invisum illis est propter Deum quem in conscientia sua gestant. — MARCUS AURELIUS, *Epistola ad Senatum:* S. Justini *Apologia I. pro Christianis*, Cap. 71.

War is one of the greatest plagues that can afflict humanity: it destroys religion, it destroys states, it destroys families. Any scourge, in fact, is preferable to it. Famine and pestilence become as nothing in comparison with it. . . . . Cannons and fire-arms are cruel and damnable machines. I believe them to have been the direct suggestion of the Devil. . . . . If Adam had seen in a vision the horrible instruments his children were to invent, he would have died of grief. — MARTIN LUTHER, *Table-Talk*, tr. Hazlitt, pp. 331 - 332.

Mulei Abdelummi, assaulted by his brother and wounded in the church, 1577, would not stirre till *sala*, or prayer, was done. — PURCHAS, *Pilgrims*, Part II. Book IX. Chap. 12, § 6, p. 1564.

A duel may still be granted in some cases by the law of England, and only there. That the Church allowed it anciently appears by this: In their public liturgies there were prayers appointed for the duellists to say; the judge used to bid them go to such a church and pray, etc. But whether is this lawful? If you grant any war lawful, I make no doubt but to convince it. — SELDEN, *Table-Talk: Duel.*

I look upon the way of Treaties as a retiring from fighting like beasts to arguing like men, whose strength should be more in their understandings than in their limbs. — *Eikon Basilike*, XVIII.

Se peut-il rien de plus plaisant qu'un homme ait droit de me tuer parce qu'il demeure au delà de l'eau, et que son prince a querelle avec le mien, quoique je n'en aie aucune avec lui? — PASCAL, *Pensées*, Part. I. Art. VI. 9.

Pourquoi me tuez-vous? Eh quoi! ne demeurez-vous pas de l'autre côté de l'eau? Mon ami, si vous demeuriez de ce côté, je serais un assassin; cela serait injuste de vous tuer de la sorte: mais puisque vous demeurez de l'autre côté, je suis un brave, et cela est juste. — *Ibid.*, Part. I. Art. IX. 3.

De tout temps les hommes, pour quelque morceau de terre de plus ou de moins, *sont convenus* entre eux de se dépouiller, se brûler, se tuer, s'égorger les uns les autres; et pour le faire plus ingénieusement et avec plus de sûreté, ils ont inventé de belles règles qu'on appelle l'art militaire: ils ont attaché à la pratique de ces règles *la gloire*, ou la plus solide réputation; et ils ont depuis enchéri de siècle en siècle sur la manière de se détruire réciproquement. — LA BRUYÈRE, *Du Souverain ou de la République.*

La calamita esser innamorata del ferro. — VICO, *Scienza Nuova*, Lib. I., *Degli Elementi*, XXXII.

> Unlistening, barbarous Force, to whom the sword
> Is reason, honor, law.
>
> THOMSON, *Liberty*, Part IV. 45, 46.

Enfin, tandis que les deux rois faisaient chanter des *Te Deum*, chacun dans son camp, il prit le parti d'aller raisonner ailleurs des effets et des causes. Il passa par-dessus des tas de morts et de mourants, et gagna d'abord un village voisin; il était en cendres : c'était un village Abare, que les Bulgares avaient brûlé, *selon les lois du droit public.* — VOLTAIRE, *Candide ou l' Optimiste*, Chap. III.

The rage and violence of public war, what is it but a suspension of justice among the warring parties? — HUME, *Essays: Inquiry concerning the Principles of Morals*, Section III., *Of Justice*, Part I.

A single robber or a few associates are branded with their genuine name; but the exploits of a numerous band assume the character of lawful and honorable war. — GIBBON, *Decline and Fall of the Roman Empire*, Chap. 50.

The glory of a warrior prince can only be written in letters of blood, and he can only be immortalized by the remembrance of the devastation of provinces and the desolation of nations. A warrior king depends for his reputation on the vulgar crowd, and must address himself to prejudice and ignorance to obtain the applause of a day, which the pen of the philosopher, the page of the historian, often annul, even before death comes to enshroud the mortal faculties in the nothingness from which they came. Consult, Sire, the laws of the King of Kings, and acknowledge that the God of the Universe is a God of Peace. — RIGHT HON HUGH ELLIOT, *British Minister in Sweden, to Gustavus III., November* 10, 1788: *Memoir*, by the Countess of Minto, p. 324.

C'est un usage reçu en Europe, qu'un gentilhomme vende, à une querelle étrangère, le sang qui appartient à sa patrie; qu'il s'engage à assassiner, en bataille rangée, qui il plaira au prince qui le soudoie; et ce métier est regardé comme honorable. — CONDORCET, *Note* 109 *aux Pensées de Pascal.*

C'était un affreux spectacle que cette déroute. Les blessés, qui ne pouvaient se traîner, se couchaient sur le chemin; on les foulait aux pieds; les femmes poussaient des cris, les enfans pleuraient, les officiers frappaient les fuyards. Au milieu de tout ce désordre, ma mère avait passé sans que je la reconnusse. Un enfant avait voulu l'arrêter et la tuer, parce qu'elle fuyait. — MADAME DE LA ROCHEJAQUELEIN, *Mémoires*, Chap. XVII. p. 301.

Let the soldier be abroad, if he will; he can do nothing in this age. There is another personage, a personage less imposing in the eyes of some, perhaps insignificant. The schoolmaster is abroad, and I trust to him, armed with his primer, against the soldier in full military array. — BROUGHAM, *Speech in the House of Commons, January* 29, 1828.

Was it possible for me to avoid the reflections which crowded into my mind, ... when I reflected that this peaceful and guiltless and useful triumph over the elements and over Nature herself had cost a million only of money, whilst fifteen hundred millions had been squandered on cruelty and crime, in naturalizing barbarism over the world, shrouding the nations in darkness, making bloodshed tinge the earth of every country under the sun, — in one horrid and comprehensive word, squandered on WAR, the greatest curse of the human race, and the greatest crime, because it involves every other crime within its execrable name? .... I look backwards with shame, with regret unspeakable, with indignation to which I should in vain attempt to give utterance, ... when I think, that, if one hundred, and but one hundred, of those fifteen hundred millions, had been employed in promoting the arts of peace and the progress of civilization and of wealth and prosperity amongst us, instead of that other employment which is too hateful to think of, and almost nowadays too disgusting to speak of (and I hope to live to see the day when such things will be incredible, when, looking back, we shall find it impossible to believe they ever happened), instead of being burdened with eight hundred millions of debt, borrowed after spending seven hundred millions, borrowed when we had no more to spend, we should have seen the whole country covered with such works as now unite Manchester and Liverpool, and should have enjoyed peace uninterrupted during the last forty years, with all the blessings which an industrious and a virtuous people deserve, and which peace profusely sheds upon their lot. — IBID., *Speech at Liverpool, July* 20, 1835.

Who can read these, and such passages as these [from Plato], without wishing that some who call themselves Christians, some Christian Principalities and Powers, had taken a lesson from the Heathen sage, and, if their nature forbade them to abstain from massacres and injustice, at least had not committed the scandalous impiety, as he calls it, of singing in places of Christian worship, and for the accomplishment of their enormous crimes, *Te Deums*, which in Plato's Republic would have been punished as blasphemy? Who, indeed, can refrain from lamenting another pernicious kind of sacrilege, an anthropomorphism, yet more frequent, — that of making Christian temples resound with prayers for victory over our enemies, and thanksgiving for their defeat? Assuredly such a ritual as this is not taken from the New Testament. — IBID., *Discourse of Natural Theology*, Note VIII.

War is on its last legs; and a universal peace is as sure as is the prevalence of civilization over barbarism, of liberal governments over feudal forms. The question for us is only, *How soon?* — EMERSON, *War: Æsthetic Papers*, ed. E. P. Peabody, p. 42.

A day will come when the only battle-field will be the market open to commerce and the mind opening to new ideas. A day will come when bullets and bomb-shells will be replaced by votes, by the universal suffrage of nations, by the venerable arbitration of a great Sovereign Senate, which will be to Europe what the Parliament is to England, what the Diet is to Germany, what the Legislative Assembly is to France. A day will come when a cannon will be exhibited in public museums, just as an instrument of torture is now, and people will be astonished how such a thing could have been. A day will come when those two immense groups, the United States of America and the United States of Europe, shall be seen placed in presence of each other, extending the hand of fellowship across the ocean. — VICTOR HUGO, *Inaugural Address at the Peace Congress of Paris, August* 22, 1849.

Clearly, beyond question, whatsoever be our theories about human nature and its capabilities and outcomes, the less war and cutting of throats we have among us, it will be better for us all. One rejoices much to see that immeasurable tendencies of this time are already pointing towards the results you aim at, — that, to all appearance, as men no longer wear swords in the streets, so neither by-and-by will nations. — CARLYLE, *Letter to the Peace Congress at London, July*, 1851.

The longer I live, the more I am convinced of the necessity of a powerful association to plead the cause of Universal Peace and International Arbitration; and I feel confident that the time is not far distant when war will be as impossible among civilized nations as duelling is among civilized men. — SIR DAVID BREWSTER, *Letter to the Peace Conference at Edinburgh, October*, 1853.

Aujourd'hui encore on bénit les drapeaux qui conduisent les hommes à de mutuels égorgements. En donnant à un Dieu de paix le nom de *Dieu des Armées*, on fait de l'Être infini en bonté le complice de ceux qui s'abreuvent des larmes de leurs semblables. Aujourd'hui encore on chante d'impies *Te Deum* pour le remercier de ces victoires obtenues au prix d'épouvantables massacres, victoires qu'il faudrait ou expier comme des crimes lorsqu'elles ont été remportées dans des guerres offensives ou déplorer comme la plus triste des nécessités quand elles ont été obtenues dans des guerres défensives. — LARROQUE, *De la Guerre et des Armées Permanentes*, Part. III. § 4.

La monarchie, sous les formes mêmes les plus tempérées, tiendra toujours à avoir à sa dévotion des armées permanentes. Or avec les armées en permanence l'abolition de la guerre est impossible. Par conséquent la grande fédération des peuples, au moins de tous les peuples Européens, dans le but d'arriver à l'abolition de la guerre par l'institution d'un droit international et d'un tribunal supérieur chargé de le faire observer, ne sera réalisable que le jour où ces peuples seront organisés sous la forme républicaine. Quand luira ce jour? — IBID., Avant-propos, p. 6.

Sir J. Lubbock quotes the case of a tribe in Baffin's Bay who "could not be made to understand what was meant by war, nor had they any warlike weapons." No wonder, poor people! They had been driven into regions where no stronger race could desire to follow them. — DUKE OF ARGYLL, *Primeval Man*, p. 177.

ADDRESS.

MR. PRESIDENT AND GENTLEMEN, — We are assembled in what may be called the Holy Week of our community, — not occupied by pomps of a complex ceremonial, swelling in tides of music, beneath time-honored arches, but set apart, with the unadorned simplicity of early custom, to anniversary meetings of those charitable and religious associations from whose good works our country derives such true honor. Each association is distinct. Gathered within the folds of each are its own members, devoted to its chosen objects: and yet all are harmonious together; for all are inspired by one sentiment, — the welfare of the united Human Family. Each has its own separate orbit, a pathway of light; while all together constitute a system which moves in a still grander orbit.

Among all these associations, none is so truly comprehensive as ours. The prisoner in his cell, the slave in his chains, the sailor on ocean wanderings, the Pagan on far off continent or island, and the ignorant here at home, will all be commended by eloquent voices. I need not say that you should listen to these voices, and answer to their appeal. But, while mindful of these interests, justly claiming your care, it is my present and most grateful duty to commend that other cause, the great cause of Peace, which in its wider embrace enfolds prisoner, slave, sailor, the ignorant, all mankind, — which to each of these charities is the source of strength and light, I may say of life itself, as the sun in the heavens.

Peace is the grand Christian charity, fountain and parent of all other charities. Let Peace be removed, and all other charities sicken and die. Let Peace exert her gladsome sway, and all other charities quicken into life. Peace is the distinctive promise and possession of Christianity, — so much so, that, where Peace is not, Christianity cannot be. It is also the promise of Heaven, being the beautiful consummation of that rest and felicity which the saints above are said to enjoy. There is nothing elevated which is not exalted by Peace. There is nothing valuable which does not gain from Peace. Of Wisdom herself it is said, that all her ways are pleasantness, and all her paths are Peace. And these golden words are refined by the saying of the Christian Father, that the perfection of joy is Peace. Naturally Peace is the longing and aspiration of the noblest souls, whether for themselves or for country. In the bitterness of exile, away from the Florence immortalized by his divine poem, and pacing the cloisters of a convent, where a sympathetic monk inquired, "What do you seek?" Dante answered, in accents distilled from the heart, "*Peace!*"[1] In the memorable English struggles, while King and Parliament were rending the land, a gallant supporter of monarchy, the chivalrous Falkland, touched by the intolerable woes of

[1] Longfellow's Poets and Poetry of Europe, p. 513.

War, cried, in words which consecrate his memory more than any feat of arms, "*Peace! peace!*"[1] Not in aspiration only, but in benediction, is this word uttered. As the Apostle went forth on his errand, as the son forsook his father's roof, the choicest blessing was, "*Peace be with you!*" When the Saviour was born, angels from heaven, amidst choiring melodies, let fall that supreme benediction, never before vouchsafed to the children of the Human Family, "*Peace on earth, and good-will towards men!*"

To maintain this charity, to promote these aspirations, to welcome these benedictions, is the object of our Society. To fill men in private with all those sentiments which make for Peace, to lead men in public to the recognition of those paramount principles which are the safeguard of Peace, above all, to teach the True Grandeur of Peace, and to unfold the folly and wickedness of the Institution of War and of the War System, now recognized and established by the Commonwealth of Nations as the mode of determining international controversies, — such is the object of our Society.

There are persons who allow themselves sometimes to speak of associations like ours, if not with disapprobation, at least with levity and distrust. A writer so humane and genial as Robert Southey left on record a gibe at the "Society for the Abolition of War," saying that it had "not obtained sufficient notice even to be in disrepute."[2] It is not uncommon to hear our aims characterized as visionary, impracticable, Utopian. Sometimes it is hastily said that they are contrary to

1 Clarendon, History of the Rebellion, Book VII. Vol. IV. p. 255.

2 Colloquies on the Progress and Prospects of Society, Vol. I. p. 224.

the nature of man, that they require for success a complete reconstruction of human character, and that they necessarily assume in man qualities, capacities, and virtues which do not belong to his nature. This mistaken idea was once strongly expressed in the taunt, that "an Anti-War Society is as little practicable as an Anti-Thunder-and-Lightning Society."[1]

Never a moment when this beautiful cause was not the occasion of jest, varying with the character of the objector. More than a century ago there was something of this kind, which arrested the attention of no less a person than Leibnitz, and afterwards of Fontenelle. It was where an elegant Dutch trifler, as described by Leibnitz, following the custom of his country, placed as a sign over his door the motto, *To Perpetual Peace,* with the picture of a cemetery, — meaning to suggest that only with the dead could this desire of good men be fulfilled. Not with the living, so the elegant Dutch trifler proclaimed over his door. A different person, also of Holland, who was both diplomatist and historian, the scholarly Aitzema, caught the jest, and illustrated it by a Latin couplet: —

> "Qui pacem quæris libertatemque, viator,
> Aut nusquam aut isto sub tumulo invenies"; —

which, being translated, means, "Traveller, who seekest Peace and Liberty, either nowhere or under that mound thou wilt find them."[2] Do not fail to observe that Liberty is here doomed to the same grave as Peace. Alas, that there should be such despair! At length Liberty is rising. May not Peace rise also?

1 Hon. Jeremiah Mason, of Boston, to Mr. Sumner.

2 Leibnitz, Codex Juris Gentium Diplomaticus, Dissert. I. § 1: Opera (ed. Dutens), Tom. IV. Pars 3, pp. 287, 288. Fontenelle, Éloge de Leibnitz: Œuvres, Tom. V. p. 456.

Doubtless objections, to say nothing of jests, striking at the heart of our cause, exert a certain influence over the public mind. They often proceed from persons of sincerity and goodness, who would rejoice to see the truth as we see it. But, plausible as they appear to those who have not properly meditated this subject, I cannot but regard them — I believe that all who candidly listen to me must hereafter regard them — as prejudices, without foundation in sense or reason, which must yield to a plain and careful examination of the precise objects proposed.

Let me not content myself, in response to these critics, with the easy answer, that, if our aims are visionary, impracticable, Utopian, then the unfulfilled promises of the Scriptures are vain, — then the Lord's Prayer, in which we ask that God's kingdom may come on earth, is a mockery, — then Christianity is no better than the statutes of Utopia. Let me not content myself with reminding you that all the great reforms by which mankind have been advanced encountered similar objections, — that the abolition of the punishment of death for theft, so long delayed, was first suggested in the "Utopia" of Sir Thomas More, — that the efforts to abolish the slave-trade were opposed, almost in our day, as visionary, — in short, that all endeavors for human improvement, for knowledge, for freedom, for virtue, all the great causes which dignify human history, and save it from being a mere protracted War Bulletin, a common sewer, a *Cloaca Maxima*, flooded with perpetual uncleanness, have been pronounced Utopian, — while, in spite of distrust, prejudice, and enmity, all these causes gradually found acceptance, as they gradually came to be understood, and the aspirations of one age became the acquisitions of the next.

Satisfactory to some as this answer might be, I cannot content myself with leaving our cause in this way. I shall meet all assaults, and show, by careful exposition, that our objects are in no respect visionary, — that the cause of Peace does not depend upon any reconstruction of the human character, or upon holding in check the general laws of man's being, — but that it deals with man as he is, according to the experience of history, — and, above all, that our immediate and particular aim, the abolition of the Institution of War, and of the whole War System, as *established* Arbiter of Right in the Commonwealth of Nations, is as practicable as it would be beneficent.

I begin by putting aside questions, often pushed forward, which an accurate analysis shows to be independent of the true issue. Their introduction has perplexed the discussion, by transferring to the great cause of International Peace doubts which do not belong to it.

One of these is the declared right, inherent in each individual, to take the life of an assailant in order to save his own life, — compendiously called the *Right of Self-Defence*, usually recognized by philosophers and publicists as founded in Nature and the instincts of men. The exercise of this right is carefully restricted to cases where life itself is in actual jeopardy. No defence of property, no vindication of what is called *personal honor*, justifies this extreme resort. Nor does this right imply the right of attack; for, instead of attacking one another, on account of injuries past or impending, men need only resort to the proper tribunals of justice. There are, however, many most respectable persons, particularly of the denomination of Friends, some of whom I may now have the honor of addressing, who believe that the exercise of this right, even thus limited, is in direct contravention of Christian precepts. Their views find faithful utterance in the writings of Jonathan Dymond, of which at least this may be said, that they strengthen and elevate, even if they do not always satisfy, the understanding. "We shall be asked," says Dymond, "'Suppose a ruffian breaks into your house, and rushes into your room with his arm lifted to murder you; do you not believe that Christianity allows you to kill him?' This is the last refuge of the cause. Our answer to it is explicit, — *We do not believe it.*"[1] While thus candidly and openly avowing an extreme sentiment of non-resistance, this excellent person is careful to remind the reader that the case of the ruffian does not practically illustrate the true character of War, unless it appears that war is undertaken simply for the preservation of life, when no other alternative remains to a people than to kill or be killed. According to this view, the robber on land who places his pistol at the breast of the traveller, the pirate who threatens life on the high seas, and the riotous disturber of the public peace who puts life in jeopardy at home, cannot be opposed by the sacrifice of life. Of course all who subscribe to this renunciation of self-defence must join in efforts to abolish the Arbitrament of War. Our appeal is to the larger number who make no such application of Christian precepts, who recognize the right of self-defence as belonging to each individual, and who believe in the necessity at times of

[1] On the Applicability of the Pacific Principles of the New Testament to the Conduct of States, p. 10.

exercising this right, whether against a robber, a pirate, or a mob.

Another question, closely connected with that of self-defence, is the asserted *Right of Revolt or Revolution.* Shall a people endure political oppression, or the denial of freedom, without resistance? The answer to this question will necessarily affect the rights of three million fellow-citizens held in slavery among us. If such a right unqualifiedly exists, — and sympathy with our fathers, and with the struggles for freedom now agitating Europe, must make us hesitate to question its existence, — then these three millions of fellow-men, into whose souls we thrust the iron of the deadliest bondage the world has yet witnessed, must be justified in resisting to death the power that holds them. A popular writer on ethics, Dr. Paley, has said: "It may be as much a duty at one time to resist Government as it is at another to obey it, — to wit, whenever more advantage will in our opinion accrue to the community from resistance than mischief. The lawfulness of resistance, or the lawfulness of a revolt, does not depend alone upon the grievance which is sustained or feared, but also upon the probable expense and event of the contest."[1] This view distinctly recognizes the right of resistance, but limits it by the chance of success, founding it on no higher ground than expediency. A right thus vaguely defined and bounded must be invoked with reluctance and distrust. The lover of Peace, while admitting, that, unhappily, in the present state of the world, an exigency for its exercise may arise, must confess the inherent barbarism of such an agency, and admire, even

[1] Principles of Moral and Political Philosophy, Book VI. ch. 3.

if he cannot entirely adopt, the sentiment of Daniel O'Connell: "Remember that no political change is worth a single crime, or, above all, a single drop of human blood."

These questions I put aside, not as unimportant, not as unworthy of careful consideration, but as unessential to the cause which I now present. If I am asked — as advocates of Peace are often asked — whether a robber, a pirate, a mob, may be resisted by the sacrifice of life, I answer, that they may be so resisted, — mournfully, necessarily. If I am asked to sympathize with the efforts for freedom now finding vent in rebellion and revolution, I cannot hesitate to say, that, wherever Freedom struggles, wherever Right is, there my sympathies must be. And I believe I speak not only for myself, but for our Society, when I add, that, while it is our constant aim to diffuse those sentiments which promote good-will in all the relations of life, which exhibit the beauty of Peace everywhere, in *national* affairs as well as *international,* and while especially recognizing that central truth, the Brotherhood of Man, in whose noonday light all violence among men is dismal and abhorred as among brothers, it is nevertheless no part of our purpose to impeach the right to take life in self-defence or when the public necessity requires, nor to question the justifiableness of resistance to outrage and oppression. On these points there are diversities of opinion among the friends of Peace, which this Society, confining itself to efforts for the overthrow of War, is not constrained to determine.

Waiving, then, these matters, with their perplexities and difficulties, which do not in any respect belong to the cause, I come now to the precise object we hope to accomplish, — *The Abolition of the Institution of War, and of the whole War System, as an established Arbiter of Justice in the Commonwealth of Nations.* In the accurate statement of our aims you will at once perceive the strength of our position. Much is always gained by a clear understanding of the question in issue; and the cause of Peace unquestionably suffers often because it is misrepresented or not fully comprehended. In the hope of removing this difficulty, I shall *first* unfold the true character of War and the War System, involving the question of Preparations for War, and the question of a Militia. The way will then be open, in the *second* branch of this Address, for a consideration of the means by which this system can be overthrown. Here I shall exhibit the examples of nations, and the efforts of individuals, constituting the Peace Movement, with the auguries of its triumph, briefly touching, at the close, on our duties to this great cause, and the vanity of Military Glory. In all that I say I cannot forget that I am addressing a Christian association, for a Christian charity, in a Christian church.

I.

AND, first, of *War and the War System in the Commonwealth of Nations.* By the Commonwealth of Nations I understand the Fraternity of Christian Nations recognizing a Common Law in their relations with each other, usually called the Law of Nations. This law, being established by the consent of nations, is not necessarily the law of all nations, but only of such as recognize it. The Europeans and the Orientals often differ with regard to its provisions; nor would it be proper to say, that, at this time, the Ottomans, or the Mahometans in general, or the Chinese, have become parties to it.[1] The prevailing elements of this law are the Law of Nature, the truths of Christianity, the usages of nations, the opinions of publicists, and the written texts or enactments found in diplomatic acts or treaties. In origin and growth it is not unlike the various systems of municipal jurisprudence, all of which are referred to kindred sources.

It is often said, in excuse for the allowance of War, that nations are independent, and acknowledge no *common superior*. True, indeed, they are politically independent, and acknowledge no common political sovereign, with power to enforce the law. But they do acknowledge a common superior, of unquestioned influence and authority, whose rules they are bound to obey. This common superior, acknowledged by all, is none other than the Law of Nations, with the Law of Nature as a controlling element. It were superfluous to dwell at length upon opinions of publicists and jurists declaring this supremacy. "The Law of Nature," says Vattel, a classic in this department, "is not less *obligatory* with respect to states, or to men united in political society, than to individuals."[2] An eminent English authority, Lord Stowell, so famous as Sir William Scott, says, "The *Conventional Law of Mankind*, which is evidenced in their practice, *allows* some and *prohibits* other modes of destruction."[3] A recent German jurist says, "A nation associating itself with the general so-

[1] Since the delivery of this Address, Turkey and China have accepted our Law of Nations.

[2] Law of Nations, Preface.

[3] Robinson's, Chr., Admiralty Reports, Vol. I. p. 140.

ciety of nations *thereby recognizes a law common to all nations*, by which its international relations are to be regulated."[1] Lastly, a popular English moralist, whom I have already quoted, and to whom I refer because his name is so familiar, Dr. Paley, says, that the principal part of what is called the Law of Nations derives its obligatory character "*simply from the fact of its being established, and the general duty of conforming to established rules* upon questions and between parties where nothing but *positive regulations* can prevent disputes, and where disputes are followed by such destructive consequences."[2]

The Law of Nations is, then, the Supreme Law of the Commonwealth of Nations, governing their relations with each other, determining their reciprocal rights, and sanctioning all remedies for the violation of these rights. To the Commonwealth of Nations this law is what the Constitution and Municipal Law of Massachusetts are to the associate towns and counties composing the State, or what, by apter illustration, the National Constitution of our Union is to the thirty several States which now recognize it as the supreme law.

But the Law of Nations, — and here is a point of infinite importance to the clear understanding of the subject, — while anticipating and providing for controversies between nations, recognizes and establishes War as final Arbiter. It distinctly says to nations, "If you cannot agree together, then stake your cause upon *Trial by Battle*." The mode of trial thus recognized and established has its own procedure, with rules and regulations,

1 Heffter, Das Europäische Völkerrecht der Gegenwart, § 2.

2 Principles of Moral and Political Philosophy, Book VI. ch. 12.

under the name of Laws of War, constituting a branch of International Law. "The Laws of War," says Dr. Paley, "are part of the Law of Nations, and founded, as to their authority, upon the same principle with the rest of that code, namely, upon the fact of their being *established*, no matter when or by whom."[1] Nobody doubts that the Laws of War are established by nations.

It is not uncommon to speak of the *practice* of War, or the *custom* of War, — a term adopted by that devoted friend of Peace, the late Noah Worcester. Its apologists and expounders have called it "a judicial trial," — "one of the highest trials of right," — "a process of justice," — "an appeal for justice," — "a mode of obtaining rights," — "a prosecution of rights by force," — "a mode of condign punishment." I prefer to characterize it as an INSTITUTION, established by the Commonwealth of Nations as Arbiter of Justice. As Slavery is an Institution, growing out of local custom, sanctioned, defined, and established by Municipal Law, so War is an Institution, growing out of general custom, sanctioned, defined, and established by the Law of Nations.

Only when we contemplate War in this light can we fully perceive its combined folly and wickedness Let me bring this home to your minds. Boston and Cambridge are adjoining towns, separated by the River Charles. In the event of controversy between these different jurisdictions, the Municipal Law establishes a judicial tribunal, and not War, as arbiter. Ascending higher, in the event of controversy between two different counties, as between Essex and Middlesex, the same Municipal Law establishes a judicial tribunal,

[1] Principles of Moral and Political Philosophy, Book VI. ch. 12.

and not War, as arbiter. Ascending yet higher, in the event of controversy between two different States of our Union, the Constitution establishes a judicial tribunal, the Supreme Court of the United States, and not War, as arbiter. But now mark: at the next stage there is a change of arbiter. In the event of controversy between two different States of the Commonwealth of Nations, the supreme law establishes, not a judicial tribunal, but War, as arbiter. War is the institution *established* for the determination of justice between nations.

Provisions of the Municipal Law of Massachusetts, and of the National Constitution, are not vain words. To all familiar with our courts it is well known that suits between towns, and likewise between counties, are often entertained and satisfactorily adjudicated. The records of the Supreme Court of the United States show also that States of the Union habitually refer important controversies to this tribunal. Before this high court is now pending an action of the State of Missouri against the State of Iowa, founded on a question of boundary, where the former claims a section of territory — larger than many German principalities — extending along the whole northern border of Missouri, with several miles of breadth, and comprising more than two thousand square miles. Within a short period this same tribunal has decided a similar question between our own State of Massachusetts and our neighbor, Rhode Island, — the latter pertinaciously claiming a section of territory, about three miles broad, on a portion of our southern frontier.

Suppose that in these different cases between towns counties, states, War had been *established* by the supreme law as arbiter; imagine the disastrous consequences; picture the imperfect justice which must have been the end and fruit of such a contest; and while rejoicing that in these cases we are happily relieved from an alternative so wretched and deplorable, reflect that on a larger theatre, where grander interests are staked, in the relations between nations, under the solemn sanction of the Law of Nations, War is *established* as Arbiter of Justice. Reflect also that a complex and subtile code, known as Laws of War, is established to regulate the resort to this arbiter.

Recognizing the irrational and unchristian character of War as established arbiter between towns, counties, and states, we learn to condemn it as established arbiter between nations. If wrong in one case, it must be wrong in the other. But there is another parallel supplied by history, from which we may form a yet clearer idea: I refer to the system of *Private Wars*, or, more properly, *Petty Wars*, which darkened even the Dark Ages. This must not be confounded with the *Trial by Battle*, although the two were alike in recognizing the sword as Arbiter of Justice. The *right to wage war* (*le droit de guerroyer*) was accorded by the early Municipal Law of European States, particularly of the Continent, to all independent chiefs, however petty, but not to vassals; precisely as the *right to wage war* is now accorded by International Law to all independent states and principalities, however petty, but not to subjects. It was mentioned often among the "liberties" to which independent chiefs were entitled; as it is still recognized by International Law among the "liberties" of independent nations. In proportion as any sovereignty was absorbed in some larger lordship, this offensive *right* or "liberty" gradually disappeared. In France it prevailed extensively, till at last King John, by an ordinance dated 1361, expressly forbade Petty Wars throughout his kingdom, saying, in excellent words, "We by these presents ordain that all challenges and wars, and all acts of violence against all persons, in all parts whatsoever of our kingdom, shall henceforth cease; and all assemblies, musters, and raids of men-at-arms or archers; and also all pillages, seizures of goods and persons illegally, *vengeances and counter-vengeances,* surprisals and ambuscades. . . . . All which things we will to be kept and observed everywhere without infringement, on pain of incurring our indignation, and of being reputed and held disobedient and rebellious towards us and the crown, and at our mercy in body and goods."[1] It was reserved for that indefatigable king, Louis the Eleventh, while Dauphin, as late as 1451, to make another effort in the same direction, by expressly abrogating one of the "liberties" of Dauphiné, being none other than the *right of war,* immemorially secured to the inhabitants of this province.[2] From these royal ordinances the Commonwealth of Nations might borrow appropriate words, in abrogating forever the Public Wars, or, more properly, the Grand Wars, with their *vengeances and counter-vengeances,* which are yet sanctioned by International Law among the "liberties" of Christian nations.

At a later day, in Germany, effective measures were taken against the same prevailing evil. Contests there

[1] Cauchy, Du Duel considéré dans ses Origines, Liv. I. Seconde Époque, Ch. V. Tom. I. pp. 91, 92.

[2] Du Cange, Dissertations sur l'Histoire de St. Louis, Diss. XXVII. (XXIX.): *Des Guerres Privées.*

were not confined to feudal lords. Associations of tradesmen, and even of domestics, sent defiance to each other, and even to whole cities, on pretences trivial as those sometimes the occasion of the Grand Wars between nations. There are still extant *Declarations of War* by a Lord of Prauenstein against the free city of Frankfort, because a young lady of the city refused to dance with the uncle of the belligerent, — by the baker and other domestics of the Margrave of Baden against Esslingen, Reutlingen, and other imperial cities, — by the baker of the Count Palatine Louis against the cities of Augsburg, Ulm, and Rottweil, — by the shoeblacks of the University of Leipsic against the provost and other members, — and, in 1477, by the cook of Eppenstein, with his scullions, dairy-maids, and dish-washers, against Otho, Count of Solms. Finally, in 1495, at the Diet of Worms, so memorable in German annals, the Emperor Maximilian sanctioned an ordinance which proclaimed a permanent Peace throughout Germany, abolished the *right* or "liberty" of Private War, and instituted a Supreme Tribunal, under the ancient name of Imperial Chamber, to which recourse might be had, even by nobles, princes, and states, for the determination of disputes without appeal to the sword.[1]

Trial by Battle, or "judicial combat," furnishes the most vivid picture of the Arbitrament of War, beyond even what is found in the system of *Petty Wars*. It was at one period, particularly in France, the universal umpire between private individuals. All causes, criminal and civil, with all the questions incident thereto, were referred to this senseless trial. Not bodily in-

[1] Coxe, History of the House of Austria, Ch. XIX. and XXI.

firmity or old age could exempt a litigant from the hazard of the Battle, even to determine differences of the most trivial import. At last substitutes were allowed, and, as in War, bravoes or champions were hired for wages to enter the lists. The proceedings were conducted gravely according to prescribed forms, which were digested into a system of peculiar subtilty and minuteness, — as War in our day is according to an established code, the Laws of War. Thus do violence, lawlessness, and absurdity shelter themselves beneath the Rule of Law! Religion also lent her sanctions. With presence and prayer the priest cheered the insensate combatant, and appealed for aid to Jesus Christ, the Prince of Peace.

The Church, to its honor, early perceived the wickedness of this system. By voices of pious bishops, by ordinances of solemn councils, by anathemas of popes, it condemned whosoever should slay another in a battle so impious and inimical to Christian peace, as "a most wicked homicide and bloody robber"[1]; while it treated the unhappy victim as a volunteer, guilty of his own death, and handed his remains to unhonored burial without psalm or prayer. With sacerdotal supplication it vainly sought the withdrawal of all countenance from this great evil, and the support of the civil power in ecclesiastical censures. To these just efforts let praise and gratitude be offered! But, alas! authentic incidents, and the forms still on record in ancient missals, attest the unhappy sanction which Trial by

[1] "Statuimus, juxta antiquum ecclesiasticæ observationis morem, ut quicumque tam impia et Christianæ paci inimica pugna alterum occiderit seu vulneribus debilem reddiderit, *velut homicida nequissimus et latro cruentus*, ab Ecclesiæ et omnium fidelium cœtu reddatur separatus," etc. — Canon XII. Concil. Valent., — quoted by Cauchy, Du Duel, Liv. I. Première Époque, Ch. III., Tom. I. p. 43, note.

Battle succeeded in obtaining even from the Church, — as in our day the English Liturgy, and the conduct of the Christian clergy in all countries, attest the unhappy sanction which the Institution of War yet enjoys. Admonitions of the Church and labors of good men slowly prevailed. Proofs by witnesses and by titles were gradually adopted, though opposed by the selfishness of camp-followers, subaltern officers, and even of lords, greedy for the fees or wages of combat. In England Trial by Battle was attacked by Henry the Second, striving to substitute Trial by Jury. In France it was expressly forbidden by that illustrious monarch, St. Louis, in an immortal ordinance. At last, this system, so wasteful of life, so barbarous in character, so vain and inefficient as Arbiter of Justice, yielded to judicial tribunals.

The Trial by Battle is not Roman in origin. It may be traced to the forests of Germany, where the rule prevailed of referring to the sword what at Rome was referred to the prætor; so that a judicial tribunal, when urged upon these barbarians, was regarded as an innovation.[1] The very words of surprise at the German custom are yet applicable to the Arbitrament of War.

The absurdity of Trial by Battle may be learned from the instances where it was invoked. Though originally permitted to determine questions of personal character, it was extended so as to embrace criminal cases, and even questions of property. In 961 the title to a church was submitted to this ordeal.[2] Some time later a grave point of law was submitted. The question was, "Whether the sons of a son ought to be reckoned

[1] "Nunc agentes gratias, quod ea Romana justitia finiret, feritasque sua novitate incognitæ disciplinæ mitesceret, et solita armis decerni jure terminarentur." — Velleius Paterculus, Lib. II. c. 118.

[2] Robertson, History of Charles V., Vol. I. Note 22.

among the children of the family, and succeed equally with their uncles, if their father happened to die while their grandfather was alive." The general opinion at first was for reference of the question to the adjudication of arbiters; but we are informed by a contemporary ecclesiastic, who reports the case, that the Emperor, Otho the First, "taking better counsel, and unwilling that nobles and elders of the people should be treated *dishonorably*, ordered the matter to be decided by champions with the sword." The champion of the grandchildren prevailed, and they were enabled to share with their uncles in the inheritance.[1] Human folly did not end here. A question of theology was surrendered to the same arbitrament, being nothing less than whether the Musarabic Liturgy, used in the churches of Spain, or the Liturgy approved at Rome, contained the form of worship most acceptable to the Deity. The Spaniards contended zealously for the liturgy of their ancestors. The Pope urged the liturgy having his own infallible sanction. The controversy was submitted to Trial by Battle. Two knights in complete armor entered the lists. The champion of the Musarabic Liturgy was victorious. But there was an appeal to the ordeal of fire. A copy of each liturgy was cast into the flames. The Musarabic Liturgy remained unhurt, while the other vanished into ashes. And yet this judgment, first by battle and then by fire, was eluded or overthrown, showing how, as with War, the final conclusion is uncertain, and testifying against any appeal, except to human reason.[2]

1 Widukindii, Res Gestæ Saxonicæ, Lib. II. c. 10: Monumenta Germaniæ Historica, ed. Pertz, Scriptorum Tom. III. p. 440.

2 Robertson, History of Charles V., Vol. I. Note 22. — The Duel has a liter-

An early king of the Lombards, in a formal decree, condemned the Trial by Battle as "impious"[1]; Montesquieu, at a later time, branded it as "monstrous"[2]; and Sir William Blackstone characterized it as "clearly an unchristian, as well as most uncertain, method of trial."[3] In the light of our day all unite in this condemnation. No man hesitates. No man undertakes its apology; nor does any man count as "glory" the feats of arms which it prompted and displayed. But the laws of morals are general, and not special. They apply to communities and to nations, as well as to individuals; nor is it possible, by any cunning of logic, or any device of human wit, to distinguish between that domestic institution, the Trial by Battle, established by Municipal Law as arbiter between individuals, and that international institution, the grander Trial by Battle, established by the Christian Commonwealth as arbiter between nations. If the judicial combat was impious, monstrous, and unchristian, then is War impious, monstrous, and unchristian.

It has been pointedly said in England, that the whole object of king, lords, and commons, and of the complex British Constitution, is "to get twelve men into

ature of its own, which is not neglected by Brunet in his *Manuel du Libraire*, where, under the head of *Les Combats Singuliers*, Tom. VI. col. 1636 - 1638, *Table Méthodique*, 28717 - 28749, will be found titles in various languages, from which I select the following: Joan. de Lignano, Tractatus de Bello, de Repressaliis, et de Duello, Papiæ, 1487; Tractatus de Duello, en Lat. y en Castellano, por D. Castillo, Taurini, 1525; Alciat, De Singulari Certamine, Lugd., 1543. In the development of civilization how can the literature of War expect more honor than that of the Duel?

1 Liutprandi Leges, Lib. VI. cap. 65: Muratori, Rerum Italic. Script., Tom. I. Pars 2, p. 74.

2 Esprit des Lois, Liv. XXVIII. ch. 23.

3 Commentaries, Book IV. ch. 33, Vol. IV. p. 418.

a jury-box"; and Mr. Hume repeats the idea, when he declares that the *administration of justice* is the grand aim of government. If this be true of individual nations in municipal affairs, it is equally true of the Commonwealth of Nations. The whole complex system of the Law of Nations, overarching all the Christian nations, has but one distinct object,—*the administration of justice* between nations. Would that with tongue or pen I could adequately expose the enormity of this system, involving, as it does, the precepts of religion, the dictates of common sense, the suggestions of economy, and the most precious sympathies of humanity! Would that now I could impart to all who hear me something of my own conviction!

I need not dwell on the waste and cruelty thus authorized. Travelling the page of history, these stare us wildly in the face at every turn. We see the desolation and death keeping step with the bloody track; we look upon sacked towns, ravaged territories, violated homes; we behold all the sweet charities of life changed to wormwood and gall. The soul is penetrated by the sharp moan of mothers, sisters, and daughters, of fathers, brothers, and sons, who, in the bitterness of bereavement, refuse to be comforted. The eye rests at last upon one of those fair fields, where Nature, in her abundance, spreads her cloth of gold, spacious and apt for the entertainment of mighty multitudes,—or, perhaps, from curious subtilty of position, like the carpet in Arabian tale, contracting for the accommodation of a few only, or dilating for an innumerable host. Here, under a bright sun, such as shone at Austerlitz or Buena Vista, amidst the peaceful harmonies of Nature, on the Sabbath of Peace, are bands of brothers, children of a common Father, heirs to a common happiness, struggling together in deadly fight,—with madness of fallen spirits, murderously seeking the lives of brothers who never injured them or their kindred. The havoc rages; the ground is soaked with commingling blood; the air is rent by commingling cries; horse and rider are stretched together on the earth. More revolting than mangled victims, gashed limbs, lifeless trunks, spattering brains, are the lawless passions which sweep, tempest-like, through the fiendish tumult.

> "'Nearer comes the storm and nearer, rolling fast and frightful on.
> Speak, Ximena, speak, and tell us, who has lost and who has won?'
> 'Alas! alas! I know not, sister; friend and foe together fall;
> O'er the dying rush the living; pray, my sister, for them all!'"

Horror-struck, we ask, wherefore this hateful contest? The melancholy, but truthful, answer comes, that this is the *established* method of determining justice between nations!

The scene changes. Far away on some distant pathway of the ocean, two ships approach each other, with white canvas broadly spread to receive the flying gale. They are proudly built. All of human art has been lavished in their graceful proportions and compacted sides, while in dimensions they look like floating happy islands of the sea. A numerous crew, with costly appliances of comfort, hives in their secure shelter. Surely these two travellers must meet in joy and friendship; the flag at mast-head will give the signal of fellowship; the delighted sailors will cluster in rigging and on yardarms to look each other in the face, while exhilarating voices mingle in accents of gladness uncontrollable. Alas! alas! it is not so. Not as brothers, not as friends, not as wayfarers of the common ocean, do they come together, but as enemies. The closing vessels now bristle fiercely with death-dealing implements. On their spacious decks, aloft on all their masts, flashes the deadly musketry. From their sides spout cataracts of flame, amidst the pealing thunders of a fatal artillery. They who had escaped "the dreadful touch of merchant-marring rocks," who on their long and solitary way had sped unharmed by wind or wave, whom the hurricane had spared, in whose favor storms and seas had intermitted their immitigable war, now at last fall by the hand of each other. From both ships the same spectacle of horror greets us. On decks reddened with blood, the murders of the Sicilian Vespers and of St. Bartholomew, with the fires of Smithfield, break forth anew, and concentrate their rage. Each is a swimming Golgotha. At length these vessels — such pageants of the sea, such marvels of art, once so stately, but now rudely shattered by cannon-ball, with shivered masts and ragged sails — exist only as unmanageable wrecks, weltering on the uncertain wave, whose transient lull of peace is their sole safety. In amazement at this strange, unnatural contest, away from country and home, where there is no country or home to defend, we ask again, Wherefore this dismal scene? Again the melancholy, but truthful, answer promptly comes, that this is the *established* method of determining justice between nations.

Yes! the barbarous, brutal relations which once prevailed between individuals, which prevailed still longer between communities composing nations, are not yet banished from the great Christian Commonwealth. Religion, reason, humanity, first penetrate the individual, next larger bodies, and, widening in influence, slowly leaven nations. Thus, while condemning the bloody contests of individuals, also of towns, counties, principalities, provinces, and denying to all these the right of *waging war*, or of appeal to *Trial by Battle*, we continue to uphold an atrocious *System* of folly and crime, which is to nations what the System of Petty Wars was to towns, counties, principalities, provinces, also what the Duel was to individuals: for *War is the Duel of Nations.*[1] As from Pluto's throne flowed those terrible rivers, Styx, Acheron, Cocytus, and Phlegethon, with lamenting waters and currents of flame, so from this established System flow the direful tides of War. "Give them Hell," was the language written on a slate by an American officer, speechless from approaching death. "Ours is a damnable profession," was the confession of a veteran British general. "War is the trade of barbarians," exclaimed Napoleon, in a moment of truthful remorse, prompted by his bloodiest field. Alas! these words are not too strong. The business of War cannot be other than the trade of barbarians, cannot be other than a damnable profession; and War itself is certainly Hell on earth. But forget not, bear always in mind, and let the idea sink deep into your souls, animating you to constant endeavor, that this trade of barbarians, this damnable profession, is part of the War System, sanctioned by International Law, — and that War itself is Hell, recognized, legalized, established, organized, by

[1] Plautus speaks in the *Epidicus* (Act III. Sc. iv. 14, 15) of one who obtained great riches by the *Duelling Art*, meaning the Art of War: —

"*Arte duellica*
Divitias magnas indeptum."

And Horace, in his Odes (Lib. IV. Carm. xv. 4–9), hails the age of Augustus, as at peace, or *free from Duels*, and with the Temple of Janus closed: —

"Tua, Cæsar, ætas
. . . . . vacuum *duellis*
Janum Quirini clausit."

the Commonwealth of Nations, for the determination of international questions!

"Put together," says Voltaire, "all the vices of all ages and places, and they will not come up to the mischiefs of one campaign."[1] This strong speech is supported by the story of ancient mythology, that Juno confided the infant Mars to Priapus. Another of nearer truth might be made. Put together all the ills and calamities from the visitations of God, whether in convulsions of Nature, or in pestilence and famine, and they will not equal the ills and calamities inflicted by man upon his brother-man, through the visitation of War, — while, alas! the sufferings of War are too often without the alleviation of those gentle virtues which ever attend the involuntary misfortunes of the race. Where the horse of Attila had been a blade of grass would not grow; but in the footprints of pestilence, famine, and earthquake the kindly charities spring into life.

The last hundred years have witnessed three peculiar visitations of God: first, the earthquake at Lisbon; next, the Asiatic cholera, as it moved slow and ghastly, with scythe of death, from the Delta of the Ganges over Bengal, Persia, Arabia, Syria, Russia, till Europe and America shuddered before the spectral reaper; and, lastly, the recent famine in Ireland, consuming with remorseless rage the population of that ill-starred land. It is impossible to estimate precisely the deadly work of cholera or famine, nor can we picture the miseries which they entailed; but the single brief event of the earthquake may be portrayed in authentic colors.

Lisbon, whose ancient origin is referred by fable to

[1] Dictionnaire Philosophique, Art. *Guerre.*

the wanderings of Ulysses, was one of the fairest cities of Europe. From the summit of seven hills it looked down upon the sea, and the bay bordered with cheerful villages,—upon the broad Tagus, expanding into a harbor ample for all the navies of Europe,—and upon a country of rare beauty, smiling with the olive and the orange, amidst grateful shadows of the cypress and the elm. A climate offering flowers in winter enhanced the peculiar advantages of position; and a numerous population thronged its narrow and irregular streets. Its forty churches, its palaces, its public edifices, its warehouses, its convents, its fortresses, its citadel, had become a boast. Not by War, not by the hand of man, were these solid structures levelled, and all these delights changed to desolation.

Lisbon, on the morning of November 1, 1755, was taken and sacked by an earthquake. The spacious warehouses were destroyed; the lordly palaces, the massive convents, the impregnable fortresses, with the lofty citadel, were toppled to the ground; and as the affrighted people sought shelter in the churches, they were crushed beneath the falling masses. Twenty thousand persons perished. Fire and robbery mingled with earthquake, and the beautiful city seemed to be obliterated. The nations of Europe were touched by this terrible catastrophe, and succor from all sides was soon offered. Within three months, English vessels appeared in the Tagus, loaded with generous contributions,—twenty thousand pounds in gold, a similar sum in silver, six thousand barrels of salted meat, four thousand barrels of butter, one thousand bags of biscuit, twelve hundred barrels of rice, ten thousand quintals of corn, besides hats, stockings, and shoes.

Such was the desolation, and such the charity, sown by the earthquake at Lisbon, — an event which, after the lapse of nearly a century, still stands without a parallel. But War shakes from its terrible folds all this desolation, without its attendant charity. Nay, more ; the Commonwealth of Nations *voluntarily agrees, each with the others*, under the grave sanctions of International Law, to invoke this desolation, in the settlement of controversies among its members, while it expressly declares that all nations, not already parties to the controversy, must abstain from any succor to the unhappy victim. High tribunals are established expressly to uphold this arbitrament, and, with unrelenting severity, to enforce its ancillary injunctions, to the end that no aid, no charity, shall come to revive the sufferer or alleviate the calamity. Vera Cruz has been bombarded and wasted by American arms. Its citadel, churches, houses, were shattered, and peaceful families at the fireside torn in mutilated fragments by the murderous bursting shell; but the English, the universal charities, which helped to restore Lisbon, were not offered to the ruined Mexican city. They could not have been offered, without offending against the *Laws of War !*

It is because men see War, in the darkness of prejudice, only as an agency of attack or defence, or as a desperate sally of wickedness, that they fail to recognize it as a form of judgment, sanctioned and *legalized* by Public Authority. Regarding it in its true character, as an *establishment* of the Commonwealth of Nations, and one of the " liberties " accorded to independent nations, it is no longer the expression merely of lawless or hasty passion, no longer the necessary incident of imperfect human nature, no longer an unavoidable, uncontrollable volcanic eruption of rage, of *vengeances and counter-vengeances*, knowing no bound; but it becomes a gigantic and monstrous Institution for the adjudication of international rights, — as if an earthquake, or other visitation of God, with its uncounted woes, and without its attendant charities, were legally invoked as Arbiter of Justice.

Surely all must unite in condemning the Arbitrament of War. The simplest may read and comprehend its enormity. Can we yet hesitate? But if War be thus odious, if it be the Duel of Nations, if it be the old surviving Trial by Battle, then must its unquestionable barbarism affect all its incidents, all its machinery, all its enginery, together with all who sanction it, and all who have any part or lot in it, — in fine, the whole vast System. It is impossible, by any discrimination, to separate the component parts. We must regard it as a whole, in its entirety. But half our work is done, if we confine ourselves to a condemnation of the Institution merely. There are all its instruments and agencies, all its adjuncts and accessaries, all its furniture and equipage, all its armaments and operations, the whole apparatus of forts, navies, armies, military display, military chaplains, and military sermons, — all together constituting, in connection with the Institution of War, what may be called the WAR SYSTEM. This System we would abolish, believing that religion, humanity, and policy require the establishment of some peaceful means for the administration of international justice, and also *the general disarming of the Christian nations*, to the end that the prodigious expenditures now absorbed by the War System may be applied to purposes of usefulness and beneficence, and that the *business* of the soldier may cease forever.

While earnestly professing this object, I desire again to exclude all question of self-defence, and to affirm the duty of upholding government, and maintaining the supremacy of the law, whether on land or sea. Admitting the necessity of Force for such purpose, *Christianity revolts at Force as the substitute for a judicial tribunal.* The example of the Great Teacher, the practice of the early disciples, the injunctions of self-denial, love, non-resistance to evil, — sometimes supposed to forbid Force in any exigency, even of self-defence, — all these must apply with unquestionable certainty to the established System of War. *Here, at least, there can be no doubt.* If the sword, in the hand of an assaulted individual, may become the instrument of sincere self-defence, if, under the sanction of a judicial tribunal, it may become the instrument of Justice also, *surely it can never be the Arbiter of Justice.* Here is a distinction vital to the cause of Peace, and never to be forgotten in presenting its claims. The cautious sword of the magistrate is unlike — oh, how unlike! — the ruthless sword of War.

The component parts of the War System may all be resolved into PREPARATIONS FOR WAR, — as court-house, jail, judges, sheriffs, constables, and *posse comitatus* are *preparations* for the administration of municipal justice. If justice were not to be administered, these would not exist. If War were not sanctioned by the Commonwealth of Nations, as the means of determining international controversies, then forts, navies, armies, military display, military chaplains, and military sermons would not exist. They would be useless and irrational, except for the rare occasions of a police,—as similar preparations would now be in Boston, for defence against our learned neighbor, Cambridge,—or in the County of Essex, for defence against its populous neighbor, the County of Middlesex,—or in the State of Massachusetts, for defence against its conterminous States, Rhode Island and New York. Only recently have men learned to question these preparations; for it is only recently that they have opened their eyes to the true character of the system, in which they are a part. *It will yet be seen, that, sustaining these, we sustain the system.* Still further, it will yet be seen, that, sustaining these, we wastefully offend against economy, and violate also the most precious sentiments of Human Brotherhood,—taking counsel of distrust, instead of love, and provoking to rivalry and enmity, instead of association and peace.

Time does not allow me to discuss the nature of these preparations; and I am the more willing to abridge what I am tempted to say, because, on another occasion, I have treated this part of the subject. But I cannot forbear to expose their inconsistency with the spirit of Christianity. From a general comprehension of the War System, we perceive the unchristian character of the preparations it encourages and requires, nay, which are the synonyms of the system, or at least its representatives. I might exhibit this character by an examination of the Laws of War, drawn from no celestial fount, but from a dark profound of Heathenism. This is unnecessary. The Constitution of our own country furnishes an illustration remarkable as a touchstone of the whole system. No town, county, or state has the "liberty" to "declare War." The exercise of any proper self-defence, arising from actual necessity, requires no such "liberty." Congress is expressly authorized to "declare War," — that is, to invoke the Arbitrament of Arms. And the Constitution proceeds to state, that all "giving aid and comfort" to the enemy shall be deemed traitors. Mark now what is said by a higher authority. "Love your enemies"; "If thine enemy hunger, feed him; if he thirst, give him drink." Under the War System, obedience to these positive injunctions may expose a person to the penalty of the highest crime known to the law. Can this be a Christian system? But so long as War exists as an Institution this terrible inconsistency must appear.

The character of these preparations is distinctly, though unconsciously, attested by the names of vessels in the British Navy. From the latest official list I select an illustrative catalogue. Most are steam-ships of recent construction. Therefore they represent the spirit of the British Navy in our day, — nay, of those War Preparations in which they play so conspicuous a part. Here are the champions: Acheron, Adder, Alecto, Avenger, Basilisk, Bloodhound, Bulldog, Crocodile, Erebus, Firebrand, Fury, Gladiator, Goliah, Gorgon, Harpy, Hecate, Hound, Jackal, Mastiff, Pluto, Rattlesnake, Revenge, Salamander, Savage, Scorpion, Scourge, Serpent, Spider, Spiteful, Spitfire, Styx, Sulphur, Tartar, Tartarus, Teazer, Terrible, Terror, Vengeance, Viper, Vixen, Virago, Volcano, Vulture, Warspite, Wildfire, Wolf, Wolverine!

Such is the Christian array of Victoria, Defender of the Faith! It may remind us of the companions of

King John, at another period of English history, — "Falkes the Merciless," "Mauleon the Bloody," "Walter Buck, the Assassin,"[1] — or of that Pagan swarm, the savage warriors of our own continent, with the names of Black-Hawk, Man-Killer, and Wild-Boar. Well might they seem to be

> "all the grisly legions that troop
> Under the sooty flag of Acheron!"

As a people is known by its laws, as a man is known by the company he keeps, as a tree is known by its fruits, so is the War System fully and unequivocally known by the Laws of War, by its diabolical ministers, typical of its preparations, and by all the accursed fruits of War. Controlled by such a code, employing such representatives, sustained by such agencies, animated by such Furies, and producing such fruits of tears and bitterness, it must be open to question. Tell me not that it is sanctioned by any religion except of Mars; do not enroll the Saviour and his disciples in its Satanic squadron; do not invoke the Gospel of Peace, in profane vindication of an *Institution*, which, by its own too palpable confession, exists in defiance of the most cherished Christian sentiments; do not dishonor the Divine Spirit of gentleness, forbearance, love, by supposing that it can ever enter into this System, except to change its whole nature and name, to cast out the devils which possess it, and fill its gigantic energies with the inspiration of Beneficence.

I need say little of military chaplains or military sermons. Like the steamships of the Navy, they come under the head of Preparations. They are part of the War System. They belong to the same school with priests of former times, who held the picture of the

[1] Matthew Paris, Historia Major, p. 274.

Prince of Peace before the barbarous champion of the Duel, saying, "Sir Knight, behold here the remembrance of our Lord and Redeemer, Jesus Christ, who willingly gave his most precious body to death in order to save us. Now ask of him mercy, and pray that on this day he may be willing to aid you, if you have right, for he is the sovereign judge."[1] They belong to the same school with English prelates, who, in the name of the Prince of Peace, consecrate banners to flaunt in remote war, saying, "Be thou in the midst of our hosts, as thou wast in the plains of India and in the field of Waterloo; and may these banners, which we bless and consecrate this day, lead them ever on to glorious victory." No judgment of such appeals can be more severe than that of Plato, who called men "most impious," who by prayer and sacrifice thought to propitiate the Gods towards slaughter and outrages upon justice, — thus, says the heathen philosopher, making those pure beings the accomplices of their crimes by sharing with them the spoil, as the wolves leave something to the dogs, that these may allow them to ravage the sheepfold.[2] Consenting to degrade the "blessedness" of the Gospel to the "impiety" of the War System, our clergy follow long established custom, without considering the true character of the system whose ministers they become. Their apology will be, that "they know not what they do."

Again I repeat, so long as the War System prevails under the sanction of International Law, these painful incongruities will be apparent. They belong to a system so essentially irrational, that all the admitted virtues of many of its agents cannot save it from judgment.

1 Cauchy, Du Duel, Liv. I. Seconde Époque, Ch. III. Tom. I. p. 74

2 Plato, Laws, Book X. ch. 13, 14.

Here the question occurs, Is the *Militia* obnoxious to the same condemnation? So far as the militia constitutes part of the War System, it is impossible to distinguish it from the rest of the system. It is a portion of the extensive apparatus provided for the determination of international disputes. From this character it borrows the unwholesome attractions of War, while disporting itself, like the North American Indian, in finery and parade. Of the latter feature I shall speak only incidentally. If War be a Christian institution, those who act as its agents should shroud themselves in colors congenial with their dreadful trade. With sorrow and solemnity, not with gladness and pomp, they should proceed to their melancholy office. The Jew Shylock exposes the mockery of street-shows in Venice with a sarcasm not without echo here:—

"When you hear the drum,
And the vile squeaking of the wry-necked fife,
Clamber not you up to the casements then,
Nor thrust your head into the public street,
To gaze on Christian fools with varnished faces;
But stop my house's ears,— I mean my casements:
Let not the sound of shallow foppery enter
My sober house."

Not as part of the War System, but only as an agent for preserving domestic peace, and for sustaining the law, is the militia entitled to support. And here arises the important practical question,—interesting to opponents of the War System as to lovers of order,—whether the same good object may not be accomplished by an agent less expensive, less cumbersome, and less tardy, forming no part of the War System, and therefore in no respect liable to the doubts encountered by the militia. Supporters of the militia do not disguise its growing unpopularity. The eminent Military Commissioners of Massachusetts, to whom in 1847 was referred the duty of arranging a system for its organization and discipline, confess that there is "either a defect of power in the State government to an efficient and salutary militia organization, or *the absence of a public sentiment in its favor*, and a consequent unwillingness to submit to the requirements of service which alone can sustain it"; and they add, that they "have been met, in the performance of their task, with information, from all quarters, of its general neglect, and of the certain and rapid declension of the militia in numbers and efficiency."[1] And the Adjutant-General of Massachusetts, after alluding to the different systems which have fallen into disuse, remarks, that "the fate of each system is indicative of public sentiment; and until public sentiment changes, *no military system whatever can be sustained in the State*."[2] Nor is this condition of public sentiment for the first time noticed. It was remarked by the Commissioners charged by the Legislature with this subject as long ago as 1839. In their Report they say, "It is enough to know that all attempts, hitherto, to uphold the system, in its original design of organization, discipline, and subordination, *are at last brought to an unsuccessful issue*."[3]

None familiar with public opinion in our country, and particularly in Massachusetts, will question the accuracy of these official statements. It is true that there is an indisposition to assume the burdens of the militia. Its offices and dignities have ceased to be an object of general regard. This, certainly, must be founded in the con-

1 Mass. Senate Documents, 1848: Doc. No. 13, pp. 4, 5.
2 Ibid., Doc. No. 15, p. 23.
3 Mass. House Documents, 1839: Doc. No. 6, p. 14.

viction that it is no longer necessary or useful; for it is not customary with the people of Massachusetts to decline occasions of service necessary or useful to the community. The interest in military celebrations has decayed. Nor should it be concealed that there are large numbers whose honest sentiments are not of mere indifference, who regard with aversion the fanfaronade of a militia muster, who not a little question the influence upon those taking part in it or even witnessing it, and look with regret upon the expenditure of money and time.

If such be the condition of the public mind, the Government must recognize it. The soul of all effective laws is an animating public sentiment. This gives vitality to what else would be a dead letter. In vain enact what is not inspired by this spirit. No skill in the device of the system, no penalties, no bounties even, can uphold it. Happily, we are not without remedy. If State Legislatures are disposed to provide a substitute for this questionable or offensive agency, as conservator of domestic quiet, it is entirely within their competency. Let the general voice demand the *substitute.*

Among powers reserved to States, under the National Constitution, is that of *Internal Police.* Within its territorial limits, a State has municipal power to be exercised according to its own will. In the exercise of this will, it may establish a system, congenial with the sentiment of the age, to supply the place of the militia, as guardian of municipal quiet and instrument of the law. This system may consist of unpaid volunteers, or special constables, like fire companies in the country, or of hired men, enrolled for this particular purpose, and always within call, like fire companies in Boston. They need not be clad in showy costume, or subjected to all the peculiarities of military drill. A system so simple, practical, efficient, unostentatious, and cheap, especially as compared with the militia, would be in harmony with existing sentiment, while it could not fail to remedy the evils sometimes feared from present neglect of the militia. Many attempts have been made to reform the militia. *It remains, that a proper effort should be made to provide a substitute for it.*

An eminent English jurist of the last century, — renowned as scholar also, — Sir William Jones, — in a learned and ingenious tract, entitled "An Inquiry into the Legal Mode of Suppressing Riots, with a Constitutional Plan of Future Defence," after developing the obligations of the citizen, under the Common Law, as part of the Power of the County, presents a system of organization independent of the military. It is not probable that this system would be acceptable in all its details to the people of our community, but there is one of his recommendations which seems to harmonize with existing sentiment. "Let companies," he says, "be taught, in the most private and orderly manner, for two or three hours early every morning, until they are competently skilled in the use of their arms; *let them not unnecessarily march through streets or high-roads, nor make any the least military parade, but consider themselves entirely as part of the civil state.*"[1] Thus is the soldier kept out of sight, while the citizen becomes manifest; and this is the true idea of republican government. In the midst of arms the laws are silent. Not "arms," but "laws," should command our homage and quicken the patriotism of the land.

1 Works, Vol. VIII. p. 494.

While divorcing the Police from the unchristian and barbarous War System, I confess the vital importance of maintaining law and order. Life and property should be guarded. Peace must be preserved in our streets. And it is the duty of Government to provide such means as are most expedient, if those established are in any respect inadequate, or uncongenial with the Spirit of the Age.

I must not close this exposition without an attempt to display the inordinate expenditure by which the War System is maintained. And here figures appear to lose their functions. They seem to pant, as they toil vainly to represent the enormous sums consumed in this unparalleled waste. Our own experience, measured by the concerns of common life, does not allow us adequately to conceive the sums. Like the periods of geological time, or the distances of the fixed stars, they baffle imagination. Look, for an instant, at the cost to us of this system. Without any allowance for the loss sustained by the withdrawal of active men from productive industry, we find, that, from the adoption of the National Constitution down to 1848, there has been paid directly from the National Treasury, —

For the Army and Fortifications,	$475,936,475
For the Navy and its operations,	209,994,428
	$685,930,903[1]

This immense amount is not all. Regarding the militia as part of the War System, we must add a moderate estimate for its cost during this period, being, according

1 American Almanac, 1849, p. 162. United States Executive Documents: 28th Cong. 1st Sess., No. 15, pp. 1018-19; 35th Cong. 1st Sess., No. 60, pp. 6, 7.

to the calculations of an able and accurate economist, as much as $ 1,500,000,000.[1] The whole presents an inconceivable sum-total of *more than two thousand millions* of dollars already dedicated by our Government to the support of the War System, — nearly twelve times as much as was set apart, during the same period, to all other purposes whatsoever!

Look now at the Commonwealth of Europe. I do not intend to speak of War Debts, under whose accumulated weight these nations are now pressed to earth, being the terrible legacy of the Past. I refer directly to the existing War System, the establishment of the Present. According to recent calculations, its annual cost is not less than a *thousand millions* of dollars. Endeavor, for a moment, by comparison with other interests, to grapple with this sum.

It is larger than the entire profit of all the commerce and manufactures of the world.

It is larger than all the expenditure for agricultural labor, producing the food of man, upon the whole face of the globe.

It is larger, by a hundred millions, than the value of all the exports sent forth by all the nations of the earth.

It is larger, by more than five hundred millions, than the value of all the shipping belonging to the civilized world.

It is larger, by nine hundred and ninety-seven millions, than the annual combined charities of Europe and America for preaching the Gospel to the Heathen.

Yes! the Commonwealth of Christian Nations, in-

[1] Jay's War and Peace, p. 13, note; and "True Grandeur of Nations," *ante*, Vol. I. p. 79.

cluding our own country, appropriates, without hesitation, as a matter of course, upwards of a thousand millions of dollars annually to the maintenance of the War System, and vaunts its three millions of dollars, laboriously collected, for diffusing the light of the Gospel in foreign lands! With untold prodigality of cost, it perpetuates the worst Heathenism of War, while, by charities insignificant in comparison, it doles to the Heathen a message of Peace. At home it breeds and fattens a cloud of éagles and vultures, trained to swoop upon the land; to all the Gentiles across the sea it dismisses a solitary dove.

Still further: every ship-of-war that floats costs more than a well-endowed college.

Every sloop-of-war that floats costs more than the largest public library in our country.

It is sometimes said, by persons yet in leading-strings of inherited prejudice, and with little appreciation of the true safety afforded by the principles of Peace, that all these comprehensive preparations are needed for protection against enemies from abroad. Wishing to present the cause without any superfluous question on what are called, apologetically, "defensive wars," let me say, in reply, — *and here all can unite,* — that, if these preparations are needed at any time, according to the aggressive martial interpretation of self-defence in its exigencies, there is much reason to believe it is because the unchristian spirit in which they have their birth, lowering and scowling in the very names of the ships, provokes the danger, — as the presence of a bravo might challenge the attack he was hired to resist.

Frederick of Prussia, sometimes called the Great, in

a singular spirit of mingled openness and effrontery, deliberately left on record, most instructively prominent among the real reasons for his war upon Maria Theresa, *that he had troops always ready to act.* Thus did these *Preparations* unhappily become, as they too often show themselves, *incentives* to War. Lord Brougham justly dwells on this confession as a lesson of history. Human nature, as manifest in the conduct of individuals or communities, has its lesson also. The fatal War Spirit is born of these preparations, out of which it springs full-armed. Here also is its great aliment; here are the seeds of the very evil it is sometimes vainly supposed to avert. Let it never be forgotten, let it be treasured as a solemn warning, that, by the confession of Frederick himself, it was the possession of *troops always ready to act* that helped to inspire that succession of bloody wars, which, first pouncing upon Silesia, mingled at last with the strifes of England and France, even in distant colonies across the Atlantic, ranging the savages of the forest under hostile European banners.[1]

But I deny that these preparations are needed for just self-defence. It is difficult, if not impossible, to suppose any such occasion in the Fraternity of Christian Nations, *if War ceases to be an established Arbitrament,*

[1] "Que l'on joigne à ces considérations *des troupes toujours prêtes d'agir*, mon épargne bien remplie, et la vivacité de mon caractère: c'étaient les raisons que j'avais de faire la guerre à Marie-Thérèse, reine de Bohême et d'Hongrie." These are the very words of Frederick, deliberately written in his own account of the war. Voltaire, on revising the work, dishonestly struck out this important confession, but preserved a copy, which afterwards appeared in his own Memoirs. Lord Brougham, in his sketch of Voltaire, says that "the passage thus erased and thus preserved is extremely curious, and for honesty or impudence has no parallel in the history of warriors." — Brougham, Lives of Men of Letters, *Voltaire*, p. 59.

or if any state is so truly great as to decline its umpirage. There is no such occasion among the towns, counties, or states of our extended country; nor is there any such occasion among the counties of Great Britain, or among the provinces of France; but the same good-will, the same fellowship, and the same ties of commerce, which unite towns, counties, states, and provinces, are fast drawing the whole Commonwealth of Nations into similar communion. France and England, so long regarded as natural enemies, are now better known to each other than only a short time ago were different provinces of the former kingdom. And there is now a closer intimacy in business and social intercourse between Great Britain and our own country than there was at the beginning of the century between Massachusetts and Virginia.

Admitting that an enemy might approach our shores for piracy or plunder or conquest, who can doubt that the surest protection would be found, not in the waste of long-accumulating preparation, not in idle fortresses along the coast, built at a cost far surpassing all our lighthouses and all our colleges, but in the intelligence, union, and pacific repose of good men, with the unbounded resources derived from uninterrupted devotion to productive industry? I think it may be assumed as beyond question, according to the testimony of political economy, that the people who spend most sparingly in Preparations for War, all other things being equal, must possess the most enduring means of actual self-defence at home, on their own soil, before their own hearths, if any such melancholy alternative should occur. Consider the prodigious sums, exceeding in all two thousand millions of dollars, squandered by the United States, since the adoption of the National Constitution, for the sake of the War System. Had such means been devoted to railroads and canals, schools and colleges, the country would possess, at the present moment, an accumulated material power grander far than any it now boasts. There is another power, of more unfailing temper, which would not be wanting. Overflowing with intelligence, with charity, with civilization, with all that constitutes a generous state, ours would be peaceful triumphs, transcending all yet achieved, and surrounding the land with an invincible self-defensive might, while the unfading brightness of a new era made the glory of War impossible. Well does the poet say with persuasive truth, —

> "What constitutes a State?
> Not high-raised battlement or labored mound,
> Thick wall or moated gate;
> Not cities proud with spires and turrets crowned;
> Not bays and broad-armed ports,
> Where, laughing at the storm, rich navies ride:
> No: MEN, high-minded MEN."[1]

Such men will possess a Christian greatness, rendering them unable to do an injury; while their character, instinct with all the guardian virtues, must render their neighbors unable to do an injury to them.

The injunction, "In time of Peace prepare for War," is of Heathen origin.[2] As a rule of international conduct, it is very questionable in a Christian age, being vindicated on two grounds only: first, by assuming that the Arbitrament of War is the proper tribunal for international controversies, and therefore the War Sys-

[1] Sir William Jones, Ode in Imitation of Alcæus: Works, Vol. X. p. 389.

[2] True Grandeur of Nations, *ante*, Vol. I., pp. 97, seqq.

tem is to be maintained and strengthened, as the essential means of international justice; or, secondly, by assuming the rejected dogma of an Atheist philosopher, Hobbes, that War is the natural state of man. Whatever may be the infirmities of our passions, it is plain that the natural state of man, assuring the highest happiness, and to which he tends by an irresistible heavenly attraction, is Peace. This is true of communities and nations, as of individuals. The proper rule is, In time of Peace cultivate the arts of Peace. So doing, you will render the country truly strong and truly great; not by arousing the passions of War, not by nursing men to the business of blood, not by converting the land into a flaming arsenal, a magazine of gunpowder, or an "infernal machine," just ready to explode, but by dedicating its whole energies to productive and beneficent works.

The incongruity of this system may be illustrated by an example. Look into the life of that illustrious philosopher, John Locke, and you will find, that, in the journal of his tour through France, describing the arches of the amphitheatre at Nismes, he says, "In all those arches, to support the walls over the passage where you go round, there is a stone laid, about twenty inches or two feet square, and about six times the length of *my sword, which was near about a philosophical yard long*."[1] Who is not struck with the unseemly incongruity of the exhibition, as he sees the author of the "Essay concerning Human Understanding" travelling with a sword by his side? But here the philosopher only followed the barbarous custom of his time. Individuals then

[1] King's Life of Locke, Vol. I. p. 99.

lived in the same relations towards each other which now characterize nations. The War System had not yet entirely retreated from Municipal Law and Custom, to find its last citadel and temple in the Law and Custom of Nations. Do not forget, that, at the present moment, our own country, the great author, among the nations, of a new Essay concerning Human Understanding, not only travels with a sword by the side, like John Locke, but lives encased in complete armor, burdensome to limbs and costly to treasury.

Condemning the War System as barbarous and most wasteful, the token and relic of a society alien to Christian civilization, we except the Navy, so far as necessary in arrest of pirates, of traffickers in human flesh, and generally in preserving the police of the sea. But it is difficult for the unprejudiced mind to regard the array of fortifications and of standing armies otherwise than obnoxious to the condemnation aroused by the War System. Fortifications are instruments, and standing armies are hired champions, in the great Duel of Nations.

Here I quit this part of the subject. Sufficient has been said to expose the War System of the Commonwealth of Nations. It stands before us, a colossal image of International Justice, *with the sword, but without the scales,*— like a hideous Mexican idol, besmeared with human blood, and surrounded by the sickening stench of human sacrifice. But this image, which seems to span the continents, while it rears aloft its flashing form of brass and gold, hiding far in the clouds "the round and top of sovereignty," can be laid low; for its feet are clay.

II.

I COME now to the means by which the War System can be overthrown. Here I shall unfold the tendencies and examples of nations, and the sacred efforts of individuals, constituting the Peace Movement, now ready to triumph, — with practical suggestions on our duties to this cause, and a concluding glance at the barbarism of Military Glory. In this review I cannot avoid details incident to a fruitfulness of topics; but I shall try to introduce nothing not bearing directly on the subject.

Civilization now writhes in travail and torment, and asks for liberation from oppressive sway. Like the slave under a weary weight of chains, it raises its exhausted arms, and pleads for the angel Deliverer. And, lo! the beneficent angel comes, — not like the Grecian God of Day, with vengeful arrows to slay the destructive Python, — not like the Archangel Michael, with potent spear to transfix Satan, — but with words of gentleness and cheer, saying to all nations, and to all children of men, "Ye are all brothers, of *one* flesh, *one* fold, *one* shepherd, children of *one* Father, heirs to *one* happiness. By your own energies, through united fraternal endeavor, will the tyranny of War be overthrown, and its Juggernaut in turn be crushed to earth."

In this spirit, and with this encouragement, we must labor for that grand and final object, watchword of all ages, the Unity of the Human Family. Not in benevolence, but in selfishness, has Unity been sought in times past, — not to promote the happiness of all, but to establish the dominion of one. It was the mad lust of power which carried Alexander from conquest to conquest, till he boasted that the whole world was one empire, with the Macedonian phalanx as citadel. The same passion animated Rome, till, at last, while Christ lay in a manger, this single city swayed a broader empire than that of Alexander. The Gospel, in its simple narrative, says, "And it came to pass in those days that there went out a decree from Cæsar Augustus that *all the world* should be taxed." History recalls the exile of Ovid, who, falling under the displeasure of the same emperor, was condemned to close his life in melancholy longings for Rome, far away in Pontus, on the Euxine Sea. With singular significance, these two contemporaneous incidents reveal the universality of Roman dominion, stretching from Britain to Parthia. The mighty empire crumbled, to be reconstructed for a brief moment, in part by Charlemagne, in part by Tamerlane. In our own age, Napoleon made a last effort for Unity founded on Force. And now, from his utterances at St. Helena, the expressed wisdom of his unparalleled experience, comes the remarkable confession, worthy of constant memory: "The more I study the world, the more am I convinced of the inability of brute force to create anything durable." From the sepulchre of Napoleon, now sleeping on the banks of the Seine, surrounded by the trophies of battle, nay, more, from the sepulchres of all these departed empires, may be heard the words, "They that take the sword shall perish by the sword."

Unity is the longing and tendency of Humanity: not the enforced Unity of military power; not the Unity of might triumphant over right; not the Unity of Inequality; not the Unity which occupied the soul of Dante, when, in his treatise *De Monarchia*, the earliest political work of modern times, he strove to show that all the world belonged to a single ruler, the successor of the Roman Emperor: not these; but the voluntary Unity of nations in fraternal labor; the Unity promised, when it was said, "There is neither Jew nor Greek, there is neither bond nor free, there is neither male nor female, for ye are all one in Christ Jesus"; the Unity which has filled the delighted vision of good men, prophets, sages, and poets, in times past; the Unity which, in our own age, prompted Béranger, the incomparable lyric of France, in an immortal ode, to salute the Holy Alliance of the Peoples,[1] summoning them in all lands, and by whatever names they may be called, French, English, Belgian, German, Russian, to give each other the hand, that the useless thunderbolts of War may all be quenched, and Peace sow the earth with gold, with flowers, and with corn; the Unity which prompted an early American diplomatist and poet to anticipate the time when nations shall meet in Congress, —

"To give each realm its limit and its laws,
Bid the last breath of dire contention cease,
And bind all regions in the leagues of Peace;
Bid one great empire, with extensive sway,
Spread with the sun, and bound the walks of day,
One centred system, one all-ruling soul,
Live through the parts, and regulate the whole";[2]

the Unity which inspired our contemporary British poet of exquisite genius, Alfred Tennyson, to hail the certain day, —

"When the war-drum throb no longer, and the battle-flags be furled,
In the Parliament of Man, the Federation of the World."[3]

1 "Peuples, formez une sainte alliance,
Et donnez-vous la main."
La Sainte Alliance des Peuples.

2 Barlow, Vision of Columbus, Book IX. 432-438.

3 Locksley Hall.

Such is Unity in the bond of Peace. The common good and mutual consent are its enduring base, Justice and Love its animating soul. These alone can give permanence to combinations of men, whether in states or confederacies. Here is the vital elixir of nations, the true philosopher's stone of divine efficacy to enrich the civilization of mankind. So far as these are neglected or forgotten, will the people, though under one apparent head, fail to be really united. So far as these are regarded, will the people, within the sphere of their influence, constitute one body, and be inspired by one spirit. And just in proportion as these find recognition from individuals and from nations will War be impossible.

Not in vision, nor in promise only, is this Unity discerned. Voluntary associations, confederacies, leagues, coalitions, and congresses of nations, though fugitive and limited in influence, all attest the unsatisfied desires of men solicitous for union, while they foreshadow the means by which it may be permanently accomplished. Of these I will enumerate a few. 1. The *Amphictyonic Council*, embracing at first twelve, and finally thirty-one communities, was established about the year 1100 before Christ. Each sent two deputies, and had two votes in the Council, which was empowered to restrain the violence of hostility among the associates. 2. Next comes the *Achæan League*, founded at a very early period, and renewed in the year 281 before Christ. Each member was independent, and yet all together constituted one inseparable body. So great was the fame of their justice and probity, that the Greek cities of Italy were glad to invite their peaceful arbitration. 3. Passing over other confederacies of Antiquity, I mention next the *Hanseatic League*, begun in the twelfth century, completed in the middle of the thirteenth, and comprising at one time no less than eighty-five cities. A system of International Law was adopted in their general assemblies, and also *courts of arbitration, to determine controversies among the cities.* The decrees of these courts were enforced by placing the condemned city under the ban, a sentence equivalent to excommunication. 4. At a later period, other cities and nobles of Germany entered into alliance and association for mutual protection, under various names, as *the League of the Rhine*, and *the League of Suabia.* 5. To these I add the combination of *Armed Neutrality* in 1780, uniting, in declared support of certain principles, a large cluster of nations, — Russia, France, Spain, Holland, Sweden, Denmark, Prussia, and the United States. 6. And still further, I refer to Congresses at Westphalia, Utrecht, Aix-la-Chapelle, and Vienna, after the wasteful struggles of War, to arrange terms of Peace and to arbitrate between nations.

These examples, belonging to the Past, reveal tendencies and capacities. Other instances, having the effect of living authority, show practically how the War System may be set aside. There is, *first*, the Swiss Republic, or *Helvetic Union*, which, beginning so long ago as 1308, has preserved Peace among its members during the greater part of five centuries. Speaking of this Union, Vattel said, in the middle of the last century, "The Swiss have had the precaution, in all their alliances among themselves, and even in those they have contracted with the neighboring powers, *to agree beforehand on the manner in which their disputes were to be submitted to arbitrators, in case they could not adjust them in an amicable manner.*" And this publicist proceeds to testify that "this wise precaution has not a little contributed to maintain the Helvetic Republic in that flourishing condition which secures its liberty, and renders it respectable throughout Europe."[1] Since these words were written, there have been many changes in the Swiss Constitution; but its present Federal System, established on the downfall of Napoleon, confirmed in 1830, and now embracing twenty-five different States, provides that differences among the States shall be referred to "special arbitration." This is an instructive example. But, *secondly*, our own happy country furnishes one yet more so. The United States of America are a National Union of thirty different States, — each having peculiar interests, — in pursuance of a Constitution, established in 1788, which not only provides a high tribunal for the adjudication of controversies between the States, but expressly *disarms* the individual States, declaring that "*no State shall, without the consent of Congress, keep troops or ships of war in time of peace, or engage in war, unless actually invaded, or in such imminent danger as will not admit of delay.*" A *third* example, not unlike that of our own country, is the *Confederation of Germany*, composed of thirty-eight sovereignties, who, by reciprocal stipulation in their Act of Union, on the 8th of June, 1815, deprived each sovereignty of the *right of war* with its confederates. The words of this stipulation, which, like those of the Constitution of the United States, might furnish a model to the Commonwealth of Nations, are as follows: "*The Confederate States likewise engage under no pretext to make war upon*

[1] Law of Nations, Book II. ch. 18, § 329.

one another, nor to pursue their differences by force of arms, but to submit them to the Diet. The latter shall endeavor to mediate between the parties by means of a commission. Should this not prove successful, and a judicial decision become necessary, provision shall be made therefor through a well-organized Court of Arbitration, to which the litigants shall submit themselves without appeal." [1]

Such are authentic, well-defined examples. This is not all. It is in the order of Providence, that individuals, families, tribes, and nations should tend, by means of association, to a final Unity. A law of mutual attraction, or affinity, first exerting its influence upon smaller bodies, draws them by degrees into well-established fellowship, and then, continuing its power, fuses the larger bodies into nations; and nations themselves, stirred by this same sleepless energy, are now moving towards that grand system of combined order which will complete the general harmony: —

> "Spiritus intus alit, totamque infusa per artus
> Mens agitat molem, et magno se corpore miscet." [2]

History bears ample testimony to the potency of this attraction. Modern Europe, in its early periods, was filled with petty lordships, or communities constituting so many distinct units, acknowledging only a vague nationality, and maintaining, as we have already seen, the "liberty" to fight with each other. The great nations of our day have grown and matured into their present form by the gradual absorption of these political bodies.

[1] Acte pour la Constitution Fédérative de l'Allemagne du 8 Juin, 1815, Art. XI. par. 4: Archives Diplomatiques, Vol. IV. p. 15.

[2] Æneid, Lib. VI. 726, 727.

Territories, once possessing an equivocal and turbulent independence, feel new power and happiness in peaceful association. Spain, composed of races dissimilar in origin, religion, and government, slowly ascended by progressive combinations among principalities and provinces, till at last, in the fifteenth century, by the crowning union of Castile and Aragon, the whole country, with its various sovereignties, was united under one common rule. Germany once consisted of more than three hundred different principalities, each with the *right of war*. These slowly coalesced, forming larger principalities; till at last the whole complex aggregation of states, embracing abbeys, bishoprics, archbishoprics, bailiwicks, counties, duchies, electorates, margraviates, and free imperial cities, was gradually resolved into the present Confederation, where each state expressly renounces the *right of war* with its associates. France has passed through similar changes. By a power of assimilation, in no nation so strongly marked, she has absorbed the various races and sovereignties once filling her territory with violence and conflict, and has converted them all to herself. The Roman or Iberian of Provence, the indomitable Celtic race, the German of Alsace, have all become Frenchmen,— while the various provinces, once inspired by such hostile passions, Brittany and Normandy, Franche-Comté and Burgundy, Gascony and Languedoc, Provence and Dauphiné, are now blended in one powerful, united nation. Great Britain, too, shows the influence of the same law. The many hostile principalities of England were first merged in the Heptarchy; and these seven kingdoms became *one* under the Saxon Egbert. Wales, forcibly attached to England under Edward the First, at last assimilated with her conqueror; Ireland, after a protracted resistance, was absorbed under Edward the Third, and at a later day, after a series of bitter struggles, was united, I do not say how successfully, under the Imperial Parliament; Scotland was connected with England by the accession of James the First to the throne of the Tudors, and these two countries, which had so often encountered in battle, were joined together under Queen Anne, by an act of peaceful legislation.

Thus has the tendency to Unity predominated over independent sovereignties and states, slowly conducting the constant process of crystallization. This cannot be arrested. The next stage must be the peaceful association of the Christian nations. In this anticipation we but follow analogies of the material creation, as seen in the light of chemical or geological science. Everywhere Nature is busy with combinations, exerting an occult incalculable power, drawing elements into new relations of harmony, uniting molecule with molecule, atom with atom, and, by progressive change, in the lapse of time, producing new structural arrangements. Look still closer, and the analogy continues. At first we detect the operation of cohesion, rudely acting upon particles near together,—then subtler influences, slowly imparting regularity of form,—while heat, electricity, and potent chemical affinities conspire in the work. As yet there is only an incomplete body. *Light* now exerts its mysterious powers, and all assumes an organized form. So it is with mankind. First appears the rude cohesion of early ages, acting only upon individuals near together. Slowly the work proceeds. But time and space, the great obstructions, if not annihilated, are now subdued, giving free scope to the powerful affinities of civilization. At last, light, thrice holy light, in whose glad beams are knowledge, justice, and beneficence, with empyrean sway will combine those separate and distracted elements into one organized system.

Thus much for examples and tendencies. In harmony with these are *efforts of individuals*, extending through ages, and strengthening with time, till now at last they swell into a voice that must be heard. A rapid glance will show the growth of the cause we have met to welcome. Far off in the writings of the early Fathers we learn the duty and importance of Universal Peace. Here I might accumulate texts, each an authority, while you listened to Justin Martyr, Irenæus, Tertullian, Origen, Augustine, Aquinas. How beautiful it appears in the teachings of St. Augustine! How comprehensive the rules of Aquinas, who spoke with the authority of Philosophy and the Church, when he said, in phrase worthy of constant repetition, that the perfection of joy is Peace![1] But the rude hoof of War trampled down these sparks of generous truth, destined to flame forth at a later day. In the fifteenth century, *The good Man of Peace* was described in that work of unexampled circulation, translated into all modern tongues, and republished more than a thousand times, "The Imitation of Christ," by Thomas-à-Kempis.[2] A little later the cause found important support from the pen of a great scholar, the gentle and learned Erasmus. At last it obtained a specious advocacy from the throne. Henry the Fourth,

1 "*Perfectio gaudii est pax.*" — Aquinas, Summa Theologica, Prima Secundæ, Quæst. LXX., Art. III. Concl.

2 De Imitatione Christi, Lib. II. cap. 3.

of France, with the coöperation of his eminent minister, Sully, conceived the beautiful scheme of blending the Christian nations in one confederacy, with a high tribunal for the decision of controversies between them, and had drawn into his plan Queen Elizabeth, of England. All was arrested by the dagger of Ravaillac. This gay and gallant monarch was little penetrated by the divine sentiment of Peace; for at his death he was gathering materials for fresh War; and it is too evident that the scheme of a European Congress was prompted less by comprehensive humanity than by a selfish ambition to humble the House of Austria. Even with this drawback it did great good, by holding aloft before Christendom the exalted idea of a tribunal for the Commonwealth of Nations.

Universal Peace was not to receive thus early the countenance of Government. Meanwhile private efforts began to multiply. Grotius, in his wonderful work on "The Rights of War and Peace," while lavishing learning and genius on the Arbitrament of War, bears testimony in favor of a more rational tribunal. His virtuous nature, wishing to save mankind from the scourge of War, foreshadowed an Amphictyonic Council. "It would be useful, and in some sort necessary," he says, — in language which, if carried out practically, would sweep away the War System and all the *Laws of War*, — "to have Congresses of the Christian Powers, where differences might be determined by the judgment of those not interested in them, and means found to constrain parties into acceptance of peace on just conditions." [1] To the discredit of his age, these moderate words, so much in harmony with his other effort for the union

1 De Jure Belli ac Pacis, Lib. II. cap. 23, § 8.

of Christian sects, were derided, and the eminent expounder was denounced as rash, visionary, and impracticable. The sentiment in which they had their origin found other forms of utterance. Before the close of the seventeenth century, Nicole, the friend of Pascal, belonging to the fellowship of Port-Royal, and one of the highest names in the Church of France, gave to the world a brief "Treatise on the Means of preserving Peace among Men,"[1] which Voltaire, with exaggerated praise, terms "a masterpiece, to which nothing equal has been left to us by Antiquity." Next appeared a little book, which is now a bibiographical curiosity, entitled "The New Cineas,"[2] — after the pacific adviser of Pyrrhus, the warrior king of Epirus, — where the humane author counsels sovereigns to govern in Peace, submitting their differences to an established tribunal. In Germany, at the close of the seventeenth century, as we learn from Leibnitz, who mentions the preceding authority also, a retired general, who had commanded armies, the Landgrave Ernest of Hesse Rhinfels, in a work entitled "The Discreet Catholic," suggested a plan for Perpetual Peace by means of a tribunal established by associate sovereigns.[3] England testified also by William Penn, who adopted and enforced what he called the "great design"

1 Traité des Moyens de conserver la Paix avec les Hommes: Essais de Morale, Tom. I. pp. 192-318. This little treatise has been printed in a recent edition of the *Pensées* of Pascal. Notwithstanding this great company, and the praise of Voltaire in his *Écrivains du Siècle de Louis XIV.*, the reader of our day will be disappointed. See Hallam, Introduction to the Literature of Europe, Part IV. ch. 4, Vol. III. p. 393.

2 Le Nouveau Cynée, ou Discours des Occasions et Moyens d'establir une Paix générale et la Liberté du Commerce par tout le Monde: Paris, 1623. A copy, found in one of the stalls of Paris, is now before me.

3 Leibnitz. Observations sur le Projet d'une Paix Perpétuelle de l'Abbé de S. Pierre: Opera (ed. Dutens), Tom. V. pp. 56, 57

of Henry the Fourth. In a work entitled "An Essay towards the Present and Future Peace of Europe," the enlightened Quaker proposed a Diet, or Sovereign Assembly, into which the princes of Europe should enter, as men enter into society, for the love of peace and order, — that its object should be justice, and that all differences not terminated by embassies should be brought before this tribunal, whose judgment should be so far binding, that, in the event of contumacy, it should be enforced by the united powers.[1] Thus, by writings, as also by illustrious example in Pennsylvania, did Penn show himself the friend of Peace.

These were soon followed in France by the untiring labors of the good Abbé Saint-Pierre, — the most devoted among the apostles of Peace, and not to be confounded with the eloquent and eccentric Bernardin de Saint-Pierre, author of "Paul and Virginia," who, at a later day, beautifully painted the true Fraternity of Nations.[2] Of a genius less artistic and literary, the Abbé consecrated a whole life, crowned with venerable years, to the improvement of mankind. There was no humane cause he did not espouse: now it was the poor; now it was education; and now it was to exhibit the grandeur and sacredness of human nature; but he was especially filled with the idea of Universal Peace, and the importance of teaching nations, not less than individuals, the duty of doing as they would be done by. This was his passion, and it was elaborately presented in a work of three volumes, entitled "The Project of Per-

[1] Clarkson, Life of William Penn, Ch. VI. Vol. II. pp. 82 - 85.

[2] Harmonies de la Nature: Œuvres, Tom. X. p. 138. Vœux d'un Solitaire: Ibid., Tom. XI. p. 168.

petual Peace,"[1] where he proposes a Diet or Congress of Sovereigns, for the adjudication of international controversies without resort to War. Throughout his voluminous writings he constantly returns to this project, which was a perpetual vision, and records his regret that Newton and Descartes had not devoted their exalted genius to the study and exposition of the laws determining the welfare of men and nations, believing that they might have succeeded in organizing Peace. He dwells often on the beauty of Christian precepts in government, and the true glory of beneficence, while he exposes the vanity of military renown, and does not hesitate to question that false glory which procured for Louis the Fourteenth the undeserved title of Great, echoed by flattering courtiers and a barbarous world. The French language owes to him the word *Bienfaisance;* and D'Alembert said "it was right he should have invented the word who practised so largely the virtue it expresses."[2]

Though thus of benevolence all compact, Saint-Pierre was not the favorite of his age. A profligate minister, Cardinal Dubois, ecclesiastical companion of a vicious regent in the worst excesses, condemned his efforts in a phrase of satire, as "the dreams of a good man." The pen of La Bruyère wantoned in a petty portrait of per-

1 Le Projet de Paix Perpétuelle. — A collection of the works of Saint-Pierre, in fourteen volumes, entitled *Œuvres de Politique*, appeared at Amsterdam in the middle of the last century. But this collection is not complete; I have several other volumes. Brunet introduces him into his Bibliographical Pantheon among "Modern Reformers"; but the space allowed is very scanty by the side of his namesake. His works are sympathetically described and analyzed in a volume published since this Address, entitled *L'Abbé de Saint-Pierre, sa Vie et ses Œuvres*, par G. de Molinari.

2 Éloge de Saint-Pierre: Œuvres, Tom. XI. p. 113. See, also, Bescherelle, Dictionnaire National, under *Bienfaisance.*

sonal peculiarities.[1] Many turned the cold shoulder. The French Academy, of which he was a member, took from him his chair, and on the occasion of his death forbore the eulogy which is its customary tribute to a departed academician. But an incomparable genius in Germany,—an authority not to be questioned on any subject upon which he spoke,—the great and universal Leibnitz, bears his testimony to the "Project of Perpetual Peace," and, so doing, enrolls his own prodigious name in the catalogue of our cause. In observations on this Project, communicated to its author, under date of February 7, 1715, while declaring that it is supported by the practical authority of Henry the Fourth, that it justly interests the whole human race, and is not foreign to his own studies, as from youth he had occupied himself with law, and particularly with the Law of Nations, Leibnitz says: "*I have read it with attention, and am persuaded that such a project, on the whole, is feasible, and that its execution would be one of the most useful things in the world.* Although my suffrage cannot be of any weight, I have nevertheless thought that gratitude obliged me not to withhold it, and to join some remarks for the satisfaction of a meritorious author, who ought to have much reputation and firmness, to have dared and been able to oppose with success the prejudiced crowd, and the unbridled tongue of mockers."[2] Such testimony from Leibnitz must have been grateful to Saint-Pierre.

I cannot close this brief record of a philanthropist, constant in an age when War was more regarded than

[1] Les Caractères, *Du Mérite Personnel*, Tom. I. p. 93.

[2] Observations sur le Projet d'une Paix Perpétuelle; Lettre à l'Abbé de S. Pierre: Opera (ed Dutens), Tom. V. pp. 56-62.

Humanity, without offering him an unaffected homage. To this faithful man may be addressed the sublime salutation which hymned from the soul of Milton: —

> "Servant of God, well done! well hast thou fought
> The better fight, who single hast maintained
> Against revolted multitudes the cause
> Of Truth, in word mightier than they in arms,
> And for the testimony of truth hast borne
> . . . . reproach, far worse to bear
> Than violence: for this was all thy care,
> To stand approved in sight of God, though worlds
> Judged thee perverse."[1]

Waking hereafter from its martial trance, the world will rejoice to salute the greatness of his career.[2] It may well measure advance in civilization by the appreciation of his character.

Contemporary with Saint-Pierre was another Frenchman, to whom I have already referred, who flashed his genius upon the game of War. La Bruyère exhibits men, for the sake of a piece of land more or less, *agreeing among themselves* to despoil, burn, and kill each other, even to cutting throats, and, for the doing of this more ingeniously and safely, inventing a beautiful system, known as the Art of War, to the practice of which is attached what is called *Glory*. The same satirist, who lived in an age of War, likens men to animals, even to dogs barking at each other, and then again to cats; and he furnishes a picture of the latter, counted by the thousand, and marshalled on an extended plain, where, after mewing their best, they throw themselves upon each other, tooth and nail, until nine or ten thousand of

1 Paradise Lost, Book VI. 29-37.

2 The *Nouvelle Biographie Générale* concludes its notice of him thus: — "Après avoir mérité le beau surnom de *Solliciteur pour le bien public*, l'Abbé de Saint-Pierre mourut, en 1743, à l'âge de quatre-vingt-cinq ans."

them are left dead on the field, infecting the air for ten leagues with an intolerable stench,—and all this for the love of Glory. But how, says the satirist, can we distinguish between those who use only tooth and nail and those others, who, first substituting lances, darts, and swords, now employ destructive balls, small and large, killing at once, while, penetrating a roof, they crash from garret to cellar, sacrificing even women and children? Wherein is the Glory?[1]

Saint-Pierre was followed by that remarkable genius, Jean Jacques Rousseau, in a small work with the modest title, "Extract from the Project of Perpetual Peace by the Abbé Saint-Pierre."[2] Without referring to those higher motives supplied by humanity, conscience, and religion, for addressing which to sovereigns Saint-Pierre incurred the ridicule of what are called practical statesmen, Rousseau appeals to common sense, and shows how much mere worldly interests would be promoted by submission to the arbitration of an impartial tribunal, rather than to the uncertain issue of arms, with no adequate compensation, even to the victor, for blood and treasure sacrificed. If this project fails, it is not, according to him, because chimerical, but because men have lost their wits, and it is a sort of madness to be wise in the midst of fools. As no scheme more grand, more beautiful, or more useful ever occupied the human mind, so, says Rousseau, no author ever deserved attention more than one proposing the means for its practical adoption; nor can any humane and virtuous man fail to regard it with enthusiasm.

1 Caractères, *Du Souverain*, Tom. I. p. 332; *Des Jugements*, Tom. II. pp. 57–59.

2 Extrait du Projet de Paix Perpétuelle de M. l'Abbé de Saint-Pierre.

The recommendations of Rousseau, reaching Germany, were encountered by a writer now remembered chiefly by this hardihood. I allude to Embser, who treats of Perpetual Peace in a work first published in 1779, under the title of "The Idolatry of our Philosophical Century,"[1] and at a later day with a new title, under the *alias* of the "Refutation of the Project of Perpetual Peace."[2] Objections common with the superficial or prejudiced are vehemently urged; the imputation upon Grotius is reproduced; and the project is pronounced visionary and impracticable, while War is exalted as an instrument more beneficent than Peace in advancing the civilization of mankind. At a later day Hegel gave the same testimony, thus contributing his considerable name to vindicate War.[3]

The cause of Saint-Pierre and Rousseau was not without champions in Germany. In 1763 we meet at Göttingen the work of Totze, entitled "Permanent and Universal Peace, according to the Plan of Henry the Fourth";[4] and in 1767, at Leipsic, an ample and mature treatise by Lilienfeld, under the name of "New Constitution for States."[5] Truth often appears contemporaneously to different minds having no concert with each other; and the latter work, though in remarkable harmony with Saint-Pierre and Rousseau, is said to have been composed without any knowledge of their labors. Lilienfeld exposes the causes and calamities of War, the waste of armaments in time of Peace, and the miserable chances of the battle-field, where, in defiance of all jus-

1 Die Abgötterei unsers Philosophischen Jahrhunderts.
2 Widerlegung des Projects von Ewigen Frieden.
3 Philosophie des Rechts, §§ 321 - 340: Werke, Band VIII. pp. 408 - 423.
4 Ewiger und Allgemeiner Friede nach der Entwurf Heinrichs IV.
5 Neues Staatsgebäude.

tice, controversies are determined as by the throw of dice; and he urges submission to Arbitrators, unless, in their wisdom, nations establish a Supreme Tribunal with the combined power of the Confederacy to enforce its decrees.

It was the glory of another German, in intellectual preëminence the successor of Leibnitz, to illustrate this cause by special and repeated labors. At Königsberg, in a retired corner of Prussia, away from the great lines of travel, Immanuel Kant consecrated his days to the pursuit of truth. During a long, virtuous, and disinterested life, stretching beyond the period appointed for man, — from 1724 to 1804, — in retirement, undisturbed by shock of revolution or war, never drawn by temptation of travel more than seven German miles from the place of his birth, he assiduously studied books, men, and things. Among the fruits of his ripened powers was that system of philosophy known as the "Critique of Pure Reason," by which he was at once established as a master-mind of his country. His words became the text for writers without number, who vied with each other in expounding, illustrating, or opposing his principles. At this period, after an unprecedented triumph in philosophy, when his name had become familiar wherever his mother-tongue was spoken, and while his rare faculties were yet untouched by decay, in the Indian Summer of life, the great thinker published a work "On Perpetual Peace."[1] Interest in the author, or in the cause, was attested by prompt translations into the French, Danish, and Dutch languages. In an

[1] Zum Ewigen Frieden, 1795; Verkündigung des nahen Abschlusses eines Tractats zum Ewigen Frieden in der Philosophie, 1796: Sämmtliche Werke, Band VI. pp. 405-454, 487-498.

earlier work, entitled "Idea for a General History in a Cosmopolitan View,"[1] he espoused the same cause, and at a later day, in his "Metaphysical Elements of Jurisprudence,"[2] he renewed his testimony. In the lapse of time the speculations of the philosopher have lost much of their original attraction; other systems, with other names, have taken their place. But these early and faithful labors for Perpetual Peace cannot be forgotten. Perhaps through these the fame of the applauded philosopher of Königsberg may yet be preserved.

By Perpetual Peace Kant understood a condition of nations where there could be no fear of War; and this condition, he said, was demanded by reason, which, abhorring all War, as little adapted to establish right, must regard this final development of the Law of Nations as a consummation worthy of every effort. The philosopher was right in proposing nothing less than a reform of International Law. To this, according to him, all persons, and particularly all rulers, should bend their energies. A special league or treaty should be formed, which may be truly called a *Treaty of Peace,* having this peculiarity, that, whereas other treaties terminate a single existing War only, this should terminate forever all War between the parties to it. A Treaty of Peace, tacitly acknowledging *the right to wage War,* as all treaties now do, is nothing more than a *Truce,* not Peace. By these treaties an individual War is ended, but not the *state of War.* There may not be constant hostilities; but there wil be constant fear of hostilities, with

1 Idee zu einer Allgemeinen Geschichte in Weltbürgerlicher Absicht: Sämmtliche Werke, Band IV. pp. 141 – 157.

2 Metaphysische Anfangsgründe der Rechtslehre, §§ 53 – 61, *Das Völkerrecht:* Sämmtliche Werke, Band VII. pp. 141 – 157.

constant threat of aggression and attack. Soldiers and armaments, now nursed as a Peace establishment, become the fruitful parent of new wars. With real Peace, these would be abandoned. Nor should nations hesitate to bow before the *law*, like individuals. They must form one comprehensive federation, which, by the aggregation of other nations, would at last embrace the whole earth. And this, according to Kant, in the succession of years, by a sure progress, is the irresistible tendency of nations. To this end nations must be truly independent; nor is it possible for one nation to acquire another independent nation, whether by inheritance, exchange, purchase, or gift. A nation is not property. The philosophy of Kant, therefore, contemplated not only Universal Peace, but Universal Liberty. The first article of the great treaty would be, that every nation is free.

These important conclusions found immediate support from another German philosopher, Fichte, of remarkable acuteness and perfect devotion to truth, whose name, in his own day, awakened an echo inferior only to that of Kant. In his "Groundwork of the Law of Nature."[1] published in 1796, he urges a Federation of Nations, with a Supreme Tribunal, as the best way of securing the triumph of justice, and of subduing the power of the unjust. To the suggestion, that by this Federation injustice might be done, he replied, that it would not be easy to find any common advantage tempting the confederate nations to do this wrong.

The subject was again treated in 1804, by a learned German, Karl Schwab, whose work, entitled "Of Una-

[1] Grundlage des Naturrechts: *Ueber das Völkerrecht*: Sämmtliche Werke, Band III. pp. 369 – 382.

voidable Injustice,"[1] deserves notice for practical clearness and directness. Nothing could be better than his idea of the Universal State, where nations will be united, as citizens in the Municipal State; nor have the promises of the Future been more carefully presented. He sees clearly, that, even when this triumph of civilization is won, justice between nations will not be always inviolate, — for, unhappily, between citizens it is not always so; but, whatever may be the exceptions, it will become the general rule. As in the Municipal State War no longer prevails, but offences, wrongs, and sallies of vengeance often proceed from individual citizens, with insubordination and anarchy sometimes, — so in the Universal State War will no longer prevail; but here also, between the different nations, who will be as citizens in the Federation, there may be wrongs and aggressions, with resistance even to the common power. In short, the Universal State will be subject to the same accidents as the Municipal State.

The cause of Permanent Peace became a thesis for Universities. At Stuttgart, in 1796, there was an oration by J. H. La Motte, entitled *Utrum Pax Perpetua pangi possit, nec ne?* And at Leyden, in 1808, there was a Dissertation by Gabinus de Wal, on taking his degree as Doctor of Laws, entitled *Disputatio Philosophico-Juridica de Conjunctione Populorum ad Pacem Perpetuam.*[2] This learned and elaborate performance, after reviewing previous efforts in the cause, accords a

[1] Ueber das Unvermeidliche Unrecht.

[2] At the Paris Peace Congress of 1849, since the delivery of this Address, with Victor Hugo as President, and Richard Cobden as an active member, Mr. Suringar, of Amsterdam, referred to this Dissertation, and announced a copy of it which had been given him for presentation to the Congress by the son of the author, John de Wal, Professor of Jurisprudence at Leyden. My own copy is a valued present from Elihu Burritt.

preëminence to Kant. Such a voice from the University is the token of a growing sentiment, and an example for the youth of our own day.

Meanwhile in England the cause was espoused by that indefatigable jurist and reformer, Jeremy Bentham, who embraced it in his comprehensive labors. In an Essay on International Law, bearing date 1786 – 89, and first published in 1839, by his executor, Dr. Bowring,[1] he develops a plan for Universal and Perpetual Peace in the spirit of Saint-Pierre. Such, according to him, is the extreme folly, the madness, of War, that on no supposition can it be otherwise than mischievous. All Trade, in essence, is advantageous, even to the party who profits by it the least; all War, in essence, is ruinous: and yet the great employments of Government are to treasure up occasions of War, and to put fetters upon Trade. To remedy this evil, Bentham proposes, first, "The reduction and fixation of the forces of the several nations that compose the European system"; and in enforcing this proposition, he says: "Whatsoever nation should get the start of the other in making the proposal to reduce and fix the amount of its armed force would crown itself with everlasting honor. The risk would be nothing, the gain certain. This gain would be the giving an incontrovertible demonstration of its own disposition to peace, and of the opposite disposition in the other nation, in case of its rejecting the proposal." He next proposes an International Court of Judicature, with power to report its opinion, and to circulate it in each nation, and, after a certain delay, to put a contumacious nation under the ban. He denies

[1] Bentham's Works, Part VIII pp. 537 – 554.

that this system can be styled visionary in any respect: for it is proved, *first*, that it is the interest of the parties concerned; *secondly*, that the parties are already sensible of this interest; and, *thirdly*, that, enlightened by diplomatic experience in difficult and complicated conventions, they are prepared for the new situation. All this is sober and practical.

Coming to our own country, I find many names for commemoration. No person, in all history, has borne his testimony in phrases of greater pungency or more convincing truth than Benjamin Franklin. "In my opinion," he says, "there never was a good War or a bad Peace"; and he asks, "When will mankind be convinced that all Wars are follies, very expensive, and very mischievous, and agree to settle their differences by arbitration? Were they to do it even by the cast of a die, it would be better than by fighting and destroying each other." Then again he says: "We make daily great improvements in natural, there is one I wish to see in moral philosophy, — the discovery of a plan that would induce and oblige nations to settle their disputes without first cutting one another's throats. When will human reason be sufficiently improved to see the advantage of this?"[1] As diplomatist, Franklin strove to limit the evils of War. To him, while Minister at Paris, belongs the honor of those instructions, more glorious for the American name than any battle, where our naval cruisers, among whom was the redoubtable Paul Jones, were directed, in the interest of univer-

[1] Letter to Josiah Quincy, Sept. 11, 1783; to Mrs. Mary Hewson, Jan. 27, 1783; to Richard Price, Feb. 6, 1780: Works, ed. Sparks, Vol. X. p. 11; IX. p. 476; VIII. p. 417.

sal science, to allow a free and undisturbed passage to the returning expedition of Captain Cook, the great circumnavigator, who "steered Britain's oak into a world unknown."[1] To him also belongs the honor of introducing into a treaty with Prussia a provision for the abolition of that special scandal, Private War on the Ocean.[2] In similar strain with Franklin, Jefferson says: "Will nations never devise a more rational umpire of differences than Force? . . . . War is an instrument entirely inefficient towards redressing wrong; it multiplies, instead of indemnifying losses."[3] And he proceeds to exhibit the waste of War, and the beneficent consequences, if its expenditures could be diverted to purposes of practical utility.

To Franklin especially must thanks be rendered for authoritative words and a precious example. But there are three names, fit successors of Saint-Pierre, — I speak only of those on whose career is the seal of death, — which even more than his deserve affectionate regard. I refer to Noah Worcester, William Ellery Channing, and William Ladd. To dwell on the services of these our virtuous champions would be a grateful task. The occasion allows a passing notice only.

In Worcester we behold the single-minded country clergyman, little gifted as preacher, with narrow means, — and his example teaches what such a character may accomplish, — in humble retirement, pained by the reports of War, and at last, as the protracted drama of

[1] Franklin's Works, ed. Sparks, Vol. V. pp 122-124. Collections of Mass. Hist. Soc., Vol. IV. pp. 79-85.

[2] Franklin's Works, ed. Sparks, Vol. II. pp. 485, 486. Lyman's Diplomacy of the United States, Vol. I. pp. 143-148.

[3] Letter to Sir John Sinclair, March 23, 1798: Transactions of the American Philosophical Society, Vol. IV. pp. 320, 321.

battles was about to close at Waterloo, publishing that appeal, entitled "A Solemn Review of the *Custom* of War," which has been so extensively circulated at home and abroad, and has done so much to correct the inveterate prejudices which surround the cause. He was the founder, and for some time the indefatigable agent, of the earliest Peace Society in the country.

The eloquence of Channing was often, both with tongue and pen, directed against War. He was heart-struck by the awful degradation it caused, rudely blotting out in men the image of God their Father; and his words of flame have lighted in many souls those exterminating fires that can never die, until this evil is swept from the earth.

William Ladd, after completing his education at Harvard University, engaged in commercial pursuits. Early, through his own exertions, blessed with competency, he could not be idle. He was childless; and his affections embraced all the children of the human family. Like Worcester and Channing, his attention was arrested by the portentous crime of War, and he was moved to dedicate the remainder of his days to earnest, untiring effort for its abolition, — going about from place to place inculcating the lesson of Peace, with simple, cheerful manner winning the hearts of good men, and dropping in many youthful souls precious seeds to ripen in more precious fruit. He was the founder of the American Peace Society, in which was finally merged the earlier association established by Worcester. By a long series of practical labors, and especially by developing, maturing, and publishing the plan of an International Congress, has William Ladd enrolled himself among the benefactors of mankind.

Such are some of the names which hereafter, when the warrior no longer usurps the blessings promised to the peacemaker, will be inscribed on immortal tablets.

Now, at last, in the fulness of time, in our own day, by the labors of men of Peace, by the irresistible cooperating affinities of mankind, nations seem to be visibly approaching — even amidst tumult and discord — that Unity so long hoped for, prayed for. By steamboat, railroad, and telegraph, outstripping the traditional movements of government, men of all countries daily commingle, ancient prejudices fast dissolve, while ancient sympathies strengthen, and new sympathies come into being. The chief commercial cities of England send addresses of friendship to the chief commercial cities of France; and the latter delight to return the salutation. Similar cords of amity are twined between cities in England and cities in our own country. The visit to London of a band of French National Guards is reciprocated by the visit to Paris of a large company of Englishmen. Thus are achieved pacific conquests, where formerly all the force of arms could not prevail. Mr. Vattemare perambulates Europe and the United States to establish a system of literary international exchanges. By the daily agency of the press we are sharers in the trials and triumphs of brethren in all lands, and, renouncing the solitude of insulated nationalities, learn to live in the communion of associated states. By multitudinous reciprocities of commerce are developed relations of mutual dependence, stronger than treaties or alliances engrossed on parchment, — while, from a truer appreciation of the ethics of government, we arrive at the conviction, that the divine injunction, "Do unto others as you would have them do unto you," was spoken to nations as well as to individuals.

From increasing knowledge of each other, and from a higher sense of duty as brethren of the Human Family, arises among mankind an increasing interest in each other; and charity, once, like patriotism, exclusively national, is beginning to clasp the world in its embrace. Every discovery of science, every aspiration of philanthropy, no matter what the country of its origin, is now poured into the common stock. Assemblies, whether of science or philanthropy, are no longer municipal merely, but welcome delegates from all the nations. Science has convened Congresses in Italy, Germany, and England. Great causes, grander even than Science, — like Temperance, Freedom, Peace, — have drawn to London large bodies of men from different countries, under the title of *World Conventions,* in whose very name and spirit of fraternity we discern the prevailing tendency. Such a convention, dedicated to Universal Peace, held at London in 1843, was graced by many well known for labors of humanity. At Frankfort, in 1846, was assembled a large Congress from all parts of Europe, to consider what could be done for those in prison. The succeeding year witnessed, at Brussels, a similar Congress, convened in the same charity. At last, in August, 1848, we hail, at Brussels, another Congress, inspired by the presence of a generous American, Elihu Burritt, — who has left his anvil at home to teach the nations how to change their swords into ploughshares and their spears into pruning-hooks, — presided over by an eminent Belgian magistrate, and composed of numerous individuals, speaking various languages, living under diverse forms of government, various in political opinions, differing in religious convictions, but all moved by a common sentiment to seek the abolition of War, and the Disarming of the Nations.

The Peace Congress at Brussels constitutes an epoch. It is a palpable development of those international attractions and affinities which now await their final organization. The resolutions it adopted are so important that I cannot hesitate to introduce them.

"1. That, in the judgment of this Congress, an appeal to arms for the purpose of deciding disputes among nations is a custom condemned alike by religion, reason, justice, humanity, and the best interests of the people, — and that, therefore, it considers it to be the duty of the civilized world to adopt measures calculated to effect its entire abolition.

"2. That it is of the highest importance to urge on the several governments of Europe and America the necessity of introducing a clause into all International Treaties, providing for the settlement of all disputes by Arbitration, in an amicable manner, and according to the rules of justice and equity, by special Arbitrators, or a Supreme International Court, to be invested with power to decide in cases of necessity, as a last resort.

"3. That the speedy convocation of a Congress of Nations, composed of duly appointed representatives, for the purpose of framing a well-digested and authoritative International Code, is of the greatest importance, inasmuch as the organization of such a body, and the unanimous adoption of such a Code, would be an effectual means of promoting Universal Peace.

"4. That this Congress respectfully calls the attention of civilized governments to the necessity of a general and simultaneous disarmament, as a means whereby they may greatly diminish the financial burdens which press upon them, remove a fertile cause of irritation and inquietude, inspire mutual confidence, and promote the interchange of good offices, which, while they advance the interests of each state in particular, contribute largely to the maintenance of general Peace, and the lasting prosperity of nations."

In France these resolutions received the adhesion of Lamartine, — in England, of Richard Cobden. They have been welcomed throughout Great Britain, by large and enthusiastic popular assemblies, hanging with delight upon the practical lessons of peace on earth and good-will to men. At the suggestion of the Congress at Brussels, and in harmony with the demands of an increasing public sentiment, another Congress is called at Paris, in the approaching month of August. The place of meeting is auspicious. There, as in the very cave of Æolus, whence have so often raged forth conflicting winds and resounding tempests, are to gather delegates from various nations, including a large number from our own country, whose glad work will be to hush and imprison these winds and tempests, and to bind them in the chains of everlasting Peace.

Not in voluntary assemblies only has our cause found welcome. Into *legislative halls* it has made its way. A document now before me, in the handwriting of Samuel Adams, an approved patriot of the Revolution, bears witness to his desire for action on this subject in the Congress of the United States. It is in the form of a Letter of Instructions from the Legislature of Massachusetts to the delegates in Congress of this State, and, though without date, seems to have been prepared some time between the Treaty of Peace in 1783 and the adoption of the National Constitution in 1789. It is as follows.

"GENTLEMEN, — Although the General Court have lately instructed you concerning various matters of very great importance to this Commonwealth, they cannot finish the business of the year until they have transmitted to you a further instruction, which they have long had in contemplation, and which, if their most ardent wish could be obtained, might in its consequences extensively promote the happiness of man.

"You are, therefore, hereby instructed and urged to move the United States in Congress assembled to take into their deep and most serious consideration, whether any measures can by them be used, through their influence with such of the nations in Europe with whom they are united by Treaties of Amity or Commerce, that National Differences may be settled and determined without the necessity of WAR, in which the world has too long been deluged, to the destruction of human happiness and the disgrace of human reason and government.

"If, after the most mature deliberation, it shall appear that no measures can be taken *at present* on this very interesting subject, it is conceived it would redound much to the honor of the United States that it was attended to by their great Representative in Congress, and be accepted as a testimony of gratitude for most signal favors granted to the said States by Him who is the almighty and most gracious Father and Friend of mankind.

"And you are further instructed to move that the foregoing Letter of Instructions be entered on the Journals of Congress, if it may be thought proper, that so it may remain for the inspection of the delegates from this Commonwealth, if necessary, in any *future* time."[1]

I am not able to ascertain whether this document ever became a legislative act; but unquestionably it attests, in authentic form, that a great leader in Mas-

[1] MSS. of Samuel Adams, belonging to the historian, George Bancroft.

sachusetts, after the establishment of that Independence for which he had so assiduously labored, hoped to enlist not only the Legislature of his State, but the Congress of the United States, in efforts for the emancipation of nations from the tyranny of War. For this early effort, when the cause of Permanent Peace had never been introduced to any legislative body, Samuel Adams deserves grateful mention.

Many years later the subject reached Congress, where, in 1838, it was considered in an elaborate report by the late Mr. Legaré, in behalf of the Committee on Foreign Affairs of the House of Representatives, prompted by memorials from the friends of Peace. While injudiciously discountenancing an Association of Nations, as not yet sanctioned by public opinion, the Committee acknowledge "that the union of all nations in a state of Peace, under the restraints and the protection of law, is the ideal perfection of civil society"; that they "concur fully in the benevolent object of the memorialists, and believe that there is a visible tendency in the spirit and institutions of the age towards the practical accomplishment of it at some future period"; that they "heartily concur with the memorialists in recommending a reference to a Third Power of all such controversies as can safely be confided to any tribunal unknown to the Constitution of our own country"; and that "such a practice will be followed by other powers, and will soon grow up into the customary law of civilized nations."[1]

The Legislature of Massachusetts, by a series of resolutions, in harmony with the early sentiments of Samuel Adams, adopted, in 1844, with exceeding unanimity, declare, that they "regard Arbitration as a practical and

[1] Reports of Committees, 25th Cong. 2d Sess., No. 979

desirable substitute for War, in the adjustment of international differences"; and still further declare their "earnest desire that the government of the United States would, at the earliest opportunity, take measures for obtaining the consent of the powers of Christendom to the establishment of a general Convention or Congress of Nations, for the purpose of settling the principles of International Law, and of organizing a High Court of Nations to adjudge all cases of difficulty which may be brought before them by the mutual consent of two or more nations."[1] During the winter of 1849 the subject was again presented to the American Congress by Mr. Tuck, who asked the unanimous consent of the House of Representatives to offer the following preamble and resolution: —

"Whereas the evils of War are acknowledged by all civilized nations, and the calamities, individual and general, which are inseparably connected with it, have attracted the attention of many humane and enlightened citizens of this and other countries; and whereas it is the disposition of the people of the United States to coöperate with others in all appropriate and judicious exertions to prevent a recurrence of national conflicts; therefore,

"*Resolved*, That the Committee on Foreign Affairs be directed to inquire into the expediency of authorizing a correspondence to be opened by the Secretary of State with Foreign Governments, on the subject of procuring Treaty stipulations for the reference of all future disputes to a friendly Arbitration, or for the establishment, instead thereof, of a Congress of Nations, to determine International Law and settle international disputes."[2]

[1] Mass. House Documents, Sess. 1844, No. 18.

[2] Congressional Globe, 30th Cong. 2d Sess., Jan. 16, 1849, p. 267. See also House Journal, Feb. 5, p. 372.

Though for the present unsuccessful, this excellent effort prepares the way for another trial.

Nor does it stand alone. Almost contemporaneously, M. Bouvet, in the National Assembly of France, submitted a proposition of a similar character, as follows: —

"Seeing that War between nations is contrary to religion, humanity, and the public well-being, the French National Assembly decrees: —

"The French Republic proposes to the Governments and Representative Assemblies of the different States of Europe, America, and other civilized countries, to unite, by their representation, in a Congress which shall have for its object a proportional disarmament among the Powers, the abolition of War, and a substitution for that barbarous usage of an Arbitral jurisdiction, of which the said Congress shall immediately fulfil the functions."

In an elaborate report, the French Committee on Foreign Affairs, while declining at present to recommend this proposition, distinctly sanction its object.

At a still earlier date, some time in the summer of 1848, Arnold Ruge brought the same measure before the German Parliament at Frankfort, by moving the following amendment to the Report of the Committee on Foreign Affairs: —

"That, as Armed Peace, by its standing armies, imposes an intolerable burden upon the people of Europe, and endangers civil freedom, we therefore recognize the necessity of calling into existence a *Congress of Nations*, for the purpose of effecting a general disarmament of Europe."

Though this proposition failed, yet the mover is reported to have sustained it by a speech which was received with applause, both in the assembly and gallery. Among other things, he used these important words: —

"There is no necessity for feeding an army of military idlers and eaters. There is nothing to fear from our neighbor barbarians, as they are called. You must give up the idea that the French *will* eat us up, and that the Prussians *can* eat us up. Soldiers must cease to exist; then shall no more cities be bombarded. These opinions must be kept up and propagated by a Congress of Nations. I vote that the nations of Europe disarm at once."

In the British Parliament the cause has found an able representative in Mr. Cobden, whose name is an omen of success. He has addressed many large popular meetings in its behalf, and already, by speech and motion in the House of Commons, has striven for a reduction in the armaments of Great Britain. Only lately he gave notice of the following motion, which he intends to call up in that assembly at the earliest moment: —

"That an humble address be presented to her Majesty, praying that she will be graciously pleased to direct her Principal Secretary of State for Foreign Affairs to enter into communication with Foreign Powers, inviting them to concur in treaties binding the respective parties, in the event of any future misunderstanding which cannot be arranged by amicable negotiation, to refer the matter in dispute to the decision of Arbitrators."

Such is the Peace Movement.[1] With the ever-flowing current of time it has gained ever-increasing strength, and it has now become like a mighty river. At first but a slender fountain, sparkling on some lofty summit, it has swollen with every tributary rill, with the friendly rains and dews of heaven, and at last with the associate waters of various nations, until it washes the feet of

[1] It will be remarked that this history stops with the date of this Address.

populous cities, rejoicing on its peaceful banks. By the voices of poets, — by the aspirations and labors of statesmen, philosophers, and good men, — by the experience of history, — by the peaceful union into nations of families, tribes, and provinces, divesting themselves of "liberty" to wage War, — by the example of leagues, alliances, confederacies, and congresses, — by the kindred movements of our age, all tending to Unity, — by an awakened public sentiment, and a growing recognition of Human Brotherhood, — by the sympathies of large popular assemblies, — by the formal action of legislative bodies, — by the promises of Christianity, are we encouraged to persevere. So doing, we act not *against* Nature, but *with* Nature, making ourselves, according to the injunction of Lord Bacon, its ministers and interpreters. From no single man, from no body of men, does this cause proceed. Not from Saint-Pierre or Leibnitz, from Rousseau or Kant, in other days, — not from Jay or Burritt, from Cobden or Lamartine, in our own. It is the irrepressible utterance of the longing with which the heart of Humanity labors; it is the universal expression of the Spirit of the Age, thirsting after Harmony; it is the heaven-born whisper of Truth, immortal and omnipotent; it is the word of God, published in commands as from the burning bush; it is the voice of Christ, declaring to all mankind that they are brothers, and saying to the turbulent nationalities of the earth, as to the raging sea, "Peace, be still!"

GENTLEMEN OF THE PEACE SOCIETY, — Such is the War System of the Commonwealth of Nations; and such are the means and auguries of its overthrow. To aid and direct public sentiment so as to hasten the coming of this day is the chosen object of this Society. All who have candidly attended me in this exposition will bear witness that our attempt is in no way inconsistent with the human character, — that we do not seek to suspend or hold in check any general laws of Nature, but simply to overthrow a barbarous Institution, having the sanction of International Law, and to bring nations within that system of social order which has already secured such inestimable good to civil society, and is as applicable to nations in their relations with each other as to individuals.

Tendencies of nations, as revealed in history, teach that our aims are in harmony with prevailing laws, which God, in his benevolence, has ordained for mankind.

Examples teach also that we attempt nothing that is not directly practicable. If the several States of the Helvetic Republic, if the thirty independent States of the North American Union, if the thirty-eight independent sovereignties of the German Confederation, can, by formal stipulation, divest themselves of the *right of war with each other*, and consent to submit all mutual controversies to Arbitration, or to a High Court of Judicature, then can the Commonwealth of Nations do the same. Nor should they hesitate, while, in the language of William Penn, such surpassing instances show that *it may be done*, and Europe, by her incomparable miseries, that *it ought to be done*. Nay, more, — if it would be criminal in these several clusters of States to reëstablish the Institution of War as Arbiter of Justice, then is it criminal in the Commonwealth of Nations to continue it.

Changes already wrought in the Laws of War teach that the whole System may be abolished. The existence of laws implies authority that sanctions or enacts, which, in the present case, is the Commonwealth of Nations. This authority can, of course, modify or abrogate what it originally sanctioned or enacted. In the exercise of this power, the Laws of War have been modified, from time to time, in important particulars. Prisoners taken in battle cannot now be killed; nor can they be reduced to slavery. Poison and assassination can no longer be employed against an enemy. Private property on land cannot be seized. Persons occupied on land exclusively with the arts of Peace cannot be molested. It remains that the authority by which the Laws of War have been thus modified should entirely abrogate them. Their existence is a disgrace to civilization; for it implies the *common consent* of nations to the Arbitrament of War, as regulated by these laws. Like the Laws of the Duel, they should yield to some arbitrament of reason. If the former, once so firmly imbedded in Municipal Law, could be abolished by individual nations, so also can the Laws of War, which are a part of International Law, be abolished by the Commonwealth of Nations. In the light of reason and religion there can be but one Law of War, — the great law which pronounces it unwise, unchristian, and unjust, and forbids it forever, as a crime.

Thus distinctly alleging the practicability of our aims, I may properly introduce an incontrovertible authority. Listen to the words of an American statesman, whose long life was spent, at home or abroad, in the service of his country, and whose undoubted familiarity with the Law of Nations was never surpassed, — John Quincy Adams. "War," he says, in one of the legacies of his venerable experience, "by the common consent and mere will of civilized man, has not only been divested of its most atrocious cruelties, but for multitudes, growing multitudes of individuals, has already been and is abolished. *Why should it not be abolished for all?* Let it be impressed upon the heart of every one of you, impress it upon the minds of your children, *that this total abolition of War upon earth* is an improvement in the condition of man entirely dependent on his own will. He cannot repeal or change the laws of physical Nature. He cannot redeem himself from the ills that flesh is heir to. But the ills of War and Slavery are all of his own creation; he has but to will, and he effects the cessation of them altogether."[1]

Well does John Quincy Adams say that mankind have but to *will* it, and War is abolished. Will it, and War disappears like the Duel. Will it, and War skulks like the Torture. Will it, and War fades away like the fires of religious persecution. Will it, and War passes among profane follies, like the ordeal of burning ploughshares. Will it, and War hurries to join the earlier institution of Cannibalism. Will it, and War is chastised from the Commonwealth of Nations, as Slavery has been chastised from municipal jurisdictions by England and France, by Tunis and Tripoli.

To arouse this *public will*, which, like a giant, yet sleeps, but whose awakened voice nothing can withstand, should be our endeavor. The true character of the War System must be exposed. To be hated, it needs only to be comprehended; and it will surely be abolished as soon as this is accomplished. See, then, that it is comprehended. Exhibit its manifold atro-

[1] Oration at Newburyport, July 4, 1837, pp. 56, 57.

cities. Strip away all its presumptuous pretences, its specious apologies, its hideous sorceries. Above all, men must no longer deceive themselves by the shallow thought that this System is the necessary incident of imperfect human nature, and thus cast upon God the responsibility for their crimes. They must see clearly that it is a monster of their own creation, born with their consent, whose vital spark is fed by their breath, and without their breath must necessarily die. They must see distinctly, what I have so carefully presented to-night, that War, under the Law of Nations, is nothing but an Institution, and the whole War System nothing but an Establishment for the administration of *international justice,* for which the Commonwealth of Nations is directly responsible, and which that Commonwealth can at any time remove.

Recognizing these things, men must cease to cherish War, and will renounce all appeal to its Arbitrament. They will forego rights, rather than wage an irreligious battle. But, criminal and irrational as is War, unhappily, in the present state of human error, we cannot expect large numbers to appreciate its true character, and to hate it with that perfect hatred making them renounce its agency, unless we offer an approved and practical mode of determining international controversies, as a *substitute* for the imagined necessity of the barbarous ordeal. This we are able to do; and so doing, we reflect new light upon the atrocity of a system which not only tramples upon all the precepts of the Christian faith, but defies justice and discards reason.

1. The most complete and permanent substitute would be a Congress of Nations, with a High Court of Judica-

ture. Such a system, while admitted on all sides to promise excellent results, is opposed on two grounds. *First,* because, as regards the smaller states, it would be a tremendous engine of oppression, subversive of their political independence. Surely, it could not be so oppressive as the War System. But the experience of the smaller States in the German Confederation and in the American Union, nay, the experience of Belgium and Holland by the side of the overtopping power of France, and the experience of Denmark and Sweden in the very night-shade of Russia, all show the futility of this objection. *Secondly,* because the decrees of such a court could not be carried into effect. Even if they were enforced by the combined power of the associate nations, the sword, as the executive arm of the high tribunal, would be only the melancholy instrument of Justice, not the Arbiter of Justice, and therefore not condemned by the conclusive reasons against international appeals to the sword. From the experience of history, and particularly from the experience of the thirty States of our Union, we learn that the occasion for any executive arm will be rare. The State of Rhode Island, in its recent controversy with Massachusetts, submitted with much indifference to the adverse decree of the Supreme Court; and I doubt not that Missouri and Iowa will submit with equal contentment to any determination of their present controversy by the same tribunal. The same submission would attend the decrees of any Court of Judicature established by the Commonwealth of Nations. There is a growing sense of justice, combined with a growing might of public opinion, too little known to the soldier, that would maintain the judgments of the august tribunal assembled in the face of the Nations, better than the swords of all the marshals of France, better than the bloody terrors of Austerlitz or Waterloo.

The idea of a Congress of Nations with a High Court of Judicature is as practicable as its consummation is confessedly dear to the friends of Universal Peace Whenever this Congress is convened, as surely it will be, I know not all the names that will deserve commemoration in its earliest proceedings; but there are two, whose particular and long-continued advocacy of this Institution will connect them indissolubly with its fame, — the Abbé Saint-Pierre, of France, and William Ladd, of the United States.

2. There is still another substitute for War, which is not exposed even to the shallow objections launched against a Congress of Nations. By formal treaties between two or more nations, Arbitration may be established as the mode of determining controversies between them. In every respect this is a contrast to War. It is rational, humane, and cheap. Above all, it is consistent with the teachings of Christianity. As I mention this substitute, I should do injustice to the cause and to my own feelings, if I did not express our obligations to its efficient proposer and advocate, our fellow-citizen, and the President of this Society, the honored son of an illustrious father, whose absence to-night enables me, without offending his known modesty, to introduce this tribute: I mean William Jay.

The complete overthrow of the War System, involving the disarming of the Nations, would follow the establishment of a Congress of Nations, or any general system of Arbitration. Then at last our aims would be accomplished; then at last Peace would be organized among the Nations. Then might Christians repeat the fitful boast of the generous Mohawk: "We have thrown the hatchet so high into the air, and beyond the skies, that no arm on earth can reach to bring it down." Incalculable sums, now devoted to armaments and the destructive industry of War, would be turned to the productive industry of Art and to offices of Beneficence. As in the dead and rotten carcass of the lion which roared against the strong man of Israel, after a time, were a swarm of bees and honey, so would the enormous carcass of War, dead and rotten, be filled with crowds of useful laborers and all good works, and the riddle of Samson be once more interpreted: "Out of the eater came forth meat, and out of the strong came forth sweetness."

Put together the products of all the mines in the world, — the glistening ore of California, the accumulated treasures of Mexico and Peru, with the diamonds of Golconda, — and the whole shining heap will be less than the means thus diverted from War to Peace. Under the influence of such a change, civilization will be quickened anew. Then will happy Labor find its reward, and the whole land be filled with its increase. There is no aspiration of Knowledge, no vision of Charity, no venture of Enterprise, no fancy of Art, which may not then be fufilled. The great unsolved problem of Pauperism will be solved at last. There will be no paupers, when there are no soldiers. The social struggles, so fearfully disturbing European nations, will die away in the happiness of unarmed Peace, no longer incumbered by the oppressive system of War; nor can there be well-founded hope that these struggles will permanently cease, so long as this system endures. The people ought not to rest, they cannot rest, while this system endures. As King Arthur, prostrate on the earth, with bloody streams pouring from his veins, could not be at ease, until his sword, the terrific Excalibar, was thrown into the flood, so the Nations, now prostrate on the earth, with bloody streams pouring from their veins, cannot be at ease, until they fling far away the wicked sword of War. King Arthur said to his attending knight, "As thou love me, spare not to throw it in"; and this is the voice of the Nations also.

Lop off the unchristian armaments of the Christian Nations, extirpate these martial cancers, that they may feed no longer upon the life-blood of the people, and society itself, now weary and sick, will become fresh and young, — not by opening its veins, as under the incantation of Medea, in the wild hope of infusing new strength, but by the amputation and complete removal of a deadly excrescence, with all its unutterable debility and exhaustion. Energies hitherto withdrawn from proper healthful action will then replenish it with unwonted life and vigor, giving new expansion to every human capacity, and new elevation to every human aim. And society at last shall rejoice, like a strong man, to run its race.

Imagination toils to picture the boundless good that will be achieved. As War with its deeds is infinitely evil and accursed, so will this triumph of Permanent Peace be infinitely beneficent and blessed. Something of its consequences were seen, in prophetic vision, even by that incarnate Spirit of War, Napoleon Bonaparte, when, from his island-prison of St. Helena, looking back upon his mistaken career, he was led to confess the True Grandeur of Peace. Out of his mouth let its praise be spoken. "I had the project," he said, mournfully regretting the opportunity he had lost, "at the general peace of Amiens, of bringing each Power to an immense reduction of its standing armies. I wished a European Institute, with European prizes, to direct, associate, and bring together all the learned societies of Europe. Then, perhaps, through the universal spread of light, it might be permitted to anticipate for the great European Family the establishment of an American Congress, or an Amphictyonic Council; and what a perspective then of strength, of greatness, of happiness, of prosperity! What a sublime and magnificent spectacle!"[1]

Such is our cause. In transcendent influence, it embraces human beneficence in all its forms. It is the comprehensive charity, enfolding all the charities of all. None so vast as to be above its protection, none so lowly as not to feel its care. Religion, Knowledge, Freedom, Virtue, Happiness, in all their manifold forms, depend upon Peace. Sustained by Peace, they lean upon the Everlasting Arm. And this is not all. Law, Order, Government, derive from Peace new sanctions. Nor can they attain to that complete dominion which is our truest safeguard, until, by the overthrow of the War System, they comprehend the Commonwealth of Nations, —

> "And Sovereign LAW, *the* WORLD'S *collected will*,
> O'er thrones and globes elate,
> Sits empress, crowning good, repressing ill."[2]

[1] Las Cases, Memorial de Sainte-Hélène, November, 1816.
[2] Sir William Jones, Ode in Imitation of Alcæus.

In the name of Religion profaned, of Knowledge misapplied and perverted, of Freedom crushed to earth, of Virtue dethroned, of human Happiness violated, in the name of Law, Order, and Government, I call upon you for union to establish the supremacy of Peace. There must be no hesitation. With the lips you confess the infinite evil of War. Are you in earnest? Action must follow confession. All must unite to render the recurrence of this evil impossible. Science and Humanity everywhere put forth all possible energy against cholera and pestilence. Why not equal energy against an evil more fearful than cholera or pestilence? Each man must consider the cause his own. Let him animate his neighbors. Let him seek, in every proper way, to influence the rulers of the Nations, and, above all, the rulers of this happy land.

The old, the middle-aged, and the young must combine in a common cause. The pulpit, the school, the college, and the public street must speak for it. Preach it, minister of the Prince of Peace! let it never be forgotten in conversation, sermon, or prayer; nor any longer seek, by specious theory, to reconcile the monstrous War System with the precepts of Christ! Instil it, teacher of childhood and youth! in the early thoughts of your precious charge; exhibit the wickedness of War and the beauty of Peace; let your warnings sink deep among those purifying and strengthening influences which ripen into true manhood. Scholar! write it in your books, so that all shall read it. Poet! sing it, so that all shall love it. Let the interests of commerce, whose threads of golden tissue interknit the Nations, enlist the traffickers of the earth in its behalf. And you, servant of the law! sharer of my own peculiar toils, mindful that the law is silent in the midst of arms, join to preserve, uphold, and extend its sway. Remember, politician! that our cause is too universal to become the exclusive possession of any political party, or to be confined within any geographical limits. See to it, statesman and ruler! that the principles of Peace are as a cloud by day and a pillar of fire by night. Let the Abolition of War, and the Overthrow of the War System, with the Disarming of the Nations, be your guiding star. Be this your pious diplomacy! Be this your lofty Christian statesmanship!

As a measure simple and practical, obnoxious to no objection, promising incalculable good, and presenting an immediate opportunity for labor, I would invite your coöperation in the effort now making at home and abroad to establish Arbitration Treaties. If in this scheme there is a tendency to avert War, — if, through its agency, we may hope to prevent a single war, — and who can doubt that such may be its result? — we ought to adopt it. Take the initiative. Try it, and nations will never return to the barbarous system. They will begin to learn War no more. Let it be our privilege to volunteer the proposal. Thus shall we inaugurate Permanent Peace in the diplomacy of the world. Nor should we wait for other governments. In a cause so holy, no government should wait for another. Let us take the lead. Let our republic, powerful child of Freedom, go forth, the Evangelist of Peace. Let her offer to the world a Magna Charta of International Law, by which the crime of War shall be forever abolished.

While thus encouraging you in behalf of Universal Peace, the odious din of War, mingled with pathetic appeals for Freedom, reaches us from struggling Italy, from convulsed Germany, from aroused and triumphant Hungary. At bidding of the Russian Autocrat, the populous North threatens to pour its multitudes upon the scene; and a portentous cloud, charged with "red lightning and impetuous rage," hangs over the whole continent of Europe, which echoes again to the tread of mustering squadrons. Alas! must this dismal work be renewed? Can Freedom be born, can nations be regenerated, only through baptism of blood? In our aspirations, I would not be blind to the teachings of History, or to the actual condition of men, so long accustomed to brute force, that, to their imperfect natures, it seems the only means by which injustice can be crushed. With sadness I confess that we cannot expect the *domestic* repose of nations, until tyranny is overthrown, and the principles of *self-government* are established; especially do I not expect imperturbable peace in Italy, so long as foreign Austria, with insolent iron heel, continues to tread any part of that beautiful land. But whatever may be the fate of the present crisis, whether it be doomed to the horrors of prolonged strife, or shall soon brighten into the radiance of enduring concord, I cannot doubt that the Nations are gravitating, with resistless might, even through fire and blood, into peaceful forms of social order, where the War System will cease to be known.

Nay, from the experience of this hour I draw the auguries of Permanent Peace. Not in any international strife, not in duel between nation and nation, not in selfish conflict of ruler with ruler, not in the unwise "game" of War, as played by king with king, do we find the origin of present commotions, "with fear of change perplexing monarchs." It is to overturn the enforced rule of military power, to crush the tyranny of armies, and to supplant unjust government, — whose only stay is physical force, and not the consent of the governed, — that the people have risen in mighty madness. So doing, they wage a battle where all our sympathies must be with Freedom, while, in sorrow at the unwelcome combat, we confess that victory is only less mournful than defeat. Through all these bloody mists the eye of Faith discerns the ascending sun, struggling to shoot its life-giving beams upon the outspread earth, teeming with the grander products of a new civilization. Everywhere salute us the signs of Progress; and the Promised Land smiles at the new epoch. His heart is cold, his eye is dull, who does not perceive the change. Vainly has he read the history of the Past, vainly does he feel the irrepressible movement of the Present. Man has waded through a Red Sea of blood, and for forty centuries wandered through a wilderness of wretchedness and error, but he stands at last on Pisgah: like the adventurous Spaniard, he has wearily climbed the mountain heights, whence he may descry the vast, unbroken Pacific Sea; like the hardy Portuguese, he is sure to double this fearful Cape of Storms, destined ever afterwards to be the Cape of Good Hope. I would not seem too confident. I know not, that, in any brief period, nations, like kindred drops, will commingle into one, — that, like the banyan-trees of the East, they will interlace and interlock, until there are no longer separate trees, but one united wood,

> "a pillared shade
> High overarched, and echoing walks between";

but I rest assured, that, without renouncing any essential qualities of individuality or independence, they may yet, even in our own day, arrange themselves in harmony; as magnetized iron rings, — from which Plato once borrowed an image, — under the influence of potent unseen attraction, while preserving each its own peculiar form, cohere in a united chain of independent circles. From the birth of this new order will spring not only international repose, but domestic quiet also; and Peace will become the permanent rule of civilization. The stone will be rolled away from the sepulchre in which men have laid their Lord, and we shall hear the new-risen voice, saying, in words of blessed truth, "Lo, I am with you alway, even unto the end of the world."

Here I might fitly close. Though admonished that I have already occupied more of your time than I could venture to claim, except for the cause, I cannot forbear to consider, for a brief moment, yet one other topic, which I have left thus far untouched, partly because it is not directly connected with the main argument, and therefore seemed inappropriate to any earlier stage, and partly because I wished to impress it with my last words. I refer to that greatest, most preposterous, and most irreligious of earthly vanities, the monstrous reflection of War, — *Military Glory.*

Let me not disguise the truth. Too true it is that this vanity is still cherished by mankind, — that it is still an object of ambition, — that men follow War, and count its pursuit "honorable," — that feats of brute force are heralded "brilliant," — and that a yet prevailing public opinion animates unreflecting mortals to "seek the bubble *reputation* even in the cannon's mouth." Too true it is that nations persevere in offering praise and thanksgiving — such as no labors of Beneficence can achieve — to the chief whose hands are red with the blood of his fellow-men.

Whatever the usage of the world, whether during the long and dreary Past or in the yet barbarous Present, it must be clear to all who confront this question with candor, and do not turn away from the blaze of truth, that any glory from bloody strife among God's children must be fugitive, evanescent, unreal. It is the offspring of a deluded public sentiment, and will disappear, as we learn to analyze its elements and appreciate its character. Too long has mankind worshipped what St. Augustine called the *splendid vices*, neglecting the simple virtues, — too long cultivated the flaunting and noxious weeds, careless of the golden corn, — too long been insensible to that commanding law and sacred example which rebuke all the pretensions of military glory.

Look face to face at this "glory." Study it in the growing illumination of history. Regarding War as an established Arbitrament, for the adjudication of controversies among nations, — like the Petty Wars of an earlier period between cities, principalities, and provinces, or like the Trial by Battle between individuals, — the conclusion is irresistible, that an enlightened civilization, when the world has reached that Unity to which it tends, must condemn the partakers in its duels, and their vaunted achievements, precisely as we now condemn the partakers in those wretched contests which disfigure the commencement of modern history. The prowess of the individual is forgotten in disgust at an inglorious barbarism.

Observe this "glory" in the broad sunshine of Christian truth. In all ages, even in Heathen lands, there has been a peculiar reverence for the relation of Brotherhood. Feuds among brothers, from that earliest "mutual-murdering" conflict beneath the walls of Thebes, have been accounted ghastly and abhorred, never to be mentioned without a shudder. This sentiment was revived in modern times, and men sought to extend the circle of its influence. Warriors, like Du Guesclin, rejoiced to hail each other as brothers. Chivalry delighted in fraternities of arms sealed by vow and solemnity. According to curious and savage custom, valiant knights were bled together, that their blood, as it spurted forth, might intermingle, and thus constitute them of *one blood*, which was drunk by each. So did the powerful emperor of Constantinople confirm an alliance of friendship with a neighbor king. The two monarchs drank of each other's blood; and then their attendants, following the princely example, caught their own flowing life in a wine-cup, and quaffed a mutual pledge, saying, "We are brothers, of *one blood*." [1]

By such profane devices men sought to establish that relation, whose beauty they perceived, though they failed to discern, that, by the ordinance of God, without any human stratagem, it justly comprehended all their fellow-men. In the midst of Judaism, which hated Gen-

[1] Du Cange, Dissertations sur l'Histoire de Saint Louys par Jean Sire de Joinville, Diss. XXI. Ibid.: Petitot, Mémoires relatifs à l'Histoire de France, 1re Série, Tom. III. p. 349. Sainte-Palaye, Mémoires sur l'Ancienne Chevalerie, Part. III. Tom. I. p. 225. The same attempt at Brotherhood appears in the "Loka-Lenna, or Strife of Loc," quoted by Sir Walter Scott in his Notes to the Metrical Romance of "Sir Tristrem," p. 350: —

"Father of Slaughter, Odin, say,
Remember'st not the former day,
When in the ruddy goblet stood,
For mutual drink, our blended blood?"

tiles, Christianity proclaimed love to all mankind, and distinctly declared that God had made of *one blood* all the nations of men. As if to keep this sublime truth ever present, the disciples were taught, in the simple prayer of the Saviour, to address God as Father in heaven, — not in phrase of exclusive worship, "*my* Father," but in those other words of peculiar Christian import, "*our* Father," — with the petition, not merely to "forgive *me my* trespasses," but with the diviner prayer, to "forgive *us our* trespasses": thus, in the solitude of the closet, recognizing all alike as children of God, and embracing all alike in the petition for mercy.

Confessing the Fatherhood of God, and the consequent Brotherhood of Man, we find a divine standard of unquestionable accuracy. No brother can win "glory" from the death of a brother. Cain won no "glory," when he slew Abel; nor would Abel have won "glory," had he, in strictest self-defence, succeeded in slaying the wicked Cain. The soul recoils from praise or honor, as the meed of any such melancholy triumph. And what is true of a conflict between *two* brothers is equally true of a conflict between *many.* How can an army win "glory" by dealing death or defeat to an army of its brothers?

The ancient Romans, not knowing this comprehensive relation, and recognizing only the exclusive fellowship of a common country, accounted *civil war fratricidal,* whose opposing forces, even under well-loved names of the Republic, were *impious;* and then, by unerring logic, these masters in War constantly refused "honor," "thanksgiving," or "triumph," to the conquering chief whose sword had been employed against *fellow-citi-*

zens, though traitors and rebels. As the Brotherhood of Man is practically recognized, it becomes impossible to restrict the feeling within any exclusive circle of country, and to set up an unchristian distinction of honor between *civil war* and *international war. As all men are brothers, so, by irresistible consequence,* ALL WAR MUST BE FRATRICIDAL. And can "glory" come from fratricide? None can hesitate in answer, unless fatally imbued with the Heathen rage of nationality, that made the Venetians declare themselves Venetians first and Christians afterwards.

Tell me not of homage yet offered to the military chieftain. Tell me not of "glory" from War. Tell me not of "honor" or "fame" on its murderous fields. All is vanity. It is a blood-red phantom. They who strive after it, Ixion-like, embrace a cloud. Though seeming to fill the heavens, cloaking the stars, it must, like the vapors of earth, pass away. Milton likens the contests of the Heptarchy to "the wars of kites or crows flocking and fighting in the air."[1] But God, and the exalted judgment of the Future, must regard all our bloody feuds in the same likeness, — finding Napoleon and Alexander, so far as engaged in War, only monster crows and kites. Thus must it be, as mankind ascend from the thrall of brutish passion. Nobler aims, by nobler means, will fill the soul. There will be a new standard of excellence; and honor, divorced from blood, will become the inseparable attendant of good works alone. Far better, then, even in the judgment of this world, to have been a doorkeeper in the house of Peace than the proudest dweller in the tents of War.

[1] History of England, Book IV.: Prose Works (ed. Symmons), Vol. IV. p. 158.

There is a pious legend of the early Church, that the Saviour left his image miraculously impressed upon a napkin which had touched his countenance. The napkin was lost, and men attempted to supply the divine lineaments from the Heathen models of Jupiter and Apollo. But the true image of Christ is not lost. Clearer than in the venerated napkin, better than in color or marble of choicest art, it appears in each virtuous deed, in every act of self-sacrifice, in all magnanimous toil, in any recognition of Human Brotherhood. It will be supremely manifest, in unimagined loveliness and serenity, when the Commonwealth of Nations, confessing the True Grandeur of Peace, renounces the War System, and dedicates to Beneficence the comprehensive energies so fatally absorbed in its support. Then, at last, will it be seen, *there can be no Peace that is not honorable, and no War that is not dishonorable.*

BE TRUE TO THE DECLARATION OF INDEPENDENCE.

Letter to a Public Meeting in Ohio, on the Anniversary of the Ordinance of Freedom, July 6, 1849.

Boston, July 6, 1849.

GENTLEMEN, — I wish I could join the freemen of the Reserve in celebrating the anniversary of the great Ordinance of Freedom; but engagements detain me at home.

The occasion, the place of meeting, the assembly, will all speak with animating voices. May God speed the work!

Let us all strive, with united power, to extend the beneficent Ordinance over the territories of our country. So doing, we must take from its original authors something of their devotion to its great conservative truth.

The National Government has been for a long time controlled by Slavery. It must be emancipated immediately. Ours be the duty, worthy of freemen, to place the Government under the auspices of Freedom, that it may be true to the Declaration of Independence and to the spirit of the Fathers!

In this work, welcome to honest, earnest men, of *all parties* and *all places!* Welcome to the efforts of Benton in Missouri, and of Clay in Kentucky! Above all, welcome to the united regenerated Democracy of the

North, which spurns the mockery of a Republic, with professions of Freedom on the lips, while the chains of Slavery clank in the Capitol!

Faithfully yours,

CHARLES SUMNER.

Messrs. JOHN C. VAUGHAN, THOMAS BROWN, } *Committee.*

WHERE LIBERTY IS, THERE IS MY PARTY.

Speech on calling the Free-Soil State Convention to Order, at Worcester, September 12, 1849.

The Annual State Convention of the Free-Soil Party, called at the time the Free Democracy, met at Worcester, September 12, 1849. It became the duty of Mr. Sumner, as Chairman of the State Central Committee, to call the Convention to order. In doing this he made the following remarks.

Fellow-Citizens of the Convention: —

IN behalf of the State Central Committee of the Free Democracy of Massachusetts, it is my duty to call this body to order.

I do not know that it is my privilege, at this stage of your proceedings, to add one other word to the words of form I have already pronounced; but I cannot look at this large and generous assembly without uttering from my heart one salutation of welcome and encouragement. From widely scattered homes you have come to bear testimony once more in that great cause containing country with all its truest welfare and honor, and also the highest aspirations of our souls. Others may prefer the old combinations of party, stitched together by devices of expediency only. You have chosen the better part, in coming to this alliance of principle.

In the labors before you there will be, I doubt not, that concord which becomes earnest men, devoted to a good work. We all have but one object in view,— the success of our cause. Turning neither to the right nor to the left, moving ever onward, we adopt into our ranks all who adopt our principles. These we offer freely to all who will come and take them. These we can communicate to others without losing them ourselves. These are gifts which, without parting with, we can yet bestow, as from the burning candle other candles may be lighted without diminishing the original flame.

It was the sentiment of Benjamin Franklin, that apostle of Freedom, uttered during the trials of the Revolution, "Where Liberty is, there is my country." I doubt not that each of you will be ready to respond, in similar strain, "Where Liberty is, there is my party."

It now remains, Gentlemen of the Convention, that I should call upon you to proceed with the business of the day.

THE FREE-SOIL PARTY EXPLAINED AND VINDICATED.

ADDRESS TO THE PEOPLE OF MASSACHUSETTS, REPORTED TO AND ADOPTED BY THE FREE-SOIL STATE CONVENTION AT WORCESTER, SEPTEMBER 12, 1849.

THE State Convention of the Free-Soil party at Worcester, 12th September, was organized with the following officers: Hon. William Jackson, of Newton, President; Bradford Sumner, of Boston, Daniel E. Potter, of Salem, C. L. Knapp, of Lowell, J. T. Buckingham, of Cambridge, John Milton Earle, of Worcester, D. S. Jones, of Greenfield, Edward F. Ensign, of Sheffield, Benjamin V. French, of Braintree, Gershom B. Weston, of Duxbury, and Job Coleman, of Nantucket, Vice-Presidents; William F. Channing, of Boston, Samuel Fowler, of Westfield, Noah Kimball, of Grafton, A. A. Leach, of Taunton, Secretaries.

On motion of Mr. Sumner, a committee of one from each county was appointed to report an Address and Resolutions, consisting of Charles Sumner, of Boston, John A. Bolles, of Woburn, J. G. Whittier, of Amesbury, John M. Earle, of Worcester, Melvin Copeland, of Chester, Erastus Hopkins, of Northampton, D. W. Alvord, of Greenfield, F. M. Lowrey, of Lee, F. W. Bird, of Walpole, Jesse Perkins, of Bridgewater, Joseph Brownell, of New Bedford, Nathaniel Hinckley, of Barnstable, and E. W. Gardner, of Nantucket.

In the course of the proceedings, speeches were made by Anson Burlingame, Esq., Hon. Charles F. Adams, Hon. Charles Allen, Hon. Edward L. Keyes, and James A. Briggs, Esq., of Ohio. From the committee of which he was chairman Mr. Sumner reported an Address to the People of Massachusetts, explaining and vindicating the Free-Soil movement, with a series of Resolutions, all of which were unanimously adopted by the Convention. Of this Address, which became the authorized declaration of the party, the *Daily Republican* remarked: "The Address, prepared by that gifted scholar and writer, Charles Sumner, is an elaborate, complete, and unanswerable vindication of the principles embodied in the Resolutions. Clear, logical, and triumphant in argument, it glows with the warm and genial spirit of love for humanity which distinguishes all the productions of its author."

Among the Resolutions was the following, which seems the prelude to the debates of twenty years later.

"*Resolved*, That we adopt, as the only safe and stable basis of our State, as well as our National policy, the great principles of Equal Rights for All, guarantied and secured by Equal Laws."

TO THE PEOPLE OF MASSACHUSETTS.

FELLOW-CITIZENS, — Another year has gone round, and you are once more called to bear testimony at the polls to those truths which you deem vital in the government of the country. By votes you are to declare not merely predilections for men, but devotion to principles. Men are erring and mortal; principles are steadfast and immortal.

If the occasion is calculated less than a Presidential contest to arouse ardors of opposition, it is also less calculated to stimulate animosities. With less passion, the people are more under the influence of reason. Truth may be heard over the prejudices of party. Candor, kindly feeling, and conscientious thought may take the place of embittered, unreasoning antagonism, or of timid, unprincipled compliance. If the controversy is without heat, there may be no viper to come forth and fasten upon the hand.

Though of less apparent consequence in immediate results, the election now approaching is nevertheless of great importance. We do not choose a President of the United States, or Members of Congress, but a Governor, Lieutenant-Governor, and other State officers. Still, the same question which entered into the election of National officers arises now. The Great Issue which has already convulsed the whole country presents itself anew in a local sphere. Omnipresent wherever any political election occurs, it will never cease to challenge attention, until at least two things are accomplished: *first*, the divorce of the National Government from all support or sanction of Slavery, — and, *secondly*, the conversion of this Government, within its constitutional limits, to the cause of Freedom, so that it shall become Freedom's open, active, and perpetual ally.

Impressed by the magnitude of these interests, devoted to the triumph of the righteous cause, solicitous for the national welfare, animated by the example of the fathers, and desirous of breathing their spirit into our Government, the Free Democracy of Massachusetts, in Convention assembled at Worcester, now address their fellow-citizens throughout the Commonwealth. Imperfectly, according to the necessity of the occasion, earnestly, according to the fulness of their convictions, hopefully, according to the confidence of their aspirations, they proceed to unfold the reasons of their appeal. They now ask your attention. They trust to secure your votes.

Our Party a permanent National Party. — We make our appeal as a *National* party, established to promote principles of paramount importance to the country. In assuming our place as a distinct party, we simply give form and direction, in harmony with the usage and the genius of popular governments, to a movement which stirs the whole country, and does not find an adequate and constant organ in either of the other existing parties. In France, under the royalty of Louis Philippe, the faithful friends of the yet unborn Republic formed a band together, and by publications, speeches, and votes sought to influence the public mind. Few at first in numbers, they became strong by united political action. In England, the most brilliant popular triumph in her history, the repeal of the monopoly of the Corn Laws, was finally carried by means of a newly formed, but wide-spread, political organization, which combined men of all the old parties, Whigs, Tories, and Radicals, and recognized opposition to the Corn Laws as a special test. In the spirit of these examples, the friends of Freedom have come together, in well-compacted ranks, to uphold their cherished principles, and by combined efforts, according to the course of parties, to urge them upon the Government, and upon the country.

All the old organizations contribute to our number, and good citizens come to us who have not heretofore mingled in the contests of party. Here are men from the ancient Democracy, believing that any democracy must be a name only, no better than sounding brass or a tinkling cymbal, which does not recognize on every occasion the supremacy of Human Rights, and is not ready to do and to suffer in their behalf. Here also are men who have come out of the Whig party, weary of its many professions and its little performance, and especially revolting at its recent sinister course with regard to Freedom, believing that in any devotion to Human Rights they cannot err. Here also, in solid legion, is the well-tried band of the Liberty Party, to whom belongs the praise of first placing Freedom under the guardianship of a special political organization, whose exclusive test was opposition to Slavery.

Associating and harmonizing from opposite quarters to promote a common cause, we learn to forget former differences, and to appreciate the motives of each other,

— also how trivial are the matters on which we disagree, compared with the Great Issue on which we all agree. Old prejudices vanish. Even the rancors of political antagonism are changed and dissolved, as in a potent alembic, while the natural irresistible affinities of Freedom prevail. In our union we cease to wear the badge of either of the old organizations. We have become a party distinct, independent, permanent, under the name of the Free Democracy, thus in our very designation expressing devotion to Human Rights, and especially to Human Freedom.

Professing honestly the same sentiments, wherever we exist, in all parts of the country, East and West, North and South, we are truly a NATIONAL party. We are not compelled to assume one face at the South and another at the North, — to blow hot in one place, and blow cold in another, — to speak loudly of Freedom in one region, and vindicate Slavery in another — in short, to present a combination where the two extreme wings profess opinions, on the Great Issue before the country, diametrically opposed to each other. We are the same everywhere. And the reason is, because our party, unlike the other parties, is bound together in support of fixed and well-defined principles. It is not a combination fired by partisan zeal, and kept together, as with mechanical force, by considerations of political expediency only, — but a sincere, conscientious, inflexible union for the sake of Freedom.

Old Issues obsolete. — Taking position as an independent party, we are cheered not only by the grandeur of our cause, but by favorable omens in the existing condition of parties. Devotion to Freedom impels us;

Providence itself seems to open the path for our triumphant efforts. Old questions which have divided the minds of men have lost their importance. One by one they have disappeared from the political field, leaving it free to a question more transcendent far. The Bank, the Sub-Treasury, the Public Lands, are all obsolete issues. Even the Tariff is not a question where opposite political parties take opposite sides. The opinions of Mr. Clay and Mr. Polk, as expressed in 1844, when they were rival candidates for the Presidency, are so nearly identical, that it is difficult to distinguish between them.

CLAY.

"Let the amount which is requisite for an economical administration of the government, when we are not engaged in war, be raised exclusively on foreign imports; and in adjusting a tariff for that purpose, let such discriminations be made as will foster and encourage our own domestic industry. All parties ought to be satisfied with a tariff for revenue and discriminations for protection." — *Speech at Raleigh, April* 13, *in the National Intelligencer of June* 29, 1844.

POLK.

"I am in favor of a tariff for revenue, such a one as will yield a sufficient amount to the treasury to defray the expenses of the government, economically administered. In adjusting the details of a revenue tariff, I have heretofore sanctioned such moderate discriminating duties as would produce the amount of revenue needed, and at the same time afford reasonable incidental protection to our home industry. I am opposed to a tariff for protection merely, and not for revenue." — *Letter to John K. Kane, June* 19, 1844.

Friends and enemies of the Tariff are to be found, more or less, in both the old organizations. From opposite quarters we are admonished that it is not a proper question for the strife of party. Mr. Webster, from the Whigs, and Mr. Robert J. Walker, from the Democrats, both plead for its withdrawal from the list of political issues, that the industry of the country may not be entangled in constantly recurring contests. And why have they thus far pleaded in vain? It is feared no better reason can be given than that certain political leaders wish to use the Tariff as a battle-horse by which to rally their followers in desperate warfare for office. The debt entailed by the Mexican War comes to aid the admonitions of wisdom, and to disappoint the plots of partisans, by imposing upon the country the necessity for such large taxation as to make the protection thus incidentally afforded satisfactory to judicious minds.

The Great Issue. — And now, instead of these superseded questions, connected for the most part only with the material interests of the country, and, though not unimportant in their time, all having the odor of the dollar, you are called to consider a cause connected with all that is divine in Religion, pure in Morals, and truly practical in Politics. Unlike the other questions, it is not temporary or local in character. It belongs to all times and to all countries. It is part of the great movement under whose strong pulsations all Christendom now shakes from side to side. It is a cause which, though long kept in check throughout our country, as also in Europe, now confronts the people and their rulers, demanding to be heard. It can no longer be avoided or silenced. To every man in the land it now says, with clear, penetrating voice, "Are you for Freedom, or are you for Slavery?" And every man in the land must answer this question, when he votes.

The devices of party can no longer stave it off. The subterfuges of the politician cannot escape it. The tricks of the office-seeker cannot dodge it. Wherever an election occurs, there this question will arise. Wherever men assemble to speak of public affairs, there again it will be. In the city and in the village, in the field and in the workshop, everywhere will this question be sounded in the ears: "Are you for Freedom, or are you for Slavery?"

The Anti-Slavery Sentiments of the Founders of the Republic. — A plain recital of facts will show the urgency of this question. At the period of the Declaration of Independence there were upwards of half a million colored persons held as slaves in the United States. These unhappy people were originally stolen from Africa, or were the children of those stolen, and, though distributed through the whole country, were to be found mostly in the Southern States. But the spirit of Freedom was then abroad in the land. The fathers of the Republic, leaders in the War of Independence, were struck with the impious inconsistency of an appeal for their own liberties, while holding fellow-men in bondage. Out of ample illustrations, I select one which specially reveals this conviction, and possesses a local interest in this community. It is a deed of manumission, made after our struggles had begun, and preserved in the Probate Records of the County of Suffolk.[1] Here it is.

"Know all men by these presents, that I, JONATHAN JACKSON, of Newburyport, in the County of Essex, gentleman, *in consideration of the impropriety I feel, and have long felt, in holding any person in constant bondage, more especially at a time when my country is so warmly contending for the liberty*

[1] Printed, since this Address, in the History of Newton, by Francis Jackson, (Boston, 1854,) p. 386.

every man ought to enjoy, and having sometime since promised my negro man, POMP, that I would give him his freedom, and in further consideration of five shillings paid me by said POMP, I do hereby liberate, manumit, and set him free; and I do hereby remise and release unto said POMP all demands of whatever nature I have against POMP. In witness whereof I have hereunto set my hand and seal, this 19th of June, 1776.

"JONATHAN JACKSON. [Seal.]

"*Witness*, MARY COBURN,
"WILLIAM NOYES."

The same conviction animated the hearts of the people, whether at the North or South. In a town-meeting at Danbury, Connecticut, held on the 12th of December, 1774, the following declaration was made.

"It is with singular pleasure we note the second article of the Association, in which it is agreed to import no more negro slaves, — as we cannot but think it a palpable absurdity so loudly to complain of attempts to enslave *us*, while we are actually enslaving *others*." [1]

The South responded in similar strain. At a meeting in Darien, Georgia, January 12th, 1775, the following important resolution speaks, in tones worthy of freemen, the sentiments of the time.

"We, therefore, the Representatives of the extensive District of Darien, in the Colony of Georgia, being now assembled in Congress, by the authority and free choice of the inhabitants of the said District, now freed from their fetters, do

Resolve, ... To show the world that we are not influenced by any contracted or interested motives, but a general philanthropy for all mankind, of whatever climate, language, or complexion, *we hereby declare our disapprobation*

[1] American Archives, 4th Series, Vol. I. col. 1038.

and abhorrence of the unnatural practice of Slavery in America, (however the uncultivated state of our country, *or other specious arguments, may plead for it*,) a practice founded in injustice and cruelty, and highly dangerous to our liberties, (as well as lives,) debasing part of our fellow-creatures below men, and corrupting the virtue and morals of the rest, and is laying the basis of that liberty we contend for (and which we pray the Almighty to continue to the latest posterity) upon a very wrong foundation. We therefore resolve at all times to use our utmost endeavors for the manumission of our slaves in this Colony, upon the most safe and equitable footing for the masters and themselves."[1]

Would that such a voice were heard once again from Georgia!

The soul of Virginia, at this period, found eloquent utterance through Jefferson, who, by precocious and immortal words, enrolled himself among the earliest Abolitionists of the country. In a paper presented to the Virginia Convention of 1774, in reference to the grievances by which the Colonies were then agitated, he openly avowed, while vindicating American rights, that "the abolition of domestic slavery is the greatest object of desire in those Colonies, *where it was unhappily introduced in their infant state*."[2] And then again in the Declaration of Independence he embodied sentiments, which, when practically applied, will give freedom to every slave throughout the land. "We hold these truths to be self-evident," said the country, speaking by his voice: "that all men are created equal; that they are endowed by their Creator with certain

1 American Archives, 4th Series, Vol. I. coll. 1135. 1136.

2 A Summary View of the Rights of British America: American Archives, 4th Series, Vol. I. col. 696. Memoir, Correspondence, and Miscellanies of Jefferson, Vol. I. p. 111; Writings, Vol. I. p. 135.

unalienable rights; that among these are life, *liberty*, and the pursuit of happiness." And again, in the Congress of the Confederation, he brought forward, as early as 1784, a resolution to exclude Slavery from all the territory "ceded or *to be ceded*" by the States to the Federal Government, and including the territory now covered by Tennessee, Mississippi, and Alabama. Lost at first by the failure of the two-thirds vote required, this measure was substantially renewed at a subsequent day by a son of Massachusetts, and in 1787 was finally confirmed, in the Ordinance of the Northwestern Territory, by a unanimous vote of the States, with only a single dissentient among the delegates.

Thus early and distinctly do we discern the Anti-slavery character of the founders, and their determination to place the National Government openly, actively, and perpetually on the side of Freedom.

The National Constitution was adopted in 1788. And here we discern the same spirit. Express provision was made for the abolition of the slave-trade. The discreditable words *Slave* and *Slavery* were not allowed to find place in the instrument, while a clause was subsequently added, by way of amendment, and therefore, according to received rules of interpretation, specially revealing the sentiments of the founders, which is calculated, like the Declaration of Independence, if practically applied, to carry freedom everywhere within the sphere of its influence. It was specifically declared, that "no person shall be deprived of life, *liberty*, or property, without due process of law."

From a perusal of the debates on the National Constitution, it is evident that Slavery, like the Slave-trade, was regarded as temporary; and it seems to have been supposed by many that they would disappear together. Nor do any words employed in our day denounce it with an indignation more burning than that which glowed on the lips of the fathers. Mr. Gouverneur Morris, of Pennsylvania, said in Convention, that "he never would concur in upholding domestic slavery: it was a nefarious institution."[1] In another mood, and with mild juridical phrase, Mr. Madison "thought it wrong to admit in the Constitution the idea that there could be property in men."[2] And Washington, in a letter written near this period, says, with a frankness worthy of imitation," There is only one proper and effectual mode by which the abolition of slavery can be accomplished, and that is by legislative authority; *and this, as far as my suffrage will go, shall never be wanting.*"[3]

In this spirit was the National Constitution adopted. Glance now at the earliest Congress assembled under this Constitution. Among the petitions presented to that body was one from the Abolition Society of Pennsylvania, signed by Benjamin Franklin, as President. This venerable man, whose active life had been devoted to the welfare of mankind at home and abroad, who as philosopher and statesman had arrested the attention of the world,—who had ravished the lightning from the skies, and the sceptre from a tyrant,—who, as member of the Continental Congress, had set his name to the Declaration of Independence, and, as member of the Convention, had again set his name to the National Constitution,—in whom was embodied, more,

1 Madison's Debates, p. 1263.

2 Ibid. p. 1429.

3 Letter to Robert Morris, April 12, 1786: Writings, ed. Sparks, Vol. IX. p. 159.

perhaps, than in any other person, the true spirit of American institutions, at once practical and humane,—than whom no one could be more familiar with the purposes and aspirations of the founders,—this veteran, eighty-four years of age, within a few months only of his death, now appeared by petition at the bar of that Congress whose powers he had helped to define and establish. "Your memorialists," he says,—and this Convention now repeats the words of Franklin,—"particularly engaged in attending to the distresses arising from Slavery, believe it their indispensable duty to present this subject to your notice. They have observed with real satisfaction that many important and salutary powers are vested in you for 'promoting the welfare and securing the blessings of Liberty to the people of the United States'; and as they conceive that these blessings ought rightfully to be administered, *without distinction of color*, to all descriptions of people, *so they indulge themselves in the pleasing expectation that nothing which can be done for the relief of the unhappy objects of their care will be either omitted or delayed.*" The memorialists conclude as follows,—and this Convention adopts their weighty words as its own: "Under these impressions they earnestly entreat your serious attention to the subject of Slavery; *that you will be pleased to countenance the restoration of liberty to those unhappy men, who alone, in this land of Freedom, are degraded into perpetual bondage*, and who, amidst the general joy of surrounding freemen, are groaning in servile subjection; that you will devise means for removing this inconsistency from the character of the American people; that you will promote mercy and justice towards this distressed race; *and that you will step to the very verge of the power vested in you for DISCOURAGING every species of traffic in the persons of our fellow-men.*

"BENJ. FRANKLIN, *President.*"[1]

Such a prayer, signed by Franklin as President of an Abolition Society, not only shows the spirit of the times, but fixes forever the true policy of the Republic.

Fellow-citizens, there are men in our day, who, while professing a certain disinclination to Slavery, are careful to add that they are not Abolitionists. Jefferson, Washington, and Franklin shrank from no such designation. It is a part of their lives which the honest historian commemorates with pride, that they were unhesitating, open, avowed Abolitionists. By such men, and under the benign influence of such sentiments, was the National Government inaugurated, and dedicated to Freedom. At this time, nowhere under the National Government did Slavery exist. Only in the States, skulking beneath the shelter of local laws, was it allowed to remain.

Change from Antislavery to Proslavery. — But the generous sentiments which filled the souls of the early patriots, and impressed upon the government they founded, as upon the very coin they circulated, the image and superscription of LIBERTY, gradually lost their power. The blessings of Freedom being already secured to themselves, the freemen of the land grew indifferent to the freedom of others. They ceased to think of the slaves. The slave-masters availed themselves of this indifference, and, though few in number, compared with the non-slaveholders, even in the Slave States, they were able, under the impulse of an imagined self-interest, by the skilful tactics of party, and espe-

[1] Annals of Congress, 1st Cong. 2d Sess., 1197, 1198.

cially by an unhesitating, persevering union among themselves, swaying by turns both the great political parties, to obtain the control of the National Government, which they have held through a long succession of years, bending it to their purposes, compelling it to do their will, and imposing upon it a policy friendly to Slavery, offensive to Freedom only, and directly opposed to the sentiments of its founders. Here was a fundamental change in the character of the Government, to which may be referred much of the evil which has perplexed the country.

Usurpations and Aggressions of the Slave Power. — Look at the extent to which this malign influence has predominated. The Slave States are far inferior to the Free States in population, wealth, education, libraries, resources of all kinds, and yet they have taken to themselves the lion's share of honor and profit under the Constitution. They have held the Presidency for fifty-seven years, while the Free States have held it for twelve years only. But without pursuing this game of political sweepstakes, which the Slave Power has perpetually played, we present what is more important, as indicative of its spirit, — the aggressions and usurpations by which it has turned the National Government from its original character of Freedom, and prostituted it to Slavery. Here is a brief catalogue.

Early in this century, when the District of Columbia was finally occupied as the National Capital, the Slave Power succeeded, in defiance of the spirit of the Constitution, and even of the express letter of one of its Amendments, in securing for Slavery, within the District, the countenance of the National Government.

Until then, Slavery existed nowhere on the land within the reach and exclusive jurisdiction of this Government.

It next secured for Slavery another recognition under the National Government, in the broad Territory of Louisiana, purchased from France.

It next placed Slavery again under the sanction of the National Government, in the Territory of Florida, purchased from Spain.

Waxing powerful, it was able, after a severe struggle, to impose terms upon the National Government, compelling it to receive Missouri into the Union with a Slaveholding Constitution.

It instigated and carried on a most expensive war in Florida, mainly to recover fugitive slaves,—thus degrading the army of the United States to slave-hunters.

It wrested from Mexico the Province of Texas, in order to extend Slavery, and, triumphing over all opposition, finally secured its admission into the Union with a Constitution making Slavery perpetual.

It next plunged the country into unjust war with Mexico, to gain new lands for Slavery.

With the meanness as well as insolence of tyranny, it compelled the National Government to abstain from acknowledging the neighbor Republic of Hayti, where slaves have become freemen, and established an independent nation.

It compelled the National Government to stoop ignobly, and in vain, before the British queen, to secure compensation for slaves, who, in the exercise of the natural rights of man, had asserted and achieved their freedom on the Atlantic Ocean, and afterwards sought shelter in Bermuda.

It compelled the National Government to seek the negotiation of treaties for the surrender of fugitive slaves, — thus making the Republic assert in foreign lands property in human flesh.

It joined in declaring the foreign slave-trade *piracy*, but insists upon the coastwise slave-trade under the auspices of the National Government.

It has rejected for years petitions to Congress against Slavery, — thus, in order to shield Slavery, practically denying the right of petition.

It has imprisoned and sold into slavery colored citizens of Massachusetts, entitled, under the Constitution of the United States, to all the privileges of citizens.

It insulted and exiled from Charleston and New Orleans the honored representatives of Massachusetts, who were sent to those places with the commission of the Commonwealth, in order to throw the shield of the Constitution over her colored citizens.

In formal despatches by the pen of Mr. Calhoun, as Secretary of State, it has made the Republic stand before the nations of the earth as the vindicator of Slavery.

It puts forth the hideous effrontery, that Slavery can go to all newly acquired territories, and have the protection of the national flag.

In defiance of the desire declared by the Fathers to limit and discourage Slavery, the Slave Power has successively introduced into the Union Kentucky, Tennessee, Louisiana, Mississippi, Alabama, Missouri, Arkansas, Florida, and Texas, as Slaveholding States, — thus, at each stage, fortifying its political power, and making the National Government lend new sanction to Slavery.

Such are some of the usurpations and aggressions of the Slave Power. By such steps the National Government is perverted from its original purposes, its character changed, and its powers subjected to Slavery. It is pitiful to see Freedom suffer at any time from any hands. It is doubly pitiful, when she suffers from a government nursed by her into strength, and quickened by her into those activities which are the highest glory.

> " So the struck eagle, stretched upon the plain,
> No more through rolling clouds to soar again,
> Viewed his own feather on the fatal dart,
> And winged the shaft that quivered in his heart.
> Keen were his pangs, but keener far to feel
> He nursed the pinion which impelled the steel,
> While the same plumage that had warmed his nest
> Drank the last life-drop of his bleeding breast."

That we may fully estimate this system of conduct in its enormity, we must call to mind the evils of Slavery, where it is allowed to exist. And here language is inadequate to portray the infinite sum of wretchedness, degradation, injustice, legalized by this unholy relation. There is no offence against religion, against morals, against humanity, which does not stalk, in the license of Slavery, "unwhipped of justice." For the husband and wife there is no marriage. For the mother there is no assurance that her infant will not be torn from her breast. For all who bear the name of Slave there is nothing which they can call their own. But the bondman is not the only sufferer. He does not sit alone in his degradation. By his side is the master, who, in the debasing influences on his own soul, is compelled to share the degradation to which he dooms his fellow-men. "The man must be a prodigy," says Jefferson, "who can retain his manners and morals undepraved by such circumstances."[1] And this is not all. The whole social fabric is disorganized; labor loses its dignity; industry sickens; education finds no schools; religion finds no churches; and all the land of Slavery is impoverished.

Shall Slavery be extended? — Now, at last, the Slave Power threatens to carry Slavery into the vast regions of New Mexico and California, existing territories of the United States, already purged of this evil by express legislation of the Mexican government. It is the immediate urgency of this question that has aroused the country to the successive aggressions of the Slave Power, and to its undue influence over the National Government. Without doubt, this is the most pressing form in which the Great Issue is presented. Nor can it be exaggerated. These territories, excluding Oregon, embrace upwards of five hundred thousand square miles. The immensity of this tract may be partially comprehended, when we consider that Massachusetts contains only 7,800 miles, all New England only 63,280, and all the original thirteen States which declared Independence only 352,000. And the distinct question is presented, whether the National Government shall carry into this imperial region the curse of Slavery, with its monstrous brood of ignorance, poverty, and degradation, or Freedom, with her attendant train of blessings.

A direct Prohibition by Congress necessary to prevent Extension of Slavery. — An attempt is made to divert attention from this question by denying the necessity of Congressional enactment to prevent the extension of Slavery into California, on the ground that climate and

[1] Notes on Virginia, Query XVIII.

physical condition furnish natural obstacles to its existence there. This is a weak device. It is well known that Slavery did exist there for many years, until excluded by law, — that California lies in the same range of latitude as the Slave States of the Union, and it may be added, also, the Barbary States of Africa, — that the mineral wealth of California creates a demand for slave labor, which would overcome any physical obstacle to its introduction, — that Slavery has existed in every country from which it was not excluded by the laws or religion of the people; and still further, it is an undeniable fact, that already slaves have been taken into California, and publicly sold there at enormous prices, and thousands are now on their way thither from the Southern States and from South America. In support of this last statement numerous authorities might be adduced. A member of Congress from Tennessee recently declared, that, within his own knowledge, there would be taken to California, during the summer just past, from ten to twelve thousand slaves. Another person states, from reliable evidence, that whole families are moving with slaves from Tennessee, Arkansas, and Missouri. Mr. Rowe, under date of May 13, at Independence, Missouri, on his way to the Pacific, writes to the paper of which he was recently the editor, the "Belfast Journal," Maine: "I have seen as many as a dozen teams going along *with their families of slaves.*" And Mr. Boggs, once Governor of Missouri, now a resident of California, is quoted as writing to a friend at home as follows: "If your sons will bring out two or three negroes who can cook and attend at a hotel, your brother will pay cash for them at a good profit, and take it as a great favor."

After these things, to which many more might be added, it will not be denied, that, in order to secure Freedom in the Territories, there must be direct and early prohibition of Slavery by Act of Congress.

POSITION OF THE FREE-SOIL PARTY.

THE way is now prepared to consider our precise position with regard to the accumulating aggressions of the Slave Power, revealed especially in recent efforts to extend Slavery.

Wilmot Proviso. — To the end that the country and the age may not witness the foul sin of a Republic dedicated to Freedom pouring into vast unsettled lands, as into the veins of an infant, the festering poison of Slavery, destined, as time advances, to show itself only in cancer and leprous disease, we pledge ourselves to unremitting endeavors for the passage of the Wilmot Proviso, or some other form of Congressional enactment prohibiting Slavery in the Territories, without equivocation or compromise of any kind.

Opposition to Slavery wherever we are responsible for it. — But we do not content ourselves with opposing this last act of aggression. We go further. Not only from desire to bring the National Government back again to the spirit of the Fathers, but also from deep convictions of morals and religion, is our hostility to Slavery derived. Slavery is wrong; nor can any human legislation elevate into any respectability the blasphemy of tyranny, that man can hold property in his fellow-man. Slavery, we repeat, is wrong, and therefore we cannot sanction it. In these convictions will be found the measure of our duties.

Wherever we are responsible for Slavery, we oppose it. Our opposition is coextensive with our responsibility. In the States Slavery is sustained by local law; and although we are compelled to share the stigma upon the fair fame of the country which its presence inflicts, yet it receives no direct sanction at our hands. We are not responsible for it there. The National Government, in which we are represented, is not responsible for it there. The evil is not at our own particular doors. But Slavery everywhere under the Constitution of the United States, everywhere under the exclusive jurisdiction of the National Government, everywhere under the national flag, is at our own particular doors. The freemen of the North are responsible for it equally with the traffickers in flesh who haunt the shambles of the South. Nor will this responsibility cease, so long as Slavery continues to exist in the District of Columbia, in any Territories of the United States, or anywhere on the high seas, beneath the protecting flag of the Republic. The fetters of every slave within these jurisdictions are bound and clasped by the votes of Massachusetts. Their chains, as they clank, seem to say, "Massachusetts does this outrage."

Divorce of the National Government from Slavery.— This must not be any longer. Let the word go forth, that the National Government shall be divorced from all support of Slavery, and shall never hereafter sanction it. So doing, it will be brought back to the condition and character which it enjoyed at the adoption of the Constitution.

The National Government must be on the side of Freedom.—Accomplishing these specific changes, a new tone will be given to the Republic. The Slave Power will be broken, and Slavery driven from its present intrenchments under the National Government. The influence of such a change will be incalculable. The whole weight of the Government will then be taken from the side of Slavery, where it has been placed by the Slave Power, and put on the side of Freedom, according to the original purposes and aspirations of its founders. This of itself is an end for which to labor earnestly in the spirit of the Constitution. Let it never be forgotten, as the pole-star of our policy, that the National Government must be placed, openly, actively, and perpetually, on the side of Freedom.

It must be openly on the side of Freedom. There must be no equivocation, concealment, or reserve. It must not, like the witches in Macbeth, "palter in a double sense." It must avow itself distinctly and firmly the enemy of Slavery, and thus give to the friends of Freedom, now struggling throughout the Slave States, the advantage of its countenance.

It must be actively on the side of Freedom. It cannot be content with simply bearing its testimony. It must act. Within the constitutional sphere of its influence, it must be felt as the enemy of Slavery. It must now exert itself for Freedom as zealously and effectively as for many years it has exerted itself for Slavery.

It must be perpetually on the side of Freedom. It must not be uncertain, vacillating, or temporary, in this beneficent policy, but fixed and constant, so that hereafter it shall know no change.

In our endeavors to give the Government this elevated character we are cheered by high examples, whose opinions have already been adduced. We ask only that the Republic should once more be inspired by their spirit and be guided by their counsels. Let it join with Jefferson in open, uncompromising hostility to Slavery. Let it unite with Franklin in giving *countenance* to the cause of Emancipation, and *in stepping to the very verge of the power vested in it for* DISCOURAGING *every species of traffic in the persons of our fellow-men.* Let all its officers and members follow Washington, declaring, that, in any legislative effort for the abolition of Slavery, THEIR SUFFRAGES SHALL NEVER BE WANTING.

Other National Matters. — Such are the principles of this Convention on the *national* question of Slavery. Other matters of national interest, on which the opinions of the party have been often expressed, are of a subordinate character. These are: cheap postage; the abolition of all unnecessary offices and salaries; election of civil officers, so far as may be practicable, by the people; retrenchment of the expenses and patronage of the National Government; improvement of rivers and harbors; and free grants to actual settlers of the public lands in reasonable portions.

Administration of General Taylor. — In support of these principles we felt it our duty to oppose the election of General Cass and General Taylor, — both being brought forward under the influence of the Slave Power: the first openly pledged against the Wilmot Proviso; and the second a large slaveholder and recent purchaser of slaves, who was not known, by any acts or declared opinions, to be hostile in any way to Slavery, or even to its extension, and who, from position, and from the declarations of friends and neighbors, was supposed to be friendly to that institution. General Taylor was elected by the people. And now, while it becomes all to regard his administration with candor, we cannot forget our duty to the cause which brings us together. His most ardent supporters will not venture the assertion that his conduct will bear the test of the principles here declared. We look in vain for any token that the National Government, while in his hands, will be placed openly, actively, and perpetually on the side of Freedom. Indeed, all that any "Free-Soil" supporters vouchsafe in his behalf is the assurance, that, should the Wilmot Proviso receive the sanction of both branches of Congress, — should it prevail in the House of Representatives, and then in that citadel of Slavery, the American Senate, — the "second Washington," as our President is called, will decline to assume the responsibility of arresting its final passage by the Presidential Veto. This is all. The first Washington freely declared his affinity with Antislavery Societies, and that in support of any legislative measure for the abolition of Slavery HIS SUFFRAGE SHOULD NEVER BE WANTING.

The character of the Administration may be inferred from other circumstances.

First. The Slave Power continues to hold its lion's share in the cabinet, and in diplomatic posts abroad, — thus ruling the country at home, and representing it in foreign lands. At the last Presidential election, the number of votes cast in the Slave States, exclusive of South Carolina, where the electors are chosen by the Legislature, was 844,890, while the number cast in the Free States was 2,027,016. And yet there are four persons in the cabinet from the Slave States, and three only from the Free States, while a Slaveholding President presides over all. The diplomatic representation of the country at Paris, St. Petersburg, Vienna, Frankfort, Madrid, Lisbon, Naples, Chili, Mexico, Guatemala, Venezuela, Bolivia, Buenos Ayres, is now confided to persons from Slaveholding States. At Rome our Republic is represented by the son of the great adversary of the Wilmot Proviso, at the Hague by a life-long Louisianian, at Brussels by the son-in-law of John C. Calhoun, and at Berlin by a late Senator who was rewarded with this high appointment in consideration of service to Slavery, while the principles of Freedom abroad are confided to the anxious care of the recently appointed Minister to England. But this is not all.

Secondly. The President, through one of his official organs at Washington, threatens to "frown indignantly" upon the movements of friends of Freedom at the North, though he has had no word of indignation, and no frown, for the schemes of disunion openly put forth by friends of Slavery at the South.

Thirdly. Mr. Clayton, as Secretary of State, in defiance of justice, and in mockery of the principles of the Declaration of Independence, refuses a national passport to a free colored citizen, alleging, that, by a rule of his Department, passports are not granted to colored persons. In marked contrast are the laws of Massachusetts, recognizing such persons as citizens, — and also those words of gratitude and commendation, in which General Jackson, after the Battle of New Orleans, addressed the black soldiers who had shared, with "noble enthusiasm," "the perils and glory of their *white fellow-citizens*."

Fourthly. The Post-Office Department, in a formal communication with regard to what are called "incendiary publications," announces that the Postmaster-General "leaves the whole subject to the discretion of postmasters under the authority of State Governments." Here is no solitary word of indignation that the mails of the United States are exposed to lawless interruption from partisans of Slavery. The Post-Office, intrusted to a son of New England, assumes an abject neutrality, while letters committed to its care are rifled at the instigation of the Slave Power.

Surely we cannot err in declaring that an administration cannot be entitled to our support, which, during the short career of a few months only, is marked by such instances of subserviency to the Slave Power, and of infidelity to the great principles of Freedom.

Necessity of our Organization. — Such is the national position of our party. We are a national party, established for national purposes, such as can be accomplished by a national party only. If the principles which we have at heart were supported openly, actively, constantly by either of the other parties, there would be no occasion for our organization. But whatever may have been, or whatever may now be, the opinions of individual members, it is undeniable, that, *as national parties,* they have never opposed Slavery in any form. Neither has ever sustained any measure for the abolition of Slavery in the District of Columbia, but, on the contrary, discountenanced all such measures. Neither has ever opposed, in any form, the coastwise slave-trade under the flag of the United States. Neither has ever opposed the extension of Slavery. Neither has ever striven to divorce the National Government from Slavery. Neither has ever labored to place the National Government openly, actively, and perpetually on the side of Freedom. Nor is there any assurance, satisfactory to persons not biased by political associations, that either of these organizations will ever, as a *national party,* espouse the cause of Freedom.

Circumstances in the very constitution of these parties render it difficult, if not impossible, for them to act in this behalf. Constructed subtly with a view to political success, they are spread everywhere throughout the Union, and the principles which they uphold are pruned and modified to meet existing sentiment in different parts of the country. Neither can venture, as a party, to place itself on the side of Freedom, because, by such a course, it would disaffect that slaveholding support which is essential to its political success. The Antislavery resolutions adopted by legislatures at the North are regarded as expressions of individual or local opinion only, and not suffered to control the action of the national party. To such an extent is this carried, that Whigs of Massachusetts, professing immitigable hostility to Slavery, recently united in support of a candidate for the Presidency in whose behalf the eminent slaveholding Whig, Mr. Berrien, had "implored his fellow-citizens of Georgia, Whig and Democratic, to forget for a time their party divisions, and to know each other only as Southern men."

Fellow-citizens, individuals in each of the old parties strove in vain to produce a change, and to make them exponents of growing Antislavery sentiments. At Baltimore and Philadelphia, in the great Conventions of these parties, Slavery triumphed. So strongly were they both arrayed against Freedom, and so unrelenting were they in ostracism of its generous supporters, — of all who had written or spoken in its behalf, — that it is not going too far to say, that, if Jefferson, or Franklin, or Washington could have descended from his sphere above, and revisited the country which he had nobly dedicated to Freedom, he could not, with his well-known and recorded opinions against Slavery, have received a nomination for the Presidency from either of these Conventions.

To maintain the principles of Freedom, as set forth in this Address, it might be well for us to take a lesson from the old parties, — to learn from them the importance of perseverance and union, and thus to see the value of a distinct political organization, — and, profiting by these instructions, to direct the efforts of the friends of Freedom everywhere throughout the country into this channel.

OBJECTIONS.

There are objections from various quarters to the establishment of our party, — some urged in ignorance, some in the sophist spirit, which would "make the worse appear the better reason." Glance at them.

Single Idea. — It is often said that it is a party of a single idea. This is a phrase, and nothing more. The moving cause and animating soul of our party is the idea of Freedom. But this idea is manifold in character and influence. It is the idea of the Declaration of Independence. It is the great idea of the founders of the Republic. In adopting it as the paramount principle of our movement we declare our purpose to carry out the Great Idea of our institutions, as originally established. In other words, it is our lofty aim to bring back the administration of the Government to the standard of a Christian Democracy, with a sincere and wide regard for Human Rights, — that it may be in reality, as in name, a Republic. With the comprehensive cause of Freedom are associated in our vows, as has been already seen, other questions important to the well-being of the people. Nor is there any cause by which mankind can be advanced that is not embraced by our aspirations. "I am a man, and regard nothing human as foreign to me," was the sentiment of the Roman poet, who had once been a slave; and these words may be adopted as the motto of our movement.

Sectional, or against the South. — Again, it is said that ours is a sectional party; and the charge is sometimes put in another form, — that it is a party against the South. The significant words of Washington are quoted to warn the country against "geographical" questions.[1] Now, if we proposed any system of measures calculated to exclude absolutely any "geographical" portion of the country from the benefit of the general laws and Constitution of the United States, or to operate exclusively and by name upon any "geographical" section, — or perhaps, if we proposed to interfere with Slavery in the States, —

1 "In contemplating the causes which may disturb our Union, it occurs as matter of serious concern, that any ground should have been furnished for characterizing parties by *geographical* discriminations, *Northern* and *Southern*, *Atlantic* and *Western*; whence designing men may endeavor to excite a belief that there is a real difference of local interests and views. One of the expedients of party to acquire influence within particular districts is to misrepresent the opinions and aims of other districts. You cannot shield yourselves too much against the jealousies and heart-burnings which spring from these misrepresentations; they tend to render alien to each other those who ought to be bound together by fraternal affection." — *Farewell Address: Writings*, ed. Sparks, Vol. XII. p. 221.

there might be some ground for this charge; but, as we propose to act against Slavery only where it exists under the National Government, and where this Government is responsible for it, nobody can say that we are sectional, or against the South. Our aim is in no respect sectional, but in every respect national. It is in no respect against the South, but against the Evil Spirit having its home at the South, which has obtained the control of the Government. As well might it be said that Jefferson, Franklin, and Washington were sectional, and against the South.

It is true that at present a large portion of the party are at the North; but if our cause is sectional on this account, then is the Tariff sectional, because its chief supporters are also in the North.

Unquestionably there is a particular class of individuals against whom we are obliged to act. These are the slave-masters, wherever situated throughout the country, constituting, according to recent calculations, not more than 248,000 in all. Those most interested are probably not more than 100,000. For years this band has acted against the whole country, and subjugated it to Slavery. Surely it does not become them, or their partisans, to complain that an effort is now made to rally the whole country against their tyranny. There are many who forget that the larger portion of the people at the South are non-slaveholders, interested equally with ourselves — nay, more than we are — in the overthrow of that power which has so long dictated its disastrous and discreditable policy. To these we may ultimately look for support, so soon as our movement is able to furnish them with the needful hope and strength.

If at the present moment our efforts seem in any

respect sectional or against the South, it is simply because the chief opponents of our principles are there. But our principles are not sectional; they are applicable to the whole Union,— nay, more, to all the human race. They are universal as Man.

Interference with other Parties.— Again, it is sometimes said that we interfere with the other parties. This is true. And it is necessary, because the other parties do not represent the principles which we consider of paramount importance. No intelligent person, careful and honest in his statements, will undertake to say that either of them does represent these. Failing thus, they are unworthy of support. They do not embody the great ideas of the Republic.

Here again it is important to distinguish between individuals and the parties to which they adhere. There are many, doubtless, in both the old parties, who subscribe to our principles, but still hug the belief that these principles can be best carried into action by the parties to which they are respectively attached. Influenced by the common bias, which indisposes distrust of the political party with which they have been associated, they continue in the companionship early adopted, and often learn to combat for an organization, which, *as a whole*, is hostile to the very principles they have at heart. *Most certainly his devotion to Freedom may well be questioned, who adheres to a national party which declines to be the organ of Freedom.* He only is in earnest who places Freedom above party, and does not hesitate to leave a party which neglects to serve Freedom. Such men we trust to welcome in large numbers from both the old organizations.

Alleged Injurious Influences in the Slave States. — Once more, it is said that the Antislavery Movement at the North, and particularly its political form, have caused unnecessary irritation among slave-owners, and thwarted a more proper movement at the South. It is sometimes declared that we have not promoted, but rather retarded, the cause of Emancipation.

To this let it be said, in the first place, that our direct and primary object is not Emancipation in the States, but the establishment of Freedom everywhere under the National Government; and there is reason to believe that we have already done something towards the accomplishment of this object. By the confession of slaveholders themselves, in one of the recent "Addresses" put forth from their conclave at Washington, it appears that we have not labored in vain. "This agitation, and the use of means," says the Address prepared by Mr. Berrien, "have been continued with more or less activity for a series of years, *not without doing much towards effecting the object intended.*" Take courage, fellow-citizens, from this confession, and do not doubt that your continued efforts must finally prevail.

But, in the second place, whatever may have been the temporary shock to Emancipation in the Slave States, it will not be denied by candid minds that the efforts in the North have hastened the great day of Freedom. They have encouraged its friends in Kentucky, Missouri, Virginia, Maryland, and Tennessee, and have contributed to diffuse the information and awaken the generous resolve which are so much needed. Nor can it be doubted, that, if the North had continued silent, Mr. Clay, in Kentucky, and Mr. Benton, in Missouri, would both have been silent. Without the moral support of the Free States, these powerful statesmen would have shrunk from the unequal battle. Let us, then, continue to plead, believing that no honest, earnest voice for Freedom can be in vain. And let us be sure to vote so as best to promote this cause, extorting yet other confessions, from other conclaves of slaveholders, that we are "*doing much towards effecting the object intended.*"

Why carry the Question of Slavery into State Elections? — Having thus reviewed the objections to our organization as a National Movement, applying its principles as a test in the choice of national officers, it only remains to meet one other objection, founded on its introduction into State elections. Here we might content ourselves by replying, that we are a national party, and, as such, simply follow the example of both the other parties. From the beginning of the Government the necessity of such a course has been recognized and acted upon uniformly by these parties; and it does not become them now to question its propriety, when recognized and acted upon by us.

But, independent of example, we are led to this course by conviction of its necessity, in the maintenance of our great cause. It is our duty so to cast our votes on all occasions as to promote the *principles* we have at heart. And it would be wrong to disregard the experience of political history, both at home and abroad, which teaches that it is through the constant, well-directed organization of party that these are best maintained. The influence already exerted over both the old parties, and over the general sentiment of the country, affords additional encouragement. Assuming, then, what few will be so hardy as to deny, that it is proper for people to combine in parties for the promotion of cherished convictions, it follows, as an irresistible consequence, that this combination should be made most effective for the purpose in view. What is worth doing is worth well doing. If men unite in constructing the powerful and complex machine of a political organization, it must be rendered complete, and thoroughly competent to its work.

Now it will be apparent to those familiar with political transactions, that such an organization, acting only in National elections, and suspending its exertions in State elections, cannot effectually do its work. People acting antagonistically in State elections cannot be brought to act harmoniously in National elections. It is practically impossible to have one permanent party in National affairs and another in State affairs. Such a course would cause uncertainty and ultimate disorganization.

Peculiar local interests may control certain local elections. These constitute the exceptions, and not the rule. They arise where, within the locality, a greater sum of good may be accomplished by sustaining a certain person, independent of party, than by voting strictly according to party. But it is clear that such instances cannot be frequent without impairing the efficiency of the movement.

It is natural that parties in our country should take their strongest complexion from National affairs, because these affairs are of the most absorbing interest. Justly important as is the election of Municipal and State officers, we feel that they are of less importance than the election of a President of the United States, — as the character of the State Government, whose influence is confined to a limited sphere, is of less importance than that of the National Government, whose influence embraces all the States, and reaches to foreign lands. Therefore the organizations of party in the States are properly treated as subordinate, though ancillary, to the National organizations. They are branches or limbs, which repay the strength they derive from the great trunk by helping to extend in all directions its protecting power. But these branches cannot be lopped off or neglected.

Again, the influence of each individual is of importance. But the State itself is a compound individual, and just in proportion to its size and character it is important that it should be arrayed as a powerful unit in support of our organization. In this way its influence can be brought to bear most effectually upon the National Government in support of our *principles.*

Fellow-citizens, the question again recurs, "Are you for Freedom, or are you for Slavery?" If you are for Freedom, do not hesitate to support the National party dedicated to this cause. Strive in all ways to extend its influence, to enlarge its means of efficiency, and to consolidate its strength. And consider well, that this can be accomplished only by casting your votes for those who, while avowing our principles, are willing to sacrifice ancient party ties in order to maintain them. By her towns, counties, and districts, by her executive and legislative departments, Massachusetts must call upon the National Government to change from the policy of Slavery to the policy of Freedom. *Massachusetts must refuse to support any Government which does not hearken to this request.*

Local Matters. — The sentiments which inspire the Party of Freedom in opposition to Slavery must naturally control their conduct on all questions of local policy. Friends of Human Rights, they cannot regard with indifference anything by which these are impaired. Recognizing Justice and Beneficence as the end and aim of Government, they must sympathize with all efforts to extend their sway. Let the Government be ever just. Let it be ever beneficent. Abuses and wrongs will then disappear, and the State will stand forth in the moral dignity of true manhood. If there be anything in the Commonwealth inconsistent with these sentiments, it must be changed. This should be done in no spirit of political empiricism, but with an honest and intelligent regard to practical results.

There is complaint in many, and even opposite quarters, of numerous corporations annually established by our Legislature, of the considerable time thus consumed in special legislation, and, still further, of the influence these corporations are able to exert over political affairs, dispensing a patronage exceeding that of the National Government within the borders of our State. Without considering these things in detail, it is impossible to avoid calling attention to the perverse influence from this source. Of this we can speak with knowledge. *The efforts to place the National Government on the side of Freedom* have received little sympathy from corporations, or from persons largely interested in them, but have rather encountered their opposition, sometimes concealed, sometimes open, often bitter and vindictive. It is easy to explain this. In corporations is the Money Power of the Commonwealth. Thus far the instinct of property has proved stronger in Massachusetts than the instinct of Freedom. The Money Power has joined hands with the Slave Power. Selfish, grasping, subtle, tyrannical, like its ally, it will not brook opposition. It claims the Commonwealth as its own, and too successfully enlists in its support that needy talent and easy virtue which are required to maintain its sway. Perhaps the true remedy for this evil will be found in a more enlightened public sentiment; meanwhile we must do what we can to restrain this influence, by watchful legislation, if need be, but especially by directing against it the finger-point of a generous indignation.

The natural influence of the Money Power is still further increased by defects in our present system of Representation. The large cities, particularly Boston, electing Representatives by a general ticket, are able to return a compact delegation, united in political opinions, while the country, through divisions into small towns, is practically subdivided into districts, and chooses Representatives differing in opinions. A careful estimate of the influence thus wrought will show that Boston alone, actually casting 13,000 votes, is able to neutralize the 26,000 votes cast by all western Massachusetts, including Berkshire, Franklin, Hampshire, and Hampden. The large cities, which are the seat of the Money Power, are thus able, though a minority, to control the State. Like the Slave Power, they are strong from union. This abuse calls for amendment; and it will be for the friends of our cause to urge such measures as the necessity of the case requires.

Our Candidates. — In the fulfilment of our duty to sustain our principles at all times, in all elections, National or State, we have nominated Hon. STEPHEN C.

PHILLIPS, of Salem, as our candidate for Governor. With confidence and pride we ask for him your support. Few in the community, by a long series of beneficent services, have entitled themselves to the same degree of kindly regard. In him we find a liberal education blended with a liberal spirit, — the experience and the wealth of the successful merchant turned into the channels of Benevolence, and the influence earned by various labors, in various posts of honor and trust, consecrated to Human Improvement. All the great causes which are doing so much to renovate the age, Temperance, Education, Peace, Freedom, have in him a discreet, practical, devoted, self-sacrificing friend. Formerly associated with the Whig party, and a member of Congress, chosen by Whig votes, he set the example of renouncing his party, when it became openly faithless to Freedom, and by unreserved and noble effort has done much to strengthen the movement in which we are engaged.

As candidate for Lieutenant-Governor, we nominate Hon. JOHN MILLS, of Springfield, a gentleman of spotless life, with ample experience in many spheres of action, formerly an honored member of the Democratic party, who has filled responsible stations under the Governments of the State and the Nation, and who, like Mr. Phillips, has testified his fidelity to Freedom by renouncing the party to which he belonged.

Fellow-citizens, such are our principles, and such our candidates. Join us in their support. Join us, all who love Freedom and hate Slavery. Join us, all who cherish the Constitution and the Union. Help us in endeavors to crown them again with their early virtue. Join us, all who reverence the memory of the fathers, and would have their spirit once more animate the Republic. Join us, all who would have the National Government administered in the spirit of Freedom, and not in the spirit of Slavery. The occasion is urgent. Active, resolute exertions must be made. It does not become the sons of the Pilgrims, and the sons of the Revolution, to be *neutral* in this contest. Such was not the temper of their fathers. In such a contest neutrality is treason to Human Rights. In questions *merely political* an honest man may stand neuter; but what true heart can be neuter, when the distinct question is put, which we now address to the people of Massachusetts, "Are you for Freedom, or are you for Slavery?"

Finally, we appeal to the moral and religious sentiments of the Commonwealth. When these are thoroughly moved, there can be no question of the result. We invoke the sympathy of the pulpit. Let it preach deliverance to the captive. We call upon good men of all sects and all parties to lend their support. You all agree in our PRINCIPLES. Do not practically oppose them by continued adhesion to a national party hostile to them. Join in proclaiming them through the new Party of Freedom.

The Resolutions at the close of the Address are omitted, being in the nature of a repetition, which, however important at the time, is of less value as a record of opinions.

WASHINGTON AN ABOLITIONIST.

LETTER TO THE BOSTON DAILY ATLAS, SEPTEMBER 27, 1849.

THE Address to the People of Massachusetts, adopted by the Free-Soil Convention, was violently attacked, as will appear from the following reply, written at a hotel in New York, where Mr. Sumner happened to be staying, when he saw the criticism.

NEW YORK, IRVING HOTEL, September 27, 1849.

GENTLEMEN, — My attention has been directed to-day to an article in your paper of the 25th September, entitled "Mr. Sumner and his Authorities," in which I am charged, among other things, with misrepresenting the opinions of Washington, particularly in the following sentence, in the Address recently adopted by the Free-Soil Convention at Worcester: —

"The first Washington freely declared his affinity with Antislavery Societies, and that in support of any legislative measure for the abolition of Slavery his suffrage should never be wanting."

A more familiar acquaintance with the opinions of our great exemplar would have prevented the writer in the Atlas from falsely accusing a neighbor. It would have prevented him from saying that the letter to Robert Morris, from which part of the above statement is drawn, was written more than ten years before the adoption of the National Constitution, and from dating it in 1776, when the letter in reality bears date in 1786.

I will not doubt your willingness to repair the injustice you have allowed in the columns of the Atlas, and therefore ask you to publish this note, with the accompanying extracts, showing the opinions of Washington.

By these it will appear that Washington freely declared to Brissot de Warville, in a conversation which took place in 1788, and was published in 1791, that he rejoiced in what was doing in other States for the emancipation of the negroes, — that he sincerely desired the extension of it to his own country, — and, contrary to the opinions of many Virginians, *expressly said that he wished the formation of an Antislavery Society, and that he would second such a society.*

It will appear, also, that Washington said to Robert Morris, in a letter dated April 12, 1786, that in support of any legislative measure for the abolition of Slavery his suffrage should not be wanting, — that he said to Lafayette, in a letter dated May 10, 1786, that gradual emancipation certainly might and assuredly ought to be effected, and that, too, by legislative authority, — that he said to John F. Mercer, in a letter dated September 9, 1786, that it was among his first wishes to see some plan adopted by which Slavery in this country may be abolished by law, — that he said to Sir John Sinclair, in a letter dated December 11, 1796, that Maryland and Virginia must have, and at a period not remote, laws for the gradual abolition of Slavery, — and that by his will, dated July 9, 1790 [1799], he expressly emancipated his slaves.

Thus acting, and thus constantly avowing his sentiments in favor of the abolition of Slavery, Washington is properly called an Abolitionist.

I cannot close without correcting the insinuation of the writer in the Atlas, that it is my wish, or that it is the wish of the Free-Soil party to interfere, through Congress, with Slavery in the States. This is a mistake. Our position is this. They who are responsible for Slavery should abolish it. Our duties are coextensive with our responsibilities. We at the North are responsible for Slavery everywhere within the jurisdiction of Congress, and it is here that we should exert ourselves, according to the principles of Washington, to abolish it by legislative action.

Still further, our sympathies and God-speed must attend every effort in the States to remove this great evil. We should join with Washington in his exclamation to Lafayette, on learning that this philanthropic Frenchman had purchased an estate in Cayenne, with the view of emancipating the slaves on it: "Would to God a like spirit might diffuse itself generally into the minds of the people of this country!"

I will not trouble you with any comment on the other criticisms upon me by the writer in the Atlas.

I am, Gentlemen, your obedient servant,

CHARLES SUMNER.

TO THE EDITORS OF THE ATLAS.

OPINIONS OF WASHINGTON ON SLAVERY.

"He has nevertheless (must I say it?) a numerous crowd of slaves; but they are treated with the greatest humanity, — well fed, well clothed, and kept to moderate labor; they bless God without ceasing for having given them so good a master. It is a task worthy of a soul so elevated, so pure, and so disinterested, to begin the revolution in Virginia, to prepare the way for *the emancipation of the negroes. This great man declared to me that he rejoiced at what was doing in other States on this subject, that he sincerely desired the extension of it in his own country;* but he did not dissemble that there were still many obstacles to be overcome, — that it was dangerous to strike too vigorously at a prejudice which had begun to diminish, — that time, patience, and information would not fail to vanquish it. Almost all the Virginians, added he, believe that the liberty of the blacks cannot soon become general. *This is the reason why they wish not to form a society,* which may give dangerous ideas to their slaves. There is another obstacle: the great plantations, of which the State is composed, render it necessary for men to live so dispersed, *that frequent meetings of a society would be difficult.*

"I replied, that the Virginians were in an error, — that, evidently, sooner or later, the negroes would obtain their liberty everywhere. It is, then, for the interest of your countrymen to prepare the way to such a revolution, by endeavoring to reconcile the restitution of the rights of the blacks with the interest of the whites. *The means necessary to be taken to this effect can only be the work of a* SOCIETY; and it is worthy the Saviour of America to put himself at their head, and to open the door of liberty to three hundred thousand unhappy beings of his own State. *He told me that he desired the formation of a* SOCIETY, *and that he would second it;* but that he did not think the moment favorable." — *Conversation with Washington, in the New Travels of Brissot de Warville in the United States in* 1788, *published in* 1791, *and translated in* 1792.

"I can only say, that there is not a man living who wishes more sincerely than I do to see a plan adopted for the abolition of it [Slavery]; but there is only one proper and effectual mode by which it can be accomplished, and that is by *legislative authority; and this, as far as my suffrage will go, shall never be wanting.*" — *Letter of Washington to Robert Morris, April* 12, 1786.

"The benevolence of your heart, my dear Marquis, is so conspicuous upon all occasions, that I never wonder at any fresh proofs of it; but your late purchase of an estate in the Colony of Cayenne, *with a view of emancipating the slaves on it,* is a generous and noble proof of your humanity. *Would to God a like spirit might diffuse itself generally into the minds of the people of this country!* But I despair of seeing it. Some petitions were presented to the Assembly, at its last session, for the abolition of Slavery; but they could scarcely obtain a reading. To set the slaves afloat at once would, I really believe, be productive of much inconvenience and mischief; *but by degrees it certainly might and assuredly ought to be effected, and that, too, by legislative authority.*" — *Letter of Washington to Lafayette, May* 10, 1786.

"I never mean, unless some particular circumstances should compel me to it, to possess another slave by purchase, *it being among my first wishes to see some plan adopted by which Slavery in this country may be abolished by law.*" — *Letter of Washington to John F. Mercer, September* 9, 1786.

"From what I have said, you will perceive that the present prices of lands in Pennsylvania are higher than they are in Maryland and Virginia, although they are not of superior quality, ... [among other reasons] because there are *laws here for the gradual abolition of Slavery,* which neither of the two States above mentioned have at present, *but which nothing is more certain than that they must have, and at a period not remote.*" — *Letter of Washington to Sir John Sinclair, December* 11, 1796.

"Upon the decease of my wife, it is my will and desire that all the slaves whom I hold in my own right shall receive their freedom. To emancipate them during her life would, though earnestly wished by me, be attended with such insuperable difficulties, on account of their intermixture by marriage with the dower negroes, as to excite the most painful sensations, if not disagreeable consequences to the latter, while both descriptions are in the occupancy of the same proprietor; it not being in my power, under the tenure by which the dower negroes are held, to manumit them. . . . . *And I do, moreover, most pointedly and most solemnly enjoin it upon my executors hereafter named, or the survivors of them, to see that this clause respecting slaves, and every part thereof, be religiously fulfilled at the epoch at which it is directed to take place, without evasion, neglect, or delay,* after the crops which may then be on the ground are harvested, particularly as it respects the aged and infirm; seeing that a regular and permanent fund be established for their support, as long as there are subjects requiring it; not trusting to the uncertain provision to be made by individuals." — *Washington's Will, dated July* 9, 1790 [1799]

EQUALITY BEFORE THE LAW:

UNCONSTITUTIONALITY OF SEPARATE COLORED SCHOOLS IN MASSACHUSETTS.

ARGUMENT BEFORE THE SUPREME COURT OF MASSACHUSETTS, IN THE CASE OF SARAH C. ROBERTS *v.* THE CITY OF BOSTON, DECEMBER 4, 1849.

THIS argument, though addressed to the Supreme Court of Massachusetts, is mainly national and universal in topics, so that it is applicable wherever, especially in our country, any discrimination in educational opportunities is founded on race or color. It is a vindication of Equal Rights in Common Schools. The term "Equality before the Law" was here for the first time introduced into our discussions. It is not found in the Common Law, nor until recently in the English language. It is a translation from the French, whence Mr. Sumner took it.

The Supreme Court heard the argument, and in their opinion complimented the advocate; but they did not take the responsibility of annulling the unjust discrimination. After stating the claim of Equality before the Law, Chief-Justice Shaw reduced it to very small proportions, when he said that it meant "only that the rights of all, as they are settled and regulated by law, are equally entitled to the paternal consideration and protection of the law for their maintenance and security."[1] This made it mean nothing; but such was the decision. The *victrix causa* was not less odious to Mr Sumner, who never ceased to regret the opportunity lost by the Court of contributing an immortal precedent to the recognition and safeguard of human rights.

The error of the Court was repaired by the Legislature of Massachusetts, which in 1855 enacted as follows: —

> "In determining the qualifications of scholars to be admitted into any Public School or any District School in this Commonwealth, no distinction shall be made on account of the race, color, or religious opinions of the applicant or scholar."[2]

1 Roberts *v.* City of Boston, 5 Cushing R., 206.

2 General Laws of Massachusetts, 1855, Ch. 256, sec. 1.

By other sections, the child excluded on such account was entitled to "damages therefor in an action of tort," with a bill of discovery to obtain evidence. Then came this supplementary protection: —

"Every person belonging to the School Committee under whose rules or directions any child shall be excluded from such school, and every teacher of any such school, shall, on application by the parent or guardian of any such child, state in writing the grounds and reasons of such exclusion."

Since this legislation, Equal Rights have prevailed in the Common Schools of Massachusetts, and nobody would go back to the earlier system.

Associated with Mr. Sumner in this case was Robert Morris, Esq., a colored lawyer.

MAY IT PLEASE YOUR HONORS: —

CAN any discrimination on account of race or color be made among children entitled to the benefit of our Common Schools under the Constitution and Laws of Massachusetts? This is the question which the Court is now to hear, to consider, and to decide.

Or, stating the question with more detail, and with more particular application to the facts of the present case, are the Committee having superintendence of the Common Schools of Boston intrusted with *power*, under the Constitution and Laws of Massachusetts, to exclude colored children from the schools, and compel them to find education at separate schools, set apart for colored children only, at distances from their homes less convenient than schools open to white children?

This important question arises in an action by a colored child only five years old, who, *by her next friend*, sues the city of Boston for damages on account of a refusal to receive her into one of the Common Schools.

It would be difficult to imagine any case appealing more strongly to your best judgment, whether you regard the parties or the subject. On the one side is the City of Boston, strong in wealth, influence, character;

on the other side is a little child, of degraded color, of humble parents, and still within the period of natural infancy, but strong from her very weakness, and from the irrepressible sympathies of good men, which, by a divine compensation, come to succor the weak. This little child asks at your hands her *personal rights*. So doing, she calls upon you to decide a question which concerns the personal rights of other colored children,—which concerns the Constitution and Laws of the Commonwealth,—which concerns that *peculiar institution* of New England, the Common Schools,—which concerns the fundamental principles of human rights,—which concerns the Christian character of this community. Such parties and such interests justly challenge your earnest attention.

Though this discussion is now for the first time brought before a judicial tribunal, it is no stranger to the public. In the School Committee of Boston for five years it has been the occasion of discord. No less than four different reports, two majority and two minority, forming pamphlets, of solid dimensions, devoted to this question, have been made to this Committee, and afterwards published.* The opinions of learned counsel have been enlisted. The controversy, leaving these regular channels, overflowed the newspaper press, and numerous articles appeared, espousing opposite sides. At last it has reached this tribunal. It is in your power to make it subside forever.

THE QUESTION STATED.

FORGETTING many of the topics and all of the heats heretofore mingling with the controversy, I shall strive to present the question in its juridical light, as becomes the habits of this tribunal. It is a question of jurisprudence on which you are to give judgment. But I cannot forget that the principles of morals and of natural justice lie at the foundation of all jurisprudence. Nor can any reference to these be inappropriate in a discussion before this Court.

Of Equality I shall speak, not only as a sentiment, but as a principle embodied in the Constitution of Massachusetts, and obligatory upon court and citizen. It will be my duty to show that this principle, after finding its way into our State Constitution, was recognized in legislation and judicial decisions. Considering next the circumstances of this case, it will be easy to show how completely they violate Constitution, legislation, and judicial proceedings, — *first*, by subjecting colored children to inconvenience inconsistent with the requirements of Equality, and, *secondly*, by establishing a system of Caste odious as that of the Hindoos, — leading to the conclusion that the School Committee have no such power as they have exercised, and that it is the duty of the Court to set aside their unjust by-law. In the course of this discussion I shall exhibit the true idea of our Common Schools, and the fallacy of the pretension that any exclusion or discrimination founded on race or color can be consistent with Equal Rights.

In opening this argument, I begin naturally with the fundamental proposition which, when once established, renders the conclusion irresistible. According to the Constitution of Massachusetts, *all men, without distinction of race or color, are equal before the law.* In the statement of this proposition I use language which, though new in our country, has the advantage of precision.

EQUALITY BEFORE THE LAW: ITS MEANING.

I MIGHT, perhaps, leave this proposition without one word of comment. The equality of men will not be directly denied on this occasion; and yet it is so often assailed of late, that I shall not seem to occupy your time superfluously, I trust, while endeavoring to show what is understood by this term, when used in laws, constitutions, or other political instruments. Here I encounter a prevailing misapprehension. Lord Brougham, in his recent work on Political Philosophy, announces, with something of pungency, that "the notion of Equality, or anything approaching to Equality, among the different members of any community, is altogether wild and fantastic."[1] Mr. Calhoun, in the Senate of the United States, assails both the principle and the form of its statement. He does not hesitate to say that the claim in the Declaration of Independence is "the most false and dangerous of all political errors," — that it "has done more to retard the cause of liberty and civilization, and is doing more at present, than all other causes combined," — that "for a long time it lay dormant, but in the process of time it began to germinate and produce its poisonous fruits."[2] Had these two distinguished authorities chosen

[1] Part II. ch. 4, p. 23.

[2] Speech on the Oregon Bill, June 27, 1848: Works, Vol. IV. pp. 507, 511, 512; Congressional Globe, 30th Cong. 1st Sess., Vol. XVIII. p. 876. These extravagances found an echo afterwards. Mr. Pettit, a Senator of the United States from Indiana, after quoting the words, "We hold these truths to be self-evident, that all men are created equal," proceeded to say: "I hold it to be a self-evident lie. There is no such thing. Sir, tell me that the imbecile, the deformed, the weak, the blurred intellect in man is my equal, physically, mentally, or morally, and you tell me a lie. Tell me, Sir, that the slave in the South, who is born a slave, and with but little over one half the volume of brain that attaches to the Northern European race, is his equal, and you tell what is physically a false-

to comprehend the extent and application of the term thus employed, something, if not all, of their objection would have disappeared. That we may better appreciate its meaning and limitation, I am induced to exhibit the origin and growth of the sentiment, which, finally ripening into a formula of civil and political right, was embodied in the Constitution of Massachusetts.

Equality as a sentiment was early cherished by generous souls. It showed itself in dreams of ancient philosophy, and was declared by Seneca, when, in a letter of consolation on death, he said, *Prima enim pars Æquitatis est Æqualitas*: "The chief part of Equity is Equality."[1]

hood. There is no truth in it at all." (Speech in the Senate of the United States, February 20, 1854: Congressional Globe, 33d Cong. 1st Sess., Appendix, Vol. XXIX. p. 214.) Mr. Choate, without descending into the same particularity, seems to have reached the same conclusion, when, in addressing political associates, he characterized the Declaration of Independence as "that passionate and eloquent manifesto of a revolutionary war," and then again spoke of its self-evident truths as "the glittering and sounding generalities of natural right." (Letter to the Maine Whig State Central Committee, August 9, 1856: Works, Vol. I. pp. 214, 215.) This great question was a hinge in the famous debate between Mr. Douglas and Mr. Lincoln in the contest for the senatorship of Illinois, when the former said, in various forms of speech, that "the Declaration of Independence only included the white people of the United States," and the latter replied, that "the entire records of the world, from the date of the Declaration of Independence up to within three years ago, may be searched in vain for one single affirmation, from one single man, that the negro was not included in the Declaration." (Political Debates between Hon. Abraham Lincoln and Hon. Stephen A. Douglas in the Campaign of 1858 in Illinois: see speech of Douglas at Springfield, July 17, and of Lincoln at Galesburgh, October 7; and *passim*.) Andrew Johnson, speaking in the Senate, showed the side to which he belonged, when he said, after quoting the great words of the Declaration: "Is there an intelligent man throughout the whole country, is there a Senator, when he has stripped himself of all party prejudice, who will come forward and say that he believes that Mr. Jefferson, when he penned that paragraph of the Declaration of Independence, intended it to embrace the African population? Is there a gentleman in the Senate who believes any such thing? . . . . There is not a man of respectable intelligence who will hazard his reputation upon such an assertion." (Congressional Globe, 36th Cong. 1st Sess., December 12, 1859, p. 100.)

[1] Epist. XXX.

But not till the truths of the Christian Religion was it enunciated with persuasive force. Here we learn that God is no respecter of persons, — that he is the Father of all, — and that we are all his children, and brethren to each other. When the Saviour gave us the Lord's Prayer, he taught the sublime doctrine of Human Brotherhood, enfolding the equality of men.

Slowly did this sentiment enter the State. The whole constitution of government was inconsistent with it. An hereditary monarchy, an order of nobility, and the complex ranks of superior and inferior, established by the feudal system, all declare, not the equality, but the inequality of men, and all conspire to perpetuate this inequality. Every infant of royal blood, every noble, every vassal, is a present example, that, whatever may be the injunctions of religion or the sentiment of the heart, men under these institutions are not born equal.

The boldest political reformers of early times did not venture to proclaim this truth, nor did they truly perceive it. Cromwell beheaded his king, but secured the supreme power in hereditary succession to his eldest son. It was left to his loftier contemporary, John Milton, in poetic vision to be entranced

"With fair Equality, fraternal state."[1]

Sidney, who perished a martyr to the liberal cause, drew his inspiration from classic, and not from Christian fountains. The examples of Greece and Rome fed his soul. The English Revolution of 1688, partly by force and partly by the popular voice, changed the succession to the crown, and, if we may credit loyal Englishmen, secured the establishment of Freedom throughout the land. But the Bill of Rights did not declare, nor did the gen-

[1] Paradise Lost, Book XII. 26.

ius of Somers or Maynard conceive the political axiom, that all men are born equal. It may find acceptance from Englishmen in our day, but it is disowned by English institutions.

I would not forget the early testimony of the "judicious" Hooker, who in his "Ecclesiastical Polity," that masterly work, dwells on the equality of men by nature, or the subsequent testimony of Locke, in his "Two Treatises of Government," who, quoting Hooker, asserts for himself that "creatures of the same species and rank, promiscuously born to all the same advantages of nature and the use of the same faculties, should also be *equal* one amongst another, without subordination or subjection."[1] Hooker and Locke saw the equality of men in a state of Nature; but their utterances found more acceptance across the Channel than in England.

It is to France that we must pass for the earliest development of this idea, its amplest illustration, and its most complete, accurate, and logical expression. In the middle of the last century appeared the renowned *Encyclopédie*, edited by Diderot and D'Alembert. This remarkable production, where science, religion, and government are discussed with revolutionary freedom, contains an article on Equality, first published in 1755. Here we find the boldest expression of this sentiment down to that time. "Natural Equality," says this authority, "is that which exists between all men by the constitution of their nature only. This Equality is the principle and the foundation of Liberty. Natural or moral equality is, then, founded upon the constitution of human nature common to all men, who are born, grow,

1 Locke on Government, Book II. ch. 2, § 4. Hooker, Ecclesiastical Polity, Book I.

subsist, and die in the same manner. Since human nature finds itself the same in all men, it is clear, that, according to Nature's law, each ought to esteem and treat the others as beings who are naturally equal to himself, — that is to say, who are men as well as himself." It is then remarked, that political and civil slavery is in violation of this Equality; and yet the inequalities of nobility in the state are allowed to pass without condemnation. Alluding to these, it is simply said that "they who are elevated above others ought to treat their inferiors as naturally their equals, shunning all outrage, exacting nothing beyond what is their due, and exacting with humanity what is incontestably their due." [1]

Considering the period at which this article was written, we are astonished less by its vagueness and incompleteness than by its bravery and generosity. The dissolute despotism of Louis the Fifteenth poisoned France. The antechambers of the King were thronged by selfish nobles and fawning courtiers. The councils of Government were controlled by royal mistresses. The King, only a few years before, in defiance of Equality, — but in entire harmony with the conduct of the School Committee in Boston, — founded a military school *for nobles only*, carrying into education the distinction of Caste. At such a period the Encyclopedia did well in uttering important and effective truth. The *sentiment* of Equality was fully declared. Nor should we be disappointed, that, at this early day, even the boldest philosophers did not adequately perceive, or, if they perceived, did not dare to utter, our axiom of liberty.

Thus it is with all moral and political ideas. First appearing as a sentiment, they awake a noble impulse,

[1] Encyclopédie, art. *Égalité Naturelle*, Tom. V. p. 415.

filling the soul with generous sympathy, and encouraging to congenial effort. Slowly recognized, they finally pass into a formula, to be acted upon, to be applied, to be defended in the concerns of life, as principles.

Almost contemporaneously with this article in the Encyclopedia our attention is arrested by a poor solitary, of humble extraction, born at Geneva, in Switzerland, of irregular education and life, a wanderer from his birthplace, enjoying a temporary home in France, — Jean Jacques Rousseau. Of audacious genius, setting at nought received opinions, he rushed into notoriety by an eccentric essay "On the Origin of the Inequality among Men," where he sustained the irrational paradox, that men are happier in a state of Nature than under the laws of Civilization. At a later day appeared his famous work on "The Social Contract." In both the sentiment of Equality is invoked against abuses of society, and language is employed tending far beyond Equality in Civil and Political Rights. The conspicuous position since awarded to the speculations of Rousseau, and their influence in diffusing this sentiment, would make this sketch imperfect without allusion to him; but he taught men to feel rather than to know, and his words have more of inspiration than of precision.

The French Revolution was at hand. That great outbreak for enfranchisement was the expression of this sentiment. Here it received distinct and authoritative enunciation. In the Constitutions of Government successively adopted, amid the throes of bloody struggle, the equality of men was constantly proclaimed. Kings, nobles, and all distinctions of birth, passed away before this mighty and triumphant truth.

These Constitutions show the grandeur of the principle, and how it was explained and illustrated. The Constitution of 1791, in its first article, declares that "Men are born and continue free and *equal in their rights.*" This great declaration was explained in the sixth article: "The law is the expression of the general will. . . . . It ought to be the same for all, whether it protect or punish. All citizens, being equal in its eyes, are equally admissible to all dignities, places, and public employments, according to their capacity, and without other distinction than their virtues and talents." At the close of the Declaration of Rights there is this further explanation: "The National Assembly, wishing to establish the French Constitution on the principles which it has just acknowledged and declared, abolishes irrevocably the institutions which bounded liberty and equality of rights. There is no longer nobility, or peerage, or hereditary distinctions, or distinction of orders, or feudal rule, or patrimonial jurisdictions, or any titles, denominations, or prerogatives thence derived, or any orders of chivalry, or any corporations or decorations for which proofs of nobility were required, or which supposed distinctions of birth, or any other superiority than that of public functionaries in the exercise of their functions. . . . . *There is no longer, for any part of the nation, or for any individual, any privilege or exception to the common right of all Frenchmen.*"[1] These diffuse articles all begin and end in the equality of men.

In fitful mood, another Declaration of Rights was brought forward by Condorcet, February 15, 1793. Here are fresh inculcations of Equality. Article First places Equality among the natural, civil, and political rights

[1] Moniteur, 1791, No. 259.

of man. Article Seventh declares: "Equality consists in this, that each individual can enjoy the same rights." Article Eighth: "*The law ought to be equal for all*, whether it recompense or punish, whether it protect or repress." Article Ninth: "All citizens are admissible to all public places, employments, and functions. Free people know no other motives of preference in their choice than talents and virtues." Article Twenty-third: "Instruction is the need of all, and society owes it equally to all its members." Article Thirty-second: "There is oppression, when a law violates the natural, civil, and political rights which it ought to guaranty. There is oppression, when the law is violated by the public functionaries in its application to individual cases."[1] Here again is the same constant testimony, reinforced by the accompanying report explaining the Constitution, where it is said: "All hereditary political power is at the same time an evident violation of natural equality and an absurd institution, since it supposes the inheritance of qualities proper for the discharge of a public function. Every exception to the common law made in favor of an individual is a blow struck at the rights of all." And in another part of the same report, "the sovereignty of the people, *equality among men*, the unity of the Republic," are declared to have been "the guiding principles always present in the formation of the Constitution."[2]

Next came the Constitution of June, 1793, announcing, in its second article, that the natural and imprescriptible rights of men are "*Equality*, liberty, security, property." In the next article we learn precisely what is meant by

[1] Moniteur, 1793, No. 49.

[2] Exposition des Principes et des Motifs du Plan de Constitution: Condorcet, Œuvres, Tom. XII. pp. 336, 413.

Equality, when it says, "All men are equal by nature *and before the law.*"[1] So just and captivating was this definition, which we encounter here for the first time, that it held its place through all the political vicissitudes of France, under the Directory, the Consulate, the Empire, the Restoration, and the Constitutional Government of Louis Philippe. It was a conquest which, when achieved, was never abandoned. Every Charter and Constitution certified to it. The Charter of Louis Philippe testifies as follows: "Frenchmen are *equal before the law,* whatever may be their titles and ranks."[2] Nor was its use confined to France. It passed into other constitutions, and Napoleon, who so often trampled on the rights of Equality, dictated to the Poles the declaration, that *all persons are equal before the law.* Thus the phrase is not only French, but Continental, although never English.

While recognizing this particular form of speech as more specific and satisfactory than the statement that all men are born equal, it is impossible not to be reminded that it finds a prototype in the ancient Greek language, where, according to Herodotus, "the government of the many has the most beautiful name of all, **ἰσονομία**, *isonomy,*" which may be defined *Equality before the Law.*[3] Thus, in an age when *Equality before the Law* was practically unknown, this remarkable language, by its comprehensiveness and flexibility, supplied a single word, not found in modern tongues, to express an

1 Moniteur, 1793, No. 178.

2 Annuaire Historique Universel pour 1830, Appendice, p. 48.

3 Book III. § 80. The same idea prevailed with Demosthenes, who, in his First Oration against Aristogiton, pictured the laws as desiring "the just and the beautiful and the useful," which, when found, is set forth in a general ordinance, "equal and alike to all." — *Orat. I. contra Aristogit.*, § 5.

idea practically recognized only in modern times. Such a word in our own language, as the substitute for Equality, might have superseded criticism to which this declaration is exposed.

EQUALITY UNDER CONSTITUTION OF MASSACHUSETTS AND DECLARATION OF INDEPENDENCE.

THE way is now prepared to consider the nature of Equality, as secured by the Constitution of Massachusetts. The Declaration of Independence, which followed the French Encyclopedia and the political writings of Rousseau, announces among self-evident truths, "*that all men are created equal;* that they are endowed by their Creator with certain unalienable rights; that among these are life, liberty, and the pursuit of happiness." The Constitution of Massachusetts repeats the same truth in a different form, saying, in its first article: "*All men are born free and equal,* and have certain natural essential, and unalienable rights, among which may be reckoned the right of enjoying and defending their lives and liberties." Another article explains what is meant by Equality, saying: "No man, nor corporation or association of men, have any other title to obtain advantages, or particular and exclusive privileges, distinct from those of the community, than what arises from the consideration of services rendered to the public; and this title being in nature neither hereditary, nor transmissible to children, or descendants, or relations by blood, the idea of a man being born a magistrate, lawgiver, or judge is absurd and unnatural." This language, in its natural signification, condemns every form of inequality in civil and political institutions.

These declarations, though in point of time before the ampler declarations of France, may be construed in the light of the latter. Evidently, they seek to declare the same principle. They are declarations of *Rights;* and the language employed, though general in character, is obviously limited to those matters within the design of a declaration of *Rights.* And permit me to say, it is a childish sophism to adduce any physical or mental inequality in argument against Equality of Rights.

Obviously, men are not born equal in physical strength or in mental capacity, in beauty of form or health of body. Diversity or inequality in these respects is the law of creation. From this difference springs divine harmony. But this inequality is in no particular inconsistent with complete civil and political equality.

The equality declared by our fathers in 1776, and made the fundamental law of Massachusetts in 1780, was *Equality before the Law.* Its object was to efface all political or civil distinctions, and to abolish all institutions founded upon *birth.* "All men are *created* equal," says the Declaration of Independence. "All men are *born* free and equal," says the Massachusetts Bill of Rights. These are not vain words. Within the sphere of their influence, no person can be *created,* no person can be *born,* with civil or political privileges not enjoyed equally by all his fellow-citizens; nor can any institution be established, recognizing distinction of birth. Here is the Great Charter of every human being drawing vital breath upon this soil, whatever may be his condition, and whoever may be his parents. He may be poor, weak, humble, or black, — he may be of Caucasian, Jewish, Indian, or Ethiopian race, — he may be of French, German, English, or Irish extraction; but before the Constitution of Massachusetts all these distinctions disappear. He is not poor, weak, humble, or black; nor is he Caucasian, Jew, Indian, or Ethiopian; nor is he French, German, English, or Irish; he is a MAN, the equal of all his fellow-men. He is one of the children of the State, which, like an impartial parent, regards all its offspring with an equal care. To some it may justly allot higher duties, according to higher capacities; but it welcomes all to its equal hospitable board. The State, imitating the divine justice, is no respecter of persons.

Here nobility cannot exist, because it is a privilege from birth. But the same anathema which smites and banishes nobility must also smite and banish every form of discrimination founded on birth, —

"Quamvis ille niger, quamvis tu candidus esses." [1]

EQUALITY BY LEGISLATION OF MASSACHUSETTS.

THE Legislature of Massachusetts, in entire harmony with the Constitution, has made no discrimination of race or color in the establishment of Common Schools.

Any such discrimination by the Laws would be unconstitutional and void. But the Legislature has been too just and generous, too mindful of the Bill of Rights, to establish any such privilege of *birth*. The language of the statutes is general, and applies equally to all children, of whatever race or color.

The provisions of the Law are entitled, *Of the Public Schools,*[2] meaning our Common Schools. To these we must look to ascertain what constitutes a Public School. Only those established in conformity with the Law can be legally such. They may, in fact, be more or less

[1] Virgil, Eclog. II. 16. [2] Revised Statutes, Ch. 23.

public; yet, if they do not come within the terms of the Law, they do not form part of the beautiful system of our Public Schools, — they are not Public Schools, or, as I prefer to call them, Common Schools. The two terms are used as identical; but the latter is that by which they were earliest known, while it is most suggestive of their comprehensive character. A "common" in law is defined to be "*open ground equally used* by many persons"; and the same word, when used as an adjective, is defined by lexicographers as "belonging equally to many or to the public," thus asserting Equality.

If we examine the text of this statute, we shall find nothing to sustain the rule of exclusion which has been set up. The first section provides, that "in every town, containing fifty families or householders, there shall be kept in each year, at the charge of the town, by a teacher or teachers of competent ability and good morals, *one school* for the instruction of *children* in Orthography, Reading, Writing, English Grammar, Geography, Arithmetic, and Good Behavior, for the term of six months, or two or more such schools, for terms of time that shall together be equivalent to six months." The second, third, and fourth sections provide for the number of such schools in towns having respectively one hundred, one hundred and fifty, and five hundred families or householders. There is no language recognizing any discrimination of race or color. Thus, in every town, the schools, whether one or more, are "for the instruction of *children*" generally, — not children of any particular class or race or color, but children, — meaning the children of the town where the schools are.

The fifth and sixth sections provide a school, in certain cases, where additional studies are to be pursued, which "shall be kept *for the benefit of all the inhabitants* of the town." The language here recognizes no discrimination among the children, but seems directly to exclude it.

In conformity with these sections is the peculiar phraseology of the memorable Colonial law of 1647, founding Common Schools, "to the end that learning may not be buried in the graves of our forefathers." This law obliged townships having fifty householders to "forthwith appoint one within their towns to teach *all such children as shall resort to him* to write and read."[1] Here again there is no discrimination among the children. *All* are to be taught.

On this legislation the Common Schools of Massachusetts have been reared. The section of the Revised Statutes,[2] and the statute of 1838,[3] appropriating small sums, in the nature of a contribution, from the School Fund, for the support of Common Schools among the Indians, do not interfere with this system. These have the anomalous character of all the legislation concerning the Indians. It does not appear, however, that separate schools are established by law among the Indians, nor that the Indians are in any way excluded from the Common Schools in their neighborhood.

I conclude, on this head, that there is but one Public School in Massachusetts. This is the Common School, equally free to all the inhabitants. There is nothing establishing an exclusive or separate school for any particular class, rich or poor, Catholic or Protestant, white or black. In the eye of the law there is but

[1] Charters and General Laws of the Colony and Province of Massachusetts Bay, p. 186.

[2] Chap. 23, sec. 68.

[3] Chap. 154.

one class, where all interests, opinions, conditions, and colors commingle in harmony,—excluding none, therefore comprehending all.

EQUALITY UNDER JUDICIAL DECISIONS.

THE Courts of Massachusetts, in harmony with the Constitution and the Laws, have never recognized any discrimination founded on race or color, in the administration of the Common Schools, but have constantly declared the equal rights of all the inhabitants.

There are only a few decisions bearing on this subject, but they breathe one spirit. The sentiment of Equality animates them all. In the case of *The Commonwealth* v. *Dedham,* (16 Mass. R., 146,) while declaring the equal rights of all the inhabitants, in both Grammar and District Schools, the Court said:—

"The schools required by the statute are to be maintained for the benefit of the whole town, *as it is the wise policy of the law to give all the inhabitants equal privileges for the education of their children in the Public Schools.* Nor is it in the power of the majority to deprive the minority of this *privilege.* . . . . Every inhabitant of the town has a right to participate in the benefits of both descriptions of schools; and it is not competent for a town to establish a grammar school for the benefit of one part of the town to the exclusion of the other, although the money raised for the support of schools may be in other respects fairly apportioned."

Here is Equality from beginning to end.

In the case of *Withington* v. *Eveleth,* (7 Pick. R., 106,) the Court say they "are all satisfied that the power given to towns to determine and define the limits of school districts can be executed only by a geographical division of the town for that purpose." A limitation of the district merely *personal* was held invalid. This same principle was again recognized in *Perry* v. *Dover*, (12 Pick. R., 213,) where the Court say, "Towns, in executing the power to form school districts, are bound so to do it as to include *every inhabitant* in some of the districts. They cannot lawfully omit any, and thus deprive them of *the benefits of our invaluable system of free schools.*" Thus at every point the Court has guarded the Equal Rights of all.

The Constitution, the Legislation, and the Judicial Decisions of Massachusetts have now been passed in review. We have seen what is contemplated by the Equality secured by the Constitution, — also what is contemplated by the system of Common Schools, as established by the laws of the Commonwealth and illustrated by decisions of the Supreme Court. The way is now prepared to consider the peculiarities in the present case, and to apply the principle thus recognized in Constitution, Laws, and Judicial Decisions.

SEPARATE SCHOOLS INCONSISTENT WITH EQUALITY.

It is easy to see that the exclusion of colored children from the Public Schools is a constant inconvenience to them and their parents, which white children and white parents are not obliged to bear. Here the facts are plain and unanswerable, showing a palpable violation of Equality. *The black and white are not equal before the law.* I am at a loss to understand how anybody can assert that they are.

Among the regulations of the Primary School Committee is one to this effect. "Scholars to go to the school nearest their residences. Applicants for admission to our schools (with the exception and provision referred to in the preceding rule) are especially entitled to enter the schools nearest to their places of residence." The exception here is "of those for whom special provision has been made" in separate schools, — that is, colored children.

In this rule — without the unfortunate exception — is part of the beauty so conspicuous in our Common Schools. It is the boast of England, that, through the multitude of courts, justice is brought to every man's door. It may also be the boast of our Common Schools, that, through the multitude of schools, education in Boston is brought to every *white* man's door. But it is not brought to every *black* man's door. He is obliged to go for it, to travel for it, to walk for it, — often a great distance. The facts in the present case are not so strong as those of other cases within my knowledge. But here the little child, only five years old, is compelled, if attending the nearest African School, to go a distance of two thousand one hundred feet from her home, while the nearest Primary School is only nine hundred feet, and, in doing this, she passes by no less than five different Primary Schools, forming part of our Common Schools, and open to white children, all of which are closed to her. Surely this is not *Equality before the Law.*

Such a fact is sufficient to determine this case. If it be met by the suggestion, that the inconvenience is trivial, and such as the law will not notice, I reply, that it is precisely such as to reveal an existing inequality, and therefore the law cannot fail to notice it. There is a maxim of the illustrious civilian, Dumoulin, a great jurist of France, which teaches that even a trivial fact may give occasion to an important application of the law: "*Modica enim circumstantia facti inducit magnam juris diversitatem.*" Also from the best examples of our history we learn that the insignificance of a fact cannot obscure the grandeur of the principle at stake. It was a paltry tax on tea, laid by a Parliament where they were not represented, that aroused our fathers to the struggles of the Revolution. They did not feel the inconvenience of the tax, but they felt its oppression. They went to war for a principle. Let it not be said, then, that in the present case the inconvenience is too slight to justify the appeal I make in behalf of colored children for *Equality before the Law.*

Looking beyond the facts of this case, it is apparent that the inconvenience from the exclusion of colored children is such as to affect seriously the comfort and condition of the African race in Boston. The two Primary Schools open to them are in Belknap Street and Sun Court. I need not add that the whole city is dotted with schools open to white children. Colored parents, anxious for the education of their children, are compelled to live in the neighborhood of the schools, to gather about them, — as in Eastern countries people gather near a fountain or a well. The liberty which belongs to the white man, of choosing his home, is not theirs. Inclination or business or economy may call them to another part of the city; but they are restrained for their children's sake. There is no such restraint upon the white man; for he knows, that, wherever in the city inclination or business or economy may call him, there will be a school open to his children near his door. Surely this is not *Equality before the Law.*

If a colored person, yielding to the necessities of position, removes to a distant part of the city, his children may be compelled daily, at an inconvenience which will not be called trivial, to walk a long distance for the advantages of the school. In our severe winters this cannot be disregarded, in the case of children so tender in years as those of the Primary Schools. There is a peculiar instance of hardship which has come to my knowledge. A respectable colored parent became some time since a resident of East Boston, separated from the mainland by water. Of course there are Common Schools at East Boston, but none open to colored children. This parent was obliged to send his children, three in number, daily across the ferry to the distant African School. The tolls amounted to a sum which formed a severe tax upon a poor man, while the long way to travel was a daily tax upon the time and strength of his children. Every toll paid by this parent, as every step taken by the children, testifies to that inequality which I now arraign.

This is the conduct of a colored parent. He is well deserving of honor for his generous efforts to secure the education of his children. As they grow in knowledge they will rise and call him blessed; but at the same time they will brand as accursed that arbitrary discrimination of color in the Common Schools of Boston which rendered it necessary for their father, out of small means, to make such sacrifices for their education.

Here is a grievance which, independent of any stigma from color, calls for redress. It is an inequality which the Constitution and the Laws of Massachusetts repudiate. But it is not on the ground of inconvenience only that it is odious. And this brings me to the next head.

SEPARATE SCHOOLS ARE IN THE NATURE OF CASTE.

The separation of children in the Schools, on account of race or color, is in the nature of *Caste*, and, on this account, a violation of Equality. The case shows expressly that the child was excluded from the school nearest to her dwelling — the number in the school at the time warranting her admission — "on the sole ground of color." The first Majority Report presented to the School Committee, and mentioned in the statement of facts, presents the grounds of this discrimination with more fulness, saying, "It is one of *races*, not of *colors* merely. The distinction is one which the All-wise Creator has seen fit to establish; and it is founded deep in the physical, mental, and moral natures of the two races. No legislation, no social customs, can efface this distinction."[1] Words cannot be chosen more apt than these to describe the heathenish relation of Caste.

This term, which has its prototype in Spanish and French, finds its way into English from the Portuguese *casta*, which signifies family, breed, race, and is generally used to designate any hereditary distinction, particularly of race. It is most often employed in India, and it is there that we must go to understand its full force. A recent English writer says, that it is "not only a distinction by birth, but is founded on the doctrine of an essentially distinct origin of the different races, which are thus unalterably separated."[2] This is the very ground of the Boston School Committee.

[1] Report to the Primary School Committee, June 15, 1846, on the Petition of Sundry Colored Persons for the Abolition of the Schools for Colored Children, p. 7.

[2] Roberts on Caste, p. 134.

This word is not now for the first time applied to the distinction between the white and black races. Alexander von Humboldt, speaking of the negroes in Mexico, characterizes them as a caste.[1] Following him, a recent political and juridical writer of France uses the same term to denote not only the distinctions in India, but those of our own country, especially referring to the exclusion of colored children from the Common Schools as among "the humiliating and brutal distinctions" by which their caste is characterized.[2] It is, then, on authority and reason alike that we apply this term to the hereditary distinction on account of color now established in the schools of Boston.

Boston is set on a hill, and her schools have long been the subject of observation, even in this respect. As far back as the last century, the French Consul here made a report on our "separate" school;[3] and De Tocqueville, in his masterly work, testifies, with evident pain, that the same schools do not receive the children of the African and European.[4] All this is only a reproduction of the Cagots in France, who for generations were put under the ban, — relegated to a corner of the church, as in a "negro pew," and even in the last resting-place, where all are equal, these wretched people were separated by a line of demarcation from the rest.[5] The Cagots are called an "accursed race," and this language may be applied to the African under our laws. Strange that here, under a State Constitution declaring the Equality of all men, we should follow the worst precedents and establish among

[1] Essai Politique sur le Royaume de la Nouvelle-Espagne, Liv. II. ch. 6.

[2] Charles Comte, Traité de Legislation, Tom. IV. pp. 129, 445.

[3] Grégoire, De la Littérature des Nègres, p. 177.

[4] Democracy in America, Vol. I. p. 461, Ch. XVIII. § 2.

[5] Michel, Histoire des Races Maudites, Tom. I. p. 3.

us a Caste. Seeing the discrimination in this light, we learn to appreciate its true character. In India, Brahmins and Sudras, from generation to generation, were kept apart. If a Sudra presumed to sit upon a Brahmin's carpet, his punishment was banishment. With similar inhumanity here, the black child who goes to sit on the same benches with the white is banished, not indeed from the country, but from the school. In both cases it is the triumph of Caste. But the offence is greater with us, because, unlike the Hindoos, we acknowledge that men are born equal.

So strong is my desire that the Court should feel the enormity of this system, thus legalized, not by the Legislature, but by an inferior local board, that I shall introduce an array of witnesses all testifying to the unchristian character of Caste, as it appears in India, where it is most studied and discussed. As you join in detestation of this foul institution, you will learn to condemn its establishment among our children.

I take these authorities from the work of Mr. Roberts to which I have already referred, "Caste opposed to Christianity," published in London in 1847. Time will not allow me to make comments. I can only quote the testimony and then pass on.

The eminent Bishop Heber, of Calcutta, characterizes Caste in these forcible terms: —

> "*It is a system which tends, more than any else the Devil has yet invented, to destroy the feelings of general benevolence, and to make nine tenths of mankind the hopeless slaves of the remainder.*"

But this is the very system now in question here. Bishop Wilson, also of Calcutta, the successor of Heber, says: —

"The Gospel recognizes no such distinction as those of Castes, imposed by a heathen usage, bearing in some respects a supposed religious obligation, condemning those in the lower ranks to perpetual abasement, placing an immovable barrier against all general advance and improvement in society, cutting asunder the bonds of human fellowship on the one hand, and preventing those of Christian love on the other. Such distinctions, I say, the Gospel does not recognize. On the contrary, it teaches us that God 'hath made of one blood all the nations of men.'"

The same sentiment is echoed by Bishop Corrie, of Madras: —

"Thus Caste sets itself up as a judge of our Saviour himself. His command is, 'Condescend to men of low estate. Esteem others better than yourself.' 'No,' says Caste, 'do not commune with low men: consider yourself of high estimation. Touch not, taste not, handle not.' Thus Caste condemns the Saviour."

Here is the testimony of Rev. Mr. Rhenius, a zealous and successful missionary: —

"I have found Caste, both in theory and practice, to be diametrically opposed to the Gospel, which inculcates love, humility, and union; whereas Caste teaches the contrary. It is a fact, in those entire congregations where Caste is allowed the spirit of the Gospel does not enter; whereas in those from which it is excluded we see the fruits of the Gospel spirit."

Another missionary, Rev. C. Mault, follows in similar strain: —

"Caste must be entirely renounced; for it is a noxious plant, by the side of which the graces cannot grow; for facts demonstrate, that, where it has been allowed, Christianity has never flourished."

So also does the Rev. John McKenny, a Wesleyan missionary: —

"I have been upward of twelve years in India, and have directed much of my attention to the subject of Caste, and am fully of opinion that it is altogether contrary to the nature and principles of the Gospel of Christ, and therefore ought not to be admitted into the Christian Church."

So also the Rev. R. S. Hardy, a Wesleyan missionary, and author of "Notices of the Holy Land": —

"The principle of Caste I consider so much at variance with the spirit of the Gospel as to render impossible, where its authority is acknowledged, the exercise of many of the most beautiful virtues of our holy religion."

So also the Rev. D. J. Gorgerly, of the same Society: —

"I regard the distinction of Caste, both in its principles and operations, as directly opposed to vital godliness, and consequently inadmissible into the Church of Christ."

So also the Rev. W. Bridgnall, of the same Society: —

"I perfectly agree with a writer of respectable authority, in considering the institution of Caste as the most formidable engine that was ever invented for perpetuating the subjugation of men: so that, as a friend of humanity only, I should feel myself bound to protest against and oppose it; but in particular as a Christian, I deem it my obvious and imperative duty wholly to discountenance it, conceiving it to be utterly repugnant to all the principles and the whole spirit of Christianity. He who is prepared to support the system of Caste is, in my judgment, neither a true friend of man nor a consistent follower of Christ."

So also the Rev. S. Allens, of the same Society: —

"During a residence of more than nine years in Ceylon I have had many opportunities of witnessing the influence of Caste on the minds of the natives, and I firmly believe it is altogether opposed to the spirit of Christianity; and it appears to me that its utter and speedy extinction cannot but be desired by every minister of Christ."

So also the Rev. R. Stoup, of the same Society: —

"From my own personal observation, during a four years' residence in Ceylon, I am decidedly of opinion that Caste is directly opposed to the spirit of Christianity, and consequently ought to be discouraged in every possible way."

I conclude these European authorities with the confirmation of Rev. Joseph Roberts, author of the work on Caste: —

"*We must in every place witness against it, and show that even Government itself is nurturing a tremendous evil, that through its heathen managers it is beguiled into a course which obstructs the progress of civilization,* which keeps in repulsion our kindlier feelings, which creates and nurses distinctions the most alien to all the cordialities of life, and which, more than any other thing, makes the distance so immense betwixt the governed and governors."

There is also the testimony of native Hindoos converted to Christianity, who denounce Caste as Jefferson denounced the despotism of Slavery. Listen to the voice of a Hindoo: —

"Caste is the stronghold of that principle of pride which makes a man think of himself more highly than he ought to think. Caste infuses itself into and forms the very essence of pride itself."

Another Hindoo testifies as follows: —

"I therefore regard Caste as opposed to the main scope, principles, and doctrines of Christianity; for either Caste must be admitted to be true and of divine authority, or

Christianity must be so admitted. If you admit Caste to be true, the whole fabric of Christianity must come down; for the nature of Caste and its associations destroy the first principles of Christianity. Caste makes distinctions among creatures where God has made none."

Another native expresses himself thus: —

"When God made man, his intention was, not that they should be divided, and hate one another, and show contempt, and think more highly of themselves than others. Caste makes a man think that he is holier than another, and that he has some inherent virtue which another has not. It makes him despise all those that are lower than himself in regard to Caste, which is not the design of God."

Still another native uses this strong language: —

"Yes, we regard Caste as part and parcel of idolatry, and of all heathen abominations, because it is in many ways contrary to God's Word, and directly contrary to God himself."

I hope that I have not occupied too much time with this testimony, which is strictly in point. There is not a word which is not plainly applicable to the present case. The witnesses are competent, and in their evidence, as in a mirror, may be seen the true character of the discrimination which I bring to judgment before this Court.

It will be vain to say that this distinction, though seeming to be founded on color, is in reality founded on natural and physical peculiarities independent of color. Whatever they may be, they are peculiarities of race; and any discrimination on this account constitutes the relation of Caste, in the most restricted sense of this term. Disguise it as you will, it is nothing but this hateful, irreligious institution. But the words Caste and Equality are contradictory. They mutually exclude each other. Where Caste is, there cannot be Equality; where Equality is, there cannot be Caste.

Unquestionably there is a distinction between the Ethiopian and the Caucasian. Each received from the hand of God certain characteristics of color and form. The two may not readily intermingle, although we are told by Homer that Jupiter did not

> "disdain to grace
> The feasts of Ethiopia's blameless race."

One may be uninteresting or offensive to the other, precisely as individuals of the same race and color may be uninteresting or offensive to each other. But this distinction can furnish no ground for any discrimination before the law.

We abjure nobility of all kinds; but here is a nobility of the skin. We abjure all hereditary distinctions; but here is an hereditary distinction, founded, not on the merit of the ancestor, but on his color. We abjure all privileges of birth; but here is a privilege which depends solely on the accident whether an ancestor is black or white. We abjure all inequality before the law; but here is an inequality which touches not an individual, but a race. We revolt at the relation of Caste; but here is a Caste which is established under a Constitution declaring that all men are born equal.

Condemning Caste and inequality before the law, the way is prepared to consider more particularly the powers of the School Committee. Here it will be necessary to enter into details.

SCHOOL COMMITTEE HAVE NO POWER TO DISCRIMINATE ON ACCOUNT OF COLOR.

THE Committee charged with the superintendence of the Common Schools of Boston have no *power* to make any discrimination on account of race or color.

It has been seen already that this power is inconsistent with the Declaration of Independence, with the Constitution and Laws of Massachusetts, and with adjudications of the Supreme Court. The stream cannot rise higher than the fountain-head; and if there be nothing in these elevated sources from which this power can spring, it must be considered a nullity. Having seen that there is nothing, I might here stop; but I wish to show the shallow origin of this pretension.

Its advocates, unable to find it among express powers conferred upon the School Committee, and forgetful of the Constitution, where "either it must live or bear no life," place it among implied or incidental powers. The Revised Statutes provide for a School Committee "who shall have *the general charge and superintendence* of all the Public Schools" in their respective towns.[1] Another section provides that "the School Committee shall determine the number and qualifications of the scholars to be admitted into the school kept for the use of the whole town."[2] These are all the clauses conferring powers on the Committee.

From them no person will imply a power to defeat a cardinal principle of the Constitution. It is absurd to suppose that the Committee in general charge and superintendence of schools, and in determining the number and qualifications of scholars, may engraft upon

[1] Chap. 23, sec. 10. [2] Chap. 23, sec. 15.

the schools a principle of inequality, not only unknown to the Constitution and Laws, but in defiance of their letter and spirit. In the exercise of these powers they cannot put colored children to personal inconvenience greater than that of white children. Still further, they cannot brand a whole race with the stigma of inferiority and degradation, constituting them a Caste. They cannot in any way violate that fundamental right of all citizens, Equality before the Law. To suppose that they can do this would place the Committee above the Constitution. It would enable them, in the exercise of a brief and local authority, to draw a fatal circle, within which the Constitution cannot enter, — nay, where the very Bill of Rights becomes a dead letter.

In entire harmony with the Constitution, the law says expressly what the Committee shall do. Besides the general charge and superintendence, they shall "determine the *number* and *qualifications* of the scholars to be admitted into the school," — thus, according to a familiar rule of interpretation, excluding other powers: *Mentio unius est exclusio alterius.* The power to determine the "number" is easily executed, and admits of no question. The power to determine the "qualifications," though less simple, must be restricted to age, sex, and fitness, moral and intellectual. The fact that a child is black, or that he is white, cannot of itself be a qualification or a disqualification. Not to the skin can we look for the criterion of fitness.

It is sometimes pretended, that the Committee, in the exercise of their power, are intrusted with a discretion, under which they may distribute, assign, and classify all children belonging to the schools *according to their best judgment*, making, if they think proper, a discrimination of race or color. Without questioning that they are intrusted with a discretion, it is outrageous to suppose that their discretion can go to this extent. The Committee can have no discretion which is not in harmony with the Constitution and Laws. Surely they cannot, in any mere discretion, nullify a sacred and dear-bought principle of Human Rights expressly guarantied by the Constitution.

REGULATIONS OF COMMITTEE MUST BE REASONABLE.

STILL further, — and here I approach a more technical view of the subject, — it is an admitted principle, that the regulations and by-laws of municipal corporations must be *reasonable*, or they are inoperative and void. This has been recognized by the Supreme Court in two different cases, — *Commonwealth* v. *Worcester*, (3 Pick. R., 462,) and in Vandine's case (6 Pick. R., 187). In another case, *City of Boston* v. *Shaw*, (1 Met. R., 130,) it was decided that a by-law of Boston, prescribing a particular form of contribution toward the expenses of making the common sewers, was void for inequality and unreasonableness.

Assuming that this principle is applicable to the School Committee, their regulations and by-laws must be *reasonable*. Their discretion must be exercised in a reasonable manner. And this is not what the Committee or any other body of men think reasonable, but what is reasonable in the eye of the Law. It must be *legally reasonable*. It must be approved by the *reason* of the Law.

Here we are brought once more, in another form, to the question of the discrimination on account of color.

Is this *legally reasonable?* Is it reasonable, in the exercise of a just discretion, to separate descendants of the African race from white children merely in consequence of descent? Passing over those principles of the Constitution and those provisions of Law which of themselves decide the question, constituting as they do *the highest reason*, but which have been already amply considered, look for a moment at the educational system of Massachusetts, and it will be seen that practically no discrimination of color is made by Law in any part of it. A descendant of the African race may be Governor of the Commonwealth, and as such, with the advice and consent of the Council, may select the Board of Education. As Lieutenant-Governor, he may be *ex officio* a member of the Board. He may be Secretary of the Board, with the duty imposed on him by law of seeing "that *all* children in this Commonwealth, who depend upon Common Schools for instruction, may have the best education which those schools can be made to impart."[1] He may be member of any School Committee, or teacher in any Common School of the State. As legal voter, he can vote in the selection of any School Committee.

Thus, in every department connected with our Common Schools, throughout the whole hierarchy of their government, from the very head of the system down to the humblest usher in the humblest Primary School, and to the humblest voter, there is no distinction of color known to the law. It is when we reach the last stage of all, the children themselves, that the beautiful character of the system is changed to the deformity of Caste, as, in the picture of the ancient poet, what above was a lovely woman terminated below in a vile, unsightly

[1] General Laws of Massachusetts, 1837, Ch. 241, sec. 2.

fish. And all this is done by the School Committee, with more than necromantic power, in the exercise of a mere discretion.

It is clear that the Committee may classify scholars according to age and sex, for the obvious reasons that these distinctions are inoffensive, and that they are especially recognized as *legal* in the law relating to schools.[1] They may also classify scholars according to moral and intellectual qualifications, because such a power is necessary to the government of schools. But the Committee cannot assume, *a priori*, and without individual examination, that all of an *entire race* are so deficient in proper moral and intellectual qualifications as to justify their universal degradation to a class by themselves. Such an exercise of discretion must be unreasonable, and therefore illegal.

SEPARATE SCHOOL NOT AN EQUIVALENT FOR COMMON SCHOOL.

BUT it is said that the School Committee, in thus classifying the children, have not violated any principle of Equality, inasmuch as they provide a school with competent instructors for colored children, where they have advantages equal to those provided for white children. It is argued, that, in excluding colored children from Common Schools open to white children, the Committee furnish an *equivalent*.

Here there are several answers. I shall touch them briefly, as they are included in what has been already said.

1. The separate school for colored children is not

1 Revised Statutes, Ch. 23, sec. 63.

one of the schools established by the law relating to Public Schools.[1] It is not a Common School. As such it has no legal existence, and therefore cannot be a *legal equivalent.* In addition to what has been already said, bearing on this head, I call attention to one other aspect. It has been decided that a town can execute its power to form School Districts only by geographical divisions of its territory, that there cannot be what I would call a *personal* limitation of a district, and that *certain individuals* cannot be selected and set off by *themselves* into a district.[2] The admitted effect of this decision is to render a separate school for colored children illegal and impossible in towns divided into districts. They are so regarded in Salem, Nantucket, New Bedford, and in other towns of this Commonwealth. The careful opinion of a learned member of this Court, who is not sitting in this case, given while at the bar,[3] and extensively published, is considered as practically settling this point.

But there cannot be one law for the country and another for Boston. It is true that Boston is not divided strictly into geographical districts. In this respect its position is anomalous. But if separate colored schools are illegal and impossible in the country, they must be illegal and impossible in Boston. It is absurd to suppose that this city, failing to establish School Districts, and treating all its territory as a single district, should be able to legalize a Caste school, which otherwise it could not do. Boston cannot do indirectly what other towns cannot do directly. This is the first answer to the allegation of equivalents.

1 Revised Statutes, Ch. 23.

2 Perry *v.* Dover, 12 Pick. R., 213.

3 Hon. Richard Fletcher.

2. The second is that in point of fact the separate school is not an equivalent. We have already seen that it is the occasion of inconvenience to colored children, which would not arise, if they had access to the nearest Common School, besides compelling parents to pay an additional tax, and inflicting upon child and parent the stigma of Caste. Still further, — and this consideration cannot be neglected, — the matters taught in the two schools may be precisely the same, but a school exclusively devoted to one class must differ essentially in spirit and character from that Common School known to the law, where all classes meet together in Equality. It is a mockery to call it an equivalent.

3. But there is yet another answer. Admitting that it is an equivalent, still the colored children cannot be compelled to take it. Their rights are found in Equality before the Law; nor can they be called to renounce one jot of this. They have an equal right with white children to the Common Schools. A separate school, though well endowed, would not secure to them that precise Equality which they would enjoy in the Common Schools. The Jews in Rome are confined to a particular district called the Ghetto, and in Frankfort to a district known as the Jewish Quarter. It is possible that their accommodations are as good as they would be able to occupy, if left free to choose throughout Rome and Frankfort; but this compulsory segregation from the mass of citizens is of itself an *inequality* which we condemn. It is a vestige of ancient intolerance directed against a despised people. It is of the same character with the separate schools in Boston.

Thus much for the doctrine of Equivalents as a substitute for Equality.

DISASTROUS CONSEQUENCES OF POWER TO MAKE SEPARATE SCHOOLS.

In determining that the School Committee have no *power* to make this discrimination we are strengthened by another consideration. If the power exists in the present case, it cannot be restricted to this. The Committee may distribute all the children into classes, according to mere discretion. They may establish a separate school for Irish or Germans, where each may nurse an exclusive nationality alien to our institutions. They may separate Catholics from Protestants, or, pursuing their discretion still further, may separate different sects of Protestants, and establish one school for Unitarians, another for Presbyterians, another for Baptists, and another for Methodists. They may establish a separate school for the rich, that the delicate taste of this favored class may not be offended by the humble garments of the poor. They may exclude the children of mechanics, and send them to separate schools. All this, and much more, can be done in the exercise of that high-handed power which makes a discrimination on account of race or color. The grand fabric of our Common Schools, the pride of Massachusetts, — where, at the feet of the teacher, innocent childhood should come, unconscious of all distinctions of birth, — where the Equality of the Constitution and of Christianity should be inculcated by constant precept and example, — will be converted into a heathen system of proscription and Caste. We shall then have many different schools, representatives of as many different classes, opinions, and prejudices; but we shall look in vain for the true Common School of Massachusetts. Let it not be said that there is little danger that any Committee will exercise a discretion to this extent. They must not be intrusted with the power. Here is the only safety worthy of a free people.

BY-LAW VOID.

THE Court will declare the by-law of the School Committee unconstitutional and illegal, although there are no express words of prohibition in the Constitution and Laws.

It is hardly necessary to say anything in support of this proposition. Slavery was abolished in Massachusetts, under the Declaration of Rights in our Constitution, without any specific words of abolition in that instrument, or in any subsequent legislation.[1] The same words which are potent to destroy Slavery must be equally potent against any institution founded on Inequality or Caste. The case of *Boston* v. *Shaw* (1 Metcalf, 130), to which reference has been already made, where a by-law of the city was set aside as unequal and unreasonable, and therefore void, affords another example of the power which I here invoke. But authorities are not needed. The words of the Constitution are plain, and it will be the duty of the Court to see that they are applied to the discrimination now waiting for judgment.

The Court might justly feel delicacy, if called to revise an act of the Legislature. But it is simply the action of a local committee that they are to overrule. They may also be encouraged by the circumstance that it is only to the schools of Boston that their decision can be applicable. Already the other towns have voluntarily banished Caste. Banishing it from the schools of Boston,

[1] Commonwealth *v.* Aves, 18 Pick. R., 210.

the Court will bring them into much-desired harmony with the schools of other towns, and with the whole system of Common Schools. I am unwilling to suppose that there can be any hesitation or doubt. If any should arise, there is a rule of interpretation which is plain. According to familiar practice, judicial interpretation is made always in favor of life or liberty. So here the Court should incline in favor of Equality, that sacred right which is the companion of those other rights. In proportion to the importance of this right will the Court be solicitous to vindicate and uphold it. And in proportion to the opposition which it encounters from prejudices of society will the Court brace themselves to this task. It has been pointedly remarked by Rousseau, that "it is precisely because the force of things tends always to destroy Equality that the force of legislation should always tend to maintain it."[1] In similar spirit, and for the same reason, the Court should always tend to maintain Equality.

ORIGIN OF SEPARATE SCHOOLS.

In extenuation of the Boston system, it is sometimes said that the separation of white and black children was originally made at the request of colored parents. This is substantially true. It appears from the interesting letter of Dr. Belknap, in reply to Judge Tucker's queries respecting Slavery in Massachusetts, at the close of the last century, that no discrimination on account of color existed then in the Common Schools of Boston. "The same provision," he says, "is made by the public for the education of the children of the blacks as for those of the

[1] Contrat Social, Liv. II. ch. 11.

whites. In this town the Committee who superintend the free schools have given in charge to the schoolmasters to receive and instruct black children as well as white." Dr. Belknap had "not heard of more than three or four who had taken advantage of this privilege, though the number of blacks in Boston probably exceeded one thousand."[1] Much I fear that the inhuman bigotry of Caste — sad relic of the servitude from which they had just escaped — was at this time too strong to allow colored children kindly welcome in the free schools, and that, from timidity and ignorance, they hesitated to take a place on the same benches with the white children. Perhaps the prejudice was so inveterate that they could not venture to assert their rights. In 1800 a petition from sixty-six colored persons was presented to the School Committee, requesting the establishment of a school for their benefit. Some time later, private munificence came to the aid of this work, and the present system of separate schools was brought into being.

These are interesting incidents belonging to the history of the Boston schools, but they cannot in any way affect the rights of colored people or the powers of the School Committee. These rights and these powers stand on the Constitution and Laws. Without adopting the suggestion of Jefferson, that one generation cannot by legislation bind its successors, all must agree that the assent of a few to an unconstitutional and illegal course nearly half a century ago, when their rights were imperfectly understood, cannot alter the Constitution and the Laws so as to bind their descendants forever in the thrall of Caste. Nor can the Committee derive from

[1] Coll. Mass. Hist. Soc., Vol. IV. pp. 206, 207.

this assent, or from any lapse of time, powers in derogation of the Constitution and the Rights of Man.

It is clear that the sentiments of the colored people have now changed. The present case, and the deep interest which they manifest in it, thronging the Court to watch this discussion, attest the change. With increasing knowledge they have learned to know their rights, and feel the degradation to which they are doomed. In them revives the spirit of Paul, even as when he demanded, "Is it lawful for you to scourge a man that is a Roman, and uncondemned?" Their present effort is the token of a manly character, which this Court will respect and cherish.

EVILS OF SEPARATE SCHOOLS.

BUT it is said that these separate schools are for the benefit of both colors, and of the Public Schools. In similar spirit Slavery is sometimes said to be for the benefit of master and slave, and of the country where it exists. There is a mistake in the one case as great as in the other. This is clear. Nothing unjust, nothing ungenerous, can be for the benefit of any person or any thing. From some seeming selfish superiority, or from the gratified vanity of class, short-sighted mortals may hope to draw permanent good; but even-handed justice rebukes these efforts and redresses the wrong. The whites themselves are injured by the separation. Who can doubt this? With the Law as their monitor, they are taught to regard a portion of the human family, children of God, created in his image, coequals in his love, as a separate and degraded class; they are taught practically to deny that grand revelation of Christianity, the

Brotherhood of Man. Hearts, while yet tender with childhood, are hardened, and ever afterward testify to this legalized uncharitableness. Nursed in the sentiments of Caste, receiving it with the earliest food of knowledge, they are unable to eradicate it from their natures, and then weakly and impiously charge upon our Heavenly Father the prejudice derived from an unchristian school. Their characters are debased, and they become less fit for the duties of citizenship.

The Helots of Sparta were obliged to intoxicate themselves, that by example they might teach the deformity of intemperance. Thus sacrificing one class to the other, both were injured, — the imperious Spartan and the abased Helot. The School Committee of Boston act with similar double-edged injustice in sacrificing the colored children to the prejudice or fancied advantage of the white.

A child should be taught to shun wickedness, and, as he is yet plastic under impressions, to shun wicked men. Horace was right, when, speaking of a person morally wrong, false, and unjust, he calls him black, and warns against him: —

"Hic niger est: hunc tu, Romane, caveto." [1]

The Boston Committee adopt the warning, but apply it not to the black in heart, but the black in skin. They forget the admonition addressed to the prophet: "The Lord said unto Samuel, *Look not on his countenance:* . . . . for the Lord seeth not as man seeth; for man looketh on the outward appearance, *but the Lord looketh on the heart.*" [2] The Committee look on the outward appearance, without looking on the heart, and thus fancy that they are doing right!

[1] Satiræ, Lib. I. iv. 85.

[2] 1 Samuel, xvi. 7.

Who can say that this does not injure the blacks? Theirs, in its best estate, is an unhappy lot. A despised class, blasted by prejudice and shut out from various opportunities, they feel this proscription from the Common Schools as a peculiar brand. Beyond this, it deprives them of those healthful, animating influences which would come from participation in the studies of their white brethren. It adds to their discouragements. It widens their separation from the community, and postpones that great day of reconciliation which is yet to come.

The whole system of Common Schools suffers also. It is a narrow perception of their high aim which teaches that they are merely to furnish an equal amount of knowledge to all, and therefore, provided all be taught, it is of little consequence where and in what company. The law contemplates not only that all shall be taught, but that *all* shall be taught *together*. They are not only to receive equal quantities of knowledge, but all are to receive it in the same way. All are to approach the same common fountain together; nor can there be any exclusive source for individual or class. The school is the little world where the child is trained for the larger world of life. It is the microcosm preparatory to the macrocosm, and therefore it must cherish and develop the virtues and the sympathies needed in the larger world. And since, according to our institutions, all classes, without distinction of color, meet in the performance of civil duties, so should they all, without distinction of color, meet in the school, beginning there those relations of Equality which the Constitution and Laws promise to all.

As the State derives strength from the unity and solidarity of its citizens without distinction of class, so the school derives strength from the unity and solidarity of all classes beneath its roof. In this way the poor, the humble, and the neglected not only share the companionship of the more favored, but enjoy also the protection of their presence, which draws toward the school a more watchful superintendence. A degraded or neglected class, if left to themselves, will become more degraded or neglected. "If any man have ears to hear, let him hear. . . . . For he that hath, to him shall be given; and he that hath not, from him shall be taken even that which he hath."[1] The world, perverting the true sense of these words, takes from the outcast that which God gave him capacity to enjoy. Happily, our educational system, by the blending of all classes, draws upon the whole school that attention which is too generally accorded only to the favored few, and thus secures to the poor their portion of the fruitful sunshine. But the colored children, placed apart in separate schools, are deprived of this peculiar advantage. Nothing is more clear than that the welfare of classes, as well as of individuals, is promoted by mutual acquaintance. Prejudice is the child of ignorance. It is sure to prevail, where people do not know each other. Society and intercourse are means established by Providence for human improvement. They remove antipathies, promote mutual adaptation and conciliation, and establish relations of reciprocal regard. Whoso sets up barriers to these thwarts the ways of Providence, crosses the tendencies of human nature, and directly interferes with the laws of God.

[1] Mark, iv. 23, 25.

DUTY OF THE COURT.

May it please your Honors: Such are some of the things which I feel it my duty to say in this important cause. I have occupied much time, but the topics are not yet exhausted. Still, which way soever we turn, we are brought back to one single proposition,— *the Equality of men before the Law.* This stands as the mighty guardian of the colored children in this case. It is the constant, ever-present, tutelary genius of this Commonwealth, frowning upon every privilege of birth, every distinction of race, every institution of Caste. You cannot slight it or avoid it. You cannot restrain it. God grant that you may welcome it! Do this, and your words will be a "charter and freehold of rejoicing" to a race which by much suffering has earned a title to much regard. Your judgment will become a sacred landmark, not in jurisprudence only, but in the history of Freedom, giving precious encouragement to the weary and heavy-laden wayfarers in this great cause. Massachusetts, through you, will have fresh title to respect, and be once more, as in times past, an example to the whole land.

Already you have banished Slavery from this Commonwealth. I call upon you now to obliterate the last of its footprints, and to banish the last of the hateful spirits in its train. The law interfering to prohibit marriage between blacks and whites has been abolished by the Legislature. Railroads, which, imitating the Boston schools, placed colored people apart by themselves, are compelled, under the influence of an awakened public sentiment, to abandon this regulation, and to allow them the privileges of other travellers. Only recently I have read that his Excellency, our present Governor,[1] took his seat in a train by the side of a negro. In the Caste Schools of Boston the prejudice of color seeks its final refuge. It is for you to drive it forth. You do well, when you rebuke and correct individual offences; but it is a higher office to rebuke and correct a vicious institution. Each individual is limited in influence; but an institution has the influence of numbers organized by law. The charity of one man may counteract or remedy the uncharitableness of another; but no individual can counteract or remedy the uncharitableness of an organized injury. Against it private benevolence is powerless. It is a monster to be hunted down by the public and the constituted authorities. And such is the institution of Caste in the Common Schools of Boston, which now awaits a just condemnation from a just Court.

One of the most remarkable expositions of Slavery is from the pen of Condorcet, in a note to the "Thoughts" of Pascal. Voltaire, in his later commentary on the same text, speaks of this "terrible" note, and adopts its conclusion. In the course of this arraignment, the philosopher, painting the character of the slave-master, says, "Such is the excess of his stupid contempt for this wretched race, that, returning to Europe, he is indignant to see them clothed as men and *placed by his side*."[2] Thus the repugnance of the slave-master to see the wretched race *placed by his side* is adduced as crowning evidence of the inhumanity of Slavery. But this very repugnance has practical sanction among us, and you are to determine whether it shall be longer permitted.

1 Hon. George N. Briggs.

2 Pensées de Pascal, Notes de Condorcet et Voltaire, No. 109.

Slavery, in one of its enormities, is now before you for judgment. Hesitate not, I pray you, to strike it down. Let the blow fall which shall end its domination here in Massachusetts.

The civilization of the age joins in this appeal. I need not remind you that this prejudice of color is peculiar to our country. You may remember that two youths of African blood only recently gained the highest honors in a college at Paris, and on the same day dined with the King of the French, the descendant of St. Louis, at the Palace of the Tuileries. And let me add, if I may refer to my own experience, that at the School of Law in Paris I have sat for weeks on the same benches with colored pupils, listening, like myself, to the learned lectures of Degerando and Rossi; nor do I remember, in the throng of sensitive young men, any feeling toward them except of companionship and respect. In Italy, at the Convent of Palazzuolo, on the shores of the Alban Lake, amidst a scene of natural beauty enhanced by historical association, where I was once a guest, I have, for days, seen a native of Abyssinia, recently from his torrid home, and ignorant of the language spoken about him, mingling, in delightful and affectionate familiarity, with the Franciscan friars, whose visitor and scholar he was. Do I err in saying that the Christian spirit shines in these examples?

The Christian spirit, then, I again invoke. Where this prevails, there is neither Jew nor Gentile, Greek nor Barbarian, bond nor free, but all are alike. From this we derive new and solemn assurance of the Equality of Men, as an ordinance of God. Human bodies may be unequal in beauty or strength; these mortal cloaks of flesh may differ, as do these worldly garments;

these intellectual faculties may vary, as do opportunities of action and advantages of position; but amid all unessential differences there is essential agreement and equality. Dives and Lazarus are equal in the sight of God: they must be equal in the sight of all human institutions.

This is not all. The vaunted superiority of the white race imposes corresponding duties. The faculties with which they are endowed, and the advantages they possess, must be exercised for the good of all. If the colored people are ignorant, degraded, and unhappy, then should they be especial objects of care. From the abundance of our possessions must we seek to remedy their lot. And this Court, which is parent to all the unfortunate children of the Commonwealth, will show itself most truly parental, when it reaches down, and, with the strong arm of Law, elevates, encourages, and protects our colored fellow-citizens.

CHARACTER AND HISTORY OF THE LAW SCHOOL OF HARVARD UNIVERSITY.

REPORT OF THE COMMITTEE OF OVERSEERS, FEBRUARY 7, 1850.

IN BOARD OF OVERSEERS, February 1, 1849.

Voted, That Hon. PELEG SPRAGUE, Hon. SIMON GREENLEAF, CHARLES SUMNER, Esq., Hon. ALBERT H. NELSON, and PELEG W. CHANDLER, Esq., be a committee to visit the Law School during the ensuing year. [Hon. WILLIAM KENT was afterwards substituted for Mr. GREENLEAF, who declined.]

IN BOARD OF OVERSEERS, February 7, 1850.

Ordered, That the Report of the Committee appointed to visit the Law School be printed.

Attest,

ALEXANDER YOUNG, *Secretary*.

THE Committee appointed by the Overseers of Harvard University to visit the Law School performed that service November 7, 1849. Among their number present on the occasion was Hon. WILLIAM KENT, of New York, who gratified his associates by coming a long distance to join in this duty.

The attention of the Committee was first directed to the actual condition of the School, and its advantages as a place of legal education. Here there is occasion for lively satisfaction. The number of students is one hundred, assembled from all parts of the Union, and constituting a representation of the whole country. Their attendance upon the lectures and other exercises, though entirely voluntary, is full and regular; while their industry, good conduct, and intelligent reception of instruction is a source of gratification to their professors.

Lectures were given, during the current term, by Professor PARKER, upon Equity Pleadings, Bailments, and Practice, — by Professor PARSONS, upon Blackstone's Commentaries, Admiralty Jurisdiction, Shipping, Bills and Notes, — and by Professor ALLEN, upon Real Law and Domestic Relations. In treating most of these branches, the professors employed text-books of acknowledged authority, to which the attention of the students was especially directed. They also examined the students in these books, and in leading cases illustrating the subject.

This system, which, with substantial uniformity, has been continued in the School since its earliest foundation, appears well adapted to instruction in the law. It is essential that the student should be directed to certain text-books, which he must study carefully, devotedly. Nor can he properly omit to go behind these, and verify them by the decided cases, letting no day pass without its fulfilled task. In this way he is prepared for examination, and enabled to appreciate the explanations and illustrations of the lecture-room, throwing light upon the text, and showing its application to practical cases. The labors of the student will qualify him to comprehend the labors of the instructor. Still further, examinations in the text-books, accompanied by explanations and illustrations, interest the student in the subject, and bring his mind in contact with that of his instructor.

These same purposes are promoted by the favorite exercise of moot-courts, held twice a week by the different professors in succession. A case involving some unsettled question of law is presented by four students, designated so long in advance as to allow time for careful preparation; and at the close of the arguments an opinion is pronounced by the presiding professor, commenting upon the arguments on each side, and deciding between them. These occasions are found to enlist the best attention, not only of those immediately engaged, but of the whole School, — while some of the efforts they call forth show distinguished research and ability. On this mimic field are trained forensic powers destined to be the pride and ornament of the bar.

The advantages for study afforded by the extensive library of the Law School should not be forgotten. This is separate from the Public Library of the University, and contains about fourteen thousand volumes. Here are all the American Reports, — the Statutes of the United States, as well as those of all the several States, — a regular series of all the English Reports, including the Year-Books, — the English Statutes, — the principal treatises on American and English law, — also a large body of works in the Scotch, French, German, Dutch, Spanish, Italian, and other foreign law, — and an ample collection of the best editions of the Roman or Civil Law, with the works of the most celebrated commentators upon that ancient text. This library is one of the largest and most valuable, relating to law, in the country. As an aid to study, it cannot be estimated too highly. Here the student may range at will through all the demesnes of jurisprudence. Here he may acquire knowledge of law-books, learning their true character and value, which will be of incalculable service in his future labors. Whoso knows how to use a library possesses the very keys of knowledge. Next to knowing the law is knowing where to find it.

There is another advantage, of peculiar character, in the opportunity of kindly and profitable social relations among the students, and also between students and professors. Young men engaged in similar pursuits are instructors to each other. The daily conversation concerns their common studies, and contributes some new impulse. Mind meets mind, and each derives strength from the contact. The professor is also at hand. In the lecture-room, and also in private, he is ready for counsel and help. The students are not alone. At every step they find an assistant ready to conduct them through the devious and toilsome passes, and to remove the difficulties which throng the way. This twofold companionship of students with each other and with their appointed teachers is full of good influence, not only in the cordial intercourse it begets, but in the positive knowledge it diffuses, and its stimulating effect upon the mind.

In dwelling on the advantages of the Law School as a seat of legal education, the Committee therefore rank side by side with the lectures and exercises of the professors the profitable opportunities afforded by the library and the fellowship of persons engaged in the same pursuits, all echoing to the heart of the pupil, as from the genius of the place, constant words of succor, encouragement, and hope.

From the present prosperity of the School, the Committee are led to look back at its early beginning, to observe its growth, and to commemorate with gratitude its benefactors.

It hardly need be added, that a Law School was not embraced by our forefathers in the original design of the College, and that it is a late graft upon the ancient stock. The College was planted at a time when law was not treated, even in England, as a part of academic instruction. The first settlers could not be expected to establish professorships unknown in the land from which they had parted; nor did there appear in those early days, or for some time later, any occasion for professional instruction. The law, as science, profession, or practical instrument of government, was scarcely recognized. Lawyers were not known as a class, nor was their business respected. Thomas Lechford, of Clement's Inn, who emigrated not long after the foundation of the College, hoping to gain a livelihood as attorney, being cautioned at a quarter court "not to meddle with controversies," went back to England. As the Colony grew, it gradually laid hold of the Common Law, and for some time before the Revolution claimed it as a birthright.

The history of the University Library exposes the poverty of the means for the study of the law in those early days. In its Catalogue, published in 1723, we find but *seven* volumes of Common Law. These are Spelman's Glossary, Pulton's Collection of Statutes, Keble's Statutes, Coke's First and Second Institutes, and two odd volumes of the Year-Books. Such were the means for the study of our law afforded by the public library, which Cotton Mather, sometime before the publication of this catalogue, described as "the best furnished that could be shown anywhere in all the American regions."

Since books are the instruments of learning, it follows, if these were wanting, that the study of the law could make little advance. Happily this is now changed.

The first professorship of law in the University was established in 1815, upon a foundation partly supplied by an ancient devise of ISAAC ROYALL, Esq., — a munificent gentleman of ample fortune, who, being connected by blood and marriage, as well as by political opinions, with the principal royalists of Massachusetts, forsook the country with them at the commencement of the Revolution, and died at Kensington, in England, in October, 1781. Though an exile, he did not forget the land he had left. Thither before death his "heart untravelled fondly turned." By his will, recorded at the Probate Office in Boston, he devised to Medford, in Massachusetts, where he had resided, certain lands in Granby, for the support of schools. The residue of his estate in that town, and other lands in the County of Worcester, he devised to the Overseers and Corporation of Harvard College, "to be appropriated towards the endowing *a Professor of Laws in the said College*, or a Professor of Physic and Anatomy, whichever the said Overseers and Corporation shall judge to be best for the benefit of the said College." The capital, with its accumulation, from the property thus devised, is $ 7,943, yielding an annual income of about four hundred dollars. It is believed that the University and the lovers of the law are indebted to the late Hon. JOHN LOWELL, while a member of the Corporation, for calling these funds — yet unappropriated to either object of the devise — from their sleep in the treasury, by procuring the establishment of a professorship of law, which was ordered, for the present, to bear the name of *Royall*, in honor of him whose will in this regard was now first executed. This was in 1815. The residue of the funds for its support have been supplied by the University, mainly from fees paid by students of law. The Hon. ISAAC PARKER, late Chief Justice of this Commonwealth, was the first professor.

In 1817 the Hon. ASAHEL STEARNS was placed upon another foundation, established by the University. The statutes of this professorship required him to open and keep a school in Cambridge for the instruction of graduates and of others prosecuting the study of the law. Besides prescribing to his pupils a course of study, it was made his duty to examine and confer with them upon their studies, to read to them a course of lectures, and generally to act the part of tutor, so as to improve their minds and assist their acquisitions. From this time may be dated the establishment of the Law School in the University.

Chief-Justice Parker never resided at Cambridge, but, in the performance of his duties as professor, every summer read lectures to the Law School and the senior class of undergraduates. These were of an elementary nature, adapted to youthful minds, — the audience being for the most part undergraduates, — and were characterized by that free and flowing style which marks the judicial opinions of this eminent Judge. They comprised a view of the Constitutions of the United States and of Massachusetts, with the early juridical history of New England, and the origin of its laws and institutions. Professor Stearns, who resided in Cambridge, was occucupied immediately with the duties of instruction. He was accustomed to hear recitations in the more important text-books, to preside in moot-courts, and to read lectures on interesting titles of law. His valuable work on Real Actions, so well known to lawyers, was prepared in the discharge of his duties as professor, and read to his pupils in a course of lectures. The first edition was dedicated by the author "To the Law Students of Harvard University, as a testimony of his earnest desire to aid them in the honorable and laborious study of American jurisprudence."

The number of students at this period was small. From 1817 to 1829 the largest class for any single year was eighteen, and the average annual number was not more than thirteen. The first important step, however, was taken. Law was admitted within the circle of University studies, while, by the learning and reputation of its professors, the cause of legal education was commended, and the idea of a Law School was shown to be practicable.

On the resignation of Chief-Justice Parker and Professor Stearns a new epoch in the history of the School began. The Hon. NATHAN DANE, in 1829, emulating the example of Viner in England, applied the profits of his extensive Abridgment and Digest of American Law to the foundation of a new professorship, still called from his name; and at his request, the late JOSEPH STORY, then a resident of Salem, and an Associate Justice of the Supreme Court, was appointed the first professor. In his communication to the University, making this endowment, the venerable founder marked out the proposed duties as follows: "It shall be the duty of the professor to prepare and deliver, and to revise for publication, a course of lectures on the five following branches of law and equity, equally in force in all parts of our Federal Republic, namely, the Law of Nature, the Law of Nations, Commercial and Maritime Law, Federal Law, and Federal Equity, in such wide extent as the same branches now are, and from time to time shall be, administered in the Courts of the United States, but in such compressed form as the professor shall deem proper, and so to prepare, deliver, and revise lectures thereon as often as the said Corporation shall think proper." The original endowment by Mr. Dane was $ 10,000, to which on his death was added $ 5,000, making the sum-total $ 15,000. Mr. Justice Story removed to Cambridge in 1829, commencing his new career as Dane Professor of Law with an inaugural discourse, where the honorable nature of legal studies, the arduous labors required in their pursuit, and the duties upon which he was entering, were reviewed with singular power and beauty. At the same time, JOHN HOOKER ASHMUN, Esq., a lawyer of remarkable acuteness and maturity, who, though young, had shown already the capacity of a jurist, was associated with him as Royall Professor of Law.

From the exertions of the new professors the Law School received fresh impulse. The number of students increased, and the fame of the institution was extended. Professor Story, though much absent in the discharge of his judicial duties, yet found time for active part in teaching. He presided in moot-courts and lecture-rooms, and, by earnest encouragement and profuse instruction, not less than by illustrious example, raised the classes to unwonted ardor. He continued in this sphere, giving and receiving happiness, for a period of sixteen years, when, as age advanced, desiring to lay down some of his cares, he proposed to resign his seat on the bench, and dedicate the remainder of his days to his professorship. As he was about to make this change he was arrested by death, September 10, 1845.

Professor Ashmun had already fallen by his side, much regretted, at the early age of thirty-three. Besides moot-courts, examinations in text-books, and oral expositions of the law, this learned teacher occasionally read written lectures. Among these was a valuable course on Medical Jurisprudence, Equity, and the Action of Assumpsit. His place was supplied in 1833 by an eminent jurist, SIMON GREENLEAF, Esq., who labored for a long period with rare success, beloved by a large circle of grateful pupils, and by his associates in instruction, till 1848, when he was compelled by ill-health to resign his connection with the Law School. Among his distinguished labors, in the discharge of his duties as professor, is a work on the Law of Evidence, which is now a manual in the courts of our country, and one of the classics of the Common Law.

On the death of Professor Story, Professor Greenleaf was made Dane Professor. Hon. WILLIAM KENT, of New York, occupied for a year the place of Royall Professor, when he felt constrained, by circumstances beyond his control, to leave Cambridge. Since then Hon. THEOPHILUS PARSONS has been Dane Professor, and Hon. JOEL PARKER, late Chief Justice of New Hampshire, Royall Professor. Hon. FRANKLIN DEXTER has lectured for a brief period on the Constitution of the United States and the Law of Nations, and Hon. LUTHER S. CUSHING on Parliamentary Law and Criminal Law. Hon. FREDERICK H. ALLEN, late a judge in Maine, at present University Professor, without any permanent foundation, is coöperating with Professor Parsons and Professor Parker in the general duties of instruction.

In reviewing the history of the School, the Committee, while gratefully remembering all its instructors, are impressed by the long and important labors of STORY. In the meridian of his fame as judge, he became a practical teacher of jurisprudence, and lent to the University the lustre of his name. Through him the Dane Professorship has acquired a renown placing it on the same elevation with the Vinerian Professorship at Oxford, to which we are indebted for the Commentaries of Sir William Blackstone. These "twin stars," each in its own hemisphere, shine rival glories. Nor is this the only parallel; for Viner, like our Dane, endowed the professorship which bears his name from the profits of his immense Abridgment of the Law. In the performance of his duties, Professor Story prepared and published the most important series of juridical works which has latterly appeared in the English language, embracing a comprehensive treatise on the Constitution of the United States, a masterly exposition of that portion of International Law known as the Conflict of Laws, and Commentaries on Equity Jurisprudence, Equity Pleading, and various branches of Commercial Law.

The extent of his labors, and their influence in building up the School, appear in an interesting passage of his last will and testament, bearing date January 2, 1842. After bequeathing to the University several valuable pictures, busts, and books, he proceeds as follows: "I ask the President and Fellows of Harvard College to accept these as memorials of my reverence and respect for that venerable institution, at which I received my education. I hope it may not be improper for me here to add, that I have devoted myself, as Dane Professor, for the last thirteen years,[1] to the labors and duties of instruction in the Law School, and have always performed equal duties and to an equal amount with my excellent colleagues, Mr. Professor Ashmun and Mr. Professor Greenleaf, in the Law School. When I came to Cambridge, and undertook the duties of my professorship, there had not been a single law student there for the preceding year. There was no law library, but a few old and imperfect books being there. The students have since increased to a large number, and for six years last past have exceeded one hundred a year. The Law Library now contains about six thousand volumes, whose value cannot be deemed less than twenty-five thousand dollars. My own salary has constantly remained limited to one thousand dollars,—a little more than the interest of Mr. Dane's donations. I have never asked or desired an increase thereof, as I was receiving a suitable salary as a Judge of the Supreme Court of the United States,—while my colleagues have very properly received a much larger sum, and of late years more than double my own. Under these circumstances, I cannot but feel that I have contributed towards the advancement of the Law School a sum out of my earnings, which, with my moderate means, will be thought to absolve me from making, what otherwise I certainly should do, a pecuniary legacy to Harvard College, for the general advancement of literature and learning therein."

From the books of the Treasurer it appears that the sums received from students in the Law School during the sixteen years of his professorship amounted to $105,000. Of this amount, only $47,800 was disbursed in salaries and current expenses. The balance, amount-

[1] His will being dated three years before his death.

ing to $ 57,200, is represented by the following items, namely: —

Books purchased for the Library and for students, including about $ 1,950 for binding, and deducting amount received for books sold	$ 29,000
Enlargement of the Hall, containing the library and lecture-rooms, in 1844-45	12,700
Fund remaining to the credit of the School in August, 1845	15,500
	$ 57,200

Thus the Law School, at the time of Professor Story's death, actually possessed, independent of the somewhat scanty donations by Mr. Royall and Mr. Dane, funds and other property, including a large library and a commodious edifice, amounting to upwards of *fifty-seven thousand dollars*, all earned during Professor Story's term of service. As during this period he declined a larger annual salary than $ 1,000, and as his high character and the attraction of his name contributed to swell the income of the School, it is evident that a considerable portion of this large sum may justly be regarded as the fruit of his bountiful labors contributed to the University.

The Committee, while calling attention to the extent of pecuniary benefaction which the Law School has received from Professor Story, feel it a duty to urge upon the Government of the University the recognition of this benefaction in some suitable form. The name of Royall, given to one of the professorships, keeps alive the memory of his early generosity. The name of Dane, given to the professorship on which Story taught, and sometimes also to the edifice containing the library and lecture-rooms, and then to the Law School itself, attests, with triple academic voice, a well-rewarded donation. But the contributions of Royall and Dane combined, important as they were, and justly worthy of honorable mention, do not equal what was contributed by Story. At the present moment Story must be regarded as the largest pecuniary benefactor of the Law School, and one of the largest pecuniary benefactors of the University. In this respect he stands before Hollis, Alford, Boylston, Hersey, Bowdoin, Erving, Eliot, Smith, M'Lean, Perkins, and Fisher. His contributions have this additional peculiarity, that they were munificently afforded from daily earnings, — not after death, but during life; so that he became, as it were, the executor of his own will. In justice to the dead, as an example to the living, and in conformity with established usage, the University should enroll his name among its founders, and in some fit manner inscribe it upon the school which he helped to rear.

Three different courses occur to the Committee. The edifice containing the library and lecture-rooms may be called after him, *Story Hall.* Or the branch of the University devoted to law may be called *Story Law School,* as the other branch of the University devoted to science, in gratitude to a distinguished benefactor, is called *Lawrence Scientific School.* Or a new and permanent professorship in the Law School may be created, with his name.

If the last suggestion should find favor, the Committee recommend that the professorship be of *Commercial Law and the Law of Nations.* It is well known to have been the desire of Professor Story, often expressed, in view of the increasing means of the Law School, and the corresponding demands for education in the law, that professorships of both these branches should be established. In his opinion that of Commercial Law was most needed. His own preëminence in this department appears in his works, and especially in numerous judicial opinions. His interest in it was attested in conversation with one of this Committee only a few days before his death. Hearing that it was proposed by merchants of Boston, on his resignation of the judicial seat he had held for nearly thirty-four years, to cause his statue in marble to be erected, he said: "If Boston merchants wish to do me honor in any way, on my leaving the bench, let it not be by a statue, but by founding in the Law School a professorship of Commercial Law." With these generous words he embraced at once his favorite law and his favorite University.

The subject of Commercial Law is of great and growing importance in the multiplying relations of mankind. Every new tie of commerce gives new occasion for its application. Besides the general principles of the Law of Contracts, it comprehends the Law of Bailments, Agency, Partnership, Bills of Exchange and Promissory Notes, Shipping, and Insurance, — branches of inexpressible interest to lawyers, merchants, and indeed to every citizen. The main features of this law are common to all commercial nations; they are recognized with substantial uniformity, whether at Boston, London, or Calcutta, at Hamburg, Marseilles, or Leghorn. In this respect they may be regarded as part of the *Private* Law of Nations. They would be associated naturally with the Public Law of Nations, — embracing, of course, the Law of Admiralty, and that other branch, which it is hoped will remain forever a dead letter, the Law of Prize.

The Committee believe that all who become acquainted with this statement will agree that something should be done to commemorate the obligations of the University to one of its most eminent professors and largest pecuniary benefactors. They have ventured suggestions as to the manner in which this may be accomplished, not with any particular confidence in their own views, but simply as a mode of opening the subject, and bringing it to attention. In dwelling on the propriety of a new and permanent professorship, they would not be understood as expressing a preference for this form of acknowledgment. It may be a question, whether the services of Professor Story, important in every respect, shedding upon the Law School a lasting fame, and securing to it pecuniary competence, an extensive library, and a commodious hall, can be commemorated with more appropriate academic honors than by giving his name to that department in the University of which he was the truest founder. The world, anticipating all formal action of the University, has already placed the Law School under the guardianship of his name. It is by the name of STORY that this seat of legal education has become known wherever jurisprudence is cultivated as a science.

For the Committee.

CHARLES SUMNER.

TO THE OVERSEERS OF HARVARD UNIVERSITY.

STIPULATED ARBITRATION, OR A CONGRESS OF NATIONS, WITH DISARMAMENT.

ADDRESS TO THE PEOPLE OF THE UNITED STATES, FEBRUARY 22, 1850.

THE history of the Peace Movement, recounted in the Address on the War System of the Commonwealth of Nations, terminates at the date of that Address, anterior to the Congress at Paris, called the Second General Peace Congress, on the 22d, 23d, and 24th of August, 1849. This Congress is briefly characterized in the Address below. There is a report of its proceedings, where may be read the able speeches and letters by which the cause was vindicated. It was arranged in Europe that the next year should witness a similar Congress, and Frankfort-on-the-Main was selected for the place of meeting, both from its central situation and the sympathy felt in the movement by leading minds of Germany.

In the United States a Committee was appointed, with Mr. Sumner as Chairman, to obtain a proper representation. The following Address was put forth by the Committee. But the question ceased to be pressed in Europe, under the influence of the prevailing reaction, while in our country it was overshadowed by Slavery, to which the general attention was now directed. It was often remarked, " One evil at a time" ; and thus the Peace Cause was postponed.

TO THE PEOPLE OF THE UNITED STATES.

THE month of August last witnessed at Paris a Congress or Convention of persons from various countries, to consider what could be done to promote the sacred cause of Universal Peace. France, Germany, Belgium, England, and the United States were represented by large numbers of men eminent in business, politics, literature, religion, and philanthropy. The Catholic Archbishop of Paris, and the eloquent Protestant preacher, M. Athanase Coquerel, — Michel Chevalier, Horace Say, and Frédéric Bastiat, distinguished political economists, — Émile de Girardin, the most important political editor of France, — Victor Hugo, illustrious in literature, — Lamartine, whose glory it is to have turned the recent French Revolution, at its beginning, into the path of Peace, — and Richard Cobden, the world-renowned British statesman, the unapproached model of an earnest, humane, and practical Reformer, — all these gave to this august assembly the sanction of their presence or approbation. Victor Hugo, on taking the chair as President, in an address of persuasive eloquence, shed upon the occasion the illumination of his genius, — while Mr. Cobden, participating in all the proceedings, impressed upon them his characteristic common sense.

The Congress adopted, with entire unanimity, a series of resolutions, asserting the duty of governments to submit all differences between them to Arbitration, and to respect the decisions of the Arbitrators; also asserting the necessity of a general and simultaneous disarming, not only as the means of reducing the expenditure absorbed by armies and navies, but also of removing a permanent cause of disquietude and irritation. The Congress condemned all loans and taxes for wars of ambition or conquest. It earnestly recommended the friends of Peace to prepare public opinion, in their respective countries, for the formation of a Congress of Nations, to revise the existing International Law, and to constitute a High Tribunal for the decision of controversies among nations. In support of these objects, the Congress solemnly invoked the representatives of the press, so potent to diffuse truth, and also all ministers of religion, whose holy office it is to encourage good-will among men.

The work thus begun has been continued since. In England and the United States large public meetings have welcomed the returning delegates. Men have been touched by the grandeur of the cause. Not in the aspirations of religion and benevolence only, but in the general heart and mind, has it found reception, filling all who embrace it with new confidence in the triumph of Christian truth.

Another Congress or Convention has been called to meet at Frankfort-on-the-Main, in the month of August next, to do what is possible, by mutual counsels and encouragement, to influence public opinion, and to advance still further the cause which has been so well commended by the Congress at Paris.

To promote the objects of this Congress generally, and particularly to secure the attendance of a delegation from the United States, in number and character not unworthy of the occasion, a Committee, representing friends of Peace throughout the country, various in opinion, has been appointed, under the name of "PEACE CONGRESS COMMITTEE FOR THE UNITED STATES." This Committee now appeal to their fellow-citizens for coöperation in this work.

The Committee hope, in the first place, to interest our Government at Washington in the objects contemplated by the proposed Congress. As this can be done only through the prompting of the people, they recommend petitions like the following: —

"PETITION FOR PEACE.

" *To the Honorable Senate* (*or H. of R.*) *of the United States.*

" The undersigned, inhabitants (or citizens, or legal voters) of ———, in the State of ———, deploring the manifold evils of War, and believing it possible to supersede its alleged necessity, as an Arbiter of Justice among Nations, by the timely adoption of wise and feasible substitutes, respectfully request your honorable body to take such action as you may deem best in favor of Stipulated Arbitration, or a Congress of Nations, for the accomplishment of this most desirable end."

As the number of delegates to the proposed Congress is not limited, the Committee hope to see States, Congressional Districts, Towns, and other bodies represented. Every delegate will be a link between the community, large or small, from which he comes, and the cause of Universal Peace.

The Committee recommend a State Convention in each State to choose a State Committee, and also two delegates at large from the State;

Also a Convention in each Congressional District to choose a delegate;

Also public meetings in towns, and other smaller localities, to explain the objects of the Congress, and to choose local delegates.

The Committee also recommend to the religious and literary bodies of the country, as churches and colleges, to send delegates to the Congress.

In making this appeal, the Committee desire to impress upon their fellow-citizens the practical character of the present movement. Instead of the *custom* or *institution* of War, now recognized by International

Law, as the Arbiter of Justice between Nations, they propose, by the consent of nations, to substitute a System of Arbitration, or a permanent Congress of Nations. With this change will necessarily follow a general disarming down to that degree of force required for internal police. The barbarous and incongruous War System, which now encases our Christian civilization as with a cumbrous coat of mail, will be destroyed. The enormous means, thus released from destructive industry and purposes of hate, will be appropriated to productive industry and purposes of beneficence. To help this consummation who will not labor?

The people in every part of the country, East and West, North and South, of all political parties and all religious sects, are now invited to join in this endeavor. So doing, while confident of the blessing of God, they will become fellow-laborers of wise and good men in other lands, and will secure to themselves the inexpressible satisfaction of aiding the advent of that happy day when Peace shall be *organized* among nations.

By order of the Peace Congress Committee for the United States.

CHARLES SUMNER, *Chairman.*

ELIHU BURRITT, } *Secretaries.*
AMASA WALKER, }

BOSTON, February 22, 1850.

OUR IMMEDIATE ANTISLAVERY DUTIES.

SPEECH AT A FREE-SOIL MEETING AT FANEUIL HALL, NOVEMBER 6, 1850.

THIS speech was made a few days before the annual election in Massachusetts, and just after the passage of the Fugitive Slave Bill. As the first open denunciation of this measure, it awakened much feeling on both sides. All who felt strongly against Slavery were grateful.

It is sometimes said to have made Mr. Sumner Senator. More than anything else, it determined his selection by the Free-Soil party shortly afterwards as their candidate. On the other hand, it was often pronounced "treasonable," and in subsequent discussions at Washington, sometimes in newspapers and repeatedly in the Senate, it was employed to point the personalities of slave-masters and their allies. It was called the "Mark Antony speech." It takes the ground to which Mr. Sumner constantly adhered, that the "Fugitive Slave Bill," as he always insisted upon calling it, — refusing to call it Law, — was absolutely unconstitutional in all respects, — not only, according to the old language of the law, "to a certain intent in general," but also "to a certain intent in every particular." Such an enactment could not be treated as law; and Mr. Sumner insisted that good citizens should refuse to it all support, as our fathers refused all support to the British Stamp Act. His effort and hope were to create a public sentiment which would render its enforcement impossible.

In all times there has been something in the human conscience which forbade certain things, even though ordained by law. "A curse on him who is not enough an honest man and enough a man of courage to be capable of the crime of hospitality towards a proscribed person!" Such is the exclamation of an eloquent historian of the French Revolution, after reciting the proposition of Saint-Just, kindred to the requirement of the Fugitive Slave Bill.[1] Guizot, in his Memoirs, records an illustrative incident. Queen Hortense, mother of Louis Napoleon, at a time when all of her family were excluded from France, suddenly arrived in Paris, when, seeing Casimir Périer, Prime-Minister of Louis

[1] Louis Blanc, Histoire de la Révolution Française, Tom. X. p. 316.

Philippe, she began: "I know, Sir, that I have violated a law; you have the right to arrest me; that would be just." "*Legal*, Madame," said the Minister, "but not *just*."[1]

At the pending election there was what was called a coalition between the Free-Soilers and Democrats, in the choice of State Senators and Representatives, with the understanding that the State officers chosen by the Legislature should be Democrats, and the United States Senator a Free-Soiler. But nothing was said at the time about candidates.

The meeting at Faneuil Hall was large and enthusiastic. It was organized by the choice of William B Spooner, Esq., President, — Edward A. Raymond, William Washburn, Henry I. Bowditch, William Bates, Ebenezer Atkins, William Dall, Caleb Gill, Theodore D. Cook, Joseph Southwick, Ephraim Allen, Richard Hildreth, and Robert E. Apthorp, Vice-Presidents, — William F. Channing and Charles List, Secretaries. On taking the chair, Mr. Spooner addressed the meeting. Dr. Luther Parks then read a series of resolutions. Mr. Sumner followed, and was received with much enthusiasm. His speech is printed with the interruptions reported at the time.

MR. CHAIRMAN, AND YOU, MY FELLOW-CITIZENS: —

COLD and insensible must I be, not to be touched by this welcome. I thank you for the cause, whose representative only I am. It is the cause which I would keep ever foremost, and commend always to your support.

In a few days there will be an important political election, affecting many local interests. Not by these have I been drawn here to-night, but because I would bear my testimony anew to that Freedom which is above all these. And here, at the outset, let me say, that it is because I place Freedom above all else that I cordially concur in the different unions or combinations throughout the Commonwealth, — in Mr. Mann's District, of Free-Soilers with Whigs, — also in Mr. Fowler's District, of Free-Soilers with Whigs, — and generally, in Senatorial Districts, of Free-Soilers with Democrats.

1 Guizot, Mémoires pour servir à l'Histoire de mon Temps, Tom. II. p. 219.

By the first of these two good men may be secured in Congress, while by the latter the friends of Freedom may obtain a controlling influence in the Legislature of Massachusetts during the coming session, and thus advance our cause. [*Applause.*] They may arbitrate between both the old parties, making Freedom their perpetual object, and in this way contribute more powerfully than they otherwise could to the cause which has drawn us together. [*Cheers.*]

Leaving these things, so obvious to all, I come at once to consider urgent duties at this anxious moment. To comprehend these we must glance at what Congress has done during its recent session, so long drawn out. This I shall endeavor to do rapidly. "Watchman, what of the night?" And well may the cry be raised, "What of the night?" For things have been done, and measures passed into laws, which, to my mind, fill the day itself with blackness. [*"Hear! hear!"*]

And yet there are streaks of light — an unwonted dawn — in the distant West, out of which a full-orbed sun is beginning to ascend, rejoicing like a strong man to run a race. By Act of Congress California has been admitted into the Union with a Constitution forbidding Slavery. For a measure like this, required not only by simplest justice, but by uniform practice, and by constitutional principles of slaveholders themselves, we may be ashamed to confess gratitude; and yet I cannot but rejoice in this great good. A hateful institution, thus far without check, travelling westward with the power of the Republic, is bidden to stop, while a new and rising State is guarded from its contamination. [*Applause.*] Freedom, in whose hands is the divining-rod of magical power, pointing the way not only to wealth untold, but to every possession of virtue and intelligence, whose presence is better far than any mine of gold, has been recognized in an extensive region on the distant Pacific, between the very parallels of latitude so long claimed by Slavery as a peculiar home. [*Loud plaudits.*]

Here is a victory, moral and political: moral, inasmuch as Freedom secures a new foothold where to exert her far-reaching influence; political, inasmuch as by the admission of California, the Free States obtain a majority of votes in the Senate, thus overturning that *balance of power* between Freedom and Slavery, so preposterously claimed by the Slave States, in forgetfulness of the true spirit of the Constitution, and in mockery of Human Rights. [*Cheers.*] May free California, and her Senators in Congress, amidst the trials before us, never fail in loyalty to Freedom! God forbid that the daughter should turn with ingratitude or neglect from the mother that bore her! [*Enthusiasm.*]

Besides this Act, there are two others of this long session to be regarded with satisfaction, — and I mention them at once, before considering the reverse of the picture. The slave-trade is abolished in the District of Columbia. This measure, though small in the sight of Justice, is important. It banishes from the National Capital an odious traffic. But this is its least office. Practically it affixes to the whole traffic, wherever it exists, — not merely in Washington, within the immediate sphere of the legislative act, but everywhere throughout the Slave States, whether at Richmond, or Charleston, or New Orleans, — the brand of Congressional reprobation. The people of the United States, by the voice of Congress, solemnly declare the domestic traffic in slaves offensive in their sight. The Nation judges this traffic. The Nation says to it, "Get thee behind me, Satan!" [*Excitement and applause.*] It is true that Congress has not, as in the case of the foreign slave-trade, stamped it as *piracy*, and awarded to its perpetrators the doom of *pirates;* but it condemns the trade, and gives to general scorn those who partake of it. To this extent the National Government speaks for Freedom. And in doing this, it asserts, under the Constitution, legislative jurisdiction over the subject of Slavery in the District, — thus preparing the way for that complete act of Abolition which is necessary to purge the National Capital of its still remaining curse and shame.

The other measure which I hail with thankfulness is the Abolition of Flogging in the Navy. ["*Hear! hear!*"] Beyond the direct reform thus accomplished — after much effort, finally crowned with encouraging success — is the indirect influence of this law, especially in rebuking the lash, wheresoever and by whomsoever employed.

Two props and stays of Slavery are weakened and undermined by Congressional legislation. Without the *slave-trade* and without the *lash,* Slavery must fall to earth. By these the whole monstrosity is upheld. If I seem to exaggerate the consequence of these measures of Abolition, you will pardon it to a sincere conviction of their powerful, though subtile and indirect influence, quickened by a desire to find something good in a Congress which has furnished occasion for so much disappointment. Other measures there are which must be regarded not only with regret, but with indignation and disgust. [*Sensation.*]

Two broad territories, New Mexico and Utah, under the exclusive jurisdiction of Congress, have been organized without any prohibition of Slavery. In laying the foundation of their governments, destined hereafter to control the happiness of innumerable multitudes, Congress has omitted the Great Ordinance of Freedom, first moved by Jefferson, and consecrated by the experience of the Northwestern Territory: thus rejecting those principles of Human Liberty which are enunciated in our Declaration of Independence, which are essential to every Bill of Rights, and without which a Republic is a name and nothing more.

Still further, a vast territory, supposed to be upwards of seventy thousand square miles in extent, larger than all New England, has been taken from New Mexico, and, with ten million dollars besides, given to slaveholding Texas: thus, under the plea of settling the western boundary of Texas, securing to this State a large sum of money, and consigning to certain Slavery an important territory.

And still further, as if to do a deed which should "make heaven weep, all earth amazed," this same Congress, in disregard of all cherished safeguards of Freedom, has passed a most cruel, unchristian, devilish law to secure the return into Slavery of those fortunate bondmen who find shelter by our firesides. This is the Fugitive Slave Bill,—a device which despoils the party claimed as slave, whether in reality slave or freeman, of Trial by Jury, that sacred right, and usurps the question of Human Freedom, — the highest question known to the law, — committing it to the unaided judgment of a single magistrate, on *ex parte* evidence it may be, by affidavit, without the sanction of cross-examination. Under this detestable, Heaven-defying Bill, not the slave only, but the colored freeman of the North, may be swept into ruthless captivity; and there is no white citizen, born among us, bred in our schools, partaking in our affairs, voting in our elections, whose liberty is not assailed also. Without any discrimination of color, the Bill surrenders all claimed as "owing service or labor" to the same tyrannical judgment. And mark once more its heathenism. By unrelenting provisions it visits with bitter penalties of fine and imprisonment the faithful men and women who render to the fugitive that countenance, succor, and shelter which Christianity expressly requires. ["*Shame! shame!*"] Thus, from beginning to end, it sets at nought the best principles of the Constitution, and the very laws of God. [*Great sensation.*]

I might occupy your time in exposing the unconstitutionality of this Act. Denying the Trial by Jury, it is three times unconstitutional: first, as the Constitution declares "the right of the people to be secure in their persons against *unreasonable seizures*"; secondly, as it further provides that "no person shall be deprived of life, *liberty*, or property, *without due process of law*"; and, thirdly, because it expressly establishes, that "in suits at Common Law, where the value in controversy shall exceed twenty dollars, *the right of trial by jury shall be preserved.*" By this triple cord the framers of the Constitution secured Trial by Jury in every question of Human Freedom. That man is little imbued with the true spirit of American institutions, has little sympathy with Bills of Rights, is lukewarm for Freedom, who can hesitate to construe the Constitution so as to secure this safeguard. [*Enthusiastic applause.*]

Again, the Act is unconstitutional in the unprecedented and tyrannical powers it confers upon Commissioners. These petty officers are appointed, not by the President with the advice of the Senate, but by the Courts of Law, — hold their places, not during good behavior, but at the will of the Court, — and receive for their services, not a regular salary, but fees in each individual case. And yet in these petty officers, thus appointed, thus compensated, and holding their places by the most uncertain tenure, is vested a portion of that "judicial power," which, according to the positive text of the Constitution, can be in "judges" only, holding office "during good behavior," receiving "at stated times for their services a compensation which shall not be diminished during their continuance in office," and, it would seem also, appointed by the President and confirmed by the Senate, — being three conditions of judicial power. Adding meanness to violation of the Constitution, the Commissioner is bribed by a double fee to pronounce against Freedom. Decreeing a man to Slavery, he receives ten dollars; saving the man to Freedom, his fee is five dollars. ["*Shame! shame!*"]

But I will not pursue these details. The soul sickens in the contemplation of this legalized outrage. In the dreary annals of the Past there are many acts of shame, — there are ordinances of monarchs, and laws, which have become a byword and a hissing to the nations. But *when we consider the country and the age*, I ask fearlessly, what act of shame, what ordinance of monarch, what law, can compare in atrocity with this enactment of an American Congress? ["*None!*"] I do not forget Appius Claudius, tyrant Decemvir of ancient Rome, condemning Virginia as a slave, — nor Louis the Fourteenth, of

France, letting slip the dogs of religious persecution by the revocation of the Edict of Nantes, — nor Charles the First, of England, arousing the patriot rage of Hampden by the extortion of Ship-money, — nor the British Parliament, provoking, in our own country, spirits kindred to Hampden, by the tyranny of the Stamp Act and Tea Tax. I would not exaggerate; I wish to keep within bounds; but I think there can be little doubt that the condemnation now affixed to all these transactions, and to their authors, must be the lot hereafter of the Fugitive Slave Bill, and of every one, according to the measure of his influence, who gave it his support. [*Three cheers were here given.*] Into the immortal catalogue of national crimes it has now passed, drawing, by inexorable necessity, its authors also, and chiefly him, who, as President of the United States, set his name to the Bill, and breathed into it that final breath without which it would bear no life. [*Sensation.*] Other Presidents may be forgotten; but the name signed to the Fugitive Slave Bill can never be forgotten. ["*Never!*"] There are depths of infamy, as there are heights of fame. I regret to say what I must, but truth compels me. Better for him, had he never been born! [*Renewed applause.*] Better for his memory, and for the good name of his children, had he never been President! [*Repeated cheers.*]

I have likened this Bill to the Stamp Act, and I trust that the parallel may be continued yet further, by a burst of popular feeling against all action under it similar to that which glowed in the breasts of our fathers. Listen to the words of John Adams, as written in his Diary at the time.

"The year 1765 has been the most remarkable year of my life. That enormous engine, fabricated by the British Parliament, for battering down all the rights and liberties of America, I mean the Stamp Act, has raised and spread through the whole continent a spirit that will be recorded to our honor with all future generations. In every colony, from Georgia to New Hampshire inclusively, the stamp distributors and inspectors have been compelled by the unconquerable rage of the people to renounce their offices. Such and so universal has been the resentment of the people, that every man who has dared to speak in favor of the stamps, or to soften the detestation in which they are held, how great soever his abilities and virtues had been esteemed before, or whatever his fortune, connections, and influence had been, has been seen to sink into universal contempt and ignominy."[1] [*A voice, "Ditto for the Slave-Hunter!"*]

Earlier than John Adams, the first Governor of Massachusetts, John Winthrop, set the example of refusing to enforce laws against the liberties of the people. After describing Civil Liberty, and declaring the covenant between God and man in the Moral Law, he uses these good words: —

"This Liberty is the proper end and object of authority, and cannot subsist without it; and it is a liberty to that only which is good, just, and honest. This liberty you are to stand for, with the hazard not only of your goods, but of your lives, if need be. *Whatsoever crosseth this is not authority, but a distemper thereof.*"[2]

Surely the love of Freedom is not so far cooled among us, descendants of those who opposed the Stamp Act, that we are insensible to the Fugitive Slave Bill. In those other days, the unconquerable rage of the people compelled the stamp distributors and inspectors to re-

1 Diary, December 18, 1765: Works, Vol. II p 154.
2 History of New England (ed. Savage), 1645, Vol. II. p. 229.

nounce their offices, and held up to detestation all who dared to speak in favor of the stamps. Shall we be more tolerant of those who volunteer in favor of this Bill? [*"No! no!"*] — more tolerant of the Slave-Hunter, who, under its safeguard, pursues his prey upon our soil? [*"No! no!"*] The Stamp Act could not be executed here. Can the Fugitive Slave Bill? [*"Never!"*]

And here, Sir, let me say, that it becomes me to speak with caution. It happens that I sustain an important relation to this Bill. Early in professional life I was designated by the late Judge Story a Commissioner of his Court, and, though I do not very often exercise the functions of this appointment, my name is still upon the list. As such, I am one of those before whom the panting fugitive may be dragged for the decision of the question, whether he is a freeman or a slave. But while it becomes me to speak with caution, I shall not hesitate to speak with plainness. I cannot forget that I am a *man*, although I am a *Commissioner*. [*Three cheers here given.*]

Could the same spirit which inspired the Fathers enter into our community now, the marshals, and every *magistrate* who regarded this law as having any constitutional obligation, would resign, rather than presume to execute it. This, perhaps, is too much to expect. But I will not judge such officials. To their own consciences I leave them. Surely no person of humane feelings and with any true sense of justice, living in a land "where bells have knolled to church," whatever may be the apology of public station, can fail to recoil from such service. For myself let me say, that I can imagine no office, no salary, no consideration, which I would not gladly forego, rather than become in any way the agent in enslaving my brother-man. [*Sensation.*] Where for me were comfort and solace after such a work? [*A voice, "Nowhere!"*] In dreams and in waking hours, in solitude and in the street, in the meditations of the closet and in the affairs of men, wherever I turned, there my victim would stare me in the face. From distant rice-fields and sugar-plantations of the South, his cries beneath the vindictive lash, his moans at the thought of Liberty, once his, now, alas! ravished away, would pursue me, repeating the tale of his fearful doom, and sounding, forever sounding, in my ears, "Thou art the man!" [*Applause.*]

The magistrate who pronounces the decree of Slavery, and the marshal who enforces it, act in obedience to law. This is their apology; and it is the apology also of the masters of the Inquisition, as they ply the torture amidst the shrieks of their victim. Can this weaken accountability for wrong? Disguise it, excuse it, as they will, the fact must glare before the world, and penetrate the conscience too, that the fetters by which the unhappy fugitive is bound are riveted by their tribunal, — that his second life of wretchedness dates from their agency, — that his second birth as a slave proceeds from *them.* The magistrate and marshal do for him here, in a country which vaunts a Christian civilization, what the naked, barbarous Pagan chiefs beyond the sea did for his grandfather in Congo: *they transfer him to the Slave-Hunter,* and for this service receive the very price paid for his grandfather in Congo, — *ten dollars!* [*"Shame! shame!"*]

Gracious Heaven! can such things be on our Free Soil? [*"No!"*] Shall the evasion of Pontius Pilate be enacted anew, and a judge vainly attempt, by washing the hands, to excuse himself for condemning one in whom he can "find no fault"? Should any court, sitting here in Massachusetts, for the first time in her history, become agent of the Slave-Hunter, the very images of our fathers would frown from the walls; their voices would cry from the ground; their spirits, hovering in the air, would plead, remonstrate, protest, against the cruel judgment. [*Cheers.*] There is a legend of the Church, still living on the admired canvas of a Venetian artist, that St. Mark, descending from the skies with headlong fury into the public square, broke the manacles of a slave in presence of the very judge who had decreed his fate. This is known as "The Miracle of the Slave," and grandly has Art illumined the scene.[1] Should Massachusetts hereafter, in an evil hour, be desecrated by any such decree, may the good Evangelist once more descend with valiant arm to break the manacles of the Slave! [*Enthusiasm.*]

Sir, I will not dishonor this home of the Pilgrims, and of the Revolution, by admitting — nay, *I cannot believe — that this Bill will be executed here.* ["*Never!*"] Among us, as elsewhere, individuals may forget humanity, in fancied loyalty to law; but the public conscience will not allow a man who has trodden our streets as a freeman to be dragged away as a slave. [*Applause.*] By escape from bondage he has shown that true manhood which must grapple to him every honest heart. He may be ignorant and rude, as poor, but he is of

1 An eloquent French critic says, among other things, of this greatest picture of Tintoretto, that "no painting surpasses, or perhaps equals" it, and that, before seeing it, "one can have no idea of the human imagination." (Taine, Italy, Florence, and Venice, tr. Durand, pp. 314, 316.) Some time after this Speech an early copy or sketch of this work fell into Mr. Sumner's hands, and it is now a cherished souvenir of those anxious days when the pretensions of Slavery were at their height.

true nobility. Fugitive Slaves are the heroes of our age. In sacrificing them to this foul enactment we violate every sentiment of hospitality, every whispering of the heart, every commandment of religion.

There are many who will never shrink, at any cost, and notwithstanding all the atrocious penalties of this Bill, from effort to save a wandering fellow-man from bondage; they will offer him the shelter of their houses, and, if need be, will protect his liberty by force. But let me be understood; I counsel no violence. There is another power, stronger than any individual arm, which I invoke: I mean that irresistible Public Opinion, inspired by love of God and man, which, without violence or noise, gently as the operations of Nature, makes and unmakes laws. Let this Public Opinion be felt in its might, and the Fugitive Slave Bill will become everywhere among us a dead letter. No lawyer will aid it by counsel, no citizen will be its agent; it will die of inanition, — like a spider beneath an exhausted receiver. [*Laughter.*] Oh! it were well the tidings should spread throughout the land that here in Massachusetts this accursed Bill has found no *servant.* [*Cheers.*] "Sire, in Bayonne are honest citizens and brave soldiers only, *but not one executioner,*" was the reply of the governor to the royal mandate from Charles the Ninth, of France, ordering the massacre of St. Bartholomew.[1] [*Sensation.*]

[1] Le Vicomte d'Orthez à Charles IX.: D'Aubigné, Histoire Universelle, Part. II. Liv. I. ch. 5, cited by Sismondi, Histoire des Français, Tom. XIX. p. 177, note. I gladly copy this noble letter. "Sire, j'ai communiqué le commandement de Votre Majesté à ses fidèles habitans et gens de guerre de la garnison; je n'y ai trouvé que bons citoyens et braves soldats, mais pas un bourreau. C'est pourquoi eux et moi supplions très humblement Votre dite Majesté vouloir employer en choses possibles, quelque hasardeuses qu'elles soient, nos bras et nos vies, comme étant, autant qu'elles dureront, Sire, vôtres."

It rests with you, my fellow-citizens, by word and example, by calm determinations and devoted lives, to do this work. From a humane, just, and religious people will spring a Public Opinion to keep perpetual guard over the liberties of all within our borders. Nay, more, like the flaming sword of the cherubim at the gates of Paradise, turning on every side, it shall prevent any SLAVE-HUNTER from ever setting foot in this Commonwealth. Elsewhere he may pursue his human prey, employ his congenial bloodhounds, and exult in his successful game; but into Massachusetts he must not come. Again, let me be understood, I counsel no violence. I would not touch his person. Not with whips and thongs would I scourge him from the land. The contempt, the indignation, the abhorrence of the community shall be our weapons of offence. Wherever he moves, he shall find no house to receive him, no table spread to nourish him, no welcome to cheer him. The dismal lot of the Roman exile shall be his. He shall be a wanderer, without *roof, fire, or water*. Men shall point at him in the streets, and on the highways.

> "Sleep shall neither night nor day
> Hang upon his penthouse-lid;
> He shall live a man forbid;
> Weary sevennights nine times nine
> Shall he dwindle, peak, and pine." [*Applause.*]

Villages, towns, and cities shall refuse to receive the monster; they shall vomit him forth, never again to disturb the repose of our community. [*Repeated rounds of applause.*]

The feelings with which we regard the Slave-Hunter will be extended soon to all the mercenary agents and heartless minions, who, without any positive obligation of law, become part of his pack. They are *volunteers*, and, as such, must share the ignominy of the chief Hunter. [*Cheers.*]

I have dwelt thus long upon the Fugitive Slave Bill especially in the hope of contributing something to that Public Opinion which is destined in the Free States to be the truest defence of the slave. I now advance to other more general duties.

We have seen what Congress has done. And yet, in the face of these enormities of legislation, — of Territories organized without the prohibition of Slavery, of a large province surrendered to Texas and to Slavery, and of this execrable Fugitive Slave Bill, — in the face also of Slavery still sanctioned in the District of Columbia, of the Slave-Trade between domestic ports under the flag of the Union, and of the Slave Power still dominant over the National Government, we are told that the Slavery Question is settled. Yes, *settled, — settled,* — that is the word. *Nothing, Sir, can be settled which is not right.* [*Sensation.*] Nothing can be settled which is against Freedom. Nothing can be settled which is contrary to the Divine Law. God, Nature, and all the holy sentiments of the heart repudiate any such false seeming settlement.

Amidst the shifts and changes of party, our DUTIES remain, pointing the way to action. By no subtle compromise or adjustment can men suspend the commandments of God. By no trick of managers, no hocus-pocus of politicians, no "mush of concession," can we be released from this obedience. It is, then, in the light of duties that we are to find peace for our country and ourselves. Nor can any settlement promise peace which is not in harmony with those everlasting principles from which our duties spring.

Here I shall be brief. Slavery is wrong. It is the source of unnumbered woes, — not the least of which is its influence on the Slaveholder himself, rendering him insensible to its outrage. It overflows with injustice and inhumanity. Language toils in vain to picture the wretchedness and wickedness which it sanctions and perpetuates. Reason revolts at the impious assumption that man can hold property in man. As it is our perpetual duty to oppose wrong, so must we oppose Slavery; nor can we ever relax in this opposition, so long as the giant evil continues anywhere within the sphere of our influence. *Especially must we oppose it, wherever we are responsible for its existence, or in any way parties to it.*

And now mark the distinction. The testimony which we bear against Slavery, as against all other wrong, is, in different ways, according to our position. The Slavery which exists under other governments, as in Russia or Turkey, or in other States of our Union, as in Virginia and Carolina, we can oppose only through the influence of morals and religion, without in any way invoking the Political Power. Nor do we propose to act otherwise. But Slavery, where we are parties to it, wherever we are responsible for it, everywhere within our jurisdiction, must be opposed not only by all the influences of literature, morals, and religion, but directly by every instrument of Political Power. [*Rounds of applause.*] As it is sustained by law, it can be overthrown only by law; and the legislature having jurisdiction over it must be moved to consummate the work. I am sorry to confess that this can be done only through the machinery of politics. The politician, then, must be summoned. The moralist and philanthropist must become for this purpose politicians, — not forgetting morals or philanthropy, but seeking to apply them practically in the laws of the land.

It is a mistake to say, as is often charged, that we seek to interfere, through Congress, with Slavery in the States, or in any way to direct the legislation of Congress upon subjects not within its jurisdiction. Our *political* aims, as well as our *political* duties, are coextensive with our *political* responsibilities. And since we at the North are responsible for Slavery, wherever it exists under the jurisdiction of Congress, it is unpardonable in us not to exert every power we possess to enlist Congress against it.

Looking at details : —

We demand, first and foremost, the instant Repeal of the Fugitive Slave Bill. [*Cheers.*]

We demand the Abolition of Slavery in the District of Columbia. [*Cheers.*]

We demand of Congress the exercise of its time-honored power to prohibit Slavery in the Territories. [*Cheers.*]

We demand of Congress that it shall refuse to receive any new Slave State into the Union. [*Cheers, repeated.*]

We demand the Abolition of the Domestic Slave-Trade, so far as it can be constitutionally reached, but particularly on the high seas under the National Flag.

And, generally, we demand from the National Government the exercise of all constitutional power to relieve itself from responsibility for Slavery.

And yet one thing further must be done. The Slave Power must be overturned, — so that the National Government may be put openly, actively, and perpetually on the side of Freedom. [*Prolonged applause.*]

In demanding the overthrow of the Slave Power, we but seek to exclude from the operations of the National Government a *political* influence, having its origin in Slavery, which has been more potent, sinister, and mischievous than any other in our history. This Power, though unknown to the Constitution, and existing in defiance of its true spirit, now predominates over Congress, gives the tone to its proceedings, seeks to control all our public affairs, and humbles both the great political parties to its will. It is that combination of Slavemasters, whose bond of union is a common interest in Slavery. Time would fail me in exposing the extent to which its influence has been felt, the undue share of offices it has enjoyed, and the succession of its evil deeds. Suffice it to say, that, for a long period, the real principle of this union was not observed by the Free States. In the game of office and legislation the South has always won. It has played with loaded dice,—*loaded with Slavery.* [*Laughter.*] The trick of the Automaton Chess-Player, so long an incomprehensible marvel, has been repeated, with similar success. Let the Free States make a move on the board, and the South says, "Check!" ["*Hear! hear!*"] Let them strive for Free Trade, as they did once, and the cry is, "Check!" Let them jump towards Protection, and it is again, "Check!" Let them move towards Internal Improvements, and the cry is still, "Check!" Whether forward or backward, to the right or left, wherever they turn, the Free States are pursued by an inexorable "Check!" But the secret is now discovered. Amid the well-arranged machinery which seemed to move the victorious chess-player is a *living force,* — only recently discovered, — being none other than the Slave Power. It is the Slave Power which has been perpetual victor, saying always, "Check!" to the Free States. As this influence is now disclosed, it only remains that it should be openly encountered in the field of *politics.* [*A voice, "That is the true way."*]

Such is our cause. It is not sectional; for it simply aims to establish under the National Government those great principles of Justice and Humanity which are broad and universal as Man. It is not aggressive; for it does not seek in any way to interfere through Congress with Slavery in the States. It is not contrary to the Constitution; for it recognizes this paramount law, and in the administration of the Government invokes the spirit of its founders. It is not hostile to the quiet of the country; for it proposes the only course by which agitation can be allayed, and quiet be permanently established. And yet there is an attempt to suppress this cause, and to stifle its discussion.

Vain and wretched attempt! [*A band of music in the street here interrupted the speaker.*]

I am willing to stop for one moment, if the audience will allow me, that they may enjoy that music. [*Several voices, "Go on! go on!" Another voice, "We have better music here." After a pause the speaker proceeded.*]

Fellow-citizens, I was saying that it is proposed to suppress this cause, and to stifle this discussion. But this cannot be done. That subject which more than all other subjects needs careful, conscientious, and kind consideration in the national councils, which will not admit of postponement or hesitation, which is allied with the great interests of the country, which controls the tariff and causes war, which concerns alike all parts of the land, North and South, East and West, which affects the good name of the Republic in the family of civilized nations, *the subject of subjects,* has now at last, after many struggles, been admitted within the pale of legislative discussion. From this time forward it must be entertained by Congress. It will be one of the orders of the day. It cannot be passed over or forgotten. It cannot be blinked out of sight. The combinations of party cannot remove it. The intrigues of politicians cannot jostle it aside. There it is, in towering colossal proportions, filling the very halls of the Capitol, while it overshadows and darkens all other subjects. There it will continue, till driven into oblivion by the irresistible Genius of Freedom. [*Cheers.*]

I am not blind to adverse signs. The wave of reaction, after sweeping over Europe, has reached our shores. The barriers of Human Rights are broken down. Statesmen, writers, scholars, speakers, once their uncompromising professors, have become professors of compromise. All this must be changed. Reaction must be stayed. The country must be aroused. The cause must again be pressed, — with the fixed purpose never to moderate our efforts until crowned by success. [*Applause.*] The National Government, everywhere within its proper constitutional sphere, must be placed on the side of Freedom. The policy of Slavery, which has so long prevailed, must give place to the policy of Freedom. The Slave Power, fruitful parent of national ills, must be driven from its supremacy. Until all this is done, the friends of the Constitution and of Human Rights cannot cease from labor, nor can the Republic hope for any repose but the repose of submission.

Men of all parties and pursuits, who wish well to their country, and would preserve its good name, must join now. Welcome here the Conservative and the Reformer! for our cause stands on the truest Conservatism and the truest Reform. In seeking the reform of existing evils, we seek also the conservation of the principles handed down by our fathers. Welcome especially the young! To you I appeal with confidence. Trust to your generous impulses, and to that reasoning of the heart, which is often truer, as it is less selfish, than the calculations of the head. [*Enthusiasm.*] Do not exchange your aspirations for the skepticism of age. Yours is the better part. In the Scriptures it is said that "your young men shall see visions and your old men shall dream dreams"; on which Lord Bacon has recorded the ancient inference, "that young men are admitted nearer to God than old, because vision is a clearer revelation than a dream."[1]

It is not uncommon to hear people declare themselves against Slavery, and willing to unite in *practical* efforts. *Practical* is the favorite word. At the same time, in the loftiness of pharisaic pride, they have nothing but condemnation, reproach, or contempt for the earnest souls that have striven long years in this struggle. To such I would say, If you are sincere in what you declare, if your words are not merely lip-service, if in your heart you are entirely willing to join in practical effort against Slavery, then, by life, conversation, influence, vote, disregarding "the ancient forms of party strife," seek to carry the principles of Freedom into the National Government, wherever its jurisdiction is acknowledged and its power can be felt. Thus, with-

[1] Essays, XLII. Of Youth and Age.

out any interference with the States which are beyond this jurisdiction, may you help to efface the blot of Slavery from the National brow.

Do this, and you will most truly promote that harmony which you so much desire. And under this blessed influence tranquillity will be established throughout the country. Then, at last, the Slavery Question will be settled. Banished from its usurped foothold under the National Government, Slavery will no longer enter, with distracting force, into national politics, making and unmaking laws, making and unmaking Presidents. Confined to the States, where it is left by the Constitution, it will take its place as a local institution, — if, alas! continue it must, — for which we are in no sense responsible, and against which we cannot exert any political power. We shall be relieved from the present painful and irritating connection with it, the existing antagonism between the South and the North will be softened, crimination and recrimination will cease, and the wishes of the Fathers will be fulfilled, while this Great Evil is left to all kindly influences and the prevailing laws of social economy.

To every laborer in a cause like this there are satisfactions unknown to the common political partisan. Amidst all apparent reverses, notwithstanding the hatred of enemies or the coldness of friends, he has the consciousness of duty done. Whatever may be existing impediments, his also is the cheering conviction that every word spoken, every act performed, every vote cast for this cause, helps to swell those quickening influences by which Truth, Justice, and Humanity will be established upon earth. [*Cheers.*] He may not live to witness the blessed consummation, but it is none the less certain. Others may dwell on the Past as secure. Under the laws of a beneficent God *the Future also is secure,* — on the single condition that we labor for its great objects. [*Enthusiastic applause.*]

The language of jubilee, which, amidst reverse and discouragement, burst from the soul of Milton, as he thought of sacrifice for the Church, will be echoed by every one who toils and suffers for Freedom. "Now by this little diligence," says the great patriot of the English Commonwealth, "mark what a privilege I have gained with good men and saints, to claim my right of lamenting the tribulations of the Church, if she should suffer, *when others, that have ventured nothing for her sake, have not the honor to be admitted mourners.* But if she lift up her drooping head and prosper, among those that have something more than wished her welfare, I have my charter and freehold of rejoicing to me and my heirs."[1] We, too, may have our charter and freehold of rejoicing to ourselves and our heirs, if we now do our duty.

I have spoken of votes. Living in a community where political power is lodged with the people, and each citizen is an elector, the vote is an important expression of opinion. The vote is the cutting edge. It is well to have correct opinions, but the vote must follow. The vote is the seed planted; without it there can be no sure fruit. The winds of heaven, in their beneficence, may scatter the seed in the furrow; but it is not from such accidents that our fields wave with the golden harvest. He is a foolish husbandman who neg-

[1] The Reason of Church Government, Book II., Introduction: Prose Works, ed. Symmons, Vol. I. p. 117.

lects to sow his seed; and he is an unwise citizen, who, desiring the spread of good principles, neglects to deposit his vote for the candidate who is the representative of those principles.

Admonished by experience of timidity, irresolution, and weakness in our public men, particularly at Washington, amidst the temptations of ambition and power, the friends of Freedom cannot lightly bestow their confidence. They can put trust only in men of tried character and inflexible will. Three things at least they must require: the first is *backbone;* the second is *backbone*; and the third is *backbone.* [*Loud cheers.*] My language is homely; I hardly pardon myself for using it; but it expresses an idea which must not be forgotten. When I see a person of upright character and pure soul yielding to a temporizing policy, I cannot but say, *He wants backbone.* When I see a person talking loudly against Slavery in private, but hesitating in public, and failing in the time of trial, I say, *He wants backbone.* When I see a person who coöperated with Antislavery men, and then deserted them, I say, *He wants backbone.* ["*Hear! hear!*"] When I see a person leaning upon the action of a political party, and never venturing to think for himself, I say, *He wants backbone.* When I see a person careful always to be on the side of the majority, and unwilling to appear in a minority, or, if need be, to stand alone, I say, *He wants backbone.* [*Applause.*] Wanting this, they all want that courage, constancy, firmness, which are essential to the support of PRINCIPLE. Let no such man be trusted. [*Renewed applause.*]

For myself, fellow-citizens, my own course is determined. The first political convention which I ever attended was in the spring of 1845, against the annexation of Texas. I was at that time a silent and passive Whig. I had never held political office, nor been a candidate for any. No question ever before drew me to any active political exertion. The strife of politics seemed to me ignoble. A desire to do what I could against Slavery led me subsequently to attend two different State Conventions of Whigs, where I coöperated with eminent citizens in endeavor to arouse the party in Massachusetts to its Antislavery duties. A conviction that the Whig party was disloyal to Freedom, and an ardent aspiration to help the advancement of this great cause, has led me to leave that party, and dedicate what of strength and ability I have to the present movement. [*Great applause.*]

To vindicate Freedom, and oppose Slavery, so far as I may constitutionally,—with earnestness, and yet, I trust, without personal unkindness on my part, — is the object near my heart. Would that I could impress upon all who now hear me something of the strength of my own convictions! Would that my voice, leaving this crowded hall to-night, could traverse the hills and valleys of New England, that it could run along the rivers and the lakes of my country, lighting in every heart a beacon-flame to arouse the slumberers throughout the land! [*Sensation.*] In this cause I care not for the name by which I am called. Let it be Democrat, or "Loco-foco," if you please. No man in earnest will hesitate on account of a name. Rejoicing in associates from any quarter, I shall be found ever with that party which most truly represents the principles of Freedom. [*Applause.*] Others may become indifferent to these principles, bartering them for political success, vain and short-lived, or forgetting the visions of youth in the dreams of age. Whenever I forget them, whenever I become indifferent to them, whenever I cease to be constant in maintaining them, through good report and evil report, in any future combinations of party, then may my tongue cleave to the roof of my mouth, may my right hand forget its cunning! [*Cheers.*]

And now as I close, fellow-citizens, I return in thought to the political election with which I began. If from this place I could make myself heard by the friends of Freedom throughout the Commonwealth, I would give them for a rallying-cry three words, — FREEDOM, UNION, VICTORY!

The peroration was received with the most earnest applause, followed by cries of "*Three cheers for Charles Sumner!*" "*Three cheers for Phillips and Walker!*" "*Three cheers for Horace Mann and the cause!*"

ACCEPTANCE OF THE OFFICE OF SENATOR OF THE UNITED STATES.

LETTER TO THE LEGISLATURE OF MASSACHUSETTS, MAY 14, 1851.

THE combinations or agreements between the Free-Soilers and Democrats throughout Massachusetts in the election of members of the State Legislature were successful. The election was more than usually interesting, because the Legislature was to choose a United States Senator for the term of six years from the ensuing fourth of March, in the place of Mr. Webster, who had become Secretary of State. Nothing had been said before the election with regard to candidates for this place, but there was a general understanding, at least among Free-Soilers, that it should be claimed for one of their party. Mr. Sumner had never regarded himself as a candidate, and the first intimation he had that he was so regarded by others came to him early in the morning after the election in a note written in pencil at his door by Seth Webb, Jr., Esq., afterwards the excellent Consul at Hayti, as follows.

"MY DEAR MR. SUMNER, —

"I called to tell you *such* good news. We have carried everything in the State. Senate sure; House nearly certain; Governor, *Senator*, all. You are bound for Washington this winter.

"Yours truly,

"SETH WEBB, JR."

Similar intimations came from various quarters. Under date of December 18th, the Rev. Joshua Leavitt, the constant Abolitionist, wrote: "I confidently hope and trust that in a month from this time you will take your seat in the Senate of the United States, as the successor of Daniel Webster. I need not say how greatly I shall be gratified at such an event, both for your sake and that of the cause. It will be a worthy rebuke of cotton arrogance, pronounced in earnest and sealed by action in the name of the good old Commonwealth." An active Free-Soiler in Vermont wrote: "I think you are nearer my ideal of a Free-Soiler of this time than anybody else; so does the whole Free-Soil heart of New England. And you may depend that the actual triumph of just such a man as you are will give a heavier blow to the conspirators against Freedom, and do more to fortify the general trust in the ultimate ascendency of uncompromising right, than that of any other living being. You cannot escape from your position." Mr. Giddings and Mr. Chase both wrote from Washington, insisting that Mr. Sumner could not refuse to be a candidate. Hon. John Mills wrote from Springfield: "C. S., I am satisfied, must be the man. He stands better with the Democrats than others, and so he does with the Free-Soilers in this section of the State." Hon. C. F. Adams "saw difficulties in alliance with the Democracy"; but he added, "If our friends decide to risk themselves in that ship, I trust we may get a full consideration for the risk, and the only full consideration that we can receive is in securing your services in the Senate. If anything can be done with that iron and marble body, you may do it. You know how hopeless I think the task."

Under the unamended Constitution of Massachusetts popular elections were determined by a majority of the votes cast, and not by a plurality. In the event of a failure to secure a majority, the election of Governor and Lieutenant-Governor was transferred to the Legislature, which made a selection from the three highest candidates. This duty was now devolved upon the Legislature. At the opening of the session there were separate caucuses of the Free-Soilers and Democrats, with committees of conference, which resulted in the understanding that the Democrats should have the Governor, Lieutenant-Governor, five of the nine Councillors, the Treasurer, and the Senator for the short term, being the few weeks till the 4th of March following, while the Free-Soilers should have the Senator for the long term, being for six years from the 4th of March. The two parties united on Mr. Sumner as their candidate for Senator. The nomination by the Free-Soilers was communicated in the following letter.

"Caucus Room, State House, ½ past 10, A. M. [Jan. 7th, 1851.]

"We have just taken the vote by ballot for Senator, and you are the man.

"Whole number

"For Charles Sumner 82

"Others 00

"We have sworn to stand by you, to sink or swim with you, AT ALL HAZARDS.

"If you shall fail us in any respect, may God forgive you! — we never shall.

"Yours truly,

"E. L. Keyes.

"Charles Sumner."

The nomination thus unanimously conferred was welcomed beyond the caucus that made it. A letter of Richard H. Dana, Jr., written the next day, congratulates Mr. Sumner. "I have just learned that you have received the unanimous nomination of the Free-Soil caucus, as their first choice for the Senate. Whether the state of parties permits your election or not, this voluntary and unanimous tribute from our party must be a deep gratification to you through life, and I heartily congratulate you upon it."

Why Mr. Sumner was selected appears from the *Commonwealth*, which was at the time the organ of the Free-Soil party, and edited by Richard Hildreth, the historian. "Mr. Sumner was selected as the candidate for the Senate, because, while true as the truest to Free-Soil principles, he was supposed to be less obnoxious than any prominent Free-Soiler in the State to the Democratic party. He was never identified with any of the measures of the Whig party, except those relating to Slavery. He never entered a Whig State Convention, except to sustain the sentiment, not of the Whig party alone, but of Massachusetts, against the annexation of Texas and the Mexican War."[1]

The Democrats in caucus were less prompt than the Free-Soilers. They began by a resolution to abide by the decision of two thirds of those present and voting, being the rule of the Baltimore Convention in 1844. This was adopted almost unanimously. Mr. Sumner then received the two thirds required, when one of those who voted against him, after stating his adverse vote, moved that he be unanimously declared the candidate of the Democratic caucus, and six only voted in the negative.

On the completion of these arrangements, the Legislature proceeded to the elections, choosing George S. Boutwell Governor, and Henry W. Cushman Lieutenant-Governor, both Democrats, and, at a later day, Robert Rantoul, Jr., a Democrat, Senator for the short term. The other Democrats were chosen according to the understanding. In the Senate, Henry Wilson, Free-Soiler, had been chosen President, and in the House of Representatives Nathaniel P. Banks, Jr., Democrat, Speaker.

On the 14th of January the House of Representatives proceeded to ballot for Senator, with the following result: Whole number, 381; necessary to a choice, 191; Charles Sumner, 186; R. C. Winthrop, 167; scattering, 28; blanks, 3. There was a second ballot on the same day, when Mr. Sumner had the same number of votes as before. The entire Free-Soil vote was 110, which he received, with 76 Democratic votes.

The *Commonwealth* announced at once the determination of the Free-Soil party as follows. "This entire unanimity of the Free-Soil members indicates a purpose, not to be changed, to stand by their candidate, come

[1] Daily Commonwealth April 2, 1851.

what may. They have taken the candidates presented by the Democratic party without pledges, without questions. They have selected for their candidate a man who stands first in the respect and affections of every true Free-Soiler in the State. Their constituents would repudiate them, if they should desert him now. We are assured *they never will.*"[1]

The failure in the House did not prevent the Senate from proceeding with the election, on January 22d, when the whole number of votes was 38: for Charles Sumner, 23; for R. C. Winthrop, 14; and for Henry W. Bishop, 1; and Mr. Sumner was accordingly chosen on the part of the Senate.

During the long contest which ensued, Mr. Sumner was constant to the end, without doing or saying anything to change or modify his position. Extracts from his speeches, printed in capitals, with hostile comments, appeared daily in the Whig and Democratic papers, and were often characterized as *treasonable*, while he was called a *disunionist*. In reply to a personal and political friend, who sought some mode of meeting these attacks, he wrote the following private letter, which was never published.

BOSTON, January 21, 1851.

MY DEAR SIR:—

The peculiar nature of your inquiry, and the friendship which prompts it, do not allow me to decline an answer.

You know well that I do not seek or desire any political office, that I am not voluntarily in my present position as candidate, and that, prescribing to myself the rule of *non-intervention*, I have constantly declined doing anything to promote my election, and have refused pledges or explanations with regard to my future course, beyond what are implied in my past life, my published speeches, and my character.

To these I now refer. They will give a sufficient refutation to the charge that I am a *Disunionist*. No honest person, acquainted with them, can make this charge.

Besides, I am closely identified, as you also are, with

[1] Daily Commonwealth, January 15, 1851.

the well-known principles of the Free-Soil party. These, while declaring the duty of opposing Slavery and its influence, wherever they exist under the National Government, always recognize that other duty of loyalty to the Union and the Constitution. We propose to wait and work patiently under and through the Constitution, that our purposes may be peaceably accomplished in the spirit of that instrument and of our fathers. We are Constitutionalists and Unionists. In this class I have always been and still am.

That I may place this matter beyond question, I beg leave to repeat and reaffirm what I said on a former occasion: "We reverence the Constitution of the United States, and seek to guard it against infractions, believing that under the Constitution Freedom can be best preserved. We reverence the Union of the States, *believing that the peace, happiness, and welfare of all depend upon this blessed bond.*"

Faithfully yours,

CHARLES SUMNER.

In another letter, written during the contest and published at its close, Mr. Sumner stated his position more fully, and released the party from all obligation to him as a candidate.

BOSTON, February 22, 1851.

MY DEAR SIR: —

I desire to repeat to you in writing what I have so constantly said to you and others by word of mouth.

Early in life I formed a determination never to hold any political office, and of course never to be a candidate for any. My hope was (might I so aspire!) to show, that, without its titles or emoluments, something might be done for the good of my fellow-men.

Notwithstanding the strength of this determination, often declared, I have, by the confidence of the friends of Freedom in Boston, more than once been pressed into the position of candidate; and now, by the nomination of the Free-Soil and Democratic members of the Legislature of Massachusetts, contrary to desires specially made known to all who communicated with me on the subject, I have been brought forward as their candidate for the Senate of the United States.

Pardon me, if I say that personal regrets mingle with gratitude for the honor done me. The office of Senator, though elevated and important, is to me less attractive than other and more quiet fields.

Besides, there are members of our party, valued associates in our severe struggle, to whom I gladly defer, as representatives of the principles we have at heart.

I trust, therefore, that the friends of Freedom in the Legislature will not, on any ground of delicacy towards me, hesitate to transfer their support to some other candidate, faithful to our cause. In this matter, I pray you, do not think of me. I have no political prospects which I desire to nurse. There is nothing in the political field which I covet. Abandon me, then, whenever you think best, without notice or apology. The cause is everything; I am nothing.

I rely upon you in some proper way to communicate this note to the Free-Soil members of the Legislature.

Believe me, my dear Sir,

Very faithfully yours,

CHARLES SUMNER.

Hon. HENRY WILSON, Chairman of the Committee of the Free-Soil Members of the Legislature.

He also wrote privately to more than one leader, proposing to withdraw. Hon. Charles Allen, who was then at Washington, said in reply: "I need no declaration from you to assure me that you did not seek nor desire political office. On that subject you have no secrets to communicate to me. Your purposes and wishes have been transparent. . . . . Though not so tall by some inches, I believe I have kept myself about as bolt upright as you have, and as far within the lines of the Free-Soil party. I shall give no more heed to the suggestion of your letter. You must be the hero of this war to the end, — the conquering hero, I trust." Hon. Stephen C. Phillips, though not sympathizing with the "Coalition," gave his best wishes to Mr. Sumner, saying: "As the case now stands, I hope you will not be disposed, and I am clear that the Free-Soil members should not allow you, to withdraw yourself; and in view of what may affect you personally, and of some probable or possible general results, I rejoice in the prospect of your election."

The issue was presented, if possible, with increased distinctness by the revival in the papers of the speech at Faneuil Hall on the eve of the election. The editor of the *Times*, a Democratic paper in Boston, calling on Mr. Sumner, invited him to modify his opinions, or, as was sometimes said, to "ease off," especially with regard to his recent speech. This Mr. Sumner declined to do, when the editor inquired how he would like that speech reprinted in the *Times*, that it might be read by the Legislature. Mr. Sumner replied at once, that nothing could give him more pleasure. The speech appeared the next day, with an appeal to the Legislature as follows. "Mr. Sumner avows that what is called his Faneuil-Hall Speech contains his calm, deliberately formed, and well-matured opinions, — opinions by which his action would be governed in the event of his election to the office of United States Senator. . . . . We hope that every Democratic member of the Legislature will read the speech of the man for whom they are asked to vote, and then consider whether it is not their duty to vote for some other person."[1]

As the discussion proceeded, the *Commonwealth* also published the speech, introducing it with these defiant words: "We treat our readers to-day to the noble speech of Charles Sumner at that great 'treasonable' meeting in Faneuil Hall. We are proud of it, and of the man who made it. We give it as it was reported by Dr. Stone for the *Traveller*, and as it was copied into the *Times*. The apologists for Slavery have heaped abuse on Mr. Sumner for this speech, and garbled it to serve their base purposes; but here it stands. Not a glorious word of it can or shall be rubbed out. We ask any member of the Legislature, whatever may be his politics or party, as a man, as a son of New England, and as an ad-

[1] Boston Daily Times, January 10, 1851.

mirer of Washington, Jefferson, Patrick Henry, John Hancock, and Samuel Adams, to read this speech, and tell us how he can do a better thing than to vote for its author next Wednesday. Here you have the intellect and heart of a man, — a man for the times, a man for Massachusetts!" [1]

The session wore on, with constantly recurring ballots, always unsuccessful, when the organ of the Free-Soil party made another appeal, in which it presented strongly the issue of principle involved. An extract will show the character of this appeal. "Circumstances have conspired to give extraordinary interest to this election in Massachusetts. Not here only, but elsewhere, both North and South, it is regarded as symbolical of the march of new opinions on an important subject. There can be no doubt in the mind of any reasonable man that there is gradually, but certainly, approaching that tremendous moral conflict in politics which was early foreseen by the wise men of the Republic as sure at some day to happen, and which no human power can do more than to retard. . . . . One peculiarity attending this election is, that it involves a true issue of principle. . . . . The question is not so much whether Mr. Sumner or any one else is to be Senator as whether the antislavery sentiment shall be understood as having established itself not only in the internal and domestic policy of the Commonwealth, where it has always been, but also in the channels through which it connects itself with the government of the Union. Tenfold importance has been attached to this decision from the fact of the apostasy to Freedom lately committed by the person who for many years was considered as the leading exponent of Massachusetts doctrines in the Senate. The election of such a man as Charles Sumner in the room of such a man as Daniel Webster may be construed to be quite as much a complete disavowal of the late conduct of the one as a sanction of the system advocated by the other. Herein it is not difficult to trace the real causes as well of the extraordinary opposition on the one side as of the tenacious adherence on the other." [2]

This was followed in a few days by the annunciation of the determination of the party. "But one course is left, — to stand by Charles Sumner, as our first, our last, our only choice. And if we fail, we fail in a good cause, true to our promises, true to our faith." [3]

On April 23d there was another ballot, when the result was announced as follows: Whole number of votes, 387; necessary to a choice, 194; Charles Sumner, 194; R. C. Winthrop, 167; scattering, 26. On the report it appeared that Mr. Sumner was elected, when it was insisted that a vote having his name printed upon it, with the name of John

[1] Daily Commonwealth, March 28, 1851. [2] Ibid., March 31, 1851.
[3] Ibid., April 2, 1851.

Mills in pencil beneath, which had been thrown out, should be counted for Mr. Mills, thus making one more necessary to a choice. It was also stated that the record of the clerk showed that only 386 votes were cast, while this count showed 388. This inconsistency was not explained. Three other ballots were had unsuccessfully. On April 24th there was another unsuccessful ballot, when, on motion of Sidney Bartlett, Esq., the eminent lawyer, and a Whig, it was ordered, that, "in the further balloting, the ballot be placed in an envelope, and that, where two votes for one person are found in the same envelope, one shall be rejected, and that, where two votes for different persons are cast, both shall be rejected; the envelopes to be of a uniform character, furnished by the Sergeant-at-Arms." At the ballot that ensued the votes were: Whole number, 384; necessary to a choice, 193; Charles Sumner, 193; R. C. Winthrop, 166; H. W. Bishop, 11; S. C. Phillips, 4; Caleb Cushing, 3; Isaac Davis, 3; John Mills, 1; H. H. Childs, 1; N. P. Banks, Jr., 1; B. F. Hallett, 1. There were also two blanks, not counted, making 386 who had voted. The Speaker read the report of the committee, and declared Mr. Sumner elected. The announcement was received with applause in the galleries, which the Speaker and Sergeant-at-Arms promptly suppressed. This was the twenty-sixth ballot.

The election had been so long in suspense, and had so much occupied the public mind, that the final result was received with much feeling. As the news spread, some were dejected and angry, others were joyous and satisfied. Mr. Sumner heard of it while at the house of Hon. Charles F. Adams, in Boston, and there received the first congratulations. A proposition for a public demonstration at his own house in the evening he discountenanced, saying, according to the published report, that, while feeling grateful to friends for their kindness, he was unwilling to do or say anything that could be construed by any one as evidence of personal triumph, — that it was the triumph of the cause, but that his heart dictated silence. In the evening there was a meeting for congratulation in State Street, where speeches were made by Hon. Henry Wilson, Joseph Lyman, and Thomas Russell. Similar meetings were held in other towns of Massachusetts, on receiving the news. The crowd in State Street moved to the house of Mr. Sumner, but he had left the city; then to the house of Mr. Adams, who said that he "was glad of the opportunity to be able to congratulate his friends upon the glorious triumph of Liberty in the election of Mr. Sumner"; then to the house of Richard H. Dana, Jr., who, being out of town, was represented by his venerable father, who said that he had "kept his bed until noon through illness, but, on learning the news of the election of Mr. Sumner, he suddenly became better."

The language of leading journals attests the prevailing interest, and the deep sense of the issue that had been tried. A few of these will be mentioned, beginning with the Free-Soil organ in Boston, which thus announced the result: "In congratulating the world on this event, we congratulate the defeated themselves: for, if they did but know it, there is no firm basis for property except the equal rights of man; there can be no durable Union contrary to our immortal Declaration of Independence and the solemn preamble of our Constitution. . . . . Those very men have the greatest reason to rejoice in our victory, for their *children*, if not for themselves."[1]

The same organ replied to the assaults on Mr. Sumner: "No man ever accepted office with cleaner hands than Charles Sumner. He consented to receive the nomination with extreme reluctance. His pursuits, his tastes, and aspirations were in a different direction. He earnestly entreated his friends to select some other candidate. After he was nominated, and an onslaught unprecedented for ferocity and recklessness in political warfare had seemed to render his election impossible, unless he would authorize some qualification of the alleged obnoxious doctrines of his speeches, particularly of his last Faneuil-Hall speech, Mr. Sumner refused to retract, qualify, or explain. Ten lines from his pen — lines that a politician might have written without even the appearance of a change of sentiment — would have secured his election in January. No solicitation, of friends or opponents, could extort a line. A delegation of Hunkers applied to him for a few words to cover their retreat; in reply, he stated that he had no pledges to give, no explanations to make; he referred them to his published speeches for his position, and added, that he had not sought the office, but, if it came to him, it must find him an independent man. To another Democrat, who called on him on the same errand, he said, 'If by walking across my office I could secure the Senatorship, I would not take a step.' In February he placed in the hands of General Wilson a letter authorizing that gentleman to withdraw his name, whenever, in his judgment, the good of the cause should require it."[2]

The *National Era*, edited by Dr. Bailey, and the organ of the Free-Soil party at Washington, after speaking of Mr. Sumner in most flattering terms, proceeded as follows: "When it is considered that he is the exponent and advocate of opinions and measures which Mr. Webster has renounced and is seeking to put down, that the whole weight of the influence of this gentleman, with that of the cotton interest, the Administration, and Hunker Democracy, has been brought to bear against him, that at no time has he consented to qualify any word he has ever written or spoken on the questions at issue between him and his opponents, or to

1 Daily Commonwealth, April 25, 1851. 2 Ibid., April 28, 1851.

give a single pledge, direct or indirect, respecting his course, his election must be regarded as one of the most brilliant, honorable, and decisive triumphs yet achieved by the opponents of Slavery and Conservatism."[1]

The *Tribune* in New York, though closely allied with the Whig party, rendered justice to Mr. Sumner. "We do not know the man who has entered the Senate under auspices so favorable to personal independence as Mr. Sumner. He has not sought the office, has not made an effort for its acquisition. No pledge has he given to any party or any person upon any question or measure. When asked as to the course he should pursue as Senator, his answer has been a reference to his past acts and published writings; in them were the only promises he had to offer. Though it would have been easy for him to secure the election three months ago by the slightest shadow of a concession to some of the Hunker members of the Legislature, he has steadily refused to say or do anything that could be construed in that manner. To every overture he has replied, that, if chosen, it must be on the footing of absolute independence, — that the Senatorship must come to him, and not he pursue the Senatorship. Such stern adherence to what he considered the path of duty and manliness has thus delayed his election. But it has not prevented it, and now Mr. Sumner enters the Senate free of all trammels whatever. This it is especially which makes us rejoice at the event. It is a new thing in our recent politics, and the loftiest success we can wish him in his Congressional career is an unflinching preservation of the same spirit and conduct."[2]

The London *Times* had a leader on the election, where, among other things, it said: "He was opposed by the Protectionists of Massachusetts as a partisan of greater freedom of trade, and by the adherents of the Government as an opponent of the Fugitive Slave Act. Yet such was the strength of feeling in Massachusetts on that point alone, that the Free-Soil party have succeeded in sending to the Senate the most active and able representative of their cause, and Mr. Sumner enters upon his ostensible political career under these remarkable and flattering circumstances. . . . . The election of Mr. Sumner to the Senate is everywhere regarded as an emphatic declaration, on the part of his own State, that the law is at least not to remain in its present form unassailed. The South responds to such an election by louder declarations of its resistance to all infractions on its local institutions, even at the sacrifice of the integrity of the Union."[3]

[1] National Era, May 1, 1851.
[2] New York Tribune, April 25, 1851.
[3] London Times, May 24, 1851.

Congratulations came from every quarter. They are alluded to here only because they belong to the history of this election. Some of them are given. One of the earliest was from Richard H. Dana, the scholar, and father of the eminent lawyer, who wrote: "I am thankful that Massachusetts is to speak through you in Washington, — through one whom neither West nor South will be able to win over or to browbeat." John G. Whittier wrote: "I rejoice, that, unpledged, free, and without a single concession or compromise, thou art enabled to take thy place in the Senate. I never knew such a general feeling of real heart pleasure and satisfaction as is manifested by all except inveterate Hunkers in view of thy election. The whole country is electrified by it. Sick abed, I heard the guns, Quaker as I am, with real satisfaction." William C. Bryant wrote: "I am glad that my native State is once more worthily represented in the United States Senate." John Bigelow, who was at the time associated with Mr. Bryant in the *Evening Post*, wrote: "I was quite overcome when I read the despatch which announced your election; and when the news was communicated through the building, it gave everybody else, including printers and clerks, almost as much pleasure as to me." Epes Sargent, who edited a Whig paper, wrote: "My private acquaintance is a sufficient assurance that your public course will be honorable and patriotic." Neal Dow wrote: "I thank God Massachusetts has at last done something effectual to redeem her character. I am sure that upon the floor of the Senate you will not forget to assert the rights of your State, and maintain with firmness and dignity the great principles upon which a free government *should be* based." Mr. Chase wrote: "*Laus Deo!* From the bottom of my heart I congratulate you — no, not you, but all friends of Freedom everywhere — upon your election to the Senate." Mr. Giddings wrote from Ohio: "A most intense interest was felt in this whole region, and I have seen no event which has given greater joy to the population generally." Judge Jay wrote: "May God enable you to leave the public service with a conscience and a reputation as unsullied as those you carry with you!" John Jay telegraphed: "Your election has made us most happy and thankful." Elihu Burritt, who was then in England, wrote: "My soul is gladdened to great and exceeding joy at the news of your election to fill the place of the late Daniel Webster. It has been hailed by the friends of human freedom and progress in this country with exultation. There are more eyes and hearts fixed upon your course than upon that of any man in America." Nobody expressed himself more cordially than John Van Buren, who wrote at once: "You will need no assurance of how delighted I was to hear that you were in fact a Senator from Massachusetts for six years"; and in another letter he said: "I was as much pleased with seeing your frank as I was with the inside of your note. Independent of the fact that it proves your election to the United States Senate, the inscription, '*Free* Charles Sumner,' seems to me mighty pretty reading."

This history brings us to the Letter of Acceptance addressed to the Legislature, which was read in the two Houses, — in the Senate by Hon. Henry Wilson, President, and in the House of Representatives by Hon. N. P. Banks, Speaker. In addressing the Legislature directly Mr. Sumner follows the precedent of John Quincy Adams, in 1808, resigning his seat in the Senate.

FELLOW-CITIZENS OF THE SENATE AND HOUSE OF REPRESENTATIVES: —

BY the hands of the Secretary of the Commonwealth I have received a certificate, that by concurrent votes of the two branches of the Legislature, namely, by the Senate on the 22d day of January, and the House of Representatives on the 24th day of April, in conformity to the provisions of the Constitution and Laws of the United States, I was duly elected a Senator to represent the Commonwealth of Massachusetts in the Senate of the United States for the term of six years, commencing on the 4th day of March, 1851.

If I were to follow the customary course, I should receive this in silence. But the protracted and unprecedented contest which ended in my election, the interest it awakened, the importance universally conceded to it, the ardor of opposition and the constancy of support which it aroused, also the principles which more than ever among us it brought into discussion, seem to justify, what my own feelings irresistibly prompt, a departure from this rule. If, beyond these considerations, any apology is needed for thus directly addressing the Legislature, I may find it in the example of an illustrious predecessor, whose clear and venerable name will be a sufficient authority.

The trust conferred on me is one of the most weighty which a citizen can receive. It concerns the grandest interests of our own Commonwealth, and also of the Union in which we are an indissoluble link. Like every post of eminent duty, it is a post of eminent honor. A personal ambition, such as I cannot confess, might be satisfied to possess it. But when I think what it requires, I am obliged to say that its honors are all eclipsed by its duties.

Your appointment finds me in a private station, with which I am entirely content. For the first time in my life I am called to political office. With none of the experience possessed by others to smooth the way of labor, I might well hesitate. But I am cheered by the generous confidence which throughout a lengthened contest persevered in sustaining me, and by the conviction, that, amidst all seeming differences of party, the sentiments of which I am the known advocate, and which led to my original selection as candidate, are dear to the hearts of the people throughout this Commonwealth. I derive, also, a most grateful consciousness of personal independence from the circumstance, which I deem it frank and proper thus publicly to declare and place on record, that this office comes to me unsought and undesired.

Acknowledging the right of my country to the service of her sons wherever she chooses to place them, and with a heart full of gratitude that a sacred cause is permitted to triumph through me, I now accept the post of Senator.

I accept it as the servant of Massachusetts, mindful of the sentiments solemnly uttered by her successive Legislatures, of the genius which inspires her history, and of the men, her perpetual pride and ornament, who breathed into her that breath of Liberty which early made her an example to her sister States. In such a service, the way, though new to my footsteps, is illumined by lights which cannot be missed.

I accept it as the servant of the Union, bound to study and maintain the interests of all parts of our country with equal patriotic care, to discountenance every effort to loosen any of those ties by which our fellowship of States is held in fraternal company, and to oppose all *sectionalism*, in whatsoever form, whether in unconstitutional efforts by the North to carry so great a boon as Freedom into the Slave States, in unconstitutional efforts by the South, aided by Northern allies, to carry the *sectional* evil of Slavery into the Free States, or in any efforts whatsoever to extend the *sectional* domination of Slavery over the National Government. With me the Union is twice blessed: first, as powerful guardian of the repose and happiness of thirty-one States, clasped by the endearing name of country; and next, as model and beginning of that all-embracing Federation of States, by which unity, peace, and concord will finally be organized among the Nations. Nor do I believe it possible, whatever the delusion of the hour, that any part can be permanently lost from its well-compacted bulk. *E Pluribus Unum* is stamped upon the national coin, the national territory, and the national heart. Though composed of many parts united into one, the Union is separable only by a crash which shall destroy the whole.

Entering now upon the public service, I venture to bespeak for what I do or say that candid judgment which I trust always to have for others, but which I am well aware the prejudices of party too rarely concede. I may fail in ability, but not in sincere effort, to promote the general weal. In the conflict of opinion, natural to the atmosphere of liberal institutions, I may err; but I trust never to forget the prudence which should temper firmness, or the modesty which becomes the consciousness of right. If I decline to recognize as my guides the leading men of to-day, I shall feel safe while I follow the master principles which the Union was established to secure, leaning for support on the great Truimvirate of American Freedom, — Washington, Franklin, and Jefferson. And since true politics are simply morals applied to public affairs, I shall find constant assistance from those everlasting rules of right and wrong which are a law alike to individuals and communities.

Let me borrow, in conclusion, the language of another: "I see my duty, — that of standing up for the liberties of my country; and whatever difficulties and discouragements lie in my way, I dare not shrink from it; and I rely on that Being who has not left to us the choice of duties, that, whilst I conscientiously discharge mine, I shall not finally lose my reward." These are words attributed to Washington, in the early darkness of the American Revolution. The rule of duty is the same for the lowly and the great; and I hope it may not seem presumptuous in one so humble as myself to adopt his determination, and to avow his confidence.

I have the honor to be, fellow-citizens,
With sincere regard,
Your faithful friend and servant,

CHARLES SUMNER.

BOSTON, May 14, 1851.

THE DECLARATION OF INDEPENDENCE AND THE CONSTITUTION OF THE UNITED STATES OUR TWO TITLE-DEEDS.

Letter to the Mayor of Boston, for July 4, 1851.

FROM the beginning, Mr. Sumner never missed an opportunity, in speech or letter, of invoking the Declaration of Independence as a rule of action. The following letter is an example.

Boston, July 3, 1851.

DEAR SIR, — I have been honored by an official invitation to unite in the celebration by our City Council of the approaching anniversary of American Independence.

Though it will not be in my power to partake of this celebration, I wish not to seem indifferent to the kind attentions of your Committee or to the hospitality of Boston.

I venture to inclose a sentiment, suggested particularly by the occasion, and in harmony, I trust, with the convictions of all sincere lovers of the Union.

I have the honor to be, dear Sir,
Your faithful servant,
Charles Sumner.

The Declaration of Independence, and the Constitution of the United States, — the two immortal title-deeds of American liberties. Defenders of the Constitution, let us not forget the principles of the Declaration, but, for the equal support of both, in the spirit of our fathers, without compromise, and with a firm reliance on the protection of Divine Providence, mutually pledge to each other our lives, our fortunes, and our sacred honor.

Hon. John P. Bigelow, &c., &c.

POSITION OF THE AMERICAN LAWYER.

LETTER TO THE SECRETARY OF THE STORY ASSOCIATION, JULY 15, 1851.

BOSTON, July 15, 1851.

DEAR SIR, — As a faithful pupil of the Law School, and an attached friend, during life, of the founder, whose illustrious name your Association bears, I feel a thrill at every act or word which does them honor. And since I may not be able to be present at your festival, I venture to send congratulations on the happy auspices of the day, and — mindful that I address a professional assembly — to inclose a sentiment commemorating the dignity and the duties of the American Lawyer.

A brief personal experience will properly introduce it. Some years ago, while at Heidelberg, in Germany, it was my fortune to see much of Thibaut and Mittermaier, both jurists of eminent fame: the first — now dead — renowned for learning in the Roman Law, and for early and constant support of a just scheme for the reduction of the unwritten law to the certainty of a written text; and the other, who is still spared, the greatest living master of Criminal Law, and of the various systems of Foreign Jurisprudence. Next after the aristocracy of birth, they were unquestionably at that moment among the most conspicuous men of Germany.

In the course of a long conversation, chiefly on matters of juridical interest, in the freedom of social intercourse at dinner, one of them asked with regard to the position of the American Lawyer, and both seemed earnest for my answer. I promptly replied: "No person is his superior. His position, Gentlemen, if you will pardon me for saying it, is what yours would be in Germany, if there were no aristocracy of birth." Both seemed penetrated by this allusion, and, looking each other in the face, exclaimed at once, in apparent consciousness of their true rank: "That is very high indeed!"

The sentiment which I now submit was suggested by this incident.

I have the honor to be, dear Sir,

Very faithfully yours,

CHARLES SUMNER.

TO THE SECRETARY OF THE STORY ASSOCIATION.

The American Lawyer: Distinguished by the lofty sphere of his influence, may he find in it new motive to the cultivation of those moral excellences, and those generous virtues of the heart, which give the truest elevation to the character! *Nobilitas sola est atque unica virtus.*

SYMPATHY WITH THE RIGHTS OF MAN EVERYWHERE.

LETTER TO A MEETING AT FANEUIL HALL, OCTOBER 27, 1851.

THIS meeting was held to consider the case of Smith O'Brien and his fellow-exiles in Australia, and to ask the intercession of our Government in their behalf. Governor Boutwell presided and addressed the meeting.

BOSTON, October 27, 1851.

DEAR SIR, — It will not be in my power to be present at Faneuil Hall this evening; nor am I entirely satisfied that it would be proper for me, holding the official position I now do, to take part in the proceeding which you propose to institute.

But though not present with you, and not undertaking to express any opinion on the precise question of national duty, I wish it to be understood that I can never fail to unite in every earnest, manly word by which the sympathies of our country are extended to all, in whatever land, who are defending the Rights of Man. To this cause we are pledged as a nation by the Declaration of Independence; and my heart warmly responds to the vow.

Nor can I forbear to add, that the clemency which you entreat from a powerful government towards those whom it classes as political offenders is in harmony with the Spirit of the Age and with the lessons of Christianity. It is a grace never otherwise than honorable to ask and honorable to bestow: —

"And 't is in crowns a nobler gem
To grant a pardon than condemn."

A recent instance enforces the appeal. Kossuth has at last passed from the house of bondage. His emancipation, promoted by the aspirations, the prayers, and the express intervention of our Republic, is an example to all nations, — while the brightness of his fame shows how vain it is for any earthly edict to stigmatize as crime a sincere and generous effort for Human Freedom. Austria brands the great Hungarian as traitor; but an enlightened Public Opinion, the predestined queen of the civilized world, already re-judges the justice of the tyrant government. To the judgments of this exalted authority mankind must bow. No people, for the sake of any seeming temporary expediency, can afford to sacrifice a principle of justice or a sentiment of humanity, and thus to peril the everlasting verdict of History.

In reaching across the sea as far as distant Turkey, to plead for the freedom of the fugitive Kossuth, our Republic has done well; and the Mahometan Sultan, in consenting to his liberation, at extraordinary hazards, has taught a lesson of magnanimity to Christian nations.

The step we have thus taken cannot be the last. With increasing power are increasing duties. The influence we now wield is a sacred trust, to be exercised firmly and discreetly, in conformity with the Laws of Nations, and with an anxious eye to the peace of the world, but always so as most to promote Human Rights. Our example can do much. The magnetism of our national flag will be felt wherever it floats; individual citizens may labor faithfully; but all these will be quickened incalculably by a system of conduct, on the part of our Government, at home and abroad, which, while avoiding all improper interference with other countries, and teaching the beauty of honesty, shall show a prompt and benevolent sympathy with those vital principles without which our Republic is but a name.

In this work, Irishmen, and the children and grand-children of Irishmen, scattered in millions throughout the land, can help. Their native love of Liberty and hatred of Oppression will here find opportunity for action.

Believe me, dear Sir,

Very faithfully yours,

CHARLES SUMNER.

TO THE COMMITTEE.

END OF VOLUME II.

University Press, Cambridge: Printed by Welch, Bigelow, & Co.

www.ingramcontent.com/pod-product-compliance
Lightning Source LLC
LaVergne TN
LVHW021132110826
845150LV00005B/1006